QUEER CLOUT

POLITICS AND CULTURE
IN MODERN AMERICA

Series Editors
Margot Canaday, Glenda Gilmore, Michael Kazin,
Stephen Pitti, and Thomas J. Sugrue

Volumes in the series narrate and analyze political and social
change in the broadest dimensions from 1865 to the present,
including ideas about the ways people have sought and wielded
power in the public sphere and the language and institutions
of politics at all levels—local, national, and transnational.
The series is motivated by a desire to reverse the fragmentation
of modern U.S. history and to encourage synthetic perspectives
on social movements and the state, on gender, race, and labor,
and on intellectual history and popular culture.

QUEER CLOUT

Chicago and the Rise of Gay Politics

Timothy Stewart-Winter

PENN

UNIVERSITY OF PENNSYLVANIA PRESS

PHILADELPHIA

Published by
University of Pennsylvania Press
Philadelphia, Pennsylvania 19104-4112
www.upenn.edu/pennpress

Printed in the United States of America
on acid-free paper
1 3 5 7 9 10 8 6 4 2

Library of Congress Cataloging-in-Publication Data

Stewart-Winter, Timothy, 1979– author.
  Queer clout : Chicago and the rise of gay politics / Timothy
Stewart-Winter.
      pages cm — (Politics and culture in modern America)
  Includes bibliographical references and index.
  ISBN 978-0-8122-4791-6 (alk. paper)
    1. Gay rights—Illinois—Chicago—History—20th century.
2. Homosexuality—Political aspects—Illinois—Chicago—
History—20th century. 3. Gays—Political activity—
Illinois—Chicago—History—20th century. 4. Minorities—
Political activity—Illinois—Chicago—History—20th century.
5. Social change—Illinois—Chicago—History—20th century.
6. Chicago (Ill.)—Politics and government—20th century. I. Title.
II. Series: Politics and culture in modern America
F548.9.G29S74 2016
323.3′2640973—dc23

                                                          2015019092

To my parents

CONTENTS

ABBREVIATIONS

ACS	Arthur C. Schenck Papers, GH
ACT UP	ACT UP/Chicago Records, Special Collections Research Center, University of Chicago Library
Booster	*Booster*, Lerner Newspapers
CD	*Chicago Defender*
CDN	*Chicago Daily News*
CGAN	*Chicago Gay Alliance Newsletter*
CGC	*Chicago Gay Crusader*
CHM	Chicago History Museum
CLL	Chicago Lesbian Liberation
CMSN	*Chicago Mattachine Society Newsletter*
CR	*Chicago Reader*
CST	*Chicago Sun-Times*
CT	*Chicago Tribune*
CWLU	Chicago Women's Liberation Union records, CHM
DOBCCN	Newsletter of the Daughters of Bilitis, Chicago Chapter
FK	Frank Kameny Papers, Library of Congress, Washington, DC
GAA	Gay Activists Alliance records, New York Public Library
GAS	Gregory A. Sprague Papers, CHM
GH	Gerber/Hart Library and Archives, Chicago
GL	Barbara Gittings/Kay Lahusen Papers, NYPL
GLCMC	Gay and Lesbian Coalition of Metropolitan Chicago records, GH
IGLTF	Illinois Gay and Lesbian Task Force records, GH
ILGTF	Illinois Lesbian and Gay Task Force records, GH
JG	John Gagnon Papers, Special Collections and University Archives, Stony Brook University, Stony Brook, NY
JR	Jack Rinella Papers, GH

KI   Kinsey Institute for Research in Sex, Gender, and
            Reproduction, Indiana University Bloomington
LAT   *Los Angeles Times*
LC   Labadie Collection, University of Michigan Special Collections
            Library
LHA   Lesbian Herstory Archives, Brooklyn, NY
LM   Phyllis Lyon/Del Martin Papers, GLBT Historical Society, San
            Francisco
LD   Leon Despres Papers, CHM
LPCA   Lincoln Park Conservation Association Records, Special
            Collections, DePaul University Library
LW   *Lavender Woman*
MMN   *Mattachine Midwest Newsletter*
MR   Mayoral Records, Harold Washington Archives & Collections,
            Chicago Public Library
MRL   Municipal Reference Library, Chicago Public Library
MSNY   Mattachine Society of New York records, NYPL
NYPL   New York Public Library
NYT   *New York Times*
REM   Robert E. Merriam Papers, Special Collections Research
            Center, University of Chicago Library
VWP   Virgil W. Peterson Papers, CHM
WBK   William B. Kelley Papers, in possession of William B. Kelley
            and Chen K. Ooi, Chicago
WCT   *Windy City Times*
WP   *Washington Post*
WS   William Simon Papers, CHM

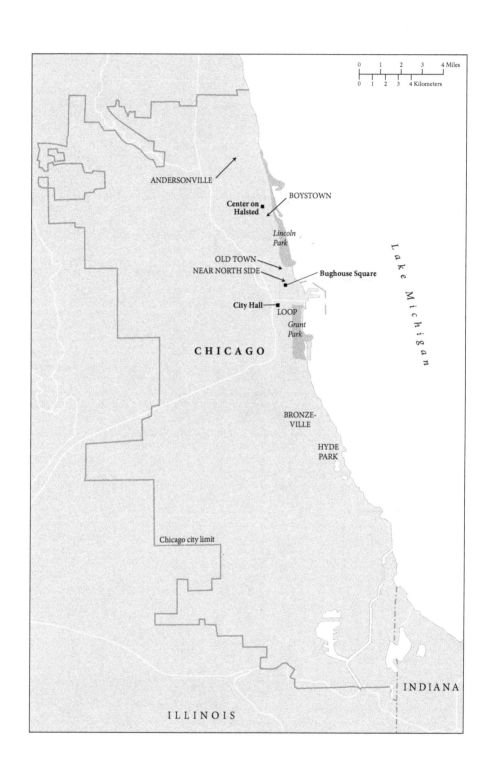

0 1 2 3 4 Miles
0 1 2 3 4 Kilometers

ANDERSONVILLE

BOYSTOWN

**Center on
Halsted** ■

*Lincoln
Park*

OLD TOWN
NEAR NORTH SIDE

Bughouse Square

City Hall ■
LOOP

*Grant
Park*

CHICAGO

L a k e   M i c h i g a n

BRONZE-
VILLE

HYDE
PARK

Chicago city limit

INDIANA

ILLINOIS

INTRODUCTION

IN 2013, the chief justice of the United States suggested that the gay-rights "lobby" was so "politically powerful" that gay couples denied equal access to marriage should not be considered a disadvantaged class deserving protection from the courts.[1] And yet, only fifty years ago, gays and lesbians were social and political pariahs, facing harassment wherever they gathered. This book traces that trajectory—from the closet to the corridors of power—and chronicles the rise of gay politics in the postwar United States.

The path of gays and lesbians to political power led through city hall and developed primarily in response to the constant threat of arrest under which they lived. Their eventual victory over police harassment, secured by allying with other urban residents who were policed with similar vigor, especially African Americans, was the prerequisite for their later triumphs. By the late 1980s, in cities where politicians had only recently sought political advantage from raiding gay bars and carting their patrons off to jail, gays and lesbians had acquired sufficient power and influence for elected officials to pursue them aggressively as a potential voting bloc—not least by campaigning in those same bars. Gays now had clout.

Gay migration to cities was a major feature of postwar urban life, one that consequentially shaped urban liberalism. After World War II, unprecedented numbers of émigrés from smaller cities, towns, rural areas, and suburbs left their families of origin and joined urban gay society, where they learned they could find both anonymity and community. As Carl Wittman wrote of San Francisco, in the most influential manifesto of the gay-liberation movement, "We came not because it is so great here, but because it was so bad there."[2] In subsequent decades, the gay-rights movement flourished and drew in predominantly white and middle-class city dwellers. As urban gay communities swelled with newly out and newly arrived gay people, their desire for recognition and their need for government protections began to realign the political views of a small but growing minority. In growing numbers, gays and lesbians chafed against their outcast status; they demanded that local government, and particularly the police, treat them as rights-bearing citizens.

The rise of the gay movement in postwar America was shaped by a liberal faith in civil liberties as well as, in the 1960s, by the Vietnam-era antiwar movement, the hippie counterculture, and the rebirth of feminism. In Chicago, where gay mobilization was weaker and routine police raids persisted longer than in the vanguard cities of New York and San Francisco, gays and lesbians joined an emerging coalition. A key factor enabling them to challenge police harassment successfully was the example of demands by blacks for police reform, and what enabled gays and lesbians to gain power—a toehold in city hall—was the emergence of progressive, black-led local electoral coalitions. The gay movement flourished in the soil of urban politics not only because gay people were concentrated in major cities but also because it was in big-city municipal government that African Americans and their white allies criticized police practices, demanded reform of the criminal-justice system, and called for inclusion and tolerance as governing ideals.

As the Democratic Party began slowly to recognize the demands of blacks and Latinos, women, and gays and lesbians, black elected officials were instrumental in cementing the importance of gays and lesbians in the new electoral coalition. The black civil rights movement provided gays not only a model but also new opportunities to gain visibility and influence at the municipal level, as black and white liberals broke open urban machines and rejected traditional political structures they viewed as corrupt and unfair. As police harassment diminished and as more gay people came out and realized they had no recourse if they were fired for being gay, they again turned to the civil rights model developed by African Americans to seek legislation to protect them, and to black elected officials to defend their civil rights. For reasons of both pragmatism and principle, African American big-city mayors in particular sought to cultivate the gay vote.

This book traces the political effects of a neglected convergence that saw blacks and gays constitute an increasing share of the urban population after white flight to the suburbs. In this period, gays and lesbians asserted a "right to the city" in a way they had not done before. They signed petitions, wrote articles, asked to meet with police commanders, filed lawsuits, and marched in the streets. In urban America, beginning in the early 1960s, gay activists learned from the tactics of African Americans who challenged police brutality through protests and lawsuits. In Chicago, as black and white liberals acquired influence in the 1970s, gay activists joined a coalition that resisted police extortion, spying, and surveillance. Driven together by their shared concern with combating the overzealous activities of law enforcement, black and gay activists sometimes found common cause with one another in the face of police harassment. These fragile alliances ultimately foundered in part because, ironically, in the very years when policing and punishment in black neighborhoods began to increase, the policing of predominantly white gay establishments and neighborhoods became far less systematic.

Much has been written about the rightward turn of American politics in the late twentieth century. And indeed all three branches of the federal government remained implacably hostile to gay mobilization into the early 2000s. But in the last quarter of the twentieth century, every major U.S. city enacted laws that its gay citizens had demanded. The gay-rights movement flourished later in the century than the other rights-based social movements on which it was modeled, and the character of gay politics bears the imprint of the 1980s and 1990s. The so-called gayborhoods on Chicago's North Side, dotted with businesses owned and patronized by gay men and by a smaller number of lesbians, reflected the uneven neoliberal economic development of metropolitan neighborhoods. By the 1990s, when gays and lesbians had mobilized to forge new institutions and to make new demands, government's capacity to remedy injustice had atrophied, and the toolkit for the delivery of services had changed. The acquired immunodeficiency syndrome (AIDS) crisis created a desperate quest for funds just as the federal government turned its back on cities. New programs serving people with AIDS and homeless lesbian, gay, bisexual, and transgender (LGBT) youth were administered by a growing nonprofit sector. However vigorously advocates strove to deliver services where they were most needed, they could not undo the growing impact of metropolitan segregation by race and class—even as the AIDS crisis worsened the impact of those inequalities.

*   *   *

Queer Clout draws together the histories of a social movement and electoral politics in the nation's great inland metropolis. Compared to the better-known stories of San Francisco and New York, the story of gay empowerment in Chicago was in many ways more representative of the dozens of other regional magnets for gay migration—from Atlanta to Seattle, Boston to Dallas. Gay migrants to urban America, no matter how numerous, have always been culturally significant despite being difficult to count. Like members of racial and ethnic minorities, their demographic quantification requires decisions about who belongs inside the group and who outside. The politics of the closet overlay these questions with a profound methodological problem: Until very recently, respondents to social surveys were typically unwilling to self-report such a concealable and highly stigmatizing trait to a stranger. Still, urban life held out the prospect of pleasure, and gays and lesbians, like African Americans, played an increasingly important role in the remaking of the American metropolitan landscape in the postwar decades.

As the industrial and population boom of the World War II years subsided, African Americans continued to migrate to the urban North. Yet many large cities, including Chicago, began to lose population to suburbs. While federal urban-renewal dollars flowed into programs that cleared or demolished struggling inner-city neighborhoods, in an attempt to reverse "blight," far more money was used to subsidize the movement of white-collar workers and corporations to sprawling suburbs where land was cheap. Gay migration to cities in the postwar era—what anthropologist Kath Weston has called the "great gay migration"—represented a trend that countervailed the much larger migration of whites to suburbs.[3] Far from gaining clout by virtue of their growing numbers, however, gays and lesbians were largely understood as people engaged in deviant behavior and as evidence of vice, decay, and disorder—not yet as a community, much less a political constituency. Routine police raids on gay establishments endured even in the most liberal places for as long as a decade after the 1969 Stonewall uprising in New York, traditionally considered the beginning of the gay-liberation movement.

Gay people most often came together to improve their lot by means other than formal political mobilization. In part because of public hostility, the mutual aid that lesbians and gay men provide one another tends to be informal, even invisible. In the late 1990s, a lifelong Chicagoan from the South Side, then in her seventies, recalled, "There was a girl who worked at Bell & Howell out in Lincolnwood, and she was black and gay, and she did the [job] interviewing." In fact, she said, "There was almost a whole production line of cameras and projectors that were nothing but gay girls. . . . She made it her business to hire every gay girl on the South Side that she could hire. So a lot of us got in at Bell & Howell."[4] This individual's quietly undertaken project—"her business"—is the reason both for its success and for its failure to leave an archival trace. Such networks emerged in every community, largely hidden from the straight majority, and they were especially crucial for women, African Americans, and others who, facing marginalization in multiple ways, were often less drawn than were white men to organize around their gay identity.

In the half century following the emergence of the American gay-rights movement, the story of gay politics was inseparable from that of big-city government in places such as Chicago. In America's large cities, gay and lesbian citizens won an end to routine police raids on gay establishments, the right to parade annually through city streets in celebration of their community, and legal protection against antigay employment discrimination. Many lesbians joined the women's movement and worked to expand protections for women living independently from men. Although the federal government legitimized the civil rights revolution in the 1960s, it was urban municipal government that expanded its scope to embrace gay men and women in the decades that followed.

Historians of queer politics have tended to emphasize the differences between the homophile organizations of the 1950s and 1960s, on the one hand, and the gay-liberation movement that flourished after the Stonewall uprising and developed into a far larger and more complex social movement, on the other. This book instead emphasizes the continuities between the 1960s and 1970s, as activists from both generations focused on challenging police brutality, entrapment, and street harassment, as well as raids on gay bars. Their concern with policing distinguished the homophile and gay-liberation movements from the movement organized around AIDS that arose later.[5]

Harassment by big-city police departments was the gay movement's first policy focus; even an arrest for disorderly conduct, or another nebulously defined crime, in practice could mean losing control over who knew about one's sexuality. This harassment was as harsh in Chicago as in any American city. In a 1967 police raid in which seven patrons were charged with indecency, eight plainclothes detectives had entered the bar separately in order to observe the activities there and establish the grounds for the charges. The next morning, a sociologist studying gay life, who heard about the raid and arranged to interview bar manager immediately, expressed surprise at the sheer number of police officers involved. "Right,"

police –harrassment

said the manager. "They do things big in Chicago."[6] The fear of arrest
thus powerfully affected even the many gays and lesbians who were never
themselves taken into custody. The decline of antigay police harassment—a
story told here as it unfolded in one large city and which took place in
some form in every large American city between the late 1960s and the late
1980s—has been almost totally neglected by historians.

Gay rights became a tool by which newly empowered African American elected officials could expand their appeal among an increasingly
important segment of urban white voters. Chicago's aldermen recognized
that, given the small size of each city ward and the low voter turnout
characteristic of local elections, a motivated segment of voters held the
power to decide their futures. As an insurgent black progressive and a
reformer, Harold Washington perceived white gays as whites who might
vote for him in very close citywide races based on his support for gay
rights. Washington was the first mayor of Chicago to welcome gay people
to city hall—indeed, his staff warned him that the members of his gay
advisory committee lacked political savvy and that most "have very little
experience with politics and city government"—but he would not be the
last.[7] Identifiably gay voters were also important because as they became
visible, they were concentrated along the North Side lakefront, in crucial
swing wards in the city's racially charged political battles of the 1980s. In
addition, the relationship between black and gay politics was not unidi-
rectional. For example, predominantly white gay voters in a key ward
joined Latinos in gradually tipping the balance of power in the city council to Washington by mid-1987.

And this was not just in Chicago. Embracing gay rights helped a startling number of black mayors win election or reelection around the country: Tom Bradley in Los Angeles, Coleman Young in Detroit, Marion Barry
in Washington, Wilson Goode in Philadelphia, Maynard Jackson and Shirley Franklin in Atlanta, and David Dinkins in New York. Black politicians
in the 1980s thus helped forge a coalition around a progressive politics
of sexuality and gender, a coalition that would become even more visible
nationally in the 1990s. One striking aspect of this story is that antigay
black pastors were not an obstacle to the successful alliance between black
and gay politicians. Indeed, Catholicism influenced council members not
because of grassroots mobilization but because of institutional ties.
Although few have argued that Roman Catholic antigay mobilization is
"white" homophobia, at least in Chicago the Catholic archdiocese exercised

far more influence on white politicians than socially conservative black pastors did on black politicians.

The urban character of gay politics sheds light on its radical roots, its growth in a neoliberal era, and its contradictory present. This book seeks to uncover the origins of gay politics as a remarkably effective challenge to the violence of state power at the local level. Influenced by the antiwar, women's liberation, and black-freedom movements, gays and lesbians increasingly sought a place within the world of party politics in the late 1960s and 1970s. The gay-pride marches of the 1970s, through the insistence of gays and lesbians on coming out, helped create the conditions that allowed middle-class, identity-based urban gay communities to emerge— something previously impossible because, with very few exceptions, holding down "good" jobs required the careful concealment of one's homosexuality. As the negative consequences associated with being identified as gay slowly lessened, an increasing number of middle-class urban gay communities became visible and even political.

It was in the 1970s that gays and lesbians made their most important early strides toward participating in local government as a recognized constituency. The movement for political reform that swept through much of American political culture in the 1970s had many effects on American life, but perhaps no community was more deeply affected than that of gays and lesbians. It was in this era that gays began to be a Democratic Party constituency. At a conference held in Chicago in February 1972, inspired by the Democratic Party's new rules requiring that minority groups and women be proportionally represented among convention delegates, gay activists from across the country passed a resolution demanding that 10 percent of the party's convention delegates be gay.[8] Even this early, it seemed less likely that the Republican Party would be responsive to such requests for inclusion. That perception had hardened by the late 1970s, as GOP leaders began to align the party's platform not with the feminist and gay-rights movements but rather with the developing religious conservative backlash against those movements' gains and visibility.

In the 1980s and 1990s, urban America was increasingly constituted as a bastion of liberalism. Although the nation's cities did not turn rightward as sharply or as quickly as the federal government did in the late twentieth century, the nation's retreat from the redistributive welfare state and the latter's supplantation by neoliberal institutions increasingly shaped big-city politics, eroding some of the dreams of radical and progressive gay activists.

By the time militant AIDS activism emerged in the 1980s, the gay movement's claims of police brutality centered almost exclusively on police behavior during arrests of activists engaged in civil disobedience, as well as on the frequent and medically unwarranted use of rubber gloves by police interacting with activists. In the late 1980s, gay activists confronted repressive legislation aimed at curbing the spread of human immunodeficiency virus (HIV) and AIDS, beating back many such proposals at the local, state, and federal levels, but they failed to block a new threat in the form of statutes criminalizing HIV transmission, laws that reinforced inequalities in the legal system.

While black and gay activists and politicians forged important political ties in the 1970s and 1980s, the social basis for black–gay alliances began to break down. In a city legendary for its racial bifurcation, the geographic centering of gay politics on the white side of town hardened a perceptual link between gayness and whiteness. In Chicago, a city-sponsored, $3.2 million gay-themed streetscape renovation project completed in 1998 in the North Side's East Lakeview district, whose commercial strip was by then known as "Boystown," epitomized the symbolic use of public funds to promote tourism by a means that, like any public project, benefited lawyers and contractors working for the city. The uneven economic development of North Side and South Side neighborhoods brought about tensions over policing and programming, and the AIDS crisis worsened those tensions by overlaying them with conflicts about respectability. A more conservative generation of black clergy began to gain clout just as the gay movement turned its focus from policing and job discrimination, which many urban blacks readily understood as matters of civil rights, to the thornier and more symbolically charged issue of marriage equality.

Even as urban white gays shook off the burden of routine police harassment and worked with police officials to institute sensitivity training and to recruit gay officers, racial tensions developed between those white gays who increasingly wielded local political clout and the queers of color who remained subject to disproportionate incarceration. Gay activists even began at times to respond to antigay violence with calls for intensified policing, a move that black, Latino, and other activists of color have resisted.[9] As recently as 1991, Chicago's police department had had no openly gay officers.[10] Breaking into law enforcement was a powerful and hard-fought alteration in the status of a group that remained a criminal class under sodomy laws in effect in more than a dozen states until 2003.[11]

The development of gay politics also shows how urban politics remained persistently gendered, as many more gay men than lesbians entered the clubby world of municipal politics. Relations between lesbians and gay men changed over time, but the struggle for gay rights always involved both. Lesbians suffered doubly from the economic discrimination of a gender-segregated metropolitan job market in which women earned far less than men. As gay-male and lesbian communities grew in the 1970s and the barriers to gay organizing fell, the two communities diverged politically on issues of consumption, sex, and objectification. A decade later, the devastating AIDS crisis paradoxically brought gay men and lesbians together. As late as the early 1970s, there were no female precinct captains in the legendary political machine over which Chicago mayor Richard J. Daley had presided since the mid-1950s. Some women gained access to the levers of power; indeed, Chicago's Jane Byrne became in 1979 the first female mayor of an American metropolis. Many gay organizations adopted policies to ensure gender parity. Yet men still had far greater access to the pinstripe patronage and campaign money that were increasingly important to local politics. "Boystown" became the center of Midwestern queer political culture in the 1990s, suggesting that the fundamentally masculine character of urban politics was reproduced in its gay variant rather than displaced altogether.

Because of its urban beginnings, the gay movement was more radical in its origins than historians have yet recognized. But as it became embedded in American public life, it reflected the contradictory character of the society in which it emerged: a society increasingly tolerant of sexual and gender diversity and willing to guarantee the civil rights of people with disabilities, gays and lesbians, and other emerging constituencies, and yet also marked by deepening economic inequality and a shrinking social safety net. Urban politics allocated clout to some gay men, and to a smaller number of lesbians, even while it marginalized many other gay and transgender citizens. Gay politics reflects neoliberalism and budgetary austerity not because of the gay-rights movement's intrinsic conservatism—indeed, radical and left-liberal figures were among the most important catalysts in legitimizing the gay movement—but because of the historical and geographic context in which it matured. In Chicago, gay political activism began to shape aldermanic races in a string of wards along the North Side lakefront. Some elected officials—even those outside these wards and seeking citywide office—began to take notice of their behavior. But their ascent to power remained tentative until the 1990s. Indeed, as recently as 2004, when many states enacted constitutional amendments banning same-sex marriage and when an antigay president won election to a second term, the gay-rights movement seemed to many to be losing ground.

Gays and lesbians have rapidly consolidated their political influence over the past two decades. Not long ago, however, the political marginality of gays and lesbians even in urban America seemed to confirm the definition of homosexuals offered by the character Roy Cohn in Tony Kushner's Pulitzer Prize–winning play *Angels in America* as "men who in fifteen years of trying cannot get a pissant antidiscrimination bill through City Council," who have "zero clout."[12] That Kushner's Cohn cited the long battle to ban antigay discrimination in New York City—finally successful in 1986—is telling. Gay rights were won in the cities.

*   *   *

This book combines the two leading methods that have characterized gay and lesbian history: the community study, which describes the first generation of scholarship on both movement activism and everyday life, and the more recent emergence of political histories, which typically center on the federal government and examine the negative effects of state power on gays and lesbians, not the dynamics of the gay movement at the national, state, or local levels.[13] By casting gay political empowerment as an aspect of urban liberalism, this book explains the roots of the movement's subsequent successes during the past decade at the federal level. The urban character of gay politics cannot be understood without taking seriously the crucial role that local and state governments played in the political reorientation by which social issues, such as sexuality and gender, moved from the margins to the center of American politics.

Queer Clout remedies a dearth of archive-based studies of gay politics after 1970. Monographs on social-movement history have fleshed out aspects of the homophile, gay-liberation, and women's liberation movements.[14] Partly because there are so few historical studies of gay politics after 1970, however, postwar historians generally have interpreted the growing electoral significance of social issues almost exclusively for its role in consolidating political conservatism.[15] One factor contributing to this problem is that until 2003 nearly all of the gay movement's successes took place at the state and local levels, out of sight of political historians who strongly emphasized the centrality of the federal government in American life since the New Deal era.

Although many scholars have examined the influence of the black-freedom struggle on subsequent mobilization by other groups, this book offers one of the first accounts to extend that approach to the gay movement—tracing the arc of that influence and taking stock of its complicated effects and dynamics.[16] Unpacking what happened on the ground in a particular city is a method well suited to examining this problem.[17] It also builds on works that examine the police and law enforcement in relation to gay life and politics,[18] as well as on the scholarship tracing the intertwined histories of race and sexuality, bringing this approach to bear for the first time on the critical setting of urban politics in the post–civil rights period.[19] Informed by the empirical work of Cathy J. Cohen and Russell K. Robinson, it extends the queer-of-color critique in sexuality studies by providing the perspective of an archive-based political history.[20]

Because gay politics until recently was urban politics, its emergence comes into clearest focus through a case study of a single city. Chicago is a major regional transportation hub and one of the nation's largest cities, and it drew gay migrants from across the Midwest. As a major battleground of the civil rights struggle in the urban North, moreover, Chicago offers a chance to examine closely the gay-rights movement's changing relationship to the black freedom struggle. In part because so little has been written on gay political history, the exceptional stories of New York and San Francisco—notably, the Stonewall rebellion in New York and the election of Supervisor Harvey Milk in San Francisco—have inflated the national significance of events that were in many respects local.[21] There were turning points in the history of Chicago's gay politics, but such exceptional stories as the Stonewall uprising and the election of Harvey Milk, were not among them. This book focuses, instead, on how gay politics developed in relation to key moments in the life of local politics, such as the Democratic National Convention, held in Chicago in August 1968, and the election of Harold Washington as the city's first black mayor in the spring of 1983.

Chicago was the birthplace, in the 1920s, of the nation's first, short-lived gay-rights organization, which quickly collapsed because of police harassment, and it was one of only four cities—along with New York, Los Angeles, and San Francisco—where the first annual gay-pride marches were held in the summer of 1970. Yet it was never one of the coastal gay meccas—like San Francisco and New York—that was so open to gay mobilization as to be unrepresentative of urban America as a whole. Indeed, Chicago may also be the largest American city *without* a strong popular association with homosexuality. Chicagoans sued for the right to operate a gay bar later than did their counterparts in New York and San Francisco.[22] Of the five most populous U.S. cities in the 1980 census, Chicago was the last with a gay-rights ordinance, passed in late 1988.[23] Gay politics there drew on local frames, events, and demographic shifts. Chicago, in short, offers the advantage of studying a large city with national importance that still claims a degree of representativeness that its coastal counterparts cannot.

This book introduces the reader to women and men who created a social movement far from the coastal meccas—where, after all, only a small minority of the nation's gays and lesbians lived. As gay Chicagoans struggled to respond to police crackdowns in the 1950s and 1960s, they turned to the criminal lawyer Pearl Hart, a radical Jewish woman from Michigan who had graduated from John Marshall Law School in the Loop before World War I. In the 1930s, she defended prostitutes in Chicago's Women's Court and helped found the left-wing National Lawyers Guild, and in the early Cold War she became nationally known for defending leftists charged under the Smith Act. Hart also defended countless gay men arrested in Chicago's gay bars and tearooms. Beginning in the mid-1950s, when she was in her mid-sixties, and for two decades, she advised nearly every Chicagoan who struggled, against the powerful forces of the closet and of a conservative era, to forge a homophile movement.

In the 1970s, Chicago's most vocal and passionate champion of enacting gay rights legislatively, Cliff Kelley, emerged not out of the gay-liberation movement but out of the 1969 Illinois constitutional convention, and the broad movement of civil rights challengers to the regime of the Jim Crow North. Kelley, a brilliant black liberal iconoclast, was born in the South Side's Washington Park neighborhood during the flood of black migrants seeking industrial jobs during World War II. Witty, idealistic, and intellectual, he introduced his gay-rights ordinance year after year, holding hearings, tweaking his arguments. At one point, Kelley, who said he was straight, told a newspaper reporter that he couldn't enact gay rights in the city council because some of his colleagues "have masculinity problems or are secret bigots."

Kelley's virtues were characteristic of his native city, and so too was the vice that brought about his political downfall. After sixteen years of service as an alderman, he was indicted in 1986 for accepting bribes from waste contractors doing business with the city, pled guilty the following year on a lesser mail-fraud charge, and served nine months in a minimum-security federal prison. After his release, he reinvented himself as a radio talk-show host, where he could be heard for many years on WVON-AM radio ("Voice of the Negro"), Chicago's sole remaining black-owned station. In 2000, he moderated the only campaign debate between the incumbent, Congressman Bobby Rush, and his challengers, Donne Trotter and Barack Obama.

Kelley's tragic flaw may have been as implausible as his heroic advocacy for gay rights. Perhaps, in a larger sense, it was nothing if not Chicagoan. We turn now to the place where these paradoxes emerged: the contradictory landscape of the postwar city.[24]

(Chicago hm)

A Little World Within a World

"I MOVED TO my own place when I was eighteen, to a building near Clark and Division, which was the place to live if you were gay," recalled John, a gay man, in 1983. The year to which he referred was 1950. The previous year, John's priest had been shocked by his disclosure at confession that he had had a sexual encounter with another teenage boy. John added that once he moved to Chicago's Near North Side, "When you applied for a job, you hesitated to give an address in that area. Quite often I gave my parents' address to avoid remarks like 'The queer North Side, eh?' or 'Is that near Clark and Perversion?'"[1] Though Americans had long viewed cities as dens of iniquity, foreignness, and political radicalism, as whites began to move to the suburbs in the 1950s, sensational depictions on television and in movies cemented the cities' reputation as dangerous. In novels and in newspapers, cops and G-men did battle to reclaim the urban jungle from dangerous criminals and sex fiends.

But cities were also places where blacks and gays could develop communities. African Americans left the Jim Crow South for Chicago in large numbers, with nearly half a million crowding into the South Side's "black belt" by 1950. As the boundaries of the black belt threatened to burst into the surrounding white residential areas, violence flared, yet African Americans found the chance for better work and pay in Chicago than in the places they had left behind. Gay men and women also found work, friends, and ways of living that were impossible in the small towns or the provincial urban neighborhoods where they had grown up. When sexologist Alfred C. Kinsey first traveled from Indiana to Chicago in the summer of 1939 in search of homosexuals to interview for a possible research project, he found himself swept up in a dizzying array of parties, clubs, and bars, "wl would be unbelievable if realized by the rest of the world," he wrote to a colleague.[2] Almost three decades later, one Chicago lesbian went so far as to lament how deeply involved younger lesbians seemed to become in the city's queer communities: "[J]ust because they're homosexual, the gay life becomes everything."[3] Many men and women were afraid to dip their toes into the gay world, but urban America offered many others access to a limited degree of freedom.

The most visible gathering places for gays and lesbians in 1950s Chicago were in the two main entertainment districts, north and south of downtown. On the South Side, just north of the historic black commercial center of Bronzeville and a block from the city's first high-rise public-housing project, which opened in 1950, the jazz trumpeter "Tiny" Davis, known as the Female Satchmo, opened a jazz club with her partner Ruby Lucas. At Tiny and Ruby's Gay Spot, later demolished to make room for the Dan Ryan Expressway in 1958, Davis recalled, "The daddies are daddies and the fems are fems."[4] At Big Lou's, a Rush Street lounge on the mostly white Near North Side, a police officer in early 1952 reported "observation of effeminate men and mannish women in the place, males dancing with males, females dancing with females, and undue demonstrations of intimacy between women at the bar."[5] Between the two places, at the Town and Country Lounge in the basement of the Palmer House hotel in the central Loop commercial district, predominantly white gay men gathered for cocktails, often under the noses of straight hotel guests, and well-heeled men mingled with male window dressers and "ribbon clerks" working in downtown department stores.[6]

As gay enclaves developed, a small number of Chicagoans, mostly gay men but some notable women as well, launched tiny organizations aimed at improving the status of homosexuals. Chicagoans founded in 1954 the first chapter outside California of the Mattachine Society, the pioneering national "homophile" group in the postwar era, which advocated greater acceptance of gays and lesbians, their successful social and cultural "adjustment" in American society, and more sympathetic views of their lot on the part of experts. Homophile groups sought to improve the status of the homosexual in American society by holding discussion groups; meeting with sympathetic doctors, lawyers, pastors, and scholars; and publishing newsletters and magazines. The homophile movement also discussed the need to reform criminal laws against same-sex acts.

how the movement started

In many ways, the federal government drove the state repression of homosexuality in the quarter century after World War II. In the so-called lavender scare, officials investigated and purged gay and lesbian federal employees, beginning in 1950. That year, Senator Kenneth Wherry of Nebraska launched an investigation of gay employees in the State Department, sparking a wave of hostile press attention that coincided with the anticommunist panic in Washington and Hollywood. In a 1953 executive order, President Dwight Eisenhower excluded gays and lesbians from federal employment on the grounds that they constituted security risks, codifying the antigay purge that Congress had initiated. The suppression of urban vice increasingly intersected with Cold War politics and the expanding mission of federal law enforcement.

But antigay policing in the 1950s entailed more variation and unevenness than the lavender-scare framework alone can explain. The federal bureaucracy's persecution of gays and lesbians became unrelenting and systematic. Local police departments across the country cracked down on gays and lesbians as well, in many cities more aggressively than in the interwar period. In the words of one gay man, however, queer life in Chicago in the years after World War II felt like "a regular wavelike pattern of freedom for homosexuals and then a period of crackdown."[7] There, politicians viewed the presence of establishments catering to gays and lesbians—especially on the North Side, where they were situated near predominantly white tourist and convention areas—as a law-enforcement and public-relations problem. Under pressure from politicians to crack down on vice, municipal police and officers of the county sheriff conducted raids on gay spots, humiliating the patrons by distributing the names of those arrested to newspapers for publication. This occurred often enough that patrons calculated the likelihood of such raids in weighing how closely to associate with other gay people. The police who launched Chicago's antigay crackdowns had typically faced demands to do so from muckraking reporters and elite reformers, especially the Chicago Crime Commission, an offshoot of the Chicago Association of Commerce and Industry. To these business-led reformers, homosexuality was to be regulated as a form of illicit vice. Not only were the operators of a gay bar potentially subject to criminal penalties in much the same manner as sex workers, pornographers, gamblers, and abortion providers, but so were the patrons. Law-enforcement agencies ensnared gay Chicagoans in small but growing numbers.

The emergence of the homophile movement in the 1950s was deeply shaped by local law enforcement. Situating homophile activism in the context of urban politics reveals two important points about the midcentury politics of sexuality. First, the tiny gay movement that arose in the course of the decade was shaped by the necessity of concealment. The figure of "the pervert" increasingly populated America's big-city newspapers, appearing abstractly as a threat to the social order or concretely as a result of being exposed and then, usually, terminated from employment. Joining the homophile movement required overcoming the fear of being blackmailed, robbed, or—above all, and most universally—simply being exposed as gay, even to relatives or friends. Pearl Hart, a lawyer who advised homophile activists in postwar Chicago, was also experienced in defending other clients—those charged as communists or prostitutes, for example—who similarly faced stigma and pressure to conceal their deviation from the American mainstream. Second, the gay world was defined as deviant because gay sex was removed from the domestic, procreative, marital relations of proper breadwinners and their families. Gay people commonly believed that politicians most often cracked down on gay life during election campaigns, appealing to voters who were assumed to consist of such families. But for many of their patrons, queer bars were crucial sources of comfort and conviviality. "When you walked through that door," recalled Esther Newton, who later published an ethnographic study of female impersonators based on her University of Chicago dissertation, "it was like you dropped through a trap door into this other world."[8] Gay bars and nightclubs served as an insecure haven from the rest of the city. Women, even more than men, frequently gathered at house parties. One woman recalled her friends carrying their party clothes, lest they attract hostile attention on the streets: "When we got to the party we'd take off the skirts, put on the pants, and have a party, and before we'd go home we'd take off our pants, put on our skirts, and bundle up the pants and go home."[9] Those who deviated from the postwar sex and gender order, no less than from its conformist political orthodoxy, were forced underground.

The gay subcultures of America's largest cities mirrored the self-consciously rough-and-tumble spirit of postwar big-city life. In *Unlike Others*, a pulp paperback novel published in 1963 and set in Chicago, Valerie Taylor captured in brilliant detail how deeply gay life was embedded in— yet marginal to—local politics. Taylor's protagonist, Jo, spends her days working in a downtown office tower as the underpaid assistant to the womanizing male editor of a corporation's in-house employee newsletter. Meticulously concealing her private life from her boss, she finds her way into the city's lesbian subculture after hours. At one point, Jo is awakened in the middle of the night by a phone call from her best friend Richard, a gay man who has been arrested in a bar raid. "Knowing the percentages," Taylor's narrator observed, "you never betrayed anyone. If you had straight friends who knew what you were and accepted you just the same, without any reservations—[Jo] never had, but some of the boys claimed it was possible—you never gave anyone away to them. It was a little world within a world."[10] Friends and lovers thus faced the risk of becoming enmeshed in the dangerous clutches of policemen, with money and influence offering the only means of escape.

The predicament of Jo and her friends offered a vivid metaphor for the status of gays and lesbians in the public sphere of America's second-largest city. Gayness, spying, and concealment were powerfully linked together in popular culture of the era. Gay people may have been "deviates," but if Taylor was right that their subculture prized "loyalty" so highly, that feature aligned them—rather ironically—with the mainstream American preoccupation in the Eisenhower years with questions of loyalty and disloyalty, even if their allegiances took an improper object. Public disapproval was forceful. Nonetheless, one gay male Chicagoan recalled, "the umbrella was still protecting us, of ignorance. I mean, not many people knew about homosexuality."[11]

"They Carry on like 'Father Time'"

During the Great Depression and World War II, queer life was more visible in Bronzeville, the bright-light district on the African American South Side, than anywhere else in Chicago. Though politically subordinate to white police and property owners, Bronzeville offered perhaps the nation's richest and densest concentration of black culture and commerce.[12] Since the early twentieth century, when the black-owned *Chicago Defender*, one of the most prominent black newspapers in the nation, exhorted its many Southern readers to come north in search of freedom, white politicians had allowed prostitution, gambling, and gay entertainment to flourish in black neighborhoods.[13] "As in all Northern cities, the lowest of the races get together," wrote the authors of a 1950 guidebook to the city's nightlife. "This is most common among the degenerates in the twilight zones of sex. They meet everywhere, but their principal point of congregation is around

Drexel Avenue and 39th Street," an intersection in the heart of Bronzeville's entertainment district.[14] For example, the multiracial Finnie's Halloween Ball, an intensely competitive contest in female impersonation, was covered extensively in the early 1950s in *Ebony* and *Jet*, African American magazines produced by Chicago's Johnson Publications and distributed nationwide. Glamorously dressed female impersonators competed for prizes. "More than 1,500 spectators milled around outside Chicago's Pershing Ballroom," said a 1953 article in *Ebony*, describing one such drag ball, "to get a glimpse of the bejeweled impersonators who arrived in limousines, taxis, Fords and even by streetcar."[15] Black queer life was thus visibly woven into the public culture of the black South Side.

For black Chicagoans in the 1950s, the daily risk of encountering police harassment did not depend on one's sexual inclinations. Life in the slums of the postwar urban North, and later in its segregated housing projects, was controlled by a police force drawn from all-white blue-collar neighborhoods. African Americans were accustomed to police brutality, and they had had little success in challenging it in the face of a dominant culture that held the police in high esteem. What little progress black activists made against police brutality in the 1950s occurred in the courts. Although the city's mainstream newspapers often ignored crime in black neighborhoods, in the second half of the 1950s the African American press increasingly covered the brutal treatment of black citizens by white officers, even in the citizens' own homes. The *Defender* had drawn attention to police brutality on the South Side in a high-profile series of articles in 1958. That year, for example, thirteen Chicago police officers broke into James Monroe's house in the middle of the night based on a false tip in a murder investigation; woke him and his wife with flashlights; and struck, pushed, and kicked him and his six children. In a landmark ruling, the U.S. Supreme Court ruled that Monroe could sue the involved officers for civil damages under a federal statute originally meant to suppress the Ku Klux Klan in the post–Civil War South.[16] Nevertheless, on the city's South Side, police harassment remained a fact of life. Not until the second half of 1963 did a sustained campaign of protest against police brutality in Chicago's black neighborhoods begin to take shape.

For white gays and lesbians, police harassment increasingly constituted their most important point of contact with the state. African Americans in Chicago in the 1950s faced police harassment regardless of whether they were queer, and in this sense being gay made less of a difference for blacks *police and queer community*

than for whites—that is, it did not separate a black gay person as much from his or her black peers as it did a white gay person from his or her white peers. White gays and lesbians faced capricious punishment by the criminal-justice system more often than other whites did. Gay men were most often targeted for physical touching, for dancing, or for propositioning undercover officers; lesbians were most likely to be arrested in bar raids for violating sartorial laws—that is, for wearing men's clothing.

To have one's name printed in the newspaper following a police raid was the quintessential punishment for being gay. In America's postwar antigay witch hunts, the fact that "such a charge will probably be dismissed the following morning" did not alter the fact that "there is a name spread on a record that will not be lost" and that ultimately "the whole of this very common procedure will surely spell 'pervert' in blazing letters for anyone who cares to take the trouble."[17] Exposure as a homosexual—especially through an arrest—jeopardized one's ties to friends and family and, especially, to one's job. Having a good job, if you were gay, meant rigorously concealing your gay life, even from family members. For example, a working-class Chicago woman recalled that her first sexual experience took place around 1954, when she was seventeen years old. "I think we were in a car," she recalled. Soon afterward, she and her new girlfriend "started going to the bars in Chicago quite a bit," even though she still lived with her parents at home at the time. Thirteen years later, she had never discussed being gay with her parents. "I don't see how they could *not* know it," she remarked, "but nothing has ever been said."[18]

Police raids, portrayed in the press as a necessary means of protecting the city from "hoodlums," reflected the linkage of gay life with criminality and the underworld. In Chicago, as in other large cities, organized crime syndicates wielded great power over gay nightlife because they possessed the means to buy protection by corrupting the police. Mob profiteering from cover charges, high prices, and diluted drinks provided funds for such protection. "It didn't make us angry because it allowed us to be somewhere," recalled Jim Darby, a patron of gay bars in Chicago in the 1950s. The police by contrast seemed only to make life dangerous. Gays and lesbians knew they could not expect authorities to treat antigay violence, extortion, and blackmail as serious crimes. Darby, for example, was on leave from the Navy, drinking in Sam's, one of the North Side's busiest gay bars, when it was raided in 1952. "I knew I was drunk already," he recalled, "and

I remember the jailer banging on his desk with his club, yelling, 'God damn you fuckin' queers, shut up and go to sleep!' " He recalls that, in sentencing him to a fine, the judge said it was a sad comment on the nation's military that a sailor would frequent such a place.[19]

Postwar American anxieties took the form of worries not only about communist subversion but also about crime. The perceptual link between crime and cities was tightened by a series of lurid congressional hearings on organized crime in 1950 and 1951, the first such hearings to receive a large national television audience. Chicago then remained strongly associated in the public mind with Al Capone, John Dillinger, and other legendary criminals of the Prohibition era; indeed, Senator Estes Kefauver of Tennessee, who presided over the hearings, declared Chicago "perhaps the one most important center of criminal activities."[20] Millions of Americans heard shocking testimony, which propagated the perception that big-city municipal governments were in fact still captive to the shadowy crime syndicates that had flourished during Prohibition.[21] The Kefauver hearings stoked a lasting preoccupation on the part of the news media with what one historian called the "notion of a vast, hydra-headed crime syndicate," and with Mafia infiltration of politics and business.[22] The hearings also proved a boon to the politicians involved in sponsoring them.

In this context, police scrutiny of gay life intensified in the first half of 1952, amid suggestions that Chicago was on the verge of returning to the lawlessness of the Prohibition era. In January of that year, Chicagoans learned that for two years they had been consuming millions of pounds of horse meat, disguised as ground beef, apparently as the result of mob profiteering.[23] In February, the acting Republican committeeman of the 31st Ward, known as an enemy of the so-called "West Side Bloc" of mob-linked politicians, was shot and killed; his murder was never solved.[24] A group of business-led civic reformers formed a Committee of Nineteen to investigate corruption. Austin L. Wyman, the chairman of the Chicago Crime Commission, charged that both Democrats and Republicans tolerated gangsters in their ranks locally. "Why have there been so few prosecutions of big-time hoodlums?" he asked U.S. Attorney Otto Kerner.[25]

The city's business-oriented, Anglo-Saxon Protestant elite, through the Crime Commission, hired investigators to examine gay nightlife, gambling, and female prostitution. The revelations turned into a full-blown quest to identify scapegoats and clean up a city portrayed as corrupt and decaying.

City officials sought advice from other cities about how best to eliminate crime and associated ills. For example, in 1953, a Washington correspondent for the *Chicago Daily News* sent his editor suggestions about how to intensify the public's demand that the city be cleaned up. "It might be worth exploring," he wrote, "whether the *Miami Herald* could suggest people, out of their cleanup experience there; the California Crime Commission, which the Kefauver committee showed was somewhat on the ball, could be helpful." In advocating for the police to crack down on deviant behavior, Chicago journalists cited the experience of Miami and of cities in California as exemplary. Miami had passed a pioneering ordinance prohibiting female impersonator performances in 1952, and California state officials had established their state government as the leading edge of the nation's postwar antigay crackdown.[26] Those lobbying for a crackdown on gay life in Chicago thus turned to counterparts in other large cities for advice and assistance, just as homophile activists would do, later, in 1954, when they first formed a Chicago chapter of the California-based Mattachine Society.

Hoping to preempt calls for an independent civilian investigator, Mayor Martin Kennelly appointed nine aldermen to an "emergency crime committee"—known as the Big Nine—to investigate organized crime in Chicago. The crime committee hired a former Pittsburgh police detective, Robert Butzler, and heard his testimony about his investigation of "conditions" in the 35th Police District on the Near North Side. Butzler appears to have focused his investigation of gay life on a bar called Big Lou's. "Approximately half the persons in this tavern were perverts, this being evident from their lewd suggestive conversation and actions," wrote an investigator, likely Butzler, in December 1952. "Other patrons observed in the booth and at the bar while dancing in the place were also very lewd in their conduct."[27] The following month, the same investigator noted that "the place continues to be a pervert hangout to both sexes but more emphasis being upon the lesbians. From the conduct of the female patrons," he concluded, "it was very evident they were lesbians and their lovers."[28] On January 26, the owner of Big Lou's, Lucille Kinovsky, was arrested in a police raid, along with three patrons.

A police raid on a gay establishment was at once a law enforcement action and a scripted ritual of exposure: a public event and a private crisis. Butzler's testimony electrified the local press with his reports of gambling, prostitution, and elusive agents of organized crime families; in the words of the *Tribune*, he threw a "spotlight" on "a segment of Chicago and a cast of characters as strange and colorful as anything ever dreamed up for a Hollywood movie."[29] Butzler also testified that one club, the Hollywood Bowl, was "full of male degenerates. They were sitting close and holding hands."[30] But the Big Lou's raid also reverberated through the social and domestic lives of those implicated. Lucille Kinovsky had grown up on the West Side of Chicago, the daughter of working-class immigrants from Bohemia. Her nephew, John Vandermeer, remembers her as an overweight, butch woman who played softball and had matching wedding rings with her partner Bernice. The nature of their relationship was never discussed, but Lou brought Bernice to family dinners on the West Side. Though family members did not speak of her explicitly as being a gay person, Lou was accepted—and even treated as one of the guys by Vandermeer's father and uncles: "When she would be at one of the family get-togethers, it would be her and the men off playing pinochle, and the women would be off in the kitchen." Kinovsky even hired Vandermeer's father to work for her: "She was looking for a bartender and he was looking for a job, and so he tended bar."[31]

Even queers who had clout under this regime, then, were nonetheless highly vulnerable. Kinovsky had her business destroyed by the Big Nine. Called to testify before the emergency crime committee, "Miss Kinovsky denied that her tavern at 731 North av. is a resort for perverts, both men and women." She acknowledged, however, that it had been raided twice in two years by police.[32] In April, she was found guilty of being the keeper of a disorderly house, fined $200, and, unable to pay the fine, was sent to Bridewell (the municipal House of Correction) to "work out the fine."[33] "What they got her on was paying off the police," Vandermeer recalled, "which she claimed to me personally—I remember this *vividly*—she claimed she never, ever did. But that's what they got her on." Vandermeer's youthful understanding was that his aunt had been "run out of town." After she was charged and convicted, she moved to Baltimore.[34]

Throughout the summer and fall of 1953, the Crime Commission hired more investigators and sent them to visit other gay establishments. The commission had two means of getting its way, partly by playing the police and the press off one another. First, "conditions" in a particular establishment would be reported to police in order to generate repressive action. Often, such direct requests for police raids were effective. One record shows, for example, "C.C.C. wrote letter to Commr. Of Police, June 2, 1953 advising that Lake Shore Lounge, 935 Rush Street was a pervert joint so packed that it was impossible to get to the bar or move around. Language filthy and obscene. *Tribune* June 6, 1953 stated 42 men were arrested at Lake Shore Lounge 935 Rush St."[35] According to the commission's executive director, if law enforcement did not respond, the next step was to leak stories about these conditions to the reporters.[36]

Raids did not always lead to the closure of the establishments where they took place, however—something that would change in the 1960s. In the 1950s, Chicago's police force lacked the administrative means to revoke a gay bar's liquor license after conducting a raid. In a fall of 1953 report on two gay bars, for example, an official of the Chicago Crime Commission noted his exasperation with downtown police district commanders: "We have already written reams of material on the Shoreline which has for years been a homo-sexual hangout and the Hague is the same type establishment." And yet, he reported, "though both have been subject of several police investigations and raids[,] they carry on like 'Father Time.'"[37] City officials had limited powers to keep a licensed establishment closed. The appeal commissions established by the state's 1934 liquor control law often reversed local officials' decision to revoke a tavern's liquor license.[38]

Political connections and graft could enable a gay bar owner with sufficient clout to keep his place open over a relatively extended period. One bar owner, Chuck Renslow, who had operated a physique photography studio that also exposed him to police and post office harassment, recalled aspects of running a gay bar in this period with something akin to nostalgia: "The Gold Coast had a 2 o'clock license, which means that we had to close at 2 [or at 3 on Saturday nights]. One year, it was a Wednesday, and in the middle of the week it was New Year's Eve. And the bar was packed! I called up the station and said, 'We got a big business, how long can I stay open?' He says, 'Fifty dollars an hour, be sure you're closed by 6 when people go to work.' That doesn't happen today."[39] Renslow drew the conclusion that, as much as payoffs and raiding posed serious problems for bar owners, they also occasionally provided certain advantages not available under today's reformed regime of liquor regulation. He recounted one evening when his downtown bar, the Gold Coast, was raided—but "they shouldn't have raided it, 'cause we were paying off. So I went to the station, and I said, 'Hey, why'd you raid?' and he says, 'Oh, my God, we made a mistake! Why didn't you *tell* the guys not to be in there?'"[40] Many bars catering to queers enjoyed relative security from police harassment only at the price of Mafia control of their operations, or graft payments to police officers or politicians. This type of freedom was a precarious one indeed.

"A City of Family Men"

Chicago's Democratic machine had bridged divisions of space and class in the decades after it was forged in the 1920s and cemented by the New Deal. In the aftermath of World War I, Mayor Anton Cermak united white Chicagoans, especially immigrant groups, into a powerful multiethnic coalition that survived his assassination in 1933. Politicians accepted and even celebrated some differences of nationality among whites—that is, among Irish, Poles, and Germans. Blacks were part of the machine, yet they had a distinctly subordinate political status. In the years after World War II, white ethnic neighborhood boundaries gave way to stark black-white divisions, as the city became increasingly segregated. The large swath of the South Side that Richard Wright called "an undissolved lump in the city's melting pot" was overcrowded already at the close of the war and continued to swell in the 1950s.[41] Chicago's "black metropolis," as St. Clair Drake and Horace Cayton called it in their famous sociological study published in 1945, was policed almost exclusively by white police officers. Time and again in the 1950s, when blacks moved beyond the edges of the ghetto, whites rioted. Black Chicagoans paid inflated prices for inferior housing and goods, and even middle-class blacks could find housing only on financially exploitative terms. Outside the South Side, police tolerated white violence against African Americans who tried to move into white neighborhoods.[42]

In the post–World War II era, Chicago politics involved a constant, always imbalanced struggle between the machine and good-government reformers. Commentators increasingly spoke of "reform" and "machine" Democrats, even though these were not neatly separable camps.[43] Except for a few diehard "goo-goos" who wielded little power, nearly all Chicago politicians accepted that the lifeblood of urban governance was the exchange of patronage for votes.[44] Most, too, at various moments in their political careers, found it advantageous to advocate reforms or to wrap themselves in reform's mantle. Precisely to tamp down the perception that his election in 1955 meant a triumph of machine patronage, for example, Daley quickly centralized the former aldermanic control over driveway permits—an especially lucrative form of graft—and other favors that city council members could do for their constituents.[45] Tacking back and forth between the politics of the machine and of reform was a well-worn path to success.

In Chicago at midcentury, the New Deal coalition embodied the aspirations of sons and daughters of the Depression for material prosperity, combined with the expectation for men to labor remuneratively outside the home and women to labor inside the home to create a comfortable home and rear children. Ordinary men in the 1950s wanted and were expected to become family men. A young man from a middle-class, predominantly white North Side neighborhood wrote that at his age, "Most Lake View guys are married, have a few kids, know a good trade and have a car."[46] A few miles to the west, social-service workers who engaged with poor and working-class young black and Latino men were making similar observations: "It is okay to remain single until around age twenty-eight, but if you have not married and settled down by that time, the male is considered 'queer.'"[47] Women were expected to marry at an even younger age.

Gays and lesbians in postwar America lived at least partly outside this framework, which the historian Robert Self has labeled "breadwinner liberalism."[48] At once provincial and self-consciously modern, the powerful men who ran Chicago's political machine embraced a welfare state whose provisions were as generous as they were narrowly premised on a white, straight, nuclear-family formation. The high tide of Daley's mayoral administration coincided with the peak of breadwinner liberalism's status in American politics. Advertisements for his first campaign, in 1955, featured his wife and seven children; "Let's elect a Family Man to represent the families of Chicago," said one."[49] For Daley, a spotlight on his large family helped focus media coverage on his blue-collar Irish Catholic parish life, rather than his ties to downtown business interests or his connections to men with syndicate ties. "Smoke filled room?" asked the caption of a photo of the Daleys at the breakfast table in one print advertisement for his campaign. "Yes, filled with the smoke of bacon and eggs frying in the pan."[50] Upon his sudden death during his sixth term in office, in 1976, the *Chicago Tribune* obituary said, "He prided himself on being a 'family man' in a city of family men."[51]

In this context of machine politics, family ties held together households, but also wards, neighborhoods, and political relationships. Alderman Vito Marzullo, one of Daley's closest allies on the city council, later described his loyalty to the mayor in terms that illustrate how deeply heterosexuality was built into local political culture: "He's a great family man. . . . I got six married children. He came to every one of their weddings. He invited me to the weddings of every one of his kids. You don't go back on people like that." Heterosexual marriages were also interlaced with the dynamics of patronage hiring, thus helping form the glue of the local political culture.[52]

Daley was elected in 1955 partly because black voters rebelled against a reform mayor who seemed to crack down only on policy gambling and jitney cabs in their areas while leaving white criminal entrepreneurs untouched. Kennelly, the city's mayor at the time of the Kefauver hearings, had been slated by the Democratic machine in 1947 as a "reformer," to replace Edward J. Kelly, who had consolidated Cermak's party organization since Cermak's death in 1933.[53] Testifying during the Kefauver hearings, Kennelly awkwardly defended the city. The episode increased the pressure on him to crack down on corruption and syndicate businesses, and he responded by cracking down on the illegal policy-gambling racket in black neighborhoods, as well as the illicit, unregulated jitney-cab regime there.[54] This crackdown, in turn, displeased black voters, who had been only recently converted to vote Democratic in local elections. In the process, Kennelly garnered the public enmity of U.S. Representative William L. Dawson, boss of the black "submachine," as well as the antipathy of many Italian and other white-ethnic voters in the city's poor, machine-dominated "river wards." Many working-class white voters, too, were more loyal to their machine precinct captains than to the mayor's downtown allies, and they had little interest in Kennelly's drive against illegal gambling.

By December 1954, Kennelly seemed so weak that the machine ousted him from the ballot, slating Richard J. Daley to run as the machine's candidate. The bitter, expensive primary contest that followed was the first local race featuring television commercials. Though a Catholic himself, Kennelly's strongest backers were the Protestant business elite. In a city with one of the most densely concentrated Catholic populations in the country, Daley, the ward heeler who had served for two years as chairman of the Cook County Democratic Organization, benefited from the perception of Kennelly as elitist and out of touch.[55] Indeed, the *Chicago Tribune* had long taunted Kennelly for his failure to marry, and his opponent exploited the opening.[56] Daley's children were featured in campaign materials labeled "A Family Man for a Family City" (see Figure 1).[57] The *Tribune* had reported on Daley's "happy family life with his wife . . . and their seven children" just before his primary win.[58]

FIGURE 1. Primary campaign placard for Richard J. Daley, February 1955.
Courtesy of Chicago History Museum.

In the equally hard-fought 1955 general election for mayor that followed, organized crime—with its corollary, vice—was a central issue. Daley's Republican general-election opponent, Robert Merriam, charged that Daley would end Kennelly's crackdown on policy gambling, and the city would become "wide open." He quoted *Variety* as saying that "strip tease joints have started to reopen in anticipation of a Daley victory and wide open conditions," according to one journalist.[59] In a veiled reference to Daley's evident willingness to tolerate policy gambling in black neighborhoods, Merriam charged, "There's no such thing as limiting the evils of a wide open city to one section."[60] Faced with these charges, Daley claimed he would wage "an all-out war on crime in every form" to make "our neighborhood streets safe for women and children" and to ensure that "the syndicate will be driven out of Chicago."[61] Daley's election as mayor made him unusually powerful because he had served as chairman of the Cook County party organization, a post he continued to hold as mayor. Moving rapidly, he centralized control of the city he would govern for two decades. Ominously for gays and lesbians, however, Daley had campaigned on a promise to fight crime and protect women and children—and the pressure for more aggressive policing would soon escalate.

"To Round Up Sex Deviates Is the Best Procedure"

Bar raids were accompanied by another, more complex but equally pernicious form of police harassment. Chicago's four daily newspapers, which competed for a readership increasingly dominated by young parents, devoted sensational coverage to violent sexual crimes against children, in a society notably obsessed with families, children, and child rearing, and at a time when men and women married at younger ages than ever before or since. Experts in psychiatry and criminology fielded questions from journalists and offered authoritative comments about sexual degenerates, sexual psychopaths, and sex fiends, as well as the broader and more loosely defined category of deviates, conflating consensual and forced acts.[62]

The occasion for Chicago's worst such panic was a triple murder in the fall of 1955. Three teenage boys disappeared and their bodies were soon found abandoned in a wooded area in a forest preserve on the city's northwestern outskirts. Police began combing the areas near where the bodies were found, as well as areas that had been condemned by eminent domain for the construction of the Northwest (later Kennedy) Expressway. Newspapers repeatedly speculated on several possible theories—was it a teenage gang or a crazed sex degenerate?—that implicated bowling alleys, schools, movie theaters, and bars as potential sites of abduction. A psychiatrist who worked frequently with the criminal courts quickly declared they "were killed by a member of Chicago's colony of sex degenerates," even though the autopsy "disclosed no signs of sexual molestation." This expert publicly called on police to "round up every known sex offender and moron," further advising police that "there are several Chicago areas where persons with abnormal sex attitudes tend to congregate."[63]

The extremely brutal nature of this crime (the Schuessler-Peterson murders), the lack of solid leads, and the dispersion of potential clues across the disparate landscape of the North Side all helped to unleash the imaginations of millions. The boys' bodies were found naked, strangled, and mutilated, not far from horse stables.[64] In the absence of leads, police sought out "sex degenerates," who, one representative expert told a reporter, "often seek their prey in movie theaters." Journalists reported that some of the county forest preserves had long "been frequented by sex degenerates." Perhaps, one expert suggested, the killer could be found if his "previous sex deviations" happened to be already "known to police." Within just a few days, city and sheriff's police were "rounding up persons whose recent actions indicated sex degeneracy or sadism."[65] Police combed through lists of paroled sex offenders, interviewed more than 300 "sex deviates" in six months, and several times released the names of suspects who were later dropped from the inquiry. In one case, police released a suspect's name with the "incriminating" fact that he had on his person, at the time of his arrest, a business card from a "gathering place for sexual degenerates."[66]

Gay men were not the only ones the police questioned—at one point, the employees of eighteen Northwest Side packing plants were interviewed —but gay men were the group to which the police kept circling back.[67] One columnist claimed that, according to "a friend of mine who is an experienced and successful policeman," it is best "to round up sex deviates" and that "in a high percentage of cases, this procedure leads to the discovery of the murderer." This, of course, implied that harsher punishment of those showing signs of "deviation" could have prevented the crime.[68] Ordinary Chicagoans, too, demanded that city elders "place under constant surveillance or remove completely from society all known and suspected sex offenders."[69]

The city's obsession with the Schuessler-Peterson murders sheds light
on how race and class determined the political meanings of violence against
children. Daley frequently repeated an offer of a $10,000 reward to anyone
who helped solve the triple murder. After the Schuessler boys' father died
of a heart attack several weeks later, Daley even proposed that the city
provide "some program of aid" to the grieving widow. It is instructive to
compare Daley's response to the triple murder with his handling of the case
of another young Chicagoan slain in a widely publicized murder during
Daley's first year as mayor. Daley proposed no reward in the murder of
Emmett Till, the fourteen-year-old Chicagoan killed two months earlier—
albeit in Mississippi—in the twentieth century's best-known lynching, and
no municipal outlay to support his mother, the grieving Mamie Till Bradley, though she, too, was a single mother. (Daley did wire President Dwight
Eisenhower, asking the federal government to become involved in the
investigation.[70]) At least one letter published in the black-owned *Chicago
Defender* invoked both crimes in a broad indictment of society's treatment
of children; Mrs. Bradley, the newspaper reported, sent her condolences to
the mothers of the three murdered white boys.[71]

The perception of gays as predators profoundly shaped the response of
law enforcement to crimes against children. This fact has been airbrushed
out of accounts of the Schuessler-Peterson case, which was for decades
among the nation's best-known unsolved murders. Even the best book
written about the murders, which was written from a law-enforcement perspective but generally avoids sensationalism, misrepresents profoundly the
reasons for the investigation's focus on gay men. "Single men living uncon-
ventional lifestyles and other persons unable to make a good accounting of
their whereabouts on the nights in question fell under suspicion," the
authors acknowledge. But they portray police harassment of gays and lesbians in a more benign light than the evidence warrants: "A rumor that
gained currency among the cops and reporters was that the slain boys and
their schoolyard chums were in the habit of extorting money from known
homosexuals—demanding cash in return for silence. For this reason, investigators took a hard look at the gay community."[72] In fact, however, gay
men were targeted for investigation not only—indeed, not *primarily*—
because they were victims of blackmail but rather because they were seen
as possible predators.

These investigations could destroy careers quietly even if no charges
were ever filed. One of those questioned and forced by the Chicago police

to take a lie-detector test was Samuel Steward, a writer and English professor at DePaul University, a Catholic university on the North Side. In March 1956, Chicago police interviewed Steward at his home and then brought him to a police station to answer questions about his whereabouts the night of the murders. In order to give an alibi, he had had to explain that he was an English professor at DePaul University. Though he passed the lie-detector test, he wrote in his journal that day, "If word of this gets to DePaul . . . it would definitely end me there." Steward later said in an interview that he was cleared of the murders "largely because I had no car" and did not know how to drive, and thus could not have dumped the bodies in the forest preserve. By the end of the same week, however, he had been called in to meet with the dean of the school and was told his contract would not be renewed. "I tried to get him to say why," Steward wrote in his diary, "but all I could force out of him was 'Shall we say for outside activities?'"[73] Steward's firing illustrates how easy it was for employers to accede to the pressure of press and police for the persecution of innocent gay citizens in the wake of a sex-crime panic. The lucky ones were those eased out of a job quietly.

Because the sex-crime panics normalized the idea that gay people did not enjoy ordinary procedural rights, the repeated investigations fostered a climate of fear. In December 1956, the disappearance of two young sisters, Barbara and Patricia Grimes, who had also gone to the movies, and the discovery of their bodies a month later, evoked a similar panic. "Chicago seems to have gone quite off its rocker about the Grimes case," wrote one gay man that spring, describing its impact on gay men sought by the police.[74] In July 1957 it was reported that a "limping blond youth" had been seen with Robert Peterson by the eye doctor who cared for his younger sister; dozens of citizens called and wrote the police with tips.[75]

In late 1959, eight detectives within the Chicago police department's sex bureau were still assigned full time to the Schuessler-Peterson investigation.[76] By the fifth anniversary of the murders, in the fall of 1960, the *Tribune* reported that 44,000 people had been interviewed and 6,500 reports and complaints investigated. Of 3,500 suspects questioned, 45 were indicted, and 40 convicted of various crimes, including crimes connected to "perversion."[77] Nearly two years later, a national gay magazine reported that the case "has led to continued police harassment of homosexuals (as alleged suspects) throughout the Midwest." And new suspects were still being rounded up.[78] It is difficult to overstate how powerfully the media-generated sex-crime panics of the 1950s—and the Schuessler-Peterson murder investigation in particular—struck fear into gay men.

Although the black press did not call for police crackdowns on deviates in the manner of the white-owned daily papers, black middle-class respectability politics increasingly shaped the coverage of queer life in the black media. The drag balls that had been a staple of *Ebony* and *Jet* received noticeably less coverage by the late 1950s, and as civil rights activism became more prominently featured, queer culture was less often portrayed in favorable ways. A *Defender* reader complained, "I saw in your paper some months ago some men dressed as women. Please don't advertise the mess."[79] In 1960, a black reformer complained that "there seems to be almost a tacit acceptance that certain conditions can and will be tolerated in a Negro community that would not be tolerated in some other sections of the city." He wrote that, along 63rd Street in the South Side's Woodlawn neighborhood, "Prostitutes, male homosexuals and drug addicts arrogantly paraded along the street with the air that it was a badge of honor to be this sort of scum."[80] For black aspirants to middle-class status, social and sexual deviance increasingly seemed not simply offensive but a threat to racial uplift as well.

Inkblots and Individual Rights

In the midst of continuing police harassment and media-generated sex-crime panics, as well as a nascent national movement for African American civil rights, Chicago's homophile movement took shape. By some twist of fate, Chicago had been the site of the nation's earliest gay-rights organization yet uncovered, the Society for Human Rights, founded in 1924 by Henry Gerber, a postal clerk and Great War veteran living on the city's North Side. The group was quickly shut down by the police, its files confiscated, and Gerber let go by the post office. In 1940, a pen pal asked Gerber about forming an organization for homosexuals. "Let me tell you from experience," he replied, "it does not pay to do anything for them. I once lost a good job in trying to bring them together."[81] Still, Gerber's activism illustrates the transatlantic influence of Magnus Hirschfeld and other German sexologists, and it was a precursor to the American gay movement of the postwar period.

The homophile movement began decades later among white liberals, most of them men. Mobilizing around an individual-level trait not shared with family members, such as one's homosexuality, often entails spatial and emotional distancing from one's family and neighborhood of origin. For this reason, participating in such a movement was perhaps inevitably both less attractive to and less possible for black than for white Chicagoans. In the working-class queer city, to be sure, there was some crosstown traffic. An African American male-to-female transgender Chicagoan living on the South Side recalls that she "was always up on north side, in and out of there," especially the mostly white, bohemian and queer enclave of Old Town, where she encountered a multiracial transgender social network— including other street queens who "introduced me to the doctor they were getting their hormones from."[82] But the racial segregation of Chicago's neighborhoods and workplaces curtailed the possibility of interracial queer political mobilization.

To most gays and lesbians in the early Cold War era, the risks of forming an organization based on their sexual orientation collectively outweighed the potential benefits. In the late 1940s or early 1950s, Shirley Willer was a young nurse in her twenties when a gay male friend died in a Catholic hospital in Chicago. Willer believed that her friend received inadequate care because he was perceived to be gay. Along with perhaps five friends, she recalled, she went to see a lawyer named Pearl Hart to ask about starting a formal organization of gays and lesbians. "We asked Pearl how you went about starting a group, and she said, 'You don't. It's too dangerous.'" At that time, Willer said, "Pearl was like everyone else. She felt that people would get further by simply doing things quietly without announcing themselves." Willer abandoned the notion of founding an organization and instead established an informal network of mutual aid. "Nothing came of that meeting, no formal organization, so my girlfriends and I did things pretty much on our own," Willer recalled. "We took in young women and sometimes young men who had been thrown out of their homes." She felt her nurse's salary enabled her to help these young people, who "wouldn't take jobs where they would be in danger of being fired because of being gay" and consequently took "the dirty jobs, the rough jobs."[83]

It was not until 1954—after the California-based Mattachine Foundation had reorganized as the Mattachine Society, at its spring 1953 convention—that Midwesterners formed their first homophile group since Gerber's. The Mattachine chapter in Chicago produced a newsletter from mid-1954 to early 1956, which published detailed, often quite well-written book reviews challenging literary conventions of gay representation. In 1954 and 1955, the Chicago group sponsored both closed and public discussions of such topics as "The Deviate and His Job" and "The Ethics of the Sex-Deviate," as well as book discussion groups and fund-raising art sales. Participants in Chicago's first homophile group looked to its West Coast progenitor as a model. One Mattachine member reported in the group's newsletter about a trip to the West Coast: "The Society in San Francisco is probably further removed from the organizational growing pains Chicago has." He was impressed, he said, that Mattachine Society pamphlets were available in the waiting room of the city health department's outpatient clinic. The man reported that a police crackdown then under way in the City by the Bay "has the approval of most deviant residents of the city" because it focused on "that minority of deviants whose promiscuity in public places is flagrant and objectionable."[84] Thus, if California was frequently held up as a model, the example was not necessarily always a radicalizing influence.

Chicago's early homophile activists, like their counterparts in coastal cities, used a patriotic rhetoric that suffused much of American life in the early Cold War. Yet, however eager they were to integrate themselves into postwar society and assert a respectable image, homophile organizers also included many leftists, who deviated in other ways from the postwar consensus. Pearl Hart, the crucial figure in the emergence of the homophile movement in Chicago, emerged out of left-wing politics (see Figure 2). Born in 1890 and raised Jewish in Traverse City, Michigan, she belonged to a generation in which there were almost no women attorneys, but she practiced law in Chicago from 1914. In 1933, Hart became a public defender in Chicago's Morals Court (later the Women's Court), where she improved the legal representation, and sharply reduced the conviction rate, of women arrested on prostitution charges.[85] Active in the Henry Wallace presidential campaign and the National Lawyers Guild, Hart was described by the journalist I. F. Stone in 1953 as "famous throughout the Midwest for a lifetime of devotion to the least lucrative and most oppressed kind of clients." She defended immigrants and Communists charged under the anticommunist Smith Act of 1950. She argued before the U.S. Supreme Court, and won, a 1957 case limiting the power of immigration officials to ask an alien awaiting deportation questions about how he used his free time and what newspapers he read.[86]

FIGURE 2. Pearl M. Hart, date unknown. Courtesy of Gerber/Hart Library
and Archives.

Hart never identified herself publicly as a lesbian, even though she did
more than any other Chicagoan in the 1950s to advance gay rights. Renee
Hanover—who later said she came to Chicago as part of the Communist
Party underground in the 1950s, then became Hart's student at John Marshall Law School in downtown Chicago, and finally joined her in opening
a legal practice focusing on cases affecting women—recalled how Hart
managed being both a lesbian and a lawyer. When they met, Hanover
recalled after Hart's death, "of course she knew I was queer and I knew she
was queer; I didn't think that *she* knew *she* was queer. To know Pearl is to
know this [feeling]! . . . She really felt that one's personal life was one's
own." She was "very conservative in that way. But *not* conservative in terms
of gay community cases. She's the one person who would take these
cases."[87] She was accustomed to representing clients despised by mainstream commentators.

Indeed, as with homophile groups in every city, organizing was hampered by the fact that pseudonyms were the custom. One of the original Chicago Mattachine chapter's first newsletters reported that the group had "formally approved Mr. Frank Beauchamp, who had generously offered to relinquish his privilege of anonymity as a member of the Society," and this would allow the group to "proceed to the next step toward legal recognition under the Illinois Not for Profit Corporation Act."[88] After its address was published in national Mattachine Society literature, mailed by the San Francisco headquarters, the organization received correspondence from readers across the Midwest. "From Illinois, Indiana, Michigan and Ohio came offers of help," wrote the newsletter editor, and "leaders throughout these States also inquired about forming chapters in their own communities."[89]

Police harassment in 1954 was harsh—yet it did not have as much of the legal architecture of the state backing it up as would be the case a decade later. The complaints described in the Chicago Mattachine Society newsletter in this era focused more on the risk of exposure in the workplace than on police practices (though, of course, the latter could and often did precipitate the former). Indeed, there was no discussion of the Chicago police department in the newsletter at any point during the chapter's first incarnation. Only one article that appeared at that time directly took up the question of the state—rather than religious and medical authorities—as persecutors of gay people, and that article lodged its complaint not against the city or state but against the federal government, as well as against corporations influenced by the example of discrimination that federal policies offered. "Not only has the Federal Government expressed its aim to refuse to employ homosexuals for the sake of 'tightening security measures' or 'improving moral standards,'" wrote the author, who published only under the initials J. B., "but an increasing number of private businesses are following the Government's lead." The author explained that federal policies had altered the climate for gay employees of local private firms. "Investigative agencies purporting to be miniature FBI's," observed another article in the Chicago Mattachine newsletter, "have sprung up to meet this demand for employee screening. Listed on the letters of one of these local agencies are the 'undesirables' this agency specializes in ferreting out; in bold print 'homosexuals' stands out."[90] Some local employers had, unfortunately for gay people, begun to take their cue from the federal government.

However timid by the standards of a later era, the Mattachine newsletter talked back to a culture that relentlessly demonized gay people. "In America at least," sociologist Erving Goffman wrote in his influential 1963 book *Stigma*, "no matter how small and how badly off a particular stigmatized category is, the viewpoint of its members is likely to be given public presentation of some kind."[91] After a psychiatrist spoke at one Mattachine meeting and advanced the view that homosexuality could be treated and cured, the editors published letters of complaint from members. After the philosopher Gerald Heard spoke at an early meeting, one member wrote a letter denouncing Heard's claims as pretentious: "As for [his] notion that the 'intergrade' has this great creative potential because he's 'relieved of the burden of procreation'—well, just ask the average invert where most of his energy goes."[92] The organization engaged in fledgling dialogues with activists in other cities, comparing their predicaments. Chicago's Mattachine chapter held a daylong benefit art show, during which viewers watched a recording of a 1954 local television program, which had been shipped from Los Angeles, where it was taped, and which most members apparently found disappointingly unsympathetic toward gay citizens.[93]

The Chicago Mattachine group also engaged in a surprisingly bold project to help produce knowledge about homosexuality. Inspired by the pathbreaking research of Evelyn Hooker, the psychologist and expert on gay men's mental health, its members volunteered to take Rorschach inkblot tests for the cause. They also recruited their friends to participate in Hooker's research. In retrospect, this may have been the chapter's most important contribution to gay equality. The collaboration began in 1954 when Hooker stopped in Chicago on a cross-country trip to meet with chapter members. Her work was pioneering because, unlike previous scholarship, it did not rely on convenience samples made up solely of those gay men who sought a cure or had trouble with the law but instead recruited participants from homophile groups.[94] After Hooker's visit, the Mattachine group "offered its services in obtaining 37 volunteers" to take Rorschach inkblot tests for a Chicago doctor interested in studying "non-institutionalized homosexuals."[95] Hooker cited her conversations with Chicago Mattachine members, along with their counterparts in San Francisco, New York, and Los Angeles, in her first published account of this research on gay men's mental health, which she presented earlier at a 1956 conference in Chicago and published that same year in the *Journal of Psychology*.[96]

Despite such activities, the Chicago Mattachine group had trouble staying afloat. By mid-1956, San Francisco activist Hal Call visited Chicago and pronounced the chapter "practically dormant," reporting a high level of fearfulness on the part of the gay Chicagoans he met, and no newsletters appear to survive from after the summer of 1955.[97] During a brief revival in 1957, the Mattachine members managed little more than to publish a pamphlet—although a significant one—written by Pearl Hart, titled "Your Legal Rights." The pamphlet might best be summarized as a description of what was likely to happen to a gay man or lesbian—though it referred only to "individuals," not homosexuals—after being arrested.

The focus of the pamphlet was on laws used against gays. The main right emphasized was the right of an arrested person not to answer questions. "No police officer," said the brochure, "has a right to question a person who has committed no offense, and the law does not require the person to answer indiscriminate questioning because the police happen to be making an investigation, or because there is a so-called 'crime wave.'" The pamphlet also included a list of Illinois criminal offenses that "are frequently invoked against individuals," including laws against public intoxication; patronizing or maintaining a disorderly house; "the infamous crime against nature"; the commission of lewd, lascivious, wanton, indecent, or lustful acts in public; and that broadest charge, "disorderly conduct." The Mattachine Society's Chicago Area Council, as it was known, offered the leaflet through the mail for 25 cents.[98]

"Your Legal Rights" drew heavily on patriotic rhetoric, claiming that the "founders . . . , wisely foreseeing the necessity for limiting the extent of the law and the methods of its enforcement, drafted the Bill of Rights." The pamphlet, even while framing its topic as the rights of "individuals," not homosexuals, gamely evoked the emotional tenor of bar raids and similar forms of police harassment: "the primary need for many arrested persons is to eliminate the feeling of fear which so many entertain because of lack of knowledge of legal procedures." But the "rights" described in "Your Legal Rights" were in fact rather few, in this age before *Miranda* and other legal precedents that augmented the rights of criminal defendants. For several brief periods in the 1950s, Chicago's gay men and women organized to give voice to their frustrations over police harassment and social and political marginalization. But it would take a national movement for civil rights to show them how to organize effectively.

*   *   *

In the second half of the 1950s, periodic sex-crime panics continued to result in police harassment of gay men. When a fifteen-year-old girl's body was found in Montrose Harbor in 1957, for example, the 44th Ward Republican committeeman, Robert Decker, railed against the leniency of judges in "loosing sex degenerates upon our streets," while Democratic alderman Charles H. Weber from the neighboring 45th Ward added that "if we want to protect the youngsters, we'll have to organize a campaign to get [them] off the streets after dark and go after the sex maniacs who make our streets dangerous."[99] After another gruesome murder on the North Side in 1960, a crime reporter said, "In the area, police know that a number of men with criminal sex records live and work," adding that they had been questioned.[100] "Chicago had quite a 'heat wave' this year," wrote a columnist for the Los Angeles–based homophile magazine *ONE* in mid-1959, using a meteorological metaphor that both punned on a slang term for police and reflected an era when police repression seemed to many gays and lesbians like a force of nature.[101]

At the same time, even though Chicago was the scene of intense—and intensifying—policing, gay citizens could sometimes carve out space for themselves in a city where the establishment was well known for corruption and graft. Chicago's Mattachine chapter struggled to attract more than a handful of members in the 1950s, but it offered a response to the increasingly systematic policing of gay life by local authorities and to the isolation and exclusion from mass society that gays and lesbians felt. Though marginal and lacking influence in the 1950s, the movement's emergence paved the way for more ambitious mobilization in later years.

In the 1950s, moreover, gay bars only erratically enforced rules against intimate contact between patrons because vice control was relatively uncoordinated and decentralized. As late as 1961, a visitor describing the Front Page Lounge on Chicago's Near North Side—one of the city's most crowded and most popular gay bars—wrote, "Dancing is allowed. They say that no close dancing is allowed, but very seldom stick to the rule."[102] By the mid-1960s, however, as we will see in the next chapter, most bars would enforce a strict prohibition on same-sex dancing altogether, as the police department's ability to suppress gay life had been dramatically increased. By the mid-1960s, gay citizens would come to feel more harassed by the Chicago police than by the military, psychiatrists, or the federal civil service, and they would think back to the 1950s as a time of relative freedom.

2

Maximum Feasible Intimidation

IN THE 1960s, as breadwinner liberalism came to dominate American politics, Chicago mayor Richard J. Daley insisted on interpreting its terms narrowly. As the Democratic Party's most powerful boss, Daley was present at the creation of America's eight years of liberal governance, playing a widely acknowledged role in the nomination of John F. Kennedy for president. Yet even as Chicago became the first major American city in which private, consensual homosexual acts were not a crime, police stepped up their war on gay nightlife. Though Daley did not protest when the Illinois legislature decriminalized same-sex acts, he lobbied that same year for changes to state liquor laws that helped shut down gay public life in his city. Gays and lesbians were no longer criminals, but for them to gather in an establishment serving alcohol became more dangerous.

Even as Daley became his party's most powerful boss, his political agenda remained strikingly parochial. His reputation as the Democrats' preeminent kingmaker was secured at the Democratic convention in Los Angeles in July 1960, where he helped engineer the nomination of Massachusetts senator John F. Kennedy for president, in part by unceremoniously dumping his own former mentor in state politics, the two-time failed presidential nominee Adlai Stevenson. Although no one can know precisely why Daley threw his support to Kennedy, the rewards he reaped went beyond the debt the young president later owed him. Having a Catholic at the top of the ticket—as well as a Protestant, Otto Kerner, running for governor—played on the enthusiasm of Catholics eager to cast a vote for the first Catholic president. Kennedy's nomination thus helped Daley defeat the incumbent state's attorney, Benjamin Adamowski, whose muckraking had exposed a police corruption scandal early in the year.[1] For Daley, a fellow Catholic at the top of the ticket would maximize the turnout of loyal white working-class voters in November, and thereby help take the pressure off corruption in his police department. As Norman Mailer would later put it, Daley "was not a national politician, but a clansman."[2]

In the liberal era that he helped to launch, Daley of Chicago played a contradictory role. He united his city's Catholic and black voters behind Kennedy in a bitterly fought election that pushed his party back into the White House in 1960.[3] Under President Lyndon Johnson, Daley took full advantage of Great Society funds for urban redevelopment. Yet he fought tooth and nail, and successfully, for the right to keep Chicago schools largely segregated.[4] He also exerted extraordinary pressure to circumvent the program's requirement that those affected at the grassroots level be permitted "maximum feasible participation" in antipoverty programs. As a machine boss, Daley perceived the program as a threat to his power; brooking no rival, he cowed Johnson with his insistence that federal funds flow through city hall. Most famously, he outmaneuvered the campaign by Martin Luther King, Jr., to protest the isolation and poverty of the city's African American ghettos during the Chicago Freedom Movement. The Chicago machine under Daley seemed to advance urban liberals without advancing urban liberalism.

Daley was deeply identified with the New Deal's vision that blue-collar white men should be able to get jobs that would allow them to support a family. With respect to questions he understood as moral rather than economic, however, Daley's vision of liberalism became more exclusionary. As urban life was increasingly sexualized, Daley did not incorporate the notion of sexual freedom into his parochial liberalism. In the neighborhoods stretching north from the Loop along the lakefront—especially along North Michigan Avenue, where offices, restaurants, and hotels began to boom in the early 1960s—the police increasingly sought not to corral and confine gay life, but to eliminate it.[5]

As city officials secured federal funds for urban renewal and highway construction and as they implemented the Daley administration's ambitious 1958 plan for construction in the Loop and on the Near North Side, middle-class reformers demanded crackdowns on vice and on organized crime, while city policy makers worked to rebuild downtown in a way that would lure white families with children to live, shop, and play there. Though Chicago was the birthplace of Hugh Hefner's *Playboy* magazine and home to the famous Playboy Mansion, the city sued Hefner under obscenity laws and confiscated copies of the magazine after actress Jayne Mansfield appeared nude in the June 1963 issue.[6] But the lawsuit was unsuccessful. Not only that, but beginning in 1965, gray-flannel-suited men visiting Chicago for conventions saw the *Playboy* moniker in illuminated white letters, nine feet tall, on top of what had formerly been the Palmolive Building. Three years later, Hefner was called "Chicago's most spectacularly successful citizen."[7] As urban life was increasingly sexualized, Daley with limited success worked to contain sexual expression and material he saw as incompatible with family life.

In the 1960s, Chicago experienced the clash between urban liberalism—characterized by its opportunist mix of machine- and reform-oriented politics, its investment in the male-breadwinner household, and its continued strength among ethnic working-class whites—and the rising tide of rights-based movements among racial and sexual minorities. In a city increasingly bifurcated—between glass-and-steel towers and brick-and-concrete public-housing projects—black civil rights activists struggled to gain traction in challenging inequality in education and housing, and local homophile groups began to reach beyond their tiny discussion groups and into the public square. It was in this moment that Daley's police department stepped up its harassment of both African Americans and queers.

"An Act Not Likely to Be Noted"

In 1961, the Illinois legislature passed two new laws affecting the policing of gay life. The first, which ostensibly liberalized the legal status of gay people, was the enactment of a criminal code reform that, among other things, decriminalized gay sex—the first successful such move in the country—by repealing the Illinois "crime against nature" statute. But the second law reform of 1961, which altered liquor regulations in a way that gave the city of Chicago more power to keep gay bars closed after a raid, had far more impact on gay life at the time. Chicago's experience thus revealed that legalizing intimate acts was not enough to make gay people feel safe when they gathered.

By adopting a package of criminal law reforms based on the Model Penal Code proposed by the American Law Institute (ALI), the Illinois legislature repealed the long-standing statutory prohibition on private

homosexual behavior between consenting adults.[8] A joint committee of the
state and Chicago bar associations had spent six years transforming the
ALI's model code into a new set of proposed criminal laws for Illinois. In
so doing, the group left in place the ALI's recommendation to repeal the
"crime against nature" statute. These liberal lawyers, according to at least
one participant, were heavily swayed by the arguments made against criminalizing sodomy by Indiana University sexologist Alfred Kinsey.[9]

Advocates for decriminalizing same-sex acts justified their position not
by asserting that people had a right to engage in those acts but by arguing
that their criminalization led to extortion and blackmail. Blackmail was in
fact a real problem. In a sample of 458 nearly all-white gay men interviewed
in Chicago in 1967, 9.4 percent said they had been blackmailed by someone
concerning their homosexuality, most often by a casual sexual partner.[10]
Liberal social scientists cited blackmail in arguing that however reprehensi-
ble a citizen's hidden, stigmatized, and victimless conduct might be, laws
prohibiting such conduct nonetheless fostered other types of crimes. The
lawyers hired to write the comments that accompanied the tentative draft
of the new criminal code, circulated to the state legislators before they cast
their votes, noted that criminalizing "an act not likely to be noted by parties
other than those admittedly involved" would foster "a secretive situation
extremely difficult of proof or disproof—and thus, lends itself . . . to the
dangers of extortion and blackmail."[11] The document referred to the acts
that were to be legalized only as "sexual conduct between consenting
adults."[12] In short, such laws would create the conditions for an *increase*
rather than a decrease in crime.

When the state criminal law reform was drafted, the principal players in
the debate were the gun lobby, defense lawyers, and the Council of Catholic
Churches.[13] Participants in the homophile movement played no part—a
testament to their marginality in 1961. And although insiders knew that the
bill decriminalized sodomy, they dared not discuss the fact publicly for fear
of threatening its passage, according to Dawn Clark Netsch, then a legal
counsel to the governor.[14] Press accounts of the criminal-code reform mentioned the sex provisions in language that appeared to be borrowed from
the bar association's committee and its spokesperson, Professor Charles
Bowman of the University of Illinois College of Law. They labeled it the
product of "a more mature attitude toward immoral conduct,"[15] or of a
need for sex offenses to be "spelled out more clearly."[16] A lawyer who wrote
a synopsis of the code for the *Illinois Bar Journal* professed that, before the

new code's passage, there was "considerable litigation and confusion . . . as to the specific acts included in the crime against nature."[17] To the limited extent that a public case was made at that time for decriminalizing private consensual homosexual acts, it centered on clarity and modernization rather than sexual freedom or homosexual rights.

Though the repeal of the Illinois sodomy law was an early harbinger of the gay-rights revolution, even most members of Chicago's homophile organizations were unaware of it at the time. "Most of the members present had no positive knowledge of the new deviant relations law until the meeting with Pearl Hart," reported the president of the new Daughters of Bilitis Chicago chapter, the month after the change went into effect.[18] The two national gay magazines of the era, both published in California, reported on the change. Del Martin, who had cofounded the Daughters of Bilitis in San Francisco in 1955, wrote in the group's magazine, *The Ladder*, that "while the homophile movement has long expounded the need to change our sex laws to this effect, now that it has happened I can't help wondering if there will be any appreciable difference in the attitude of law enforcement regarding the homosexual."[19] In Chicago, the sodomy-law reform had no discernible effect on the trajectory of gay mobilization in Chicago—nor, as we shall see, on policing. By September 1970, when members of Chicago Gay Liberation spoke at the plenary session of the Black Panther Party–sponsored Revolutionary People's Constitutional Convention in Philadelphia, their statement declared, "Any homosexual from Chicago, where homosexuality is legal, will tell you that changing the law makes no difference."[20]

At Daley's behest, the legislature also passed, in the very same session, a law that enabled Daley to keep taverns shut during license-revocation-appeal proceedings. This law's impact on gay communal life was far more immediate and concrete than the theoretical benefit gays and lesbians might derive from the new criminal code. Because the statute dealt with liquor regulations, Daley could not enact this more significant measure municipally. Rather, it required an act of the state legislature, where downstate Republicans initially opposed it. Politicians from more rural parts of Illinois "contended enactment of the bill could lead to harassment of legitimate business men."[21] The Democratic Senate majority leader and a key Chicago machine politician, George W. Dunne, assured his colleagues otherwise: "This bill is not directed at the ma and pa taverns," he said, "but at the dens of iniquity that are operating in Chicago."[22] Yet it was squeezed through the legislature by limiting its application to Chicago—a provision that would, nearly a decade later, lead the state's high court to strike it down. (The final law was written so that it applied to cities with more than half a million residents, of which Illinois had only one.) This debate departed from the usual pattern of partisan conflict in Springfield, in which Chicago Democrats typically argued for, and downstate Republicans against, higher spending and taxes. In the padlock law, the machine fought for the power to crack down more harshly on nightlife, while Republicans prevented such power from being exercised outside Chicago's city limits.[23]

The new measure effectively strangled those best positioned to fight back against the war on gay sociability. By depriving bar owners of revenue while they appealed a liquor-license revocation, a process that could drag on for months or even years, the new measure added significantly to the financial risk involved in running a gay bar in Chicago. Daley portrayed the measure as a step against organized crime. One reporter said, referring to the mayor's power before the new law's passage, "When he closes a tavern for serious offenses, the operator can reopen for as long as two years while appealing the revocation."[24] The presence of "deviates" was clearly among the "serious offenses" that politicians and journalists alike understood to be a legitimate ground for closing a tavern. For the mayor of Chicago, homosexuality became a political question almost exclusively in the context of the regulation of vice. So far were gays and lesbians from being deemed a political constituency that they lacked, in some sense, even the right to assemble.

War on Vice

Even more consequential for gay citizens than the sodomy-law repeal and the law allowing the padlocking of taverns appealing license revocation was still another transformation that occurred in 1960, unfolding in Chicago rather than Springfield: a churning of the cycle of scandal and reform in the police department. A major scandal broke in January 1960, in which a police station on the Northwest Side (on Foster Avenue just east of Damen Avenue) was revealed as the epicenter of a large-scale burglary ring. Though Daley had consolidated his authority yet further after his reelection to a second term in 1959, the so-called Summerdale scandal that erupted early in 1960—named for the police station at its center—seemed to confirm the

FIGURE 3. New Chicago police superintendent O. W. Wilson being filmed by
WGN-TV, 1960. Courtesy of Chicago History Museum.

harshest charges of the machine's critics. Daley had in fact loosened the
regulation of organized crime after taking office, adding to his vulnerability:
As a favor to his backers in the organized-crime syndicate, he had abolished
the police intelligence unit, known as "Scotland Yard," in 1956.[25]

The mayor managed not only to avoid being tarnished but even to
benefit from the Summerdale affair through a politically brilliant step: He
hired a new police superintendent, a reformer from outside, and authorized
him to revamp the department from top to bottom. The choice of O. W.
Wilson, a nationally prominent police reformer and the dean of the School
of Criminology at the University of California, Berkeley, restored confidence in Daley and showed his commitment to professionalism (see Figure
3).[26] Arriving in the spring of 1960, Wilson was given wide authority to
revamp the department. The Chicago job enabled him to implement his
ideas about reorganizing big-city police departments, which involved a
costly modernization of facilities and centralization of operations. The most

up-to-date equipment was purchased, psychological profiling was adopted as a means of identifying officers for promotion, and a new intelligence division—the existence of which was widely publicized even as its actual operations were kept secret—was established.[27]

Wilson was a strong believer in policing vice aggressively. At the same time as the State Department's dismissals of "security risks" at the national level decreased overall by focusing more exclusively on homosexuals than it did in the 1950s, it was local political authorities who most directly organized antigay policing in the Windy City.[28] Newspapers spread the word that the new chief was cracking down on all manner of illicit activity, from horse betting to women's being hired by bars to solicit drinks from male patrons.[29] This upstanding Protestant clashed with local traditions in a city in which the police force and public life were heavily Catholic. In his first weeks on the job, Wilson stopped the practice of routinely allowing Catholic churches and other charities to raise money by holding bingo games, because this was technically illegal gambling. It did not endear this former university administrator to many of his officers, or to the city council, who for more than a year afterward pursued the idea of legalizing bingo by state law or referendum.[30] Police confiscated bingo equipment in a raid at the Belgium-American Club.[31] Slot machines were seized in Veterans of Foreign Wars halls.[32] "There can be no compromise with vice any more than there can be compromise with other crime," Wilson wrote in the second edition of his best-selling textbook *Police Administration*, which was released during his time at the helm in Chicago, following revisions made by his wife.[33]

Highly attentive to public relations, Wilson was a masterful superintendent in an era of intense competition between local newspapers to cover crime and policing. In planning a department's public-relations efforts, he wrote in his textbook, "One story each day is better than three stories every third day."[34] The mainstream press, and many middle-class whites, credited Wilson with professionalizing the department, investing in technological improvements, and centralizing operations to reduce corruption. But the new chief's need to justify budget increases, and his commitment to accurate and detailed crime statistics, generated pressure to increase arrests. He launched a phase of aggressive policing of black life that was invisible to most whites and with civil liberties implications that were ignored by the predominantly white media. Wilson believed that police officers should not simply respond to crime but should engage in aggressive, "preventive" action on the streets, and the brunt of this new style of policing fell on

Chicago's segregated black neighborhoods. The intelligence division that Wilson created in 1961 even included a special Gang Intelligence Unit, an early signal of the militarization of the department in the coming decade—as was the imposition of the 24-hour-clock military time system on police recordkeeping.[35]

In the streets of Chicago, and in his textbook on police administration, Wilson was a proponent of using undercover officers extensively, and under his leadership the department expanded the contexts in which these were used. To control vice, he wrote, "undercover operators and funds are needed for the intensive investigation, which is essential for successful enforcement."[36] Most controversially, he assigned—or at least told reporters that he was assigning—undercover police officers to the task of identifying officers willing to accept graft or bribes so that such officers could be prosecuted.[37] This policy was extremely unpopular with the rank and file and opposed by the Patrolmen's Association and the department's Catholic chaplain. Together with his new limits on officers' outside employment and his firm opposition to graft and what he called "political interference" with crime-fighting, these policies led to what Wilson's biographer called "a serious morale problem" at the grass roots.[38]

Plainclothes cops and their swashbuckling antics, which appealed to a society obsessed with espionage and spying, became a staple of Wilson's aggressive approach to public relations. Newspapers reported on cops "posing as conventioneers from New York" and hiring women from an escort service for sexual encounters at the Palmer House hotel in the Loop.[39] Crime reporters were invited to come along with undercover officers and chronicle their operations. The resulting "true crime" news articles became fodder for the intense competition for readers among the city's four main daily papers. The stories covered the heroic feats, for example, of ten police officers "dressed in the tattered fashion of skid row" who prevented a robbery, or a pair of cops who witnessed and stopped a crime while "wearing shabby clothing and pretend[ing] to be intoxicated."[40] The publicity-obsessed Wilson gave his blessing to a television program about one of the police plainclothes units, telling reporters at the preview that it would be a corrective to a society he believed was too "concerned about the rights of the criminal."[41]

Wilson launched harsh and well-publicized crackdowns on predominantly white queer nightlife, using plainclothes officers in several ways. Gay men risked police action when plainclothes officers, who had been sent to monitor bars undercover, witnessed men dancing together, kissing, touch-ing, or "soliciting" sex. When places that catered to women witnessed mass arrests, it was more often because lesbians, simply by being part of a subcul-ture organized around the butch/femme subcultural forms of gender expression, were treated as violators of city laws.[42] Narcotics charges were also frequently used against gay establishments—often, according to Valerie Taylor, using planted evidence. "A guy would go into the men's room and leave a joint on the window sill," she recalled. "Pretty soon another man, also in plain clothes, would go into the men's room, come out with the joint, making little cries of happy surprise."[43] The spike in plainclothes surveillance thus enlisted officers in a semiotics of disguise and disclosure that mirrored the architecture of the closet.

As he mounted a sweeping war on vice, Wilson accepted suggestions from unelected antivice reformers while ignoring pleas from aldermen who found the crackdowns excessive. In 1962, for example, Virgil Peterson, a business-backed reformer and longtime director of the Chicago Crime Commission, wrote to Wilson proposing a new ordinance tightening enforcement of a ban on "B-girls"—women employed by taverns to induce men to buy them drinks. The superintendent quickly proposed such an ordinance. Though it took two years for the city council to enact it, Wilson promptly embarked on an aggressively publicized "war" on B-girls.[44] Some South Side aldermen argued that this bill was bad for small businesses; "with Wilson as police boss, [2nd Ward alderman William H.] Harvey asserted, barmaids supporting families have lost their jobs." In fact, at least one club owner thought launching a female impersonator show would make his business *safer* from the police: This Near North Side establish-ment, the Talk of the Town, reportedly "after a prostitution raid changed its entertainment policy to one featuring female impersonators." The strategy apparently did not work, as the place was raided again within a year, this time with nine male dancers arrested and one charged with impersonating a female.[45]

The intensified police harassment under Wilson was reflected in the activities of a new chapter of the Mattachine Society founded late in 1959. In the spring of 1960, the group held a dinner meeting at the La Salle hotel, at which Pearl Hart spoke to sixteen men, and plans were made to reissue the 1957 pamphlet "Your Legal Rights" in "a new pocket-sized edition," though this plan does not seem to have come to fruition.[46] In a particularly large February 1961 raid on a blue-collar lesbian bar on the Northwest

Side, the C & C Club, more than fifty women were arrested along with the bartender. The following month, the newsletter of the new Chicago chapter of the Mattachine Society linked antigay harassment to the bingo debacle, which had continued to attract ink: "Upon taking office as Chicago's police commissioner several months ago, Orlando Wilson struck a mighty blow against crime and vice in Cook County by outlawing bingo. On February 18 the forces of law and order took another giant step by raiding one of the city's more sedate gay bars and arresting more than fifty women, plus the bartender." The article appeared under the headline "Civic Virtue Triumphs Again."[47] At the police station, "those women wearing 'fly fronts,' regardless of whether they wore lipstick, long hair, or earrings, were made partially to undress in order to determine whether they wore jockey shorts," according to the account of a woman named Del Shearer.[48] Although this newest Mattachine incarnation was, like its predecessors, unable to sustain itself beyond a small number of newsletter issues, the article's tone anticipated the backlash that Wilson's war on vice would stimulate by lesbians and gay men by mid-decade. As we will see, the C & C Club raid led Shearer to found a chapter of the Daughters of Bilitis, the San Francisco-based all-female homophile organization.

Policing was perhaps harshest on working-class queer teenagers. The municipal police and county sheriff were not the only agency involved in policing gays and lesbians; the Illinois Youth Commission incarcerated children deemed troublesome. Around 1960, a white sixteen-year-old teenager was taken to a Chicago police station by his parents, who were angry that he stayed out late at night and sneaked into gay bars. The police shuttled him to the youth commission, which deemed him "incorrigible" and sent him to the State Industrial School for Boys. There, "they immediately locked me up and kept me away from all the other boys. This is the way that they handle homosexuals: they lock them up and that's it." Released after two months, he said nearly all the other boys were kept for six. "It's awfully strange some of the kids they have in there that shouldn't be there," he recalled several years later.[49] Working-class black queer teenagers were treated even more coercively. Thus, Ron Vernon, a "flamboyant" black teenager who grew up on Chicago's South Side, recalls that when he began high school in the early 1960s, he was "sent to a counselor immediately . . . because of my overt femininity."[50] Later, a family court judge asked the boy's father during a hearing if he were "aware that your son is a homosexual?" The son recalled, "My father is a very honest man, and just said,

'Yeah.' So they said, 'Well, we're going to send him to Galesburg Mental Institution to try to correct his homosexuality.'" The boy, twelve or thirteen at the time of the hearing, would spend much of his adolescence in and out of the custody of the state of Illinois.[51]

In the first half of the 1960s, it became more common for newspapers to publish the names and addresses of all those arrested in a bar raid, a practice that peaked in the spring and summer of 1964 with a merciless series of raids. Cook County Sheriff Richard Ogilvie, a Republican with aspirations to higher office, escalated the war on vice by orchestrating a huge raid on an outlying gay club, Louie's Fun Lounge, on a barren stretch of road in an unincorporated area on the western edge of Cook County. Commercialized vice had flourished on Mannheim Road since the construction of O'Hare airport nearby was completed in 1955. The patrons referred to the place as "Louie Gage's" or "Louie Gauger's," after the club's proprietor, Louis Gauger. Like other owners of gay bars, Gauger had mob ties. He had angered the sheriff by refusing to testify against Mafia kingpin Tony "Big Tuna" Accardo when Ogilvie unsuccessfully prosecuted the latter in 1960 for income-tax fraud.

Not only journalists but also politicians competed to show they were tough on vice. Aggressive raids on gay establishments in the mid-1960s were partly a manifestation of the race for voters' allegiances between the Cook County Democratic Organization—that is, the machine—and the Republican Party, which traditionally was powerful downstate but could also win elections in suburban areas both outside Cook County and just within its borders. In fact, a promise to escalate the war on vice in outlying parts of the county had been the cornerstone of Ogilvie's campaign strategy in 1962: He promised to "raid and close the syndicate gambling casinos and vice dens which have flourished for decades." He even singled out the Fun Lounge specifically for criticism, in a campaign that focused on which candidate was "best qualified to turn the heat on the mob."[52] In the first months of 1964, as Republican and Democratic candidates geared up for the April primary election, charges and countercharges flew, hinting that a crackdown on vice might be in the offing.[53] A Republican candidate for state's attorney "accused Mayor Daley of 'looking the other way' instead of cleaning up syndicated crime in Cook County"[54] and promised to reopen the "Sex Bureau" of the state's attorney's office "because the streets of Chicago are not safe for our women."[55]

Ogilvie's officers humiliated the bar patrons in a spectacular fashion. Early on the morning of Saturday, April 25, 1964, the sheriff blockaded the front and back doors of the Fun Lounge. Undercover sheriff's police officer John Chaconas later testified that just before the raid he had seen "10 or 15 male couples dancing and half a dozen male couples embracing."[56] "They just burst in the front door and lined up inside so no one could go out the front door," recalled one gay man. "They had sent somebody around the back," he said, noting that he escaped arrest by passing through the beer storage room into owner Louie Gauger's own living space behind the club, where the man waited out the raid.[57] They arrested six women and 103 men; loaded them onto school buses; paraded them in front of news photographers while those arrested tried to cover their faces; and supplied reporters with the names, ages, addresses, and occupations of most of those arrested in time for that information to be printed in the Saturday afternoon newspapers (see Figure 4). They kept them overnight. In the morning, they were charged with being "inmates of a disorderly house" and, in a few cases, "lewd and lascivious conduct" as well.

After this raid, which became the stuff of local gay legend, the *Chicago Daily News* published the name, age, home address, and occupation of most of the 109 arrested. They ranged in age from 19 to 56; the median age was 27, eighteen patrons being 21 or 22 years old. The group included many students and teachers; office workers, clerks, salesmen, and a Teletype operator; a hair stylist and a beautician; and a laborer, a dock worker, and a trucker; an accountant, an insurance claim examiner, and a laboratory technician; and a 24-year-old office manager living at tony 3600 Lake Shore Drive. It was a predominantly suburban crowd: of the ninety-three whose addresses were published, thirty-four lived in the city of Chicago, thirty-three elsewhere in Cook County, eleven in Du Page County west of the city, and three in Kane County farther to the west. Six other Illinois counties were represented by one patron each.[58]

As in the purges of gay federal employees in the same era, job dismissals were the most feared outcome of such raids. Some of those arrested reportedly were terminated after what the Los Angeles–based gay magazine *ONE* called their "conviction by publicity." At trial, defense attorneys objected to photographers' presence in the courtroom, but they were overruled.[59] Ogilvie stressed that those arrested included two employees of the Chicago police department, as well as a county employee and school district officials.

FIGURE 4. *Chicago Daily News*, April 25, 1964.

He drew particular attention to the presence of seven schoolteachers and one suburban school principal. Ogilvie effectively challenged other law-enforcement officials to conduct crackdowns of their own by sending letters to the districts that employed the arrested teachers, and by telling reporters, "School districts should keep an eye on people who maintain such close contact with youngsters in the community." The superintendent of the Du

Page County public schools suggested that state authorities revoke the licenses of the teachers.[60] In calling on public-sector employers to fire any of their employees who were arrested, Ogilvie implicitly sanctioned private-sector dismissals as well.[61]

Though the firing of gay teachers was widely praised, at least one school district departed from the pattern. A thirty-year-old schoolteacher living in Dundee, Illinois, and arrested during the raid, was allowed to keep his job, at least initially, as officials "said they were convinced he would be acquitted, and that he claimed all he knew was that he was going to a night club."[62] The *Chicago Tribune* also published a wry letter to the editor from one citizen who found the harassment hypocritical. The fact that "only teachers, as an occupational group, were singled out for attention," observed Russell Doll of Chicago, apparently because of their "contact and assumed influence" with children, suggested "an importance to society" higher than that of other occupations. "It is, therefore, amusing that when it comes to paying teachers, this implied importance decreases," he wrote.[63] But Doll's apparent sympathy toward those arrested was shared by very few public commentators. A few days after the raid, a popular "bad boy" radio host told a *Tribune* interviewer that he was in favor of "sex"—then added, "but not those 109 wig wearers at the Fun Lounge."[64] Even commentators otherwise sympathetic to the sexual revolution, in short, excluded the gay subculture from the circle of acceptable deviation.

Politicians, police, journalists, and employers thus together cast a pall of fear over gay and lesbian life, while advancing their own careers and often extorting money from bar patrons and owners. The men and women caught up in the escalating harassment struggled to make their case to the judges they faced. Pleas for journalists to withhold the names of those arrested from publication were rejected. Splashy raids helped Ogilvie deflect attention from the persistence of organized crime—and from rumors that his own officers were linked to the very syndicate they were supposed to be rooting out. Remarkably, by the end of the year, both Richard Cain, who led the raid, and John Chaconas, the plainclothes officer who testified in court about what he had observed at the Fun Lounge, would be convicted and sentenced to one to three years in prison. Both were indicted as double agents for the very crime syndicate to which the club's owner was thought to be connected.[65] "It is a little hard to tell who are the cops and who the robbers in this script," observed the *Tribune* when the two men were sentenced.[66]

The Fun Lounge incident launched a wave of aggressive raids, and the Chicago police evidently did not want to be outdone by their counterparts in county employment.[67] Days later, Lieutenant Thomas Kernan of the Chicago police department's vice division raided another "hangout for sex deviates," telling reporters afterward, "[T]here has been an increase recently in night spot performances by female impersonators."[68] A few weeks later, Chicago police arrested thirty-three men in the Lincoln Baths in Old Town. Kernan announced not only that "the bathhouse has been a national meeting place for perverts" but that "files of the bathhouse confiscated in the raid listed various meeting places for perverts throughout the United States."[69] The spring 1964 crackdown in Chicago indeed reverberated across the country.

The intense news coverage of the Fun Lounge raid attracted significant attention from *ONE*, the gay magazine published in Los Angeles. "I imagine that you have been receiving clippings on the Chicago raids," a Milwaukee man wrote; he had heard from a friend in Chicago that "there are an awful lot of people looking for new jobs."[70] The editor also explained that the raids justified one of the editorial policies: "[W]e have been often asked to print and distribute lists of gay bars, baths, and other places where homosexuals congregate so that our friends will know where to go when they visit strange towns." However, he said, "We have never felt it would be wise to print such a list," a stance he felt was justified given that the officers in the Fun Lounge raid "found a copy of such a guidebook" and now seemed to be investigating "the other bars listed in the publication." In short, "Why should the homosexual always make it easy for the police? Why print a list that in the wrong hands can be used against us?" With a tone of gallows humor, he encouraged readers to seek out information by word of mouth instead: "Anyway, no self-respecting, enterprising homosexual should ever confess to the need for such a guide." Most devastating, he suggested at the same time, "it probably would be advisable to have a copy of the March 1961 issue of *ONE* magazine if you happen to be unlucky enough to live in Chicago. The March '61 issue contains the editorial telling you what to do in case of arrest."[71]

In the 1950s, police raids on gay bars had been sporadic; in the early 1960s, they had become systematic. The 1964 Fun Lounge raid, like the C & C Club raid three years earlier, angered gay citizens. "Illinois took a giant step forward two years ago," wrote one gay man in a letter to *ONE*. "We up-dated our laws in this state at that time. But the two raids and attendant publicity recently here in Chicago was a black eye for us." The writer primarily blamed the press: "The law has come a long way in Illinois. Now justice must catch up through responsible reporting that makes it impossible for publicity hungry public servants to destroy the innocent before trial."[72] These raids led a small group of gay Chicagoans to found a new organization of people like themselves, determined to act boldly to challenge the authorities.

"A Transparent Curtain of Homosexuality"

Daley's breadwinner liberalism, however resonant in city hall, was increasingly difficult to square with the rising visibility of a cultural liberalism that allowed artistic and cultural experimentation, built on the urban bohemian subcultures that dated at least to the early twentieth century. By the late 1950s, the flourishing of a predominantly white bohemia in Chicago's Old Town and Near North Side was unmistakable. The area had been a site of cultural ferment and dissidence and a magnet for artists and writers from across the Midwest since World War I, but it grew in the prosperous postwar years into a center of beatnik visibility. The celebrated comedy troupe Second City, founded there in 1955, included a pioneering skit on its 1963 program about a young gay man in Chicago who tries to hint to his family members visiting from downstate Illinois about his homosexuality.[73] The landscape was filled with places that catered to these locals. One man recalled an all-night diner on Clark Street, just south of Division, called Feast on a Bun, "just a counter, no tables, and a lot of street hustlers, street cruisers, drag queens—anybody who frequented that area. . . . And I think a lot of cops used the place, too."[74]

The Daley machine reacted against the liberalization of intimate norms in the late 1950s and early 1960s, yet it gradually narrowed its target to focus increasingly on gay life. In his first term in office, Daley launched an ambitious "slum clearance" and redevelopment program, targeting the Loop and the Near North Side, a program that was all but overtly intended to remake downtown to appeal to whites. For Daley, however, not all whites were equally desirable. Rather, he specifically wanted to lure white *families* to live downtown and thus privileged their needs over those of single people. In his influential 1961 study of political power in Chicago, the political scientist Edward Banfield claimed that in 1959 Daley nixed a particular

Near North development project, known as Fort Dearborn, precisely because "the residential part of the Project would have to be mainly high-rise 'economy' apartments for elderly people and childless couples." For Banfield, the mayor's decisive preoccupation with social reproduction was rooted in his Catholic background. "[H]e was against development of a kind that might discourage people from having children or interfere with family life," he wrote.[75]

The redevelopment of the Near North Side may have been aided by the growth of bohemia, but it was primarily driven by downtown business interests. The alliance between the real-estate industry and Daley's city hall was strengthened in 1958 when Daley released a downtown redevelopment plan, which was meant both to prevent black encroachment from residential neighborhoods to the south and to limit the visibility of gays and female prostitutes on the Near North Side. As whites fled to suburban areas to live and shop and the city's black population grew, South Side blacks were increasingly visible as patrons of Loop establishments, where they could purchase goods and services unavailable in slums where commercial developers were unwilling to invest in retail stores. The developer Arthur Rubloff told a reporter that among the major concerns of downtown retailers was that the growing visibility of African Americans on the street was scaring away whites.[76]

Near Old Town, the city entered into a partnership in the early 1960s with a group of private investors to build a giant high-rise apartment complex, Sandburg Village, intended as an attractive urban alternative for affluent white families thinking of moving to the suburbs. The project required many existing buildings along Clark Street to be razed: "I think they were trying to clean up the neighborhood *for* Sandburg Village and get rid of the old businesses," recalled William B. Kelley. Sam's, the most popular gay bar in the area, closed, and other longtime bars followed suit.[77] Rent for apartments in the new buildings was out of reach for many of the area's existing tenants. By the second half of the 1960s, the neighborhood's bohemian history was increasingly being commodified.[78] Newspapers profiled white couples who had chosen to raise children in the revitalized Near North, such as Mrs. Herman Fell, who raised two young children while her husband was at work as a television producer. "It's a nice neighborhood with nice kooky people who do a lot of different things," Mrs. Fell said. The reporter for the *Tribune* explained, "Folk singers, actors, and newspaper persons are among their neighbors."[79] Making the area safe for "squares," however, entailed aggressive police action to shut down unwholesome establishments. Near North Side police rounded up women nightly on suspicion of engaging in sex work.[80]

Black insurgency increased after Daley's reelection, early in 1963, in the aftermath of the high-profile civil rights campaign in Birmingham, Alabama, and the March on Washington for Jobs and Freedom in August. Protest centered on the dramatic racial inequalities in the Chicago public schools. That fall, African American parents staged two massive daylong boycotts of the public school system to protest overcrowding in many all-black schools. Daley's school policies reflected his loyalty to white working-class constituents who held supremacist ideals about the right of white residents to send their children to all-white neighborhood schools. African American activists drew attention in particular to the highly visible use of mobile classrooms outside overcrowded all-black schools. Black parents led a campaign to oust Benjamin Willis, Daley's schools superintendent, who became a symbol of white resistance to integration. Daley, however, was intransigent and refused to fire Willis.[81] The *Defender* drew more attention to police brutality, although the main focus of mobilization in these years remained the school system. The boycotts failed to oust Willis, but their boldness and their identification of city hall as the source of injustice in the neighborhoods marked a watershed for the black freedom struggle locally.[82]

In what became a turning point for the Daley machine's approach to the censorship of sexual material, the Chicago city council rather suddenly became engulfed in the winter of 1964–65 in a lengthy debate over a proposal to prohibit James Baldwin's novel *Another Country* from being used as required reading in an English course in a city-funded two-year college. This major controversy, which captured the attention of the news media locally and even nationally, revealed how central sexuality was to the volatile politics of race, class, and education. The sponsor of the ban was one of the few Republicans on the city council, Alderman John Hoellen of the Northwest Side's 47th Ward. Hoellen objected to the book because, he said, it "extensively dwells upon homosexuality as though it had redeeming social value," a phrase that alluded to the legal definition of obscenity promulgated by the Supreme Court in 1957 in *Roth v. United States*.[83]

Throughout the debate on the city-council floor—the city council's most in-depth discussion of homosexuality in a half century—the assumption prevailed among most participants that gay visibility in the city signified moral decline.[84] The key problem with *Another Country*, according to its critics among local politicians, was that in its pages, as one columnist put it, "Boy gets girl, to be sure, but boy also gets boy."[85] At its height, the controversy involved a seven-hour hearing attended by 200 people while some 30 student picketers weaved back and forth in front of city hall. "Objections to the book centered on charges that it makes interracial homosexuality appear to be a 'joyous' experience and that it is overloaded with sex and vulgarity," wrote one reporter.[86] The spirited public debate over the novel touched on fundamental political questions of censorship, parenting, and state control over the educational system, and it generated commentary about the novel's portrayal of interracial sex, illegal drug use, and obscenity.

Many critics of the book asserted the right of parents to control their children's educational materials, illustrating concern about social reproduction in a child-obsessed society. Wright Junior College, the institution where the controversy arose, was attended largely by working-class whites from the city's nearly all-white bungalow districts. The Chicago man who first contacted Alderman Hoellen to complain about the assignment of the book had objected primarily to its homosexual content, explaining that his twenty-six-year-old daughter should not have been assigned the text because "this is a filthy book. I don't think you have to know the details of how homosexuality is performed to be a whole person."[87] The ensuing city-council debate reified the alignment of interracial with homosexual sex that pervaded much of the novel's reception in white-owned newspapers. "The fine job you have done to keep our city streets clean to make Chicago a city to be proud of is to be commended," testified Mrs. Kenneth Kantor before the aldermen. "Don't allow the dirt and garbage to find it's [sic] way into the classroom." She argued that "accounts of deviates and degenerates' activities" should be used "for medical study only" and not in English classes.[88] The Roman Catholic archdiocese editorialized against teachers who would "shove filth down the throats of students."[89] A suburban Berwyn father of five wrote to the city council that he would not give up "my God-given right to keep a voice in how my children's morals are to be influenced."[90] Precisely because it would interfere with their control over the classroom, teachers' unions opposed the measure.[91]

The black-owned *Chicago Defender*, which had covered Baldwin's meteoric rise to mainstream white acclaim as well as his Chicago appearances, condemned Hoellen's resolution. The paper's editorial board argued that "what these critics are objecting to, is not so much the moral content of the novel, but the free interracial association that is described with such skill and literary brilliance."[92] Indeed, there is ample evidence to support this claim. One Evanston woman, for example, wrote to Alderman Leon Despres, a Hyde Park liberal well known for supporting racial integration and civil rights, sarcastically expressing her gratitude for his vocally backing the book. "Thank you for advocating wide circulation of Baldwin's book *Another Country*," she wrote. "This book tells exactly and in detail just how negroes [sic] live, and it should be read by *all* white people *everywhere*." This, she said, would help them become aware of the "many reasons" why they should oppose the integration of neighborhoods.[93]

Testimony by whites before the city council emphasized the idea that *Another Country* constituted smut. Even Despres, the leading defender of the book, shied away from dignifying its wide-ranging sexual content. He taunted Hoellen by asking, on the council floor "What exists in your mind that glorified homosexuality when you read the book[?]"[94] Despres in this sense more or less gay-baited his opponent. Perhaps because it allowed a respectable means for talking about race and sexual politics, local newspapers were consumed with the controversy. Defenders of the book typically labeled the resolution's proponents as would-be censors. The liberal *Daily News* was lukewarm, editorializing that students who were "old enough to fight, or marry, or both" were adults and should know "what immorality and amorality are."[95] Studs Terkel, the radio journalist, called the council hearing "an incredible charade," defended the literary representation of homosexuality and even alluded to Baldwin's own gayness: "*Ulysses* will be next on the list. Then Walt Whitman will be next because that great American poet was a homosexual."[96]

The discussion of *Another Country* revealed that vice control involved not only the regulation of public space but also the relations and exchange between public and private spaces. The right-wing *Tribune* repudiated its own favorable review of the book, published two years earlier, calling the book "a compilation of perverted interracial sexual relationships" and comparing it to "a guest at a dinner party in your home who was so uncouth as to spout filth at the table and embarrass your other guests with accounts of sexual deviation." Under such circumstances, "you would lose no time handing him his hat and coat, ushering him to the door, and returning to apologize to the company for such behavior."[97] In a city riven by white racial violence against the presence of African Americans, even temporarily, in white neighborhoods, such a metaphor hinted at a segregationist impulse insofar as it conjured a scene of expulsion at the threshold of the home.

The black press, too, associated homosexuality with social or sexual mixing across the color line, sometimes depicting it as a peril to be kept beyond the threshold of the home. In a column written in the early 1960s, and reprinted in the South Side's *New Crusader* in 1964 after the writer's death, Dan Burley—an influential black pianist, journalist, and editor of the Nation of Islam newspaper *Muhammad Speaks*—suggested that blacks might think twice about racial integration, on the ground that "white no-gooders," after being "chased out of respectable white neighborhoods, are only too happy to move into mixed communities and buildings." As an example of "white no-gooders," he conjures a scenario in which one's neighbor, a "young assistant pastor" with a "chubby wife and brood," is "called to the pulpit in a small town faraway" and is replaced by a man who hosts late-night interracial gay parties.[98] Burley's storyline is based on the precariousness of middle-class black existence, in contrast to the *Tribune*'s implicit appeal to the white supremacist to patrol the boundaries of racial purity. Yet both discussions propose policing the boundary of the domestic sphere to exclude sexual deviance.

The black press faced a conundrum given the fact that Baldwin, the nation's most celebrated black writer, was both widely known to be gay and also the author of the postwar era's most prominent gay-themed novels. One strategy was to downplay his gayness. The *Defender*, a middle-class paper committed to keeping black life respectable, largely portrayed the queerness of *Another Country* as an incidental feature. The paper's own editors offered a different interpretation, suggesting that "it was the interracial setting of the plot that aroused the ire of the critics. They hid that motive behind a transparent curtain of homosexuality."[99] In calling homosexuality a red herring, the city's daily black paper thus implied that the book's critics had invoked it only for tactical reasons to conceal their racial prejudices. More explicit was a published letter to the editor from a reader who called the book "an affront to the Negro" for its depiction of "suicide, homosexuals, fornication, and adultery."[100] Still, the wording suggests that in the era of the Civil Rights Act, an African American paper concerned with respectability nonetheless advanced a sense of racial solidarity that securely encompassed Baldwin, whose homosexuality was then widely known among blacks and some whites. Conservative white journalists were frustrated, in fact, by the failure of their black counterparts to line up to criticize the author. "It is a libel to depict Negroes as homosexuals," declared an editorial in the conservative *Tribune*, which supported banning the book and complained bitterly about the failure of black aldermen to join the crusade.[101]

But Daley quashed the measure. If *Another Country* seemed to the black press to contain one sort of public-relations problem, for the mayor it instead threatened to portray municipal government as out of step with modernity and churlishly censorious. Eventually, in the second half of January, Daley's allies on the council killed the proposal.[102] Although they did not give a reason publicly, one city hall reporter speculated that Daley did not want Chicago to acquire "a reputation as the new Boston in the book banning field."[103] A city government that only five years earlier had successfully defended all the way to the U.S. Supreme Court its regime for strictly censoring movies now viewed too strong an association with censorship as potentially damaging.[104] The collapse of the effort to censor the book testified as well to the degree to which young people had begun to challenge long-standing sexual norms. As Professor Perrin Lowrey of the University of Chicago English department said of the novel, "It might shock parents, but I don't think that it would shock their children."[105] Indeed, the generational divide to which he gestured would only become more prominent in the second half of the 1960s.

The racial politics of urban neighborhoods was charged in part because of the way the issue was suffused with sexual imagery and fears, as white Chicagoans repeatedly used violence and threats in the face of black residential encroachment on all-white neighborhoods. By the fall of 1965, the growth of Chicago's Daughters of Bilitis chapter showed "no signs of slacking off," according to its newsletter. "Obviously," it continued, "it will no longer be feasible to meet at the homes of members, so we've begun shopping for an office."[106] But the group had a very difficult time locating a suitable space. In a cartoon in the group's February 1966 newsletter, one member poked fun at the issue, mocking homophobic landlords by comparing the difficulties of the group's members to the concept of social equality then so often used as a bogeyman by white opponents of racial integration. A real-estate office is labeled "Elegant Realty Co." and has a map on the wall labeled, "Blight Survey—Blockbust Map Co.," with a cigar-smoking white real-estate agent and a sign saying, "Use the spittoon."

The caption says, "Now they want an office . . . next thing you know they'll be wanting to marry our daughters."[107] The turn of phrase alluded to the experience of many lesbians for whom taking on a lesbian identity had meant straining or ending a heterosexual marriage. But it also referred to, and made light of, the constrant refrain by segregationists that racial integration would lead to black men's having sex with or even marrying white women.[108]

"The Airing of a Hush-Hush Subject"

Even as the "war on vice" was heating up and politicians fought smut and immorality, and the press and politicians treated gay life as dangerous and deviant, homophile activists tried to cultivate more favorable press coverage. There were liberal reporters, too, after all, and homophile activists began to seek them out. The pioneer in this effort was the city's Daughters of Bilitis chapter, especially its first president, Del Shearer, the first local activist to appear on television. In 1962, a producer for a popular local talk show, "Off the Cuff," hosted by Norman Ross, had approached the group to inquire whether a representative might be willing to appear in a forum on homosexuality. At that time, Shearer considered the idea but decided she was unwilling to take on something so risky.[109] She very much liked the forum when it aired in February 1963, however. "The program in accomplishing one goal—the airing of a hush-hush subject—was tremendously successful," stated the chapter's meeting minutes. "Ross did an excellent job in rounding the presentation to include the many sides of the story."[110]

Later that year, when the same television producers again approached her, Shearer changed her mind about the costs and benefits of appearing on television, now that she trusted the producers. "My friends have advised me against this possible exposure to ridicule and similar types of aggravation," she wrote in a letter to Meredith Grey, the Daughters of Bilitis national publicity director in San Francisco. But she had decided to reject the advice. "I must admit," she wrote, "that I have reached a point in my life when I must show my belief in people and in myself." She believed that "a presentation properly handled," something she now knew she could expect from Ross's show, would be less likely to harm her. She concluded, "I will not wear a mask," which she meant figuratively and perhaps literally as well.[111]

During the televised forum, Shearer tried to convey to the show's viewers what it felt like to be gay in a straight world. "So much public life has this heterosexual overtone," she said, "so much heterosexuality surrounds homosexuals. If they are going to move in society and be a part of it, they have to be able to withstand the pressures of this heterosexual atmosphere."[112] She disputed a psychiatrist's claims that homosexuals are mentally arrested in adolescence and strenuously argued one could be both happy and homosexual. She bristled, however, at what she considered the outlandish claims of the two other homophile activists who appeared with her—Frank Kameny, visiting from Washington, and Randy Wicker, from New York. Wicker compared the gay movement to the African American civil rights movement, declaring that he, too, wanted his rights. The fourth participant, a liberal Episcopal priest named James G. Jones, had complained on the program, "We've got enough troubles now here in Chicago without equating the Negro problem with the homosexual problem!"[113] Later, Shearer wrote to the host of the show, who apparently had found Wicker's claims excessive or unpersuasive. "I agree," he replied. "Our friends from New York and Washington dwelled so much on their crusade against being parts of a put-upon minority."[114] (The episode aired on April 4, 1964, just weeks before the Fun Lounge raid.)

The black press, perhaps as a result of its tendency to view the police more critically, covered white homophile activism more sympathetically than did its white mainstream counterparts. When Shearer wrote letters to newspaper editors all over Chicago in the spring of 1964, "as a means of gaining publicity for DOB," only the New Crusader, a militant African American paper, covered the issue. The story appeared under the remarkably sympathetic headline, "Local Lesbians Also Fight for Integration; Open Office Here." The account of the Daughters of Bilitis's activities stressed the lesbian activists' interest in changing laws and police practices, including "integration of the penal code as it pertains to the homosexual" and the pursuit of "equitable handling of cases involving this minority group." Shearer praised the article after it ran, in a letter to the Daughters of Bilitis national board, saying it "carried no detrimental slant," but said that in her view "the term integration was somewhat over-played." Indeed, before even local white gay activists had tried to get a public forum to draw the analogy between black and gay activism—after all, Shearer didn't even like the word "integration"—the black press articulated this connection.[115]

Not all journalists were sympathetic. As Chicago's gay nightlife, along with the war on vice and the ascendant political issue of street crime, received increasing media attention, some reporters even directly forwarded information about gay bars to the police, taking on a role more often played by the Crime Commission a decade earlier. For example, Robert Wiedrich of the *Tribune* discovered information that "the mobsters are muscling in on distressed tavern owners and converting their joints to deviate hangouts in exchange for a silent 50 per cent partnership." Wiedrich then passed this information along to the municipal police prostitution unit, leading to a series of police raids. He subsequently reported on the resulting raid on "the headquarters of a near north side vice ring," which, the paper reported, revealed "ledgers showing that one of 14 sex dens alone is grossing more than $150,000 annually."[116] Although the mob may have been increasing its control over gay life by "muscling in" during this period, Wiedrich had fashioned a narrative around the ledgers that his friends in the police department supplied him.

The attitudes of journalists began to change, however, partly because liberal journalists adopted more tolerant approaches to their material than did Wiedrich. A breakthrough for gay visibility in the local news media came in mid-1966, when the *Daily News* published a series of four major articles on gay men in Chicago. "Our city editor at the time, Jim McCartney, had noticed a bunch of arrests for sex crimes," recalls Lois Wille, who wrote the series. McCartney assigned Wille to the story but felt she should have a male escort. The colleague who accompanied her to the gay bars was a police reporter "dressed badly," she says—and two "quite elegant" places they visited did not allow him in, so he had to wait for her outside on the street while she went inside to have a look. Wille had previously won a Pulitzer Prize for a 1962 series on the failures of local hospitals and clinics to provide birth control to poor women; perhaps, having brought prestige on her employer in this way, she had greater leeway than other reporters might have had to treat her material unconventionally.

The series appeared on the newspaper's front page on four successive days in late June 1966. In her first article, Wille said it was an "all-too-obvious and disturbing facet of life in Chicago" that "homosexuals—male deviates—are emerging openly in the city as never before." Yet the body of the article treated the city's male homosexual world with unprecedented sympathy, observing that "flagrant effeminates" are "only a small portion of a great unknown mass, most of them not 'sissyish' at all."[117]

Though the article's lede suggested that the increase in gay visibility was troubling, Wille nonetheless painted a clear picture of the intense hostility and discrimination that gay men faced. Her three subsequent articles highlighted the significance for gay Chicagoans of churches, the vice squad, and psychiatrists. As problematic as some of Wille's language may seem today, that she quoted a gay activist's opinions about police harassment in a front-page article alone reflected a more tolerant view of gay life than was the norm among reporters. And although she reported that homosexuality might be a changeable defect in the eyes of mainstream psychiatric science, she also noted the dissident voices that were increasingly suggesting otherwise.[118]

Crucially, Wille recast gays as victims, rather than associates, of mobsters. Organized-crime syndicates, she suggested, exploited the need of gay-bar patrons for protection from the police. "In the last four months . . . there has been increasing evidence that the crime syndicate is taking over some of the gay bars and bathhouses," said James O'Grady, head of the prostitution and obscene-matter unit, who later became the superintendent of police. "Hoodlums," Wille explained, would approach the owner of a struggling tavern, strike a deal to convert the establishment into a gay bar, raise drink prices "by as much as 50 per cent," and "invite homosexuals to this new hangout" (in a sense ratifying what Wiedrich had reported earlier). She vividly portrayed the hostility and discrimination gay men faced, explicitly comparing these to the racial exclusions that would have been familiar to *Daily News* readers. In perhaps the series' most inadvertently revealing passage, Wille quoted a police detective who told her, "They call us and say, 'A pair of them moved in just across the hall.' . . . But the public is unaware . . . that you can't arrest a homosexual just because he's a homosexual." If indeed some members of the public did believe that it was possible to ask for someone to be arrested "just because he's a homosexual," perhaps in Chicago in 1966 they could not be blamed for holding this impression, given the intensity of police harassment.

Wille's series, which was published at the height of Martin Luther King, Jr.'s Chicago campaign, also used an analogy to compare the treatment of blacks and gays by hostile neighbors in apartment buildings and in dense urban neighborhoods. Wille wrote that in the Lakeview neighborhood, on the North Side, "residents in expensive apartments talk about the homosexual 'move-in' the way some white neighborhoods decry Negroes." At that time, with King demanding that the Daley administration enact open-housing policies and drawing attention to antiblack violence in Chicago and suburban neighborhoods, the reference would have been instantly familiar to readers. Though the parallel was, of course, exaggerated, Wille's language humanized gay men, casting them both as members of a persecuted minority and also as people with jobs, homes, and neighbors.[119]

Unlike the crime reporters who typically penned journalistic representations of gays, Wille distinguished between the motives and the economic roles of gay bars' syndicate bosses and their patrons, rather than treating them as undifferentiated denizens of an evil demimonde. What is more, she even reported on the skepticism of the gay activist she quoted—a member of Mattachine Midwest, founded in 1965 and independent of the San Francisco–based Mattachine Society that had maintained earlier chapters in Chicago—concerning police motives: "Aren't [mobsters moving into bars] up and down Rush St. and other places around town? Why pick on the homosexual bars? I think it's just an excuse for police harassment." And she concluded with a suggestion that gays needed police *protection* from blackmailers and violent attackers, and that the police failed to provide it. She quoted the Mattachine leader's view that police paid too little attention to the illegal activities of extortionists who blackmail homosexuals by threatening to "tattle to the man's boss or wife."[120] In suggesting not only the ways gay life was overpoliced but also the underpolicing of those who committed crimes against gay people, Wille's series paved the way for more realistic and more complex public representations of gay life.

*   *   *

In tandem with the more frequent newspaper articles about gays, the notion that gays were increasing in visibility, and possibly also in numbers, became a staple of news coverage by mid-decade. By 1967, when the Illinois state senate voted in favor of funds for studying the problem of sex "deviation," the Democratic state senator and Chicagoan Arthur Swanson declared, "I don't think we have to worry about embarrassing any of these people. They are perfectly frank and open about their way of life. They even publish magazines devoted to the subject."[121] The bill's downstate Republican sponsor "asserted that the problem concerning sex deviates is becoming acute in the state" and was quoted as calling it "a threat to the children in schools" and saying that "the problem is growing by leaps and bounds."[122] For gays and lesbians, increased publicity seemed double-edged.

In the years between the Selma and Birmingham campaigns in the spring of 1963 and the assassination of Martin Luther King, Jr., in the spring of 1968, black and gay Chicagoans both bore the brunt of newly aggressive approaches to policing, at the same time that their expectations were raised by the successes of nonviolent mobilization in the face of police violence in the South. On a significant scale, African Americans and Latinos challenged long-standing forms of police harassment that the state had rarely recognized as such: Ordinary men and women publicized their grievances, and civil rights groups won important victories from the Supreme Court that circumscribed the powers of law enforcement. White gays and lesbians observed these developments, and some began to redefine their everyday fears of the police as an element of an unjust system. A few began to use homophile organizations to enter the public square to articulate that notion.

White liberals became more conscious of racial inequality, and the federal civil rights apparatus expanded significantly. As in other cities in the North, Chicago's Democratic machine had enthusiastically embraced and benefited from the New Deal, but it had a more complex relationship with the rights-based claims pressed by African Americans in the 1960s. White politicians readily incorporated demands for equal access to public accommodations, voting rights, and even fair employment practices legislation, but they balked at school desegregation, opening the bifurcated housing market, or dismantling the financial practices that enriched wealthy real-estate men at the expense of ordinary African Americans. They aggressively resisted Great Society redistributive programs that threatened to replace their own power with alternative bureaucracies or authorities. They also aggressively resisted sexual freedom, including gay visibility, and they increasingly tried to suppress it altogether rather than merely confining it to specific areas of the city.[123]

In April 1964, in his first appearance in Chicago since taking office following Kennedy's assassination the previous November, President Lyndon Johnson spoke to Cook County Democrats to raise campaign funds. Highlighting his new poverty proposals, and pandering to his party's urban base, he declared that although for the first time two-thirds of Americans now lived in metropolitan areas, "too few of those people really live the good life."[124] Johnson spoke the evening before the Fun Lounge raid. As he

returned to Washington the next day, and gay men and lesbians com-
menced an evening of carousing, the county sheriff prepared to raid the
Fun Lounge and then to hound a group of schoolteachers out of their jobs.

The intensified repression of the mid-1960s laid the groundwork for a
new phase of the gay movement, as a smattering of gay activists went public
with their complaints and others became resentful of the war on vice. "It is
very strange indeed," said one middle-aged gay man late in 1967, "that
Chicago, since we have had the law, has become a much more difficult and
dangerous city to live in," a reference to the sodomy-law repeal. He
explained, "There is no such thing as a safe bar in Chicago today." Only a
few years earlier, he said, bars were not only open, but "you might say
roaring," their atmosphere "convivial, lively, happy," and "people felt that
they had been sort of liberated . . . at least in regard to a full and happy
night life, only to have this completely crushed in a very short time." Nowa-
days, he said, when you go to a bar, "you may be placing yourself in a
position that you're not just going to a bar but you're going to jail that
night."[125] In response to this state repression, a more militant phase of the
homophile movement emerged.

generations!

education → school rebellion against rumor sexuality

3

Freaking Fag Revolutionaries

BETWEEN 1962 AND 1968, facing increasing police harassment, Chicago's homophile movement coalesced. Gay Chicagoans created three organizations in the 1960s—a chapter of ONE, a chapter of the Daughters of Bilitis, and Mattachine Midwest—each lasting longer than the three Mattachine chapters founded between 1955 and 1960. Each group held meetings, appointed officers, and sponsored parties. One or two members of the Daughters of Bilitis chapter, and a larger number of Mattachine Midwest participants, also differed from members of the previous groups in their willingness to shed their anonymity and appear in public. Although antiwar and civil liberties activism were important influences on the mobilization of gays, it was the challenge that black Chicagoans were posing to place-based forms of institutional racism that most significantly influenced the trajectory of the local gay movement in this period.

The Northern civil rights movement framed homophile activists' analysis of the urban political landscape, shaping the movement's growth and inspiring its greater militancy. Black activists in Chicago, as Mike Royko wrote in 1971, "began by coming downtown with picket signs and demanding better schools."[1] Many of Chicago's white ethnic voters were drawn to a new politics of law and order, for which their mayor became an emblem. Where breadwinner liberals had called for positive state action to aid orderly households, law-and-order Democrats now called for negative state action to control disorderly individuals. Yet white gay activists instead began to borrow the language of black and New Left challenges to police brutality, using some of the same language and the same tools with which African Americans were challenging the ossified urban machine. Black and gay activists in the late 1960s shared a concern with police behavior because they both encountered aggressive policing in the streets, and their gathering places were disproportionately subjected to police harassment and extortion. Gay leaders staked claims to city streets, parks, offices, and residential buildings; in so doing, they claimed the right to the city. In the spring of 1968, Daley controversially declared, after the uprisings that followed the assassination of Martin Luther King, Jr., that the police should "shoot to kill" arsonists and "shoot to maim" looters. As his party became divided over the war abroad and crime and unrest at home, Daley came to epitomize the defense of "law and order." A new liberal political faction that supported civil liberties and questioned Daley's police department began to emerge in Chicago, and gay activists were part of it.

The more involved you were in gay networks—unless you studiously avoided bars and exclusively attended house parties, which were less likely to be raided—the more you worried about the police. Gay activists viewed police with great suspicion; middle-class gays and lesbians simply had more negative experiences with the police than did similarly situated heterosexuals. Cruising on city streets brought gay men into conflict with law enforcement even more frequently than did bar raids. In 1967, gay men in Chicago, nearly all of them white, were asked how often they worried about five possible consequences "when out looking for sex with other men." The worry that the greatest proportion of respondents said they "often" felt at such moments was "being caught by the police"; 50 percent reported having this worry either "often" or "sometimes." Of 458 respondents, 115 said they "often" felt this worry, compared to 89 (19 percent) who reported "often" worrying about the second-most common consequence, which was "catching a disease."[2]

The makeup of the homophile movement in Chicago in the 1960s does not match the persistent notion that the movement was preoccupied with respectability and elite concerns. Two of Chicago's new gay organizations were both more diverse in their class makeup and less hostile to the city's bar-based queer subcultures than one might expect, compared to similar organizations in San Francisco and New York.[3] They differed from the chapter of ONE, established in 1965, which shared a name and Los Angeles roots with ONE magazine and was largely a social group for upper-middle-class and professional white men.[4] By contrast, the officers of Mattachine Midwest, which was founded in 1965, included left-wing social radicals, a leader of the early 1960s struggle for racial integration in a Chicago suburb, and the manager of a gay bar, as well as some more conservative individuals.[5] A prominent Kansas City female impersonator, Skip Arnold, was a featured speaker at one of its early public meetings.[6] And the Daughters of Bilitis chapter, founded in 1962 and active through about 1967, was described by the anthropologist Esther Newton as a "group of lower middle-class girls."[7] The editors of the group's newsletter wrote, "It is true that the women in our organization are mostly non-professionals, but never let it be said that professional people alone make the world go 'round."[8] Although many lesbian activists across the country had begun to leave all-male homophile organizations for the women's movement, lesbians in Chicago continued to work alongside gay men because the two groups found unity of purpose in opposing police harassment.

Chicago's homophile movement also gradually began to shed some of the protections that secrecy had provided it. As some Mattachine Midwest members opened the group up to public view in the mid-1960s, the members increasingly discussed the relationship between gays and lesbians and the public sphere, including city streets and the police who patrolled them. While police raids continued, gay activists increased their visibility, expanded their protest repertoires, and built their mailing lists. In so doing, they positioned themselves to exploit a political opportunity they could not have foreseen when, in the aftermath of the 1968 Democratic National Convention, the Chicago police department came under intense public scrutiny. First, liberal Americans were troubled by spectacular police brutality directed at mostly white, peaceful demonstrators at the convention. Second, and just as important, journalists—many of whom were treated roughly or beaten by Chicago cops during the convention—were more willing to question police activities. Although the importance of the convention violence to the direction of the New Left has been widely discussed, its importance for gay politics has been overlooked. After the police killing of Illinois Black Panther leaders Fred Hampton and Mark Clark in December 1969, at least some local gay activists swerved toward a more radical view yet on policing.

"If the Gay Element Wants Its Freedom, It Has No Choice But to Fight"

Black Chicagoans had numerous grievances in the postwar years. For more than two decades after the end of World War II, police departments across

the urban North turned a blind eye as whites violently resisted blacks' moving into their neighborhoods. As we have seen, Chicago laws, real-estate
practices, and unwritten codes forced African Americans to live in segregated slums, to send their children to inferior schools, and to suffer unequal
treatment from white police officers. Real-estate speculators used blockbus-
ting, panic peddling, and contract sales, profiting from a citywide housing
market in which the valuation of a home fell sharply once even a single
African American family moved onto a block.[9] Black communities were
also underpoliced—police failed to respond adequately to crimes committed against blacks or in black neighborhoods—as well as overpoliced.

Police brutality was a particularly troubling problem because it seemed
to worsen as black militancy increased. Since 1963, the issue had received
increasing attention from the *Chicago Defender*.[10] In the spring of 1963,
Eugene "Bull" Connor, the public-safety commissioner of Birmingham,
Alabama, made antiblack police brutality a major national news story for
the first time. Although the Chicago public-school boycott in the fall of
1963 did not succeed in ousting Superintendent Benjamin Willis, a crony
of Daley's who enforced his desire for continued school segregation, it represented a mass mobilization in protest against a major element of local
state power and was thus a turning point in the growth of black insurgency.[11] Lawmakers gave the police new weapons to fight this new effort.[12]

As the enforcer of public order and as the most visible representative of
the municipal government, Chicago's overwhelmingly white police department was a focus of mounting African American resentment. By the mid-
1960s, the Chicago police operated the largest city-sponsored secret police
"red squad" in the United States, an antisubversive unit that spied on the
lawful activities of a wide range of even quite mainstream political and social
groups. So intense was the preoccupation of Daley's city hall with maintaining law and order that Frank Donner, in his study of police spying on Americans in the postwar decades, called Chicago the "national capital of police
repression."[13] Politicians began to demand from the police a tough response
to street crime—and they got such a response. Although the department had
begun a long process of opening hiring to African Americans, only 17 percent
of officers were black in 1965, compared to 27 percent of the city's population.[14] Police brutality in urban black ghettoes was a major factor in the urban
uprisings of the 1960s. It provided the spark for most rebellions in the urban
North between 1964 and 1968, with the exception of those that followed the
King assassination.[15] "To many Negroes," wrote President Johnson's Kerner

Commission, in its March 1968 report on the causes of the urban rebellions of the previous three summers, "police have come to symbolize white power, white racism and white repression. And the fact is that many police do reflect and express these white attitudes."[16]

For white gays and lesbians, too, the police were the focus of mounting frustration, and this was reflected in the emergence of larger and more effective homophile groups. Del Shearer seemed to anticipate the decade's later militancy when she founded Chicago's Daughters of Bilitis chapter in 1961. In her letter to *The Ladder* about the February 1961 C & C Lounge raid, Shearer complained, "If the gay element wants its freedom, it has no choice but to fight, for freedom in this country or any country is not a thing given or guaranteed to anyone who does not hold it in highest esteem."[17] In the spring of 1965, frustrated by the war on vice, Bob Basker, Pearl Hart, Valerie Taylor, Ira Jones, Bruce Scott, Don Blythe, and Polly Adams met to plan the launching of a new gay civil rights group in the Midwest.[18] The short life spans of the previous Mattachine Society chapters that had been founded between 1955 and 1960 left the founders of Mattachine Midwest with concerns about the risks involved in trying again. "It would be almost criminal making another false start at this time," wrote Bob Basker, the group's chief founder, who used the pseudonym Robert Sloane, in the spring of 1965; "it could throw us back many years."[19] To avoid such a scenario, they carefully planned the organization's launch. They worked to smooth their relationship to the existing Daughters of Bilitis chapter and initiated a series of discussions about the issues involved in speaking to the public about homosexuality.[20]

From the beginning, the group anticipated the need for addressing unexpected arrests of its members. At one early planning meeting, thirteen participants envisioned an "emergency committee," by which an answering service would enable those arrested or otherwise facing dire circumstances to be connected with assistance.[21] Like their forebears in the 1950s, the founders of Mattachine Midwest initially were loath even to use the dreaded "H" word in delineating the group's aims. Taylor, who helped write an organizing document for the group, recalled, "We were so timorous that the word 'homosexual' was not mentioned in the first draft." She observed that when veteran homophile leader Frank Kameny "came in from Washington, D.C., to lend us a hand, he was quite disgusted by our caution."[22] After some debate, they decided the risks of a public kickoff meeting were outweighed by the benefits.

The public meeting marked the official launch of Mattachine Midwest and occurred on July 25, 1965, at the downtown Midland Hotel, whose owner Eugene Pekow had inherited it from his father and carved out an economic niche by opening its meeting spaces to groups that could not go elsewhere.[23] The attendance was estimated at between 100 and 200 people. Pearl Hart, Bob Sloane, and several others gave speeches, making the case that the audience members should become involved with the group. Though the organization shared a name (even if not a corporate identity) with the Chicago Mattachine chapters of the 1950s, this public meeting represented a major departure from the under-the-radar style of 1950s and early 1960s homophile activists. Jim Osgood, whose pseudonym was Jim Bradford and who would serve as the group's president several times, recalled in 1980, "Everyone was very, very reluctant to go public. We didn't know who would come. . . . We were afraid of police infiltration, even for a number of years after that."[24]

More gender-integrated than the city's two other gay organizations (though female participation dropped off by the late 1960s), Mattachine Midwest's leaders were far more explicit than their predecessors about mimicking the efforts of militant civil rights protesters. As Chicago became the civil rights movement's most visible Northern battleground in the second half of the 1960s, Mattachine Midwest eclipsed the Daughters of Bilitis in its militancy. At the public launch, the introductory address by Robert Sloane, the new organization's president, powerfully invoked civil rights. "Who could have imagined, a generation ago," he asked the audience, "the 1954 Supreme Court ruling barring segregated schooling, the 1964 Civil Rights Act, the law soon to be enacted on voting rights?" Sloane attached the 1961 Illinois sodomy-law repeal to this illustrious lineage, squarely situating the new group's goals in line with the revolution in African American civil rights then under way.[25] Among the "things that are in it for you" was securing the "right to assemble without police interference," said Roland Lancaster, who went by the pseudonym Roland Keith, in his speech at the same event.[26]

William B. Kelley, who was among the new organization's energetic young members, was in many ways the epitome of a young white left-liberal drawn toward gay activism by virtue of his dismay at police harassment. In February 1966, he attended and served as secretary of a national homophile planning conference in Kansas City, and that August he attended the second national homophile conference meeting in San Francisco. In July of 1967, he traveled to Philadelphia to participate in the third Annual Reminder picket

FIGURE 5. Protestors for gay rights in front of Independence Hall in Philadelphia, July 4, 1967, including William B. Kelley of Chicago (fourth from left). Courtesy of Associated Press.

held outside Independence Hall, the nation's first annual gay political event (see Figure 5). Kelley had joined the American Civil Liberties Union (ACLU) while a high-school student in small-town Missouri in the 1950s and written to the other left-wing and liberal groups, including the Congress of Racial Equality, "just to get their literature." By 1965, as a twenty-three-year-old former University of Chicago student, Kelley had attended some meetings of organizations in downtown auditoriums and conference rooms. One of the meetings was organized in honor of the antiracist and social-justice activists Anne and Carl Braden on Carl's release from a Kentucky prison sentence for "sedition." "I was used to going to such meetings," where radicals or social critics would give speeches to large groups. "It was something I had wanted to have happen in a gay context, and now finally [with the formation of Mattachine Midwest] it was here." Kelley also recalled that by the mid-1960s he had been attuned to black civil rights concerns for at least ten years, and "I saw this as fitting into the same space on the political spectrum."[27] The emerging national network of homophile activists drew together his activist interests in civil liberties and sexual freedom.

From the beginning, Mattachine Midwest's leaders were strongly influenced by civil rights organizations' response to police brutality. Like similar groups in other cities, Mattachine Midwest's mission included a speaker's bureau and the aspiration to provide social services to gay people in need.[28] But from 1965 until 1969, the group was distinctive in its rhetoric that homosexuals must challenge an unjust system, not just survive it. "The homosexual charged with being an 'inmate of a disorderly house' who refuses to fight for a 'not guilty' decision," opined the editor in an unsigned piece, "continues to put every drinking homosexual in jeopardy."[29] From the standpoint of political theory, then, a key innovation brought to bear by Mattachine Midwest was the notion that each gay man or lesbian had an obligation to take the risks involved in associating with, and defending, the rights of the group as a whole.

Founded in the same year in which the Supreme Court first recognized the right to privacy, the organization's policy efforts framed police problems as civil liberties issues. In response to stepped-up police harassment in the spring of 1966, for example, Mattachine Midwest members met with William Brackett of the ACLU of Illinois, where they discussed the "inmate of a disorderly house" charge that was so frequently invoked by police against their community. As a result of the meeting, they agreed to help organize a subcommittee of the local ACLU to deal with "civil liberties problems and the homosexual."[30] Pearl Hart, who remained a key figure, continued to pass along to the group's officers information gleaned from her clients about where they had been arrested, by whom, and under what circumstances, and the newsletter began to report, on the basis of her sources, "which part of the parks," especially Lincoln Park, a favorite for summertime cruising, "were currently hot."[31] By year's end, Bradford wrote, "As children, we were told that the policeman was there to protect and help us. To the homosexual citizen such thoughts are pure nonsense." Writing more than two years before the Stonewall uprising and the emergence of gay liberation, he added, "The time for shrinking violets and closet queenery is over."[32]

"Fear That I Was 'the Fuzz'"

As the Chicago police department increasingly embraced crime prevention, including the idea of stop-and-frisk policing, Mattachine Midwest took a

all cases not "right to privacy"

strong stance against the politics of law and order. Crime and policing became increasingly important political issues nationally after the August 1965 Watts uprising in California. Early in 1966, for instance, the group expressed concern about a proposal to expand police powers, which allowed the police to maintain files on persons stopped for suspicious behavior even if they were not arrested.[33] When, later that spring, Chicago police orchestrated yet another series of raids on gay bars and baths, gay activists met with Chicago police for the first time. "Chicago's homosexual community once again faces the dangers of a jittery police department as election time draws near," and, consequently, "a series of raids that shook responsible homosexuals to the core." They were told that police felt "forced to act" when pressured to crack down on gay life by "clergymen, ward politicians, chambers of commerce and individuals."[34]

By late summer, members were sharing stories about their experiences of harassment: "At a recent membership meeting of Mattachine Midwest, several members told of recent experiences they or their friends had had with the police," including charges of loitering and harassment in parks and bus terminals and washroom arrests by policemen "hiding in closets" and watching for sexual activity. And these activists increasingly pointed out the hypocrisy of the state of Illinois's having decriminalized private, consensual homosexual relations while the Chicago police continued to liberally apply catch-all "disorderly conduct" charges against gays and lesbians.[35]

Even a Mattachine Midwest–sponsored potluck was the subject of worry on the part of its organizers, according to a Kinsey Institute ethnographer who recorded a strong fear of police infiltration or surveillance. "I was apprehensively greeted at the door by persons I had not met before," he wrote. There followed "a wave of silence and anxiety," which continued "until I was recognized by men appearing from nether rooms as being their guest." Only then was he "informed that there had been several anonymous tips (or harassing calls) about the prospect of the police raiding the Pot Luck gathering and that until someone recognized me there was fear that I was 'the fuzz.'"[36] Because homophile gatherings in other cities not only had been infiltrated but on occasion had been disrupted by police raids and arrests, the fear was not irrational.[37]

As with African Americans, the daily lives of gay men were shaped not only by excessive police harassment but also by the failure of police to take seriously the crimes to which they were routinely subjected as a result of being gay. Of the 458 gay men in Chicago sampled by the mid-1967 Kinsey Institute study, 101, or 22 percent, reported that they had been "arrested by the police" for a reason "related to homosexuality" in their lifetime.[38] Even more—159 respondents, or 35 percent—answered in the affirmative when asked if he had "ever been rolled or robbed by a sexual partner or someone who knew that [he] was homosexual."[39] Of these 159, only 34—21 percent of those who had been robbed—said they had reported the robbery to the police; 79 percent had not reported the robbery.[40] One man said in 1967 that although he had had some fear about the risk of being involved in a homophile organization, "I'm very tempted to join the Mattachine Society and give them a little bit of money because I might need them one of these days."[41] People knew they might need help against the police, and that drove the organization's further growth.

Some Mattachine Midwest members began a gradual shift away from the use of pseudonyms in favor of self-disclosure and toward a more confrontational approach to the public, even as high-profile police raids on gay bars continued, spiking again in the summer of 1968. That June, Valerie Taylor wrote in the group's newsletter that "the telephone began to ring" because the May issue had accidentally been sent out with the name of the organization on the envelope—"a simple error on the part of the mailing service" but one that violated the informal contract that then obtained between *all* gay publications and their subscribers. Although Taylor apologized, she added, remarkably, "We don't feel that anyone ought to be upset over receiving mail from a (horrors) homophile organization. Most people get bales of unsolicited mail, some of it blush-making. We ourselves recently got a letter inviting us to vote for George Wallace, which we flushed down the etcetera rather than have the garbage man see it."[42] Although activists in the gay-liberation era dropped the earlier homophile movement's policy of organizational officers' always using pseudonyms, the shift was never complete and was never mapped cleanly onto generational lines.

Only in 1968 did Chicago catch up to the pattern of legal challenges to the bar-raid regime that had begun earlier in other cities. In a letter to Mattachine Society of Washington founder Frank Kameny, who had urged the group to press the police harder, Jim Bradford of Mattachine Midwest wrote, "In Chicago, unlike Washington, the chief of police is not really concerned unless you wield power, threaten suit, or can or threaten to make life complicated for him."[43] A high-profile January 1968 raid on the Trip, a place patronized by professional-class white men, reflected both the escalation of the war on vice and the growing resistance to it, including a frontal attack in the courts on its legal foundation. "More than 140 men," the *Tribune* reported, "including prominent professors, business men and several clergymen, were questioned by police last night after a raid on a reputed private club for homosexuals on the near north side." Only fourteen were arrested, however, and the Tribune did not print the names or addresses of the eight patrons charged with public indecency for same-sex dancing, nor of two co-owners charged as keepers of a disorderly house. Only one manager and three bartenders were subjected to having their names and addresses included in the *Tribune* article.[44] Objectively speaking, the punishments imposed by the police were far less harsh than during the Fun Lounge raid. Yet gay activists were far more mobilized to mount a response than they had been four years earlier.

Because it occurred on a Sunday night, during a weekly scheduled "private club" evening affair that its upper-middle-class clientele perceived as relatively safe, the Trip raid was yet another indication that not only blacks but even some whites had to worry about the risk of mass police actions. As a restaurant, it drew a mainstream, nongay weekday crowd at lunchtime from nearby offices, and it operated as primarily a gay bar at night. But on Sunday nights it was technically a membership club: each patron had to pay $10 for an identification card. If even a place like the Trip was risky, it was not clear gays could be safe anywhere. As Bill Kelley recalled, "Practically any place occasionally had police trouble" if it catered to gay people.[45] The police seized the club's mailing list, which contained, according to the *Tribune*, "several thousand names of persons throughout the United States." O. W. Wilson had retired as police superintendent in 1967, but his successor James B. Conlisk continued his emphasis on eliminating rather than confining gay life. The raid on the Trip, like so many other bar raids, would have frightened not only those gay men who were present but also those who read about it in the papers the next day.[46]

Chicago 1968

After a summer in which rioting in more than one hundred cities fueled many Americans' sense that the nation was coming unglued, the Democratic Party met in Chicago in August to nominate its presidential and vice

White gay men → better treated than lesbians

presidential candidates. Daley, the mayor of the host city, had also been the party boss who helped usher in two successive Democratic presidencies. But since January, as the country seemed to be losing control of the Vietnam War and President Johnson announced he would not run for reelection for the good of the nation, the party had been deeply roiled by conflict and scarred by the assassination of Robert F. Kennedy just two months earlier, moments after he had declared victory in the California presidential primary.

For Chicago's gay activists, the 1968 Democratic National Convention was a local crisis as well as a national one. Although Chicago police had engaged in high-profile, dramatic bar raids since the early 1960s, the raids had increased in severity and frequency during the summer of 1968. Earlier that summer, Mattachine Midwest president Bradford, who continually pressed his organization toward more radical action (though without using his own real name), complained that he needed men and women "willing to stick their necks out, walk the picket line, go on radio and television, and even get arrested if need be to bring real equality to the homosexual in Chicago and the Middle West."[47] The newsletter noted that Jan Sutton, a popular local drag queen, "is appearing at the Isle of Capri in the suburbs, since police pressure closed her act at a Near North Side lounge. It's convention time again, you know."[48]

Immediately before the far larger meeting of the Democrats, Mattachine Midwest had had its first experience hosting a national convention of gay activists. The convention of the North American Conference of Homophile Organizations (whose acronym NACHO rhymes with "Waco") was attended by about a hundred gay activists from cities all across the United States. Members of Mattachine Midwest made no secret of their displeasure at the curtailment of gay life in Chicago that summer—not that they could have concealed their displeasure had they wished to do so. Indeed, the owners of the Trip, now closed because of the revocation of its liquor license following the January raid, had generously offered the venue for use by the conference—"a plush restaurant-club recently closed by Mayor Daley's bullyboys," as one California participant later wrote. When the convention attendees took an evening off to see a local drag show, they went to see Jan Sutton—which required driving out to the suburbs, where she was performing in exile. The NACHO convention formally adopted "Gay Is Good" as its official slogan, a proposal made by longtime activist Frank Kameny that was explicitly modeled on Stokely Carmichael's slogan "Black

Is Beautiful," and which perhaps anticipated the self-affirming politics of gay liberation. Kameny's resolution further compared gays to Catholics and Jews, saying that in "our pluralistic society" gays should similarly be "free of insolent and arrogant pressures to convert." Although the conference adopted a "homosexual bill of rights," attendees were largely consumed with procedural issues and failed to approve a permanent basis for national federation.[49]

In the weeks before the Democratic convention, it was clear that the police were prioritizing the surveillance of black neighborhoods. Known civil rights activists and other dissidents found mysterious, windowless vans parked ominously in front of their homes.[50] Yet white gay and lesbian nightlife, too, was shut down. As Democrats, antiwar protesters, and journalists descended on the city, a *Los Angeles Times* reporter wrote that in the North Side's "tawdry mecca of the homosexual set," many of the bars displayed signs saying they were "closed for two weeks 'for redecoration.'"[51] And then, in the morning hours of Tuesday, August 20, 1968, with the city in the midst of a heat wave and daytime temperatures climbing into the nineties, Chicago police entered Sam's, at Clark and Division, and the Annex, near Clark and Diversey—two large, crowded bars and epicenters of North Side gay nightlife. Jim Flint, who worked as a bartender at Sam's, recalled, "During the Convention we paid off the night before and got raided and closed anyhow."[52] At both locations, in a style familiar to gay activists in Chicago of the era, plainclothes police had infiltrated the bars long enough to be "propositioned" by patrons, then brought in uniformed colleagues to conduct the raid. In the Annex, a judge later summarized, a plainclothes detective named "Sullivan testified that he observed two different pairs of men standing against the south wall fondling each other in the area of the penis, thighs and buttocks."[53] The arriving uniformed officers announced that everyone present, some seventy people, was under arrest. However, officers in fact proceeded to arrest people "at random on a 'you, you, and you' basis." In the end, seventeen patrons and employees of the two bars were arrested.[54]

Perhaps because they had hosted a national convention of homophiles just weeks earlier, local leaders responded boldly to these two major raids.[55] Outraged Mattachine Midwest members took the almost unprecedented step of seeking attention from the press. They wrote an open letter to Superintendent James B. Conlisk, complaining about the recent "increased plainclothes and uniformed police surveillance and . . . intimidation." The letter stressed, "*we are tired of receiving 'special' treatment as a minority group in Chicago*. . . . Unfounded arrests, trumped-up charges, entrapment and constant surveillance of homosexuals and their social institutions must stop." The letter also alleged that one police officer told an arrestee at the Annex "that he was part of a minority group and should expect to be treated like it."[56] Copies of the press release were dropped off at gay bars.[57] Thus, even before the infamous chant "The whole world is watching" drew attention to Chicago police excesses, local activists had begun to rewrite the usual script for police raids—a script in which publicity itself was the most terrifying weapon in the police department's arsenal.

Members of Mattachine Midwest also made plans to circulate a petition protesting the bar raids and present the petition to Governor Samuel Shapiro on Monday, August 26.[58] Some members even asked the antiwar demonstrators gathered in Lincoln and Grant parks—most of whom, of course, were straight—to sign it. Gay activists in Chicago had, in 1966, picketed in front of the *Sun-Times* office to protest rejection of advertising, but this was perhaps the first time Chicago gay activists had circulated a petition in public, asking strangers to sign in support of their cause.[59]

Under the headline "Forgotten Citizens Unite," the petition echoed the New Left anti-authoritarianism of the antiwar movement, notably and argumentatively reframing the concepts of "citizen" and "crime." "Every time there is an election or a political convention," the authors explained, "the bars frequented by homosexuals are raided," because officials "deem it a crime" for gay people to congregate. The authors contended instead that "the true crime is the corruption this policy engenders," leading "the homosexual to be treated as a criminal and a sub-citizen." The petition, in short, at once acquitted homosexuals and indicted the state that harassed them.[60] Although the convention protesters were likely among the most sympathetic audiences imaginable in America at the time, the willingness of gay activists to ask the straight majority to lend their signatures to a document protesting antigay harassment was somewhat unprecedented.

The convention was a gathering place for dissenters and the left-wing avant-garde from across the country—though fewer than the many thousands Daley had warned of in order to justify the massive police presence—and they mingled with local radicals of various stripes. The French writer Jean Genet, who had been commissioned by *Esquire* to report on the convention, met Allen Ginsberg and also William S. Burroughs for the first time during that week. Genet and Burroughs, both widely known to be gay, had both been hired by *Esquire* to write about the subject.[61] Bill Kelley remembers that Ginsberg "stole my would-be trick" when they shared a ride after an Old Town party.[62] Many of the most dramatic incidents of police brutality, as documented by the Walker Report on the convention-week events, took place in the side streets near Lincoln Park on the North Side, an area where there were a number of gay and gay-friendly bars.[63] According to several accounts, the first protesters to be driven out of Lincoln Park by tear gas that week consisted of a group that had been seated in a quiet circle, led by Ginsberg in chanting the mantra "Om."[64] One gay man, perhaps describing the same event, recalled being at the Inner Circle, a gay bar across from the park at Lincoln Avenue and Wells Street, when "all of a sudden a group of 'hippie-types' came running into the bar in an attempt to dodge the cops."[65] Buddy King, a former bartender at the Inner Circle, recalled Ginsberg's coming into the bar during the convention. "We talked and he got drunk," he said.[66]

The events of the convention week, particularly the police violence against protesters, polarized the opinions of white Americans concerning the police. Some whites came to see police brutality, a cause associated mainly with black communities and civil rights protesters, as troubling. A young black woman told a *New York Times* reporter that Chicago police were beating young New Left demonstrators "because they don't consider them to be white." "Maybe now people will listen when we're talking about police brutality," said one black man, now that "they've seen it on television and it's white kids."[67] Police officers gay-baited male antiwar activists, mocking their long hair.[68] Much of white America, however, sided with Daley and the police. On Wednesday, August 28, the date of the most spectacular police violence, during which many journalists were injured, ten million Americans watched live on national television as William F. Buckley called Gore Vidal a "queer," in response to Vidal's calling Buckley a "crypto-Nazi."[69] Gay and lesbian citizens' experiences with the police set the terms by which they participated in the public culture of their city in an era of crisis.

In the convention's aftermath, gay activists stepped up their struggle against the Chicago police. Mattachine Midwest held a press conference to publicize the raiding and closure of some of the city's most popular gay bars, taking advantage of the political opportunity offered by the diminished confidence of local elites in Daley's police force. Linking antigay oppression with the televised police riot, Mattachine Midwest's president

Jim Bradford asked readers of the October 1968 *Newsletter* if they were "Tired of hearing The Subject treated with tea and sympathy—or Mace and nightsticks?"[70] Bradford also worked with Pearl Hart to update her pamphlet, "Your Rights If Arrested," which appeared in the September 1968 newsletter and was also printed separately by the thousands.[71] September's membership meeting was an open forum about the relationship between homosexuals and the police.[72] Under Bradford, the group kept the pressure on the police issue, comparing the Chicago police unfavorably to those in New York and decrying systematic police abuse.[73]

In the following months, Chicago homophile activists challenged police harassment in the courts, in the media, and in meetings with police officials. They met with a commander of the police department's vice control division, although to little avail.[74] They created ways of monitoring the police and drawing media attention to their excesses, responding to increased harassment by borrowing the publicity-oriented strategies of black and anti-war activists. They organized a "bar patrol" to monitor and challenge trumped-up police allegations. Kelley organized a "Know Your Candidates" forum at a Lincoln Park church, which Bill Singer attended during his insurgent campaign for 44th Ward alderman. In further evidence that the group had become more able to win over heterosexuals, an attorney for the ACLU, Bill Brackett, persuaded fourteen of his colleagues to agree to be added to a list of lawyers willing to take telephone calls should a gay man or lesbian call from jail. (A designated Mattachine Midwest volunteer who had arranged to be at home would receive a call from an answering service employed by the group, upon someone's calling the answering service from jail.[75])

All this occurred in the ten months between the Democratic convention and the Stonewall rebellion in New York. In this sense, the events of August 1968 thus set Mattachine Midwest on a path toward more militant political protest. Though Stonewall is often described as the turning point in the birth of a more militant phase of the gay movement, it barely registered with Chicago's gay-activist community at the time, consumed as they were by the fallout from the convention and related matters. The *Mattachine Midwest Newsletter*, for example, included only a brief mention of Stonewall in a report on developments in New York City that gave equal weight to vigilantes' chopping down trees and bushes in a park in Queens where men met for anonymous sex.[76]

Gay activists also established contact with other radical social movements. Bill Kelley, for example, attended an April 1969 conference on police treatment of minorities, held at the University of Chicago Law School, and reported back to his Mattachine Midwest colleagues that police used disorderly conduct and other catchall charges in somewhat similar fashion against both blacks and gays. He was particularly struck, he said, by a talk by Renault Robinson, who had founded the Afro-American Patrolmen's League the previous summer: "He found the disorderly conduct charge discriminatorily applied to Chicago's black population, in approximately the same manner as homosexuals frequently find it." Kelley's report indicates, in addition, that Robinson said police made excessive arrests of blacks for "victimless" crimes such as drunkenness, just as gay men were frequently arrested for cruising in public. The seeds of an interracial coalition against police harassment, and sharing of strategies, had been sown.[77]

In the Public Eye

Just as the events around the Democratic National Convention led black students in the Chicago public schools to adopt a more pugnacious stance toward civic authorities, so too did gay activists begin responding more vocally to police controversy in the public eye.[78] In this effort, they drew on tactics pioneered by the Black Panther Party and the antiwar movement, and they were also aided by local reporters sympathetic to claims of police excesses.

The case of David Stienecker illustrates the ratcheting up of tensions between gays and the police. As a young editor of the *Mattachine Midwest Newsletter*, Stienecker published a highly provocative article in the fall of 1969 about a particular plainclothes "youth officer," John Manley, suggesting that he was a deeply closeted gay man who had been lucky enough to find a job where he could "cruise in the public interest."[79] (Manley, in fact, had also been responsible for "the only fatality remotely connected with the Democratic National Convention of 1968," the death of a seventeen-year-old American Indian runaway late on August 22 in Old Town.[80]) Manley was blond, muscular, and known to gay men who frequented Lincoln Park toilets as the most aggressive of the plainclothes officers who cruised there, racking up an impressive number of arrests of men he charged with allegedly soliciting him for sex.

In a remarkable departure from normal police procedure, Manley came in person to Stienecker's home, arrested the young volunteer reporter, and filed charges against him under a criminal defamation law that criminalized someone whose defamation was likely to cause public disorder. Stienecker's arrest shocked Mattachine members and was the subject of coverage in gay papers elsewhere and a sympathetic article in the left-wing *Chicago Journalism Review*—itself a creature of the convention and a reflection of journalists being pulled to the left by what appeared to be uncontrolled repression of activists by the state. Manley's actions only increased the attention Stienecker had already tried to place on a questionable police practice—"the pretty-cop-in-faggy-clothes-horny-as-hell-begging-for-love routine like the New York cops used to use," as one New York publication put it in covering the Stienecker affair. (Police entrapment had already been curbed in New York City as a result of successful negotiations between the Mattachine Society and that city's liberal mayor, John Lindsay.[81]) Stienecker won his court case but lost his job at World Book Encyclopedia.[82]

In the fall of 1969, when another police crackdown occurred, Mattachine activists took it upon themselves to police the police—and to do it in plainclothes. The group organized a "bar patrol" on weekend nights. The idea, they said, was to "put a significant crimp in police raid plans" by supplying "responsible observers who would be prepared to testify to the falsity of police allegations of public indecency."[83] Following the convention, the federal government attempted to prosecute leading radicals for supposedly participating in a criminal conspiracy to disrupt the Democrats' meeting. The so-called Chicago Seven conspiracy trial exacerbated the nation's divisions over law-and-order matters. At first, it was known as the Chicago Eight case, but Bobby Seale—the Black Panther Party leader and the sole African American in the group—refused to remain silent during the proceedings. For a time, he was physically bound and gagged in the courtroom on the judge's instructions before his case was separated from that of the other seven. There was also one openly gay defendant, the poet Allen Ginsberg, who testified for the defense and was cross-examined by the prosecutor, Thomas Foran, about gay-themed poems he had published.[84]

In February 1970, Foran declared in a speech at Loyola Academy, a private high school in the North Shore suburb of Wilmette, "We are losing our kids to the freaking fag revolution." The specificity of the charge led to an equally specific response: Mattachine Midwest quickly condemned the antigay slur. The resulting article in the *Chicago Daily News*, under the headline "Homosexuals Blast Foran," was likely the first time that a mainstream daily newspaper in the city published a news article in response to a press release issued by a gay organization. The article quoted Mattachine Midwest president Bradford, who said Foran sounded "like a dirty-mouthed little boy who has discovered new swear words."[85] Several months later, a book reviewer said, of Foran's phrase, "The distance between the factions contending for power in our country today is nowhere better displayed than in this language."[86] The assertion reverberated as a reflection of the ideological gap between American parents and their children, while also playing powerfully on the notion that a gay child was, by definition, a child that his or her parents had "lost."

The State Police Power and the Gay Movement

Driven together by their shared concern with combating the overzealous operations of both local and federal law enforcement, black and gay activists found common cause with one another, as well as with a small number of straight white leftists. From the late 1960s to the early 1980s, gay activists latched onto the critique of overzealous exercise of the police power on the part of the state, its leaders periodically steeped in the reaction against police surveillance of black militants. Although historians have focused on the coastal gay meccas of New York and San Francisco, it is in cities such as Chicago that the importance of black-gay organizing against police harassment comes into clearest focus and helps clarify the gay movement's radical roots.

In December 1969, Fred Hampton and Mark Clark, leaders in the Illinois Black Panther Party, were shot and killed in a pre-dawn raid on their West Side apartment by officers working for the Cook County state's attorney together with Chicago police. The so-called Panther raid sharply divided Chicagoans between those sympathetic to Daley's "law and order" politics and those suspicious of it. Locally, its impact on gay activists' trust in law enforcement was far greater than that of the Stonewall riots; indeed, more than anything else this event would cement the fragile black-gay alliance in Chicago, and would unify liberals and leftists more generally, for a decade to come. Leaders of Mattachine Midwest attended a tour of Hampton and Clark's bullet-riddled apartment by Panther leaders, and they issued a rare joint statement with Chicago Gay Liberation, siding with those challenging the police account of the raid. "The Black Panthers are getting support from a surprising source—the Mattachine Midwest, a society for homosexuals," Irv Kupcinet told the readers of Chicago's most widely read daily newspaper column.[87] Eventually, nearly every aspect of the police account of events would be discredited by forensic evidence and witness testimony. Racial tensions flared on Chicago's West and South sides. The killings spurred multiple government inquiries and became a major flashpoint in the national debate over public safety and law enforcement. Commentators interpreted the assassinations by the police as evidence that the government was on a mission to wipe out black militants by killing them. Following shortly afterward, the killings of student protesters at Kent State University in Ohio and Jackson State College in Mississippi further seemed to confirm the possibility that violent state repression of the black and antiwar movements was under way.[88]

The gay movement's increasing public profile, its militancy, and its growing alliance with black activists, all heightened after the killings of Hampton and Clark, further crystallized in November 1970, when two Chicago police officers chased James Clay, Jr., a twenty-four-year-old African American man, fired eight shots into his back, and killed him. Clay, who was wearing women's clothing when police encountered him, would likely have been understood, in the language of the day, as a "street fairy," and he had a long arrest record that included charges of impersonating the opposite sex and solicitation to commit prostitution. Though it didn't receive national attention, Clay's killing was covered by the local papers, including the *Sun-Times*, the countercultural *Seed*, and the black-owned *Defender* (on the front page), and had a significant impact on local gay politicization. The Chicago Gay Alliance, founded a few months earlier, demanded an FBI investigation into whether Clay's rights were violated. On the first anniversary of Clay's death, Ortez Alderson, a "former go-go dancer from Chicago's South Side," organized a memorial march on the city's 18th District police station in his memory.[89] As historian John D'Emilio has noted, Clay's death also led to the formation in 1971 of the Transvestites Legal Committee, Chicago's first transgender political organization.[90]

Although the protests and organizing that occurred around the deaths of Hampton, Clark, and Clay served the cause of black politicians by making whites more aware of police violence as a problem, they were even more consequential for the gay movement. The decade after the assassination of Martin Luther King, Jr., saw a flourishing of black gay and lesbian organizations in Chicago, whose founders theorized the dual nature of their struggle.[91] One such organization was Third World Gay Revolution, created by the zealous Alderson to address the specific concerns of black lesbians and gay men.[92] Alderson's organizing with the caucus was cut short when, as one of the "Pontiac Four," he was arrested and convicted for stealing draft files from a federal facility in Pontiac, Illinois, and sent to the federal prison in Ashland, Kentucky.[93] He was released in August 1971, not before having tried to organize a gay-liberation chapter inside the prison.[94]

Some white gay liberationists were also influenced by the militant perspectives of the Black Panthers. "What had Ray done? He walked down the street being unmistakably black and gay. *That* was his crime," wrote the author of an article in the New Left underground newspaper *Chicago Seed*, after a black gay man was arrested and charged with solicitation for prostitution. "During the past few weeks there has been increased harassment of gay people just going about their business. Third world gay people in mainly white areas are in particular danger of being arrested." The paper reported that "the police are busting an increasing number of brothers on the charge of solicitation for prostitution," adding, "it is warfare on all gay people being carried out by the Chicago Pig Department."[95] As noted by a white gay activist who bailed out a black friend arrested for solicitation, "I called in sick Tuesday morning—sick of being harassed by pigs with nothing better to do with their time than chase gays and blacks and freaks around Chicago in the wee hours of the dawn."[96]

In 1972, radical gay activists in Chicago joined African Americans and Latinos to protest a police crackdown in the Lincoln Park neighborhood, a North Side lakefront area where urban renewal pitted progressive housing activists and clergy against new homeowners and developers.[97] At a community-relations meeting arranged by the police, activists demanded to know "why homosexuals in the district are arrested for kissing and holding hands."[98] When the district commander said the "gay community" should really be called the "sad community," because of its high suicide rate, gays in the audience demanded an apology. When he suggested that "his boys in blue didn't hassle the gay bars," the audience was unimpressed. " 'Yeah, $1,500 a month is why!' someone yelled," a reference to an ongoing federal investigation of police extortion of bar owners that would soon produce indictments.[99] Gay-liberation activists noted afterward that Latino speakers at the meeting "came up with names, dates, times and places of Pig harassment and brutality," and that this was "a very effective tactic with even the middle-class members of the audience." And they suggested that gay activists should "begin to do the same thing."[100]

Black and white activists forged institutional links through the Alliance to End Repression (AER), a coalition of organizations that shared a concern with challenging repressive and authoritarian institutions, founded in the wake of the killing of Hampton and Clark. Both Mattachine Midwest and Chicago Gay Liberation (and, later, the Illinois Gay Rights Task Force, which AER spawned) became institutional members of this umbrella organization. The larger group successfully challenged the Chicago police department's late-1960s spike in surveillance and undercover infiltration of radical and left-wing organizations. Its lawsuit has been called the most successful grassroots effort to control police antisubversive activity in U.S. history.[101]

The Alliance addressed a range of issues related to the reform of law enforcement. Many of its organizers were veterans of the radical Catholic social-action movement of the late 1960s and early 1970s; some of the leaders were radical priests and nuns. One early project sought recognition by the courts of the right to bail. "There were a hundred people at our first organizational meeting," recalled John Hill, the group's first executive director, "the most colorful I had ever been at. We had Black Panther Party members. Black street gangs were represented. We had gay and lesbian people. Then there were nuns and priests and the religious laypeople."[102] The group won an increase in the proportion of criminal defendants released on recognizance instead of being jailed while awaiting trial.

At an Alliance planning retreat in late March 1974, members held sessions in which they selected new issues for the group to take up. This resulted in a recommendation to form a Gay Rights Task Force within the Alliance, which held its first meeting on June 18, 1974, at the AER offices.[103] The Gay Rights Task Force and its successor autonomous organization, the Illinois Gay Rights (later Gay and Lesbian) Task Force, were for nearly a decade the principal vehicle for gay activists pushing for the passage of a local antidiscrimination ordinance. They worked closely with the measure's longtime legislative advocate, Cliff Kelley, a straight black alderman from the South Side's 20th Ward. The AER encouraged other radical activities that linked gay equality with other causes. In 1974, for example, the Alliance's police-monitoring committee reached out to six gay men arrested at a lakefront cruising spot, to work up a complaint for the new Police Board.[104] And in alignment with the Alliance or under its auspices, beginning as early as 1970, members of gay organizations took formal part in a campaign to ratify a new Illinois constitution and in an effort cosponsored by the Japanese American Citizens League to repeal Title 2 of the federal Internal Security Act.[105] Through such activities, gay activists met and began working with others engaged in liberal and left-wing reform causes at the local level.

*   *   *

Though queer historians have often emphasized differences between the homophile movement and the gay-liberation movement that quickly overtook it after the 1969 Stonewall uprising in New York, this book instead emphasizes their shared focus on police brutality. In America's largest cities, gays and lesbians who organized against police harassment beginning in the 1960s allied with black communities who also sought to rein in police aggression. Placing urban politics at the center of analysis points to the centrality of urban policing as a major target of gay political mobilization—not only in the pre-Stonewall period but throughout the 1970s and into the 1980s.

The 1968 election year saw a triumph for law-and-order politics in Illinois, as in the nation. The same year that Richard Nixon was elected president on a campaign that promised to restore law and order to the nation's cities, Richard Ogilvie, who in his four years as Cook County sheriff had escalated law-enforcement persecution of local gays and lesbians, won election as governor of Illinois. Chicago homophile activists watched with dismay, but they did not have the means to mount a serious challenge to his campaign.[106] The courts, however, began to offer relief from antigay police harassment. After the January 1968 raid on the Trip, while the club's owners appealed the revocation of its liquor license, the city shut down the club under the padlock law passed in 1961, discussed in Chapter 2. The owners then sued to challenge that law.[107] The attorney for the Trip's owners, Ralla Klepak, persuaded her friend Elmer Gertz, a celebrated Chicago activist attorney, and his associate Wayne Giampietro to institute the case challenging the padlock law. Though no one on the night of the raid would have expected it, the state Supreme Court ruled in favor of the club owners in April 1969, offering a ray of hope by invalidating the padlock law on the narrow grounds that the state could not apply such a statutory regulation solely to the state's largest city.[108]

That decision came too late to prevent the closure of the bars raided in the run-up to the Democratic National Convention. But bar owners had begun to turn to the courts for relief from excessive police targeting of gay establishments. Though Daley exercised his power to suspend the license of the Annex, one of the bars targeted in the August 20, 1968, raids, the owners sued the city's License Appeal Commission, arguing that the revocation was improper.[109] After more than five years, the Illinois Appellate Court ruled against the commission. In the ruling, the court referenced the 1961 sodomy decriminalization, rhetorically though not legally directing Chicago officials to adhere not only to its letter but to its spirit.[110] The violence at the Democratic National Convention marked a turning point not only for the city but for the Daley machine, in that it sparked more white liberal antipathy toward corruption and, to a lesser extent, toward police brutality. Although the local newspapers had usually ignored the police crackdown against gay life and the homophile response, they proved more receptive to news coverage about police misbehavior in years to come.

Thus, police misconduct was the first issue around which Chicago gay activists collaborated in a sustained way with other groups. Raids on gay bars brought about petition drives in the late 1960s; direct-action protests in the late 1970s; and, in a couple of cases, civil damages in the 1980s awarded by juries to plaintiffs who pursued legal action against the city. But police brutality was only the first issue that would lead gay activists to look to the black community. As more gay people came out and realized they had no recourse if they were fired for being gay, they again turned to the civil rights model developed by African Americans to seek legislation to protect them.[111]

4

Clark and Diversey Is *Our* Ghetto!

ON SATURDAY, June 27, 1970, Chicago became one of four American cities where gay men and lesbians marched to commemorate the first anniversary of the Stonewall rebellion. The procession began with a rally in Washington Square Park, better known as Bughouse Square, on the Near North Side. Once associated with political and artistic radicalism, Bughouse Square had been a major cruising area since the interwar era, and the march's planners began there to show they were "renouncing the guilt, repression, fear and shame" involved in the stigmatization of their erotic lives, as the countercultural *Chicago Seed* newspaper said in a special gay-liberation supplement. The group, numbering 150 to 200, marched to Michigan Avenue and then downtown to the Civic Center (now Daley Center) Plaza, where they listened to speeches and danced around the famous Picasso statue there while chanting "Gay power to gay people!"[1]

The invented tradition of the gay-pride march gave concrete expression to the notion of coming out of the closet, disclosing one's homosexuality, and becoming visible, which were central tenets of the movement for gay liberation that flourished beginning in late 1969. By marching publicly and proudly, queer Chicagoans pressed at the boundaries of the closet and staked a claim to city streets. Paradoxically, although gay liberation was a radical movement suffused with rhetoric of revolution, it set in motion the greater visibility of gay life on the North Side as well as in participation in urban machine politics.[2] By the mid-1970s, this commemoration of the Stonewall anniversary had become an annual ritual; by the second half of the decade, it had evolved from a protest march into a Pride parade, and moved north to Lakeview. By 1973, there were 1,500 to 2,000 in attendance.[3]

Tracing the relationship between queer communities and gay politics in the 1970s requires recognition of two broader factors. First, the class bias in the available evidence on gay activism and politics is stronger than that which shapes the historical record regarding the social, recreational, and domestic lives of gays and lesbians. Moreover, those for whom gay identity was politicizing were overwhelmingly both white and male. For queer people of color and white women, the gay movement was often not the movement that spoke most directly to their daily concerns. Second, many gay men were—and are—simultaneously privileged by race and class at the same time that they were victimized by antigay discrimination. To be sure, white gay men are hardly universally privileged economically; in fact, the economic penalties for being gay were often harsh. However, their race and gender status could make them insiders even as their sexual orientation made them outsiders.[4] They could be despised and fired if their sexuality were known, and yet a sizable and growing number of white gay men held economically comfortable positions in the city.

These simultaneous dynamics of inclusion and exclusion were central to the rise of gay urban politics, and in particular to how gays and lesbians—primarily white gay men—began to insinuate themselves into urban-machine politics. "Gays are like an ethnic group," wrote a gay journalist in 1987, "one that has been crystallizing before our very eyes over the last ten to fifteen years." Surveying the array of gay groups and facilities in the North Side's Lakeview neighborhood, he attributed their emergence to the fact that "gays started building those same sorts of institutions that other groups had."[5] This analogy between gayness and race or ethnicity as a force for collective clout in municipal politics seemed obvious to many white gay men, and to some people of color—including Alderman Clifford P. Kelley of the South Side's 20th Ward, who, as we will see, became a crucial figure in the incorporation of gays and lesbians into Chicago politics.

However, to many people of color in Chicago, especially to those who were poor or working-class, this gradually developing connection between gay people and political power was problematic because many white gay men seemed to be relatively economically privileged. By the late 1970s, the nation began to debate gay rights after the 1977 repeal of Miami-Dade County's gay-rights ordinance, and urban blacks began to gain real access to the levers of power in municipal government. In this era, a black man living on Chicago's West Side was quoted anonymously in a news article

insiders   vs   outsider

about Kelley's gay-rights ordinance, saying, "You wouldn't believe how many gays there are in good jobs, on the management level. And especially when it comes to blacks, most likely the gay will be doing the firing, rather than getting fired."[6] Other African Americans rejected the notion that being homosexual—a trait that could be concealed—could be compared to being black. One black minister in Chicago "dashed cold water" on the analogy, saying, "When you're black it sticks."[7] To be sure, white gay men were highly vulnerable to being fired because of their sexuality.[8] Yet a significant number of white gay men, who dominated most gay organizations, held comfortable positions where they could be "out."

can't conceal blackness

Inventing the Gay-Pride Parade

The defining issue for the gay-liberation movement in Chicago during its first year in existence, and its greatest policy victory, was the right to dance with a person of the same sex. In the fall of 1969, Henry Wiemhoff and Vernita Gray founded a Gay Liberation Front organization at the University of Chicago. The group quickly spread to other campuses, as well as to nonacademic populations. By the spring and summer of 1970, gay liberationists held one large, public event after another. Wiemhoff, Gray, and their colleagues, frustrated by the fact that the city's gay bars did not allow dancing, tested their ability to sponsor dances where same-sex couples could embrace without facing arrest, using the relatively safe space of the university for this purpose. After the university shut down the dances because too many nonstudents were attending, gay liberationists decided to hold a citywide gay dance at the Chicago Coliseum—a once-grand venue, the site of national party conventions in decades past, and more recently of the annual gay Halloween balls—on April 18, 1970.[9]

Two days in advance, on April 16, 1970, a rally for gay freedom drew 250 people into Grant Park, downtown along the lakefront, followed by a march down Washington Street (see Figures 6, 7, and 8). This rally brought together women and men from a wide political spectrum. Surviving images show many on the grass listening to speakers, with a few wearing buttons or holding signs. Many of them appeared simply curious. Among the core members of the group, some saw their role as championing liberation for all of society's underdogs. They would have liked to see the group take on the name "Gay Liberation Front," as did the New York group after which

Univ of chicago]

FIGURE 6. Gay-liberation rally in Grant Park, April 1970, with New York activist
Martha Shelley addressing the crowd through a megaphone.
Photograph: Margaret Olin.

they modeled themselves, while others believed in working methodically
and carefully through legal channels and targeted protests to achieve equal
rights and recognition for gays. These tensions would come to a head later
in 1970.

The dance on April 18 drew a much larger crowd to the Coliseum.
When the planners could not locate an insurer to underwrite a policy for
an event with such a high risk of police involvement, they turned to Renee
Hanover, the radical lawyer and former student of Pearl Hart's at John
Marshall Law School. Hanover used her own network of contacts on the
South Side to find an African American insurance broker who did business
with the Nation of Islam and who was willing to write a policy.[10] One man
recalls "being terribly energized by the idea of two thousand people . . . in
one place, just being free to express themselves, via dance in this case, and
not worrying about the consequences."[11] Despite many fears, precautions,
and inconclusive negotiations, the dance was not raided by the police.

Following their success in sponsoring the Coliseum dance, gay-liberation
activists next picketed the owners of a large North Side gay bar, the Normandy Inn, just a few blocks from the Chicago Avenue (18th) Police District headquarters. The protesters called on the bar's owners to use their

FIGURE 7. Close-up of protestors at gay-liberation rally in Grant Park, April 1970.
Photograph: Margaret Olin.

influence with police to force toleration of same-sex dancing.[12] When they
succeeded—the Normandy owners negotiated directly with district police
to allow dancing—gay Chicagoans celebrated. "Thanks are due to Gay Liberation," noted the *Mattachine Midwest Newsletter*, "for getting dancing in
gay bars," reflecting its importance to people of many ages.[13] Even years
later, the excitement over the moment was remembered: "When the Nor-
mandie [sic] opened a dance floor to gay men in 1970, the first such occasion in Chicago's history, there was widespread jubilation over the
supposedly new era gays were entering," recalled one commentator.[14] By
the time of the first Pride march at the end of June, gay liberation had
spawned individual campus gay-liberation groups and a loose citywide
cluster of gay-liberation groups, which continued throughout 1971 to offer
a subversive challenge to the city's heteronormative political culture (see
Figure 9).

In September 1970, however, more moderate activists left Chicago Gay
Liberation and founded Chicago Gay Alliance (CGA) to pursue a militant

FIGURE 8. Onlookers and gay-liberation protestors on Loop sidewalk after Grant Park rally, April 1970. The protestors are carrying banners and flags at right. Photograph: Margaret Olin.

but largely "single-issue" approach to mobilization (see Figure 10). Like the Gay Activists Alliance in New York City on which it was modeled, CGA represented a partial assimilation of the movement into the emerging pattern of interest-group politics. The group's members had a civil rights orientation and a belief that rights could be protected only by using political levers and changing political structures.[15]

Energized by the new universe of possibilities offered by freedom from concealment, CGA members began to challenge local opinion leaders, such as leading newspaper columnist Mike Royko, when he wrote disparagingly about homosexuals.[16] In the wake of the founding of CGA, gay liberationists continued to speak out. An informant for the Chicago police "red squad"—the undercover anti-subversive unit, which had grown dramatically under O. W. Wilson—noted that they attended "whatever Left Wing Demonstrations or activities there are," where, "if given an opportunity to speak" a member would describe "the advantages of Homosexuality, and the discrimination that is shown to Homosexuals."[17] But CGA, unlike its liberationist counterparts, endured past the end of 1970. Members of the new group sent

big audience

FIGURE 9. Gay Pride Week schedule with line drawing by Steve Fabus, 1971. Courtesy of Manuscripts and Archives Division, The New York Public Library, Astor, Lenox, and Tilden Foundations.

speakers to hundreds of church, school, and community groups through the first half of the 1970s, spreading by their very presence the then-novel idea that one's homosexuality could be publicly proclaimed. Gay activists solicited and accommodated requests for speakers on talk shows, in club meetings, at churches, and on radio and television. From early on, they placed a municipal gay-rights ordinance on their agenda. They lobbied the nation's professional organizations for lawyers and doctors, both headquartered in Chicago, to change their influential antigay positions.[18]

As gays and lesbians built and staffed the city's first gay and lesbian community centers, counseling agencies, medical clinics, and religious congregations, they confronted the fact that losing control of knowledge of one's sexuality could entail the very real risk of losing one's job. After newspapers covered journalist David Stienecker's speech at the April 16, 1970, Grant Park demonstration, for example, he was fired from his job at World Book Encyclopedia.[19] In a similar vein, Margaret Wilson confronted Governor Daniel Walker at an "accountability session," demanding an

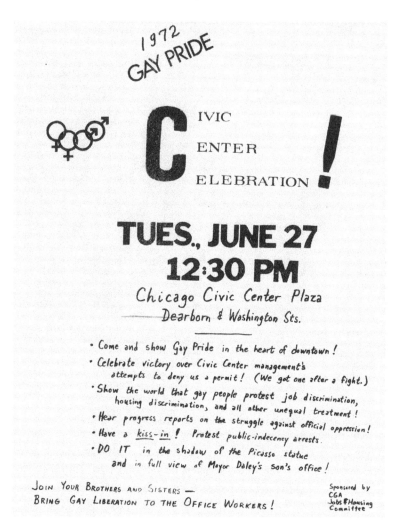

FIGURE 10. Chicago Gay Alliance flyer for Pride event, 1972.
Courtesy of William B. Kelley.

executive order to protect gay state employees from job discrimination. Wilson's boss saw her on television and fired her the next day.[20] Two women who were highly active volunteers at Beckman House—a storefront community center in Lakeview—told a reporter that "they would probably be in serious trouble with their employers if their activism ever got too much notoriety."[21] By advancing a political strategy centered on visibility, the Pride parade constituted a stunningly effective challenge to the specific experiences of discretion and concealment that characterized gay life in the postwar decades. But the existence of gay-pride marches and, later, parades did not transform the limitations of the closet overnight. Indeed, an individual's attendance at a gay-pride event did not necessarily signal a willingness to go public about one's sexuality. As during the homophile era, that is, even many of those most involved in gay activism continued in the early 1970s to avoid having their names become associated with the cause.

The growth and institutionalization of gay liberation by the mid-1970s helped realize some of the radical goals of the earlier gay movement, and solidarity with other social minorities remained central to activists' agenda. As early as October 1970, Chicago Gay Liberation—part of the loose network of militant gay groups that sprang up in U.S. cities after Stonewall—organized a picket outside a coffee shop near Diversey and Clark, where black drag queens and effeminate gay men had been refused service. Gay liberationists echoed the rhetoric of Carl Wittman's influential 1969 manifesto, reprinted in the radical press nationwide, that portrayed gay enclaves as "ghettoes" exploited by straight profiteers. One group member asked: "Could a restaurant at 63rd and Cottage refuse Blacks? Could one at 18th and Blue Island refuse Mexicans? Could one at 45th and Archer refuse Lithuanians, or at Halsted and Jackson refuse Greeks? After all, Clark and Diversey is *our* ghetto!"[22] Yet, by positing an isomorphism between gay and racial/ethnic identities, the question—like its underlying premise of single-issue mobilization—elided the very existence of queers of color.

During the dramatic and short-lived upsurge of radical gay activism in 1970 and 1971, the racial politics of the rapidly growing and changing gay movement shifted. In the initial flush of gay liberation, black gay activists created a Black Caucus in August 1970. Its first Statement of Purpose declared that "white racism exists in the homosexual ghettos as it does in our total society." The black activists also called on their need to "create a dialogue with other movement groups in the black ghettos where we for the most part live. . . . We will not be denied our sexuality to perpetuate the myth that homosexuality doesn't exist among black folk."[23] Within a month, the group became Third World Gay Revolution. "We must align ourselves with our Black heritage in our fight for Black equality," wrote Elandria V. Henderson in an early manifesto. "Before we can even begin to

Change identity

do this we have to demand acceptance from our Black people."[24] Joining a wave of rhetoric and activism organized around the concept of remaking society on wholly new principles, black activists theorized the dual nature of the black-gay struggle.

At the same time, because gay liberation cast the active disclosure of one's gay identity as a mark of liberation, it obscured other ways of affirmation and belonging that did not rely on active disclosure. "Unlike the white gay community, black gays are not about the business of advertising themselves," observed a reporter for the *Defender*. To be sure, there were forms of acceptance within nongay institutions on the South Side: "In some groups, it may be the 'norm,' as is reportedly the case within many of the smaller churches' choirs." Code-switching became even more critical to survival for African American gays and lesbians. "One minute, we've gotta be a Miss Thing, the next we've gotta be Mr. So & So, and after that maybe we're Brother," one man told the reporter. "You've got to change to cope."[25] Black queer Chicagoans thus had two ghettoes to code-switch between: the black one and the gay one.

Marches and activism were crucial to the increasing visibility of gay life in Chicago; so too were demographic changes. On Chicago's North Side, several of the lakefront wards were also home to gay and lesbian bars and to the city's largest residential enclaves that were significantly gay. The center of gravity of gay life moved from Old Town in the 1960s to "New Town," just to the north—a brand-new label for a neighborhood known to its longtime inhabitants as Lake View (later, Lakeview)—in the 1970s. To be sure, many white gay people joined their straight counterparts in moving to the suburbs—and gay activism even bore some fruit there. At Elk Grove High School, a suburban public school, three CGA members spoke to assembled students in 1972, and one of them even told the group, "There are more gay people here than just us three."[26] But urban gay enclaves only continued to grow in size, complexity, and visibility by the late 1970s, when 64 percent of gay male gathering places in Chicago were situated on less than 1 percent of the city's total land mass.[27]

In the decade after 1968, the residential composition of the North Side's lakefront wards became younger, better educated, and more white-collar, and land in the area increased in value. Gay men were part of a proliferation of nonnuclear households. Though commercial establishments were important to the "gayification" of areas like Lakeview, grassroots organizations were also crucial. New gay organizations, formal and informal, ranged from weight-loss groups to softball teams, from counseling centers to churches to organizations of social workers and tenants.[28] The *Reader* proclaimed, "In Chicago they are tireless organizers, setting up everything from volleyball teams to phone newslines," and counting "more than 70 gay businesses in town, most of them on the north side." A new telephone recorded-message service told hundreds of callers daily about gay community events.[29]

"Tireless Organizers"

Gay men created community-based groups to address unmet needs of the growing gay population, with one group often forming the seed for another. In 1973, Michael Bergeron created the Gay Switchboard, from the apartment he shared with his then-lover Bill Kelley, and promoted its helpline number, 929-HELP (929–4357). When Bergeron opened Beckman House, the Gay Switchboard operations became part of its program, and the phone was housed there rather than in the apartment he shared with Kelley. Some of the earliest nonprofit institutions founded in the gay-liberation era centered on the unmet health needs of gay men, who often encountered homophobic reactions from doctors and hospitals. An example is the Gay VD Clinic. The clinic was founded in May 1974 and staffed by volunteers; it was located on the second floor of an old Wobbly (Industrial Workers of the World) location called Liberty Hall. Eventually, the clinic was acquired by Gay Horizons, which in turn spun it off into the Howard Brown Memorial Clinic (later, the Howard Brown Health Center), which incorporated in 1975.[30]

Meanwhile, in much the same way that Chicago Gay Alliance had split off from Chicago Gay Liberation, a group called Gay Horizons was later formed by people splitting off from CGA because they preferred social service to political action. Later, both the Gay Switchboard and the community-center functions of Beckman House were inherited by Gay Horizons, which then acquired the helpline number. The switchboard's helpline number was used for decades afterward by Horizons and remains the helpline number used by the successor organization of Horizons, the Center on Halsted, though it no longer uses the letters "HELP" in its publicity materials.[31] The creation of Chicago Gay Alliance, in short, inaugurated a period of extraordinary organizational proliferation.

The growth of gay enclaves, like that in Lakeview, tracked the larger process by which an increasing percentage of U.S. households did not conform to the traditional heterosexual family form. The family wage system that was the ideological foundation of New Deal social-welfare programs—although one that always only partially corresponded to economic life on the ground—eroded by the 1970s.[32] Though we often think of "gayborhoods" as the outcome of gay mobilization, the decisions of architects and urban planners were just as important as those of gay activists in paving the way for the identification of gayness with the North Side. In this sense, Chicago's mostly white gay enclaves should be seen as part of the broader trajectory of the postwar city, rather than apart from it. To take another example, the massive Chicago Housing Authority high-rise projects built alongside the new South (later Dan Ryan) Expressway in the 1950s were deliberately built to concentrate large families and to exclude small families and single people.[33]

In the 1960s, after builders created publicly financed, massive concrete high-rise housing projects on the South Side, private real-estate developers remade the landscape of the North Side lakefront neighborhoods. They built so-called "four-plus-one" apartment buildings on the North Side lakefront, rising to the maximum height limits and filling every inch of their lots. These cheaply constructed apartment buildings sharply increased residential density and increased developers' profits. They also usually replaced single-family homes with efficiencies, studios, and one-bedroom apartments that were unappealing to people with children. In 1969, one neighborhood group estimated that some forty-eight such buildings either had been completed or were under construction in an area partly overlapping Boystown.[34]

Before and during the construction of four-plus-ones, countless gay people moved into the many older apartment buildings and high-rises already in the area, but the new buildings provoked a major controversy in Lakeview in which discussions of real estate converged with rhetoric about family life. Reformers who opposed the new apartment buildings—widely derided as cheap and ugly, though they were clearly also profitable and attracted many tenants—drew on the prejudiced grammar of urban real estate in leveling their critiques. The Lake View Citizens' Council, a neighborhood group dominated by middle-class white homeowners, complained to Mayor Daley that "the rising tide of four plus ones in our area is forcing families out of the city."[35] The group circulated letters in the neighborhood, saying, "Dear Neighbor, Are you willing to add your voice to our fight to protect family housing from four plus ones?"[36] To be sure, activists against the four-plus-ones objected not only to single residents but also to developers being given free rein to seek "large quick profits." Nonetheless, the sign carried by two women promoting the sale of a Victorian home in Lincoln Park—"For Sale to Family Only"—suggested unmistakably which neighbors were desirable and which undesirable. Other critics were more specific, charging that "transients and single persons, not interested in the welfare of the neighborhood, are the main inhabitants of the 'four plus ones.'"[37] In their opposition to developers' profit motives, these reformers were progressive, yet in casting families with children as model citizens, they portrayed those living otherwise as outsiders.

As gays became increasingly visible and concentrated in Lakeview and adjacent neighborhoods, then, they encountered resistance, regardless of whether they occupied four-plus-ones or older housing stock. One 1972 news article quoted a story about a gay couple who "invested several hundred dollars in fixing up an apartment" in Lincoln Park, only to have their lease not renewed without explanation.[38] By 1977, the *Sun-Times* reported, "there are landlords who believe neighborhoods deteriorate when significant numbers of homosexuals move in." The owner of a building in Lakeview, near the corner of Pine Grove Avenue and Surf Street, a notoriously cruisy area in the 1970s, had "decided to sell five years ago as a result of the neighborhood atmosphere he attributes to the presence of gay hustlers." The reporter quoted the new owner as saying that gay men had broken the lights in the courtyard in order to keep their sexual encounters hidden. But as a result, "[w]hen you saw them at night, you didn't know if they were homosexuals or guys who might rob you."[39]

On the one hand, Chicago's gayborhoods—the eastern half of Lakeview, for example—were and are more racially integrated than its other white neighborhoods. The gay in-migration of the 1960s and 1970s predominantly drew whites who chose not to live near their families of origin, but it also coincided with sharp increases in the residential racial diversity of the majority-white neighborhoods along the North Side lakefront where families had long lived.[40] In the 1970s, these neighborhoods were welcoming enough of at least some individual blacks that a black gay schoolteacher quoted in *Playboy* could claim in 1979 that "the blacks who go to the North Side are just trying to get away from momma."[41] Yet, on the other hand, Lakeview, where the largest burgeoning enclave was located, was far away

from the South Side black metropolis. Moving to New Town on the North
Side would have meant, for most blacks, leaving one's community of origin,
which was both more difficult and less desirable for many black gay Chicagoans than for white gays. Some black gays and lesbians gravitated toward
the mostly white North Side gay enclaves, others socialized primarily
in mostly straight black South Side and West Side communities, and still
others code-switched between the two.

The gay world may have been more racially integrated than the straight
world, but not by much, and not enough to alleviate the resentment of
many African Americans. As new gay commercial establishments opened
in New Town, black gays and lesbians often found them harder to get to
and harder to enter than white people did. Max Smith recalls that he was
often willing to brave the North Side white clubs alone, "but a lot of times
if I were going out with other people, and they didn't want to deal with the
hassle of being carded," they would stay on the South Side.[42] However,
Smith attended church at the Good Shepherd Parish Metropolitan Community Church in Lakeview, part of a national network of predominantly
gay congregations founded in Los Angeles in 1969 by the Reverend Troy D.
Perry. The fact that Smith remained a churchgoer helped his grandmother,
also black, reconcile herself to his being gay. "In her mind, if you go to
church every Sunday—it doesn't matter what church it is, Catholic, Baptist,
Methodist, doesn't matter—just go to church every Sunday and worship
God, and then you're okay."[43] Precisely because, as a gay church, it deviated
so radically from the general pattern of religious life in Chicago, Good
Shepherd Parish was relatively racially mixed.[44]

The emergence of gay-pride parades and more-visible gay businesses in
the 1970s coincided with a transformation in the significance of ethnicity
among white Americans. Indeed, gay politics adopted what some social
scientists have called an "ethnic model" at the very moment that national
identifications, so long the basis of "ethnic" identification among urban
whites, gave way in the face of sharp black-white racial polarization. "In
the early 1970s race had replaced nationality as the major cultural and political factor in the life of the city," wrote one observer, "and the ethnic neighborhoods are changing into racial areas of blacks, browns, and whites."
Black mobilization, he noted, "has unified the ethnic whites on a single
issue—blocking the movement of the blacks and Latins into white neighborhoods."[45] Gay neighborhoods bore crucial differences from the white
ethnic neighborhoods out of which they developed, not least because

becoming part of them frequently entailed a partial or total loss of contact with one's family of origin. The similarities, however, were striking.

Even as Irish, Italian, German, and Polish ethnic neighborhood businesses continued to decline through the assimilation of successive generations into the U.S. mainstream, gay businesses began to proliferate rapidly. In 1979, in one of the first scholarly accounts of how gay neighborhoods seemed to be reworking traditional forms of urban ethnicity, Stephen O. Murray drew on an earlier study by Raymond Breton that had defined "institutional completeness" as a key feature of ethnic communities. Institutional completeness, Breton claimed, "would be at its extreme whenever the ethnic community could perform all the services required by its members. Members would *never have to* make use of native institutions for the satisfaction of any of their needs."[46] In contrast to urban ethnic communities, which were becoming less institutionally complete, gay communities were becoming more so.

As gay politics became spatialized in Lakeview in the 1970s, queers of color thus began to associate it not only with sexual liberalism but also with whiteness and with property ownership. Black gay activism more often focused on gay racism than on black homophobia, and especially on the problem of racially discriminatory door policies in North Side gay bars and clubs. A particularly well-known case, in which state liquor regulators became involved, was that of one of the most popular lesbian bars on the North Side, Augie & C.K.'s. Discrimination complaints brought by a group calling itself the Black Lesbian Discrimination Investigation Committee, and represented by the white lesbian lawyer Renee Hanover, led to a settlement that was covered in the gay press across North America. The deal required the bars to post the requirements for entry, fire one bouncer, and agree not to engage in any reprisals against protesters.[47] The location of gay institutions in Lakeview was not deliberately an act of racial exclusion, and yet it represented one of the ways in which even as gay people became more visible everywhere, gay visibility came to be associated with whiteness.

Reform in Black and White

The mobilization by gays and lesbians and civil libertarians that had developed within the radical left in the 1960s gained a toehold on the fringe of the Democratic Party in the early 1970s. In 1972, as the Democratic Party nationwide was flooded by progressive mobilization of all kinds, Michael Bergeron, then in his early twenties, ran for delegate-at-large to the Democratic National Convention, the city's first campaign for elected office by an out gay person.[48] Early in 1972, Chicago gay activists hosted the first national planning conference for gay activists hoping to influence the two major political parties during their quadrennial conventions that summer. "I hope quite frankly that we take an active role," said John Abney, the president of Chicago Gay Alliance. "That means seeking delegate positions to the conventions, and especially the Democratic convention under the new convention rules that were put through in Chicago in 1968." A single well-known public figure attended: Dr. Benjamin Spock, the author of the famous child-rearing manual, who had become active in the antiwar movement. One of the major strategic discussions was about "candidate confrontation," a practice about which the Gay Activists Alliance members from New York were the experts, having recently successfully confronted or "zapped" Mayor John Lindsay several times over his failure to push the gay-rights bill under consideration in the city council. The conference passed a national platform, much of which was apparently based on planks proposed by Frank Kameny.[49]

As gays and lesbians participated in electoral politics for the first time, they drew on a broader challenge to Chicago's patronage-based machine politics. Although a majority of white Chicagoans continued to support the Daley regime's association with law-and-order politics, the minority of whites who recoiled from it were concentrated in the North Side lakefront wards. "The 'lakefront liberal' political movement that would challenge Daley's machine was formed out of the violent struggle at the convention," as the political scientist William Grimshaw put it.[50] In a string of lakefront wards on the city's North Side, voters began to elect "independent" politicians who increasingly challenged ossified local structures of public power and who did not depend on the Cook County Democratic Organization for their support. The independents—the tiny band of antimachine, anti-Daley, reformist, good-government challengers who had sprung up on the North Side lakefront—were practically the only politicians interested in listening to gay activists. This small faction was the first element in Chicago's political culture to explicitly welcome the political concerns of gay activists.

In the spring of 1969, two special city-council elections ushered in the hope that this "independent" political movement could serve as a semiviable electoral force, unifying black and white progressive reformers behind a challenge to the Daley machine's stranglehold on local politics. In this pair of aldermanic elections, antimachine candidates shocked Chicagoans by defeating the party organization's slated candidates. One, Fred Hubbard, was a black insurgent elected from the 2nd Ward on the South Side. The other, in the 44th Ward on the North Side, home to a significant Jewish population, was William Singer, a twenty-eight-year-old lawyer who had worked for Robert Kennedy's presidential campaign and won narrowly on an explicitly antimachine platform.[51] Noting the confluence of interests between gays and reform candidates, Bill Kelley wrote at the time that Singer's election "may be of some help to homosexuals in the area who are up against the Town Hall district police."[52]

The pressure of the independent movement pushed machine regulars to adopt more-liberal positions on a number of issues, including gay rights. It is telling, perhaps, that Chuck Renslow, the first openly gay precinct captain in the Daley machine and the only one to come out before the mayor's death, served in the early 1970s in one of the most antimachine wards in the city, the 43rd Ward on the North Side (see Figure 11). Precinct captains occupied the first rung on the ladder of local politics, the essential starting point for members of any ethnic group who hoped to rise in the Cook County Regular Democratic Organization. The precinct captain's job was to be the face of the machine at ground level, serving as an intermediary for citizens in need of constituent services or desiring favors, and pounding the pavement to turn out votes at elections. It illustrates the distance between the spectrum of gay political opinion and the American mainstream that Renslow—a former physique photography entrepreneur and a bar and bathhouse owner, who would later found the International Mr. Leather pageant—was viewed in Chicago as politically conservative, even square. At the same time, he was rightly seen as a pioneer in the political incorporation of gay people into urban machine politics.

Renslow created and owned some of the earliest "quasi-ethnic" gay institutions. He owned a series of gay-oriented businesses since the 1950s, and they expanded significantly in the 1970s to include, beginning in 1975, the city's first commercial newspaper aimed at gays and lesbians. He had first opened a physique photography studio, Kris Studio, in 1952, and had owned a gay leather bar called the Gold Coast since the 1950s.[53] In 1974, as if to literalize the flow of gay men into spaces being vacated by white ethnic migration to the suburbs, Renslow opened a glitzy gay bathhouse in the

FIGURE 11. Chuck Renslow (left) receives plaque from Mayor Richard J. Daley
commemorating city-council designation of Dewes Mansion as historic landmark,
1974. Courtesy of Chuck Renslow.

former headquarters of the Swedish Society, in a longtime Swedish enclave
on the North Side.[54] Man's Country quickly became a booming business,
featuring an array of drag performers and entertainment amenities. The
following year, when the founder of a new weekly newspaper called *GayLife*
ran into financial difficulties, Renslow bought it from him and published it
thereafter. The new publication took over the role previously played by the
monthly *Chicago Gay Crusader*, but where the latter had been created by
Michael Bergeron and Bill Kelley in 1973 as a labor of love, with volunteer
writers and photographers, *GayLife* was a commercial venture.

Like other precinct captains for the machine, Renslow performed constituent services in his neighborhood. For decades, ambitious Chicagoans
of all ethnicities had acquired power through this role, positioning themselves as conduits of information and authority between specific neighborhoods and the Democratic Party. After Daley died in December 1976,
Renslow got out the vote in his precinct for the late boss's handpicked

successor, Michael Bilandic. Renslow described his visits to voters like this: "I said, 'I don't care who you vote for at the top of the ticket; vote for my people at the bottom. We can trim your trees.'"[55] In the March 1977 mayoral primary election, when surrounding precincts went for Roman Pucinski or Harold Washington by 20 or 30 votes each, Chuck Renslow pulled his in for Bilandic.[56] On the left wing of local political culture, then, electoral mobilization by gays and lesbians occurred on both sides of the machine-independent divide.

"The Real Gut of This Problem Is the Policing of Vice"

For all its impact, gay liberation did not end gay-bar raids—a police scandal did. As late as 1972, police raids on gay bars and arrests in parks and public restrooms (or "tearooms") remained widespread. "We get a lot of calls for bail, but we don't maintain a bail fund," said Tom Erwin (a pseudonym), the twenty-seven-year-old president of Mattachine Midwest, that year. Hanover, the radical lawyer, told a reporter, "I would say a male homosexual is more apt to be arrested in Chicago than almost anywhere."[57]

Though Daley maintained control of his city after the tumult and controversy of 1968, his power steadily began to erode. He won reelection to a fifth term in 1971, but the vaunted power of his machine to turn out large majorities had clearly declined. Over time, he came to depend not on the votes of African Americans, as he had earlier in his mayoral career, but on an increasingly reactionary white working class. After 1968, as once-crucial black support for Daley steadily declined, African American votes were replaced in the 1971 and 1975 mayoral elections by higher margins for Daley in blue-collar white neighborhoods. By contrast, some middle-class and professional white liberals, along with white radicals, joined blacks in increasingly questioning the machine.[58]

At the same time, Daley faced a challenge from other quarters that had the side effect—remarkably quickly—of transforming gay life. In the reform-oriented and scandal-conscious 1970s, James R. Thompson, a young Republican prosecutor whom President Richard Nixon appointed as U.S. attorney for the Northern District of Illinois in 1970, investigated and prosecuted what he portrayed as widespread corruption on the police force, anchored in vice control. Thompson asserted federal control over what Daley had understood to be a local matter. Thompson took an aggressive

tack against police corruption, both by using an obscure 1946 antiracketeering law known as the Hobbs Act to charge police with a federal crime,
and by giving bar owners and some police who cooperated immunity from
prosecution. In a crucial decision, which foreshadowed his later prosecution of former governor Otto Kerner, Thompson chose not to charge bar
owners who had paid off police but rather to grant them immunity so
that they could testify against officers.[59] Thompson conceded that "federal
prosecutors face a dilemma in trying to determine whether an offense is
extortion or bribery," but he took the view that because bar owners had no
choice but to pay off the police, they were the victims in this particular
exchange.[60] Thompson publicized what had been an open secret, widely
known but rarely disclosed, much less questioned, since the 1960 scandal
that led to the hiring of Wilson: Many underpaid police officers supple-
mented their income by demanding cash payments from businesses.
Thompson, in turn, prosecuted some officers for this crime while inducing
others to testify against their colleagues, again by promising immunity from
prosecution.[61]

    With the Thompson inquiry, the long postwar oscillation between
police corruption and reform for the first time aligned gay bar owners with
prosecutors, bringing them into the circle of respectability from which vice
squad officers were being newly ejected. Notably, *Tribune* crime-reporter-
turned-columnist Robert Wiedrich went from helping make gay bar raids
happen in the 1960s to questioning and exposing the corruption behind
them in the 1970s. As recently as 1966, Wiedrich had published investigations that led directly to police harassment of Near North gay establishments. Now, Wiedrich argued that enlisting every officer in the war on vice
and decentralizing the endeavor by designating a vice coordinator for each
police district had actually bred corruption on a massive scale. "The real
gut of this problem," he wrote, "is the policing of vice, particularly in
taverns"—precisely the kind of policing that he had vigorously called for.
He cited New York as a place where vice control had been highly centralized, which decreased the authority of beat cops to initiate vice-related
investigations.[62] Wiedrich also argued that state liquor laws gave police too
much power: "The threat of liquor-license revocation . . . gives the police
extortionist a magic hammer with which to beat tavern owners . . . into
submission without ever going to court."[63] Because police actions could
lead to the revocation of an establishment's liquor license, bar owners were
wholly at the mercy of individual officers.

gay
ppl
alung
with
prosecutors
↓
bringing
gay
movement
to
a
reform

and
national
level → not
fringe   group
anymore

The ensuing criminal trial made clear that if a bar's patrons were gay, its owners faced a choice between systematically paying off vice cops and systematic police intimidation of their patrons. A former member of the vice squad, John Cello, a "bagman" who collected payoffs for his colleagues, testified under a grant of immunity that he solicited $100 a month from each bar under his watch. "In return, there would be no harassment," he testified. Specifically, there would be no "premise checks, I.D. checks of individuals in the bars. If it was a gay bar, you would not go in there with flashlights and harass the patrons of the bar." If a bar's management had paid off, then as soon as you came across "any knowledge or any information that VCD [the central Vice Control Division] was going to come into the district to make a raid on these taverns, you would forewarn them."[64]

Citywide, the owners of bars and other small businesses were not infrequently subject to lower-level police shakedowns, as police officers either accepted, or made clear that they would be delighted to accept, gifts at Christmas time. It had become routine on the Near North Side for officers to demand large monthly cash payments in return for the survival of the business. Thompson's decision to grant immunity to several former members of the vice squad was controversial—some viewed it as a partisan move meant to undermine confidence in Daley; indeed, Thompson leveraged his record prosecuting municipal corruption to win election as governor.

In a fairly short period of time, aided by the cascade of revelations of government corruption and criminality, police extortion and mob control came to be viewed as a more serious threat to the social order than the threat posed by lesbian and gay social life. The *Chicago Gay Crusader*, the volunteer-staffed gay newspaper that Bergeron and Kelley had founded in 1973, cheered the indictment of vice squad members in the Town Hall Police District.[65] Jim Bradford called it a "break-through" that "should liberate everyone—bars, bar employees and individual gays—to assert their right to pursue their happiness unmolested by authorities."[66] The police extortion scandal of the early 1970s not only brought down the superintendent of police, James B. Conlisk, the handpicked successor to O. W. Wilson, but precipitated the collapse of systematic police shakedowns of gay establishments. Gay bar owners and bartenders felt vindicated as they were called to testify about the details of police extortion.[67] By 1975, in the twilight of the Daley era, the mainstream press reported on the proliferation of gay bars, as well as on the fact that more of them were gay-owned. The local

m press would soon report in detail, for the first time, on the
s of being out in the workplace.[68]

"Gays Fear Fact of Life on Job"

Before the gay-liberation movement popularized "coming out of the
closet," almost all gay people concealed their sexuality at least some of the
time, and especially at work. The 1967 Kinsey Institute study revealed that
only 6 percent of gay men interviewed on the North Side said "all" of their
coworkers on their last full-time job knew of their homosexuality, 3 percent
said "most" of their coworkers knew, and 6 percent said "some" knew. By
contrast, 35 percent said "few" such coworkers knew and 46 percent said
that "none" knew. For most of those interviewed, the prospect of being
outed at work was a source of fear. Some 26 percent of those interviewed
said they were very or somewhat worried about "being identified as homosexual in a work situation," 31 percent said they were "a little" worried,
and 42 percent said they were "not at all" worried.[69]

Being out of the closet exacted a toll that was emotional as well as
economic. In 1972, a reporter spoke with twenty-four-year-old Linda
Shear, who told her she had worked as a high-school teacher in an experi-
mental Chicago school from October 1971 until January 1972: "She found
her students and teaching responsibilities 'gradually phased out' when her
lesbianism became quietly known. Now she is trying to start a career as a
folk singer who happens to be a lesbian and who will not work straight
bars." Shear was careful to emphasize to the reporter, "But not for a second
do I forget what I have left behind."[70] For women, the necessity of concealment exacerbated the toll taken by antiwoman job discrimination and sexual harassment. As one Chicago woman put it, "I have to put on this big
scene of being heterosexual. And I don't like putting on fronts. But the men
who come in like to flirt and expect me to flirt back."[71]

Things were slow to change. In 1970, the Chicago-based newspaper columnist Ann Landers told a man who longed to bring his male lover to his
office Christmas party, "If you want to lose your cover—go ahead," but
that he would be wise to "have another job lined up—just in case."[72] In
this period, people who lost a job or who were not hired for a job as a
result of being gay had no expectation of legal recourse or remedy. In 1975,
fully 57 percent of readers polled by GayLife, then Chicago's gay newspaper,

said they would lose their jobs if their homosexuality were discovered.[73] For men as well as women, holding down a good job, with very few exceptions, required carefully concealing one's homosexuality.[74]

The rapid decline in police harassment had the effect of making job discrimination the top issue for gay activists. This development has been almost totally ignored by historians partly because so little is known about how and why antigay police practices declined. As more gays and lesbians weighed disclosing their sexuality in more spheres of their lives, they faced the risk of losing their livelihoods as a result. Today, being fired as a result of being outed is considered discrimination, but on the cusp of the gay-liberation era it was a risk nearly all gay employees faced. Many people outed at work were not explicitly fired but rather pushed out. Bill Kelley and his friend Larry Gulian, on letterhead titled Illinois Gays for Legislative Action, sent a survey to corporate employers and real-estate firms asking if they were willing to employ or rent an apartment to homosexuals.[75] In an unusually blunt reply, a personnel manager at Helene Curtis, the Chicago-based beauty-products manufacturer, described his experiences with gay employees like this: "Some good, some bad experiences, the latter attrib-uted to the individuals' blatant disregard for the feelings and mores of co-workers. The homosexual will usually end up finding him/herself in a situa-tion so uncomfortable that he/she resigns."[76] It was perfectly legal to fire an employee solely because of homosexuality. But often neither employee nor employer would have had reason to put such grounds for dismissal in writing.

For protection from job discrimination to become a key issue required the readily available template for such protections offered by the state fair-employment laws of the postwar era; the Civil Rights Act of 1964, and the subsequent federal, state, and local legislation inspired by that act that stretched its umbrella of protections over a growing number of Americans. Employment nondiscrimination had been one of the five "basic rights" included in the "Homosexual Bill of Rights" adopted at the August 1968 NACHO convention in Chicago.[77] The new Illinois constitution, developed by a convention of delegates elected from across the state and enacted by the voters in a special election in late 1970, had included an explicit prohibi-tion of sex discrimination.[78] In 1971, when Daley supported amendments to add "sex" to local antidiscrimination ordinances dealing with "race" and "color," CGA members attended the city-council hearings and unsuccess-fully made the case for adding homosexuals and "transvestites."[79]

Most legislators would not touch the issue. At the February 1972 national convention of gay activists, for example, a CGA member noted that Dick Simpson, by then the independent 44th Ward alderman who gay activists had hoped would be an ally, had not publicly backed any pro-gay policy measure besides the city funding a gay venereal disease clinic on the North Side—and they had only gotten that endorsement after confronting him publicly.[80] But in 1973, that changed. A young black alderman from the South Side, Clifford P. Kelley (no relation to Bill), first introduced a proposed ordinance to ban job discrimination against gays and lesbians (see Figure 12). Kelley advocated its passage for a decade afterward despite little chance of its passing. The first time he introduced the ordinance, the *Chicago Gay Crusader*, a movement publication, reported with great enthusiasm on the upcoming first hearings on the bill: "A lineup of lesbians, gay males, and transvestites who have been discriminated against, as well as experts in religion, sociology, psychology, law, and homosexuality, will appear as witnesses in favor of the bills."[81] Yet members of the Judiciary Committee expressed "fears that the proposed ordinances would turn Chicago into a haven for homosexuals."[82]

Kelley began his city-council career loyal to the Daley machine but with reformist credentials as well. Kelley had been a law student in the late 1960s and was elected as a delegate to the 1969–70 Illinois Constitutional Convention.[83] A former vice president of the Illinois Young Democrats, he was tapped by the machine following the death of the 20th Ward alderman at the end of 1970.[84] He quickly came to be seen as "more than slightly a maverick."[85] In 1974, he even called for a black caucus on the council without Daley's approval.[86]

Because Kelley was a prominent figure in black reform politics, his role in backing the gay-rights measure ensured it would receive steady coverage in the city's African American press throughout the 1970s. In discussing his proposal with journalists, he frequently mentioned black gay people; indeed, the first time he introduced it, the measure was joined with a separate bill to repeal the city's ban on cross-dressing in public, with Kelley telling the *Defender* that most arrests of black transvestites were made by white policemen.[87] The following year, the paper reported on a "kiss-in," held in the plaza in front of city hall in support of the law, and published a photograph of two men kissing on its front page—a first among the city's dailies.[88] In a majority-white 50-seat city council, a majority-black group of aldermen served as his cosponsors, a testament to how strongly the black

THE CHICAGO GAY CRUSADER

ISSUE NO. 23   25¢

ALD. CLIFFORD P. KELLEY

FIGURE 12. Alderman Clifford P. Kelley, sponsor of proposed gay-rights ordinance, on the cover of the *Chicago Gay Crusader*, January 1973. Courtesy of Manuscripts and Archives Division, The New York Public Library, Astor, Lenox, and Tilden Foundations.

○ Other groups turning now under fire
like trans people

○ Public turned against the police

freedom struggle was identified with the concept of expanding the powers of the state to suppress discrimination.[89]

Commentators puzzled over Kelley's motivations. In predominantly white gay and liberal publications, the involvement of a black elected official in the struggle for gay rights was itself worthy of news coverage. Gay activists, the *Reader* reported, "never expected to find themselves working closely with a straight black alderman from a machine ward on the South Side."[90] Kelley represented the South Side's 20th Ward, "deep in the heart of the city's ghetto," as the national gay magazine the *Advocate* put it.[91] Kelley consistently said he acted because he viewed gay rights as precisely analogous to African American civil rights. He told the *Advocate* in 1975, "[W]here do you think black people would be today if back in the '60s all the decent white folks would have said to themselves, if I go out and march for civil rights people are going to call me a nigger lover[?]" He added, "When I sign up for a war, I sign up for the duration."[92] He told me, "I do not believe that people who are gay make any more choice in being gay than I made in being black, and I truly believe that, and that is the major reason that I did what I did."[93]

Kelley's stance was striking because it was not clear he stood to benefit from it politically in the slightest. The 20th Ward had few openly gay residents, and none who were mobilized. Kelley recalled that once his sponsorship of the ordinance became known, "I even went to a few black parties on the South Side. I would get a lot of calls from people, some people would call anonymously—a lot of folks was closet queens, that's for sure." Because Kelley was a bachelor, some said that he himself must have been gay. "I was the only gay womanizer around," he recalls. "I was either a womanizer or I was gay. I don't know how those match."[94] When he first proposed the ordinance in 1973, Kelley could not have expected any financial reward for his reelection campaign. In January 1975, however, white gay activists on the North Side, who could not vote for Kelley, held a grassroots fund-raiser for his campaign at the North Side disco LePub (see Figure 13).

If Kelley's constituents appeared largely indifferent to Kelley's gay-rights crusade, some of his fellow African American aldermen were less than pleased. Kelley seemed almost to relish the homophobic opposition of his colleagues to the ordinance. In 1975, he told a reporter that he and his supporters were having trouble passing the bill because many "of my colleagues have masculinity problems or are secret bigots."[95] As if to confirm

FIGURE 13. Flyer for Cliff Kelley fund raiser at LePub, 1975.
Courtesy of William B. Kelley.

his hypothesis, Alderman Niles Sherman of the 21st Ward said, "I've had a number of constituents call to tell me they don't want me to turn gay, that I should stand up and be a man. And I will be voting against it." Kelley, moreover, certainly goaded the opposition with statements such as "I'm the prince of the fags." He said this to Ron Grossman of the *Advocate*—"with a certain glee, as if to indicate to his listeners that he has earned the right to use a word which, coming from another's lips, he would personally find offensive."[96] By the decade's end, one South Side alderman, who requested anonymity, acknowledged, "We sound just like conservative whites. As in, 'some of my best friends are . . . gay.'" Yet another South Side alderman said, in frustration, "Frankly I wish Cliff had never brought the damn thing up."[97] But Kelley continued to do so. Black legislators in general—not just Kelley—played an outsize role in casting votes for gay rights not only in city hall but in Springfield. In the first state-legislature vote on gay rights, a larger proportion of the legislature's African American members voted for it than did any other group, including women.[98]

The first attempt by gay activists to lobby aldermen about the proposal took place in the fall of 1974. Though Kelley's gay-rights ordinance had failed to pass the city council's Judiciary Committee in 1973, the Watergate revelations had given hope to reformists of various stripes at all levels of government. That year, the new Gay Rights Task Force of the Alliance to End Repression again set about trying to take concrete steps toward passing the bill. A subcommittee of the task force had elicited the backing of a tiny number of independent aldermen—Anna Langford, Seymour Simon, Leon Despres, and Bill Singer, who had succeeded Simpson in the 44th Ward—started approaching allies and sympathetic contacts whom they felt might have influence on the members of the council's Judiciary Committee. These contacts fell into two main groups: black civil rights leaders and liberal Catholic priests. Some members of the group began creating a list of "black organizations which might support gay rights," and Langford promised the group "she would have 'kind words' for any mailing done for black groups." By December 1974, the group was still working on an endorsement from Operation PUSH (People United to Save Humanity)—Jesse Jackson's South Side civil rights group—though Jackson's aide Willie Barrow offered a personal endorsement. Another member of the group wrote to the individual members of the Association of Chicago Priests to ask them to endorse the gay-rights bill, which generated more positive responses than expected. And an endorsement from the Van Ecko brothers—both priests, and brothers-in-law of Daley's daughter—offered a "ray of hope."[99]

Activists failed to anticipate how hard it would be to pass a gay-rights law; indeed, the legislative record is filled with misplaced optimism. When Alderman Edward Burke in 1974 appealed to Archbishop John Patrick Cody to intervene in opposition to gay-rights laws, organizers of the new gay Catholic organization Dignity believed Cody would likely ignore the entire issue—little imagining the central role the archdiocese would play in delaying the city's gay-rights ordinance in the 1980s.[100] Meeting minutes from November 1974 indicate that an aide to Cliff Kelley told Betty Plank, a member of the AER Gay Rights Task Force, that if Kelley were able to move the proposal out of the Judiciary Committee, "it is expected to pass on the floor."[101] As late as February 1977, some believed the gay-rights bills held up in the Illinois legislature might soon be passed quickly, as there had been "no organized effort against the bills," so "they might have a chance to pass before such homophobic action can develop."[102]

Reformers' pro-gay stance prodded those machine candidates facing independent challengers to back gay rights or, at a minimum, to meet with and listen to gay activists. The forward momentum by the Gay Rights Task

Force of the Alliance, notably, was only possible because of the core support of "lakefront liberal" politicians. The leading lakefront liberal political group, the Independent Voters of Illinois, agreed to ask aldermanic candidates their views about gay rights.[103] Bill Singer, the alderman elected to represent the 44th Ward in 1969, reflected the civil-libertarian and racially progressive tendencies of these lakefront "independents." When Singer ran a somewhat quixotic mayoral campaign against Daley in 1975, Bill Kelley penned a letter in the *Chicago Gay Crusader* that endorsed Singer over Daley in no uncertain terms: "The plain fact is that the majority of Daley-ites have been apathetic-to-hostile toward gay rights."[104]

In the mid-1970s, the fate of gay rights tracked the fate of the independent movement opposed to machine control. That movement faltered in the February 1975 citywide election, when Daley was reelected to a sixth term and the machine's get-out-the-vote operation defeated most of the Gay Rights Task Force's allies on the city council. With the independents having failed to deliver and the machine seemingly resurgent, it seemed unclear where the next jolt of energy for the movement might come from. Daley's death at the end of 1976, however, offered another opening. "For the past ten years, increasing numbers of Chicago gays have been tumbling and clunking out of the closet," observed Denise DeClue, in a remarkable 1977 cover article in the weekly alternative *Chicago Reader*, "and finally it looks as though they're ready to clank out of the bedroom and make some political noise."

In this same period, the state legislature also saw the first interest-group mobilization by gays and lesbians from the same areas of the North Side. DeClue had noted that in the North Side's 12th and 13th state legislative districts, along the lakefront, all six state representatives were backers of the gay-rights bill. "They're all aware of the gay vote in their districts," DeClue opined, "and they're not about to be left out."[105] Some of these politicians had openly gay staff members, such as Glynn Sudbury, who worked in the leadership of the winning 1972 joint campaigns of State Senator Dawn Clark Netsch and State Representative Jim Houlihan. Sudbury became, in 1974, the executive director of the Independent Precinct Organization, a key independent political group, while remaining actively involved in gay organizations.[106]

In the Illinois state capital, the first politician closely identified with gay rights was a white Republican woman, Susan Catania, who represented a majority-black South Side district. In fact, Illinois legislative rules—which at the time required at least one of the three House members elected from each district to be elected from the minority party—had enabled gays and lesbians to help elect two pro-gay Republicans, Elroy Sundquist as well as Catania, in the second half of the 1970s. A mother of seven, Catania had run for office after testifying in support of a bill requiring employers to justify enforced maternity leaves. She was enraged when "the legislators treated the whole thing as a joke." Though she was a Catholic and staunchly opposed legalized abortion, Catania opposed the amendment proposed by her fellow Chicago Republican, Henry J. Hyde, to ban Medicaid coverage for abortions, out of a belief that financial ability should not determine women's access to the procedure.[107] In the 1970s, gay activists viewed liberal Republicans as well as Democratic politicians as potential targets for organizing. Soon, though, the parties would diverge on "social issues"—chiefly abortion but also gay rights—a new fault line in U.S. politics as the 1970s came to an end.

"A New Barrier Being Broken Down in Chicago"

A turning point in the formation of a national gay movement came in 1977 when the singer and Florida orange juice spokeswoman Anita Bryant launched a campaign to repeal the new gay-rights law in Miami-Dade County by a citizen referendum. Gay Chicagoans joined activists in other cities in giving money to help the fight against her effort, with Chuck Renslow sponsoring a giant "Orange Ball" to raise funds. Bryant's repeal effort won at the ballot box, however. The backlash against the movement had put gay activists on the defensive even before they had won statewide protection anywhere in the United States. In this respect, Bryant exploited the public's uncertainty surrounding the causes of homosexuality as well as the long-standing association between homosexuality and child molestation.[108]

Bryant charged that gay activists' goal was to recruit children to the gay lifestyle, and the charge was taken up by backers of a narrowly defeated referendum the following year that would have prohibited openly gay schoolteachers in California. Opponents of gay rights in Chicago drew on Bryant's invocation of the gay teacher as the linchpin of her case against gay rights. The same year as the Briggs Initiative in California, for example, a Chicago voter-registration program targeting high-school students rejected several openly gay activists from serving as voter registrars.[109] The

Chicago Tribune published a series of articles exposing child pornography and purporting to link it to homosexuality, which was believed to fuel the overwhelming defeat of gay rights in the Illinois House. Alderman Edward M. Burke held hearings about these reports and even invited Bryant to appear in person and testify, indicating that antigay politics had gone national.[110]

Fears of backlash in Illinois centered on "downstate" regions, a reflection of the longtime divide that had shaped state politics since the New Deal era. Though the antigay religious right that developed in the late 1970s was most strongly associated with Florida and California, southwestern Illinois was the home of New Right activist Phyllis Schlafly, and activists feared that downstate antigay mobilization might emerge. A 1977 article in the *Chicago Reader* explained the slow pace of progress of the Illinois gay-rights bill both as a result of the conservatism of the state legislature and because "nobody wants to trigger an Anita Bryant flip-out in Illinois."[111]

In June 1977, one week after her victory in Miami, Bryant came to Chicago for the first time in her singing career to give a Flag Day concert, an episode that unexpectedly led more gays and lesbians to protest publicly in the city than ever before—or since, for that matter. Far more people showed up to protest outside Bryant's concert than to hear her perform—as many as 5,000—and they encircled her venue, the Medinah Temple (see Figure 14).[112] "What makes you think I'd molest your child?" read one homemade sign.[113] Ron Helizon, who grew up in a Polish neighborhood, recalls speaking in Polish to a Polish American police officer working the protest site, and telling the visibly startled cop that there are Polish gay people, too.[114] At the year's end, *GayLife* called the protest the "greatest show of strength ever" on the part of the city's gay communities.[115]

The Bryant protest was a pivotal moment for the rise of gay politics in Chicago, and it led directly to the first campaign for public office by an out gay Chicagoan. Weeks earlier, at the height of the campaign to stop Bryant's gay-rights repeal, journalist Denise DeClue had predicted, "Sometime soon, it's going to make sense to run a real gay, not just a pro-gay, on the north side. Right now, the speculation is about who will do it first: the regulars or the independents?" The answer would come almost a year later, in early 1978, when a twenty-nine-year-old named Gary Nepon ran for the state legislature. Nepon recalled, "I spent the day of the march in personal crisis. Should I go? After all, I was a respectable businessman with a good job and might even be seen!" Though he had no political experience or previous

FIGURE 14. Approximately two thousand demonstrators in front of the Tribune Tower protest a concert by the singer Anita Bryant, one week after the success of her effort to repeal a Florida gay-rights ordinance, June 1977. Courtesy of Associated Press.

involvement with gay activism, Nepon became Chicago's first "real gay" to run for office. The theme of his candidacy was "Human Rights Here at Home," emphasizing the Equal Rights Amendment, which Illinois had failed to ratify.[116] But he acknowledged that both of the incumbent candidates, Daniel O'Brien and James Houlihan, had voted for gay-rights legislation, making it difficult for Nepon to press his case.[117] A friend who worked as Nepon's campaign strategist wrote him that of the district's nongay residents, "high risers" were "probably the most sympathetic and easily reached block [sic] of voters."[118] The high-rise buildings, those closest to the lake, were more cosmopolitan and affluent, and more disproportionately Jewish as well as liberal, than the district as a whole.

Nepon's candidacy was a flash in the pan from the standpoint of Chicago electoral politics, but it received considerable press coverage from outlets around the country as a novelty and a breakthrough. Though he ran as an independent, Nepon sought the backing of the regular Democrats, even claiming, "I cried when Mayor Daley died."[119] Even if he had had a track record as a precinct captain or playing some other role for the regular Democrats, however, Nepon's views, including his support for the legalization of prostitution and pornography, made it highly implausible that the regulars would support his candidacy.[120] To Chuck Renslow, the precinct captain, Nepon's brief campaign had violated the unwritten rule that gays would need to wait their turn in the machine's ethnic "queue." Offended by Nepon's decision to run, Renslow told a reporter that Nepon had had "an extremely slim chance" to be slated by the machine. "This is no way to reward a friend," he said, referring to the incumbent Danny O'Brien, who was also the 43rd Ward Democratic committeeman for whom Renslow had worked as a precinct captain.[121]

Nepon's campaign, in fact, became another instance of outsiders pushing the machine to embrace gay rights.[122] In a joint radio interview with Nepon, Renslow was asked how many gay voters there were in the 13th District. "Well, two weeks ago I don't think I could have answered that question," he replied, but "right now I know that in the 13th District there are five thousand gay people." He explained that he used "a mailing list which I've developed through my business, and I've just had somebody sort it—the people who live in those districts and who don't." The *Sun-Times* reported that in these same two districts, "the Democratic candidates for state representative are falling all over each other to represent the consumer, the tenant, the condominium owner, the elderly, the poor, the gay—just about every popular cause of today." This outsider campaign thus apparently lit a fire under Renslow—the bathhouse and *GayLife* owner and machine precinct captain—leading him to take steps toward using his business mailing list for political purposes for the first time in support of O'Brien, and surely also prodding him to emphasize his voting record in support of the gay rights bill in Springfield.[123]

In what became the highlight of Nepon's campaign, the nation's highest-profile gay elected official, Supervisor Harvey Milk of San Francisco, flew in to hold two campaign fund raisers for Nepon. Milk referred to Nepon's candidacy as "a new barrier being broken down in Chicago." Responding to the concern that gay candidates might be unstable or unreliable, he declared, "With elected officials today so often on the take, we don't have to worry about that." Milk pointed out that his candidacy, too, had been opposed by "the self-appointed gay leaders in San Francisco," but it had succeeded nonetheless.[124] But Renslow's newspaper, *GayLife*, endorsed the straight incumbents over Nepon. The paper did print an opinion piece by a gay businessman in support of his effort, under the headline "Why Gays Must Vote Gay," that commanded, "Do not be complacent about your bars, baths, movies and bookstores being open now; this can change and will at the mayor's whim."[125] A letter to the editor complained about the paper's failure to endorse Nepon. "Not only does Mr. Renslow run the baths and bars, he runs the newspaper," the author wrote. The paper's editor, Grant Ford, published a response observing that Milk, after all, "had to run several times before he became a Supervisor in San Francisco." Ford also described his own differences with Renslow concerning other races, asserting that his editorial viewpoint was independent of the publisher.[126]

Nepon's candidacy nonetheless represented a breakthrough, after which there would be many more gay candidates—nearly all of them men and all similarly proclaiming that they were not running solely as gay candidates or on gay issues—in municipal elections. Although Renslow's support for O'Brien surely weakened Nepon's chances, most independent candidates on the North Side were defeated in a drive by the regulars to retake their seats that spring.[127] Nepon inspired a short-lived effort by Les Trotter, a progressive gay African American and resident of the North Side's Lincoln Park neighborhood, to run for a seat on the Cook County Board of Commissioners. Trotter narrowly failed, however, to collect the required signatures to win a spot on the ballot.[128] Renslow himself ran for delegate to the

1980 Democratic National Convention, pledged to Massachusetts Senator Edward M. Kennedy.[129] Ford, in turn, who as editor of *GayLife* had refused to endorse Nepon, launched his own campaign in 1979 for 44th Ward alderman. Although Nepon had been covered by the press as "the first gay candidate," Ford found himself resisting that label. "Perhaps because he is not the first openly gay candidate to run in Chicago," claimed the *Sun-Times*, "Ford's campaign has gained a respectability that makes him a serious contender. Although he cannot escape the label, Ford insists he is not running as 'the gay candidate.'"[130] But Ford's campaign faltered, and he withdrew before election day.[131] The following year, a second black gay man living on the North Side, Michael Harrington, ran for office, this time as 44th Ward alderman; he received nearly 20 percent of the vote on election day.[132] Yet it would be another two decades before an openly gay man was elected to Chicago's city council.[133]

*   *   *

Gays and lesbians achieved higher visibility in part by locating themselves on the map of the pluralist metropolis—and comparing themselves to an ethnic minority group. In the context of Chicago's machine politics, this was an effective strategy. In the 1970s, the machine became slightly more open than it had previously been to the participation of gay men—far more than lesbians—on these terms. The movement unmistakably shifted "toward a gay *politik*," as *Chicago* magazine put it in 1979—toward participating in mainstream local power politics in ways reminiscent of the political behavior of ethnic groups.[134] By the early 1980s, the notion of New Town as "*our* ghetto" had solidified. To one twenty-six-year-old gay man interviewed by *Chicago* magazine in 1983, "Anywhere outside of New Town, you can't be openly gay. What goes on in our ghetto means nothing to a gay boy in Bridgeport or the South Side."[135]

For all their revolutionary aspects, gay-pride parades nonetheless assimilated gays and lesbians into the existing landscape of the city. The trajectory of the gay movement in the decade after Stonewall was profoundly shaped by the politics of respectability that had so long been central to how Americans understood struggles for civil rights. For example, Robert Sheehan, the commander of the lakefront East Chicago Avenue police district, said in 1977 that "gays are generally no more of a problem than straights." He explained, "We don't have a problem with those who are legitimate community members, with those who hold jobs. Occasionally, we do have a problem with male prostitutes, with the hustlers."[136] As establishment institutions began to express their openness to gays and lesbians, they drew distinctions between those whose inclusion they would consider and others they continued to view as a threat to the social order.

In Chicago, as in other large cities, the efforts to push a proposed gay-rights ordinance in the 1970s never progressed beyond committee hearings onto the council floor. Yet the effort had a secondary consequence: defining as "discrimination" (in the minds of gay employees if not necessarily their bosses) the experience of losing a job as a result of being gay. Gay-rights lobbying in Chicago in the 1970s, though unsuccessful, made participants more comfortable with speaking to their elected officials about the experience of being gay.

Gay Chicagoans gradually began to participate as such in the Democratic Party. Between 1968 and 1976, Bill Kelley went from protesting gay-bar raids outside the party's convention to requesting that the platform committee support a gay-rights plank on behalf of the Gay and Lesbian Coalition of Metropolitan Chicago. Upon Kelley's return from the convention, the Coalition "endorse[d] the concept of 'every gay and lesbian a voter.'" It also endorsed and undertook efforts to promote voter registration in members' businesses, and to research, collect, and distribute information to gay voters about the views on gay rights of every candidate for every office.[137] If asking politicians to state their views on gay-rights questions was disruptive in the early 1970s, it had become routine in North Side lakefront state and local legislative districts by the late 1970s.[138] Thousands of gay Chicagoans had paraded, picketed, or joined a gay mailing list. Non-gay politicians in North Side lakefront districts took notice and expected to be asked about gay rights.

By the late 1970s, the progress of the gay movement in influencing politicians was dramatic but relatively geographically confined. Grant Ford even declared it was "entirely conceivable" that "if gay people were really mobilized to vote . . . we could put in our own alderman in the 43rd ward, maybe the 44th ward."[139] And yet, wrote another observer, "For all their progress, gays have yet to solidify into a formidable political force. Along the lake, they may be movers and shakers, but just one ward west they are still voters *non grata*." As the Regular Democrats proved that reports of the

death of the machine were at least somewhat exaggerated, *Chicago* magazine asked if gays and lesbians might truly mobilize under its aegis. To the
writer, "the willingness of gay leaders to align with Regular Democrats"
was a sign of the movement's maturity, "for in Chicago politics those who
can help are the Regular Democrats"—at least, so it would seem, until
Harold Washington's upset victory in the 1983 mayoral race.[140]

Not all of the newly open gay political activists of the 1970s were working inside the system, however. Even as the gay movement reconfigured the
relationship between blacks and whites, it also intensified tensions between
gay men and lesbians. Gay men and women interacted more often, and in
more ways. And as radical feminism emerged, it drew many lesbians into
its orbit. Many gay women came to identify more with other women than
with gay men, and many rejected the brokered, male-dominated world of
local electoral politics.

5

Lesbian Survival School

"ONE OF THE main reasons for lesbian involvement in Women's Lib movements," activist Marie Kuda observed in a 1970 article in the *Mattachine Midwest Newsletter*, "is that in the job market women traditionally lose the battle of the sexes."[1] Lesbian activism in the 1970s focused, to a degree little recognized by its latter-day chroniclers, on the economic status of women. Women without husbands in the 1970s frequently faced difficulty even obtaining loans, credit cards, and mortgages. Because most lesbians could not depend on the income of a husband, the cause of pay equity for women was especially resonant for lesbians. Even before the formulation of lesbian feminism as a fully articulated political ideology, jobs and economic equality were central issues for urban women who wanted to live separately from men. Lesbian organizing in Chicago emerged out of the city's women's liberation and antiwar movements and the counterculture, drawing together women of all races, students and young college-educated women, hippies, and radicals. Radical lesbians declared their unwillingness "to sit calmly while men receive the best jobs, the best degrees, the most money, the best part of the world," as one writer put it. She added, seeming to aim her prose at male leftists and skeptical straight women, "As lesbians we are as much or more political than any group on the face of this earth. We stand as the greatest threat to this society, far more than gun-carrying revolutionaries or bomb-scare groups blowing up the White House or the Chase Manhattan Bank."[2] Since the emergence of gay liberation, lesbian politics has been far more inflected by radicalism than has gay male politics.

Many lesbians struggled to make ends meet, partly because they were disadvantaged by metropolitan job markets that assumed women would be supported by a male breadwinner who earned a "family wage." Indeed, lesbians experienced more financial insecurity than either straight women or gay men.[3] The conditions of their lives as women and as lesbians led some women to begin to formulate what they called lesbian feminism. At once a theory with ramifications for everyday life and way of living with philosophical implications, this new framework was empowering because its vision of sisterhood offered alternatives to the rigid norms of American political economy and culture, which in the postwar decades assumed marriage and childrearing as the appropriate activities for adult women.

Lesbian feminism gave women alternatives to the limited options offered by breadwinner liberalism by raising their consciousness. The nascent lesbian feminist press helped women understand and analyze their experiences in the job market and the hidden forms that sexism often took. In Chicago, *Lavender Woman*, founded in 1971, ran a first-person article by a woman describing her experiences working for an employment agency as a job counselor, under a headline—"I Was a Flesh Peddler"—that mocked the sensationalist language of the metropolitan press. "There were some details that didn't get written down," noted the story's author, "but passed by word of mouth from counselor to counselor: A company wouldn't see blacks, B wouldn't see fatties, C wanted women with big tits."[4] Such articles served simultaneously to raise readers' "consciousness" about experiences that many women had faced in the workplace, while also helping to recruit new participants for workplace activism.

In late 1973, the collective that ran the Women's Center on North Halsted Street created a series of courses they called "Lesbian Survival School." Modeled on the Chicago Women's Liberation Union's "Liberation School for Women," the program included courses that taught concretely usable skills like crafts, auto mechanics, "home mechanics," and "street fighting," as well as courses to enrich women's intellectual development and to educate them about lesbian politics, theory, and culture. Lesbian Survival School exemplified several features of lesbian feminist mobilization. Lesbian *survival* implied women living independently in a society structured by heterosexual male desires.[5] And survival *school* was a form of cultural education, not electoral or legislative mobilization, or even protest. The woman-oriented communities that flourished between 1968 and the early 1980s reflected a grassroots, do-it-yourself ethos. Many lesbians and bisexual women put their political energy in these years not into electoral politics but into grassroots communities that valued women's writing, art, and other creative pursuits.

"Do It Yourself"

As legal and cultural constraints on institutions catering to homosexuals eroded, the gay-male and lesbian subcultures developed in different directions. The differences between lesbian and gay-male politics, and the tensions between them, can best be understood in the context of the breakdown of the family wage system. The expanding gay male consumer sphere of the 1970s in some ways represented an intensification and reworking of the new styles of masculinity in post–World War II America. In the 1970s, young straight white men's desire for premarital or unserious sexual encounters became increasingly acceptable to mainstream taste.[6] Gay men, increasingly above ground legally, became attractive to advertisers as well, at least in theory, because they were free of the financial burden of wives, children, and mortgages. Although many men who cruised Chicago's lakefront parks looking for sexual encounters in fact were married men leading straight lives, the growing number of out gay-identified men could be imagined as a market.[7]

Lesbians often faced problems involving child care, custody fights, and legal and financial troubles. Many lesbians, in contrast to gay men, felt that by far their most pressing problem was their right to work, not their right to consume: "We have a house, a child, the responsibilities of marriage, yet none of the legal or social sanctions of institutionalized heterosexual marriage to protect us," wrote one woman.[8] Some gay men were trapped in heterosexual marriages they felt they could not afford to leave, and some gay men had children who depended on them for the daily work of caretaking and social reproduction. Lesbians were far more likely to be in either or both of these situations.

Although gay men dominated "gay" institutions, lesbians were highly overrepresented in new institutions meant for women. Indeed, in the 1970s "women's" became almost a code word for "lesbian" in certain circles. In Chicago, lesbian women in Hyde Park on the South Side and in Lincoln Park on the North Side met in church basements, staffed telephone switchboards, hosted meetings, and joined softball teams. Some women joined the Chicago Women's Liberation Union, a large, grassroots socialist-feminist organization that developed out of the West Side Group, one of the nation's first women's liberation organizations, in 1969. Others volunteered to paint the walls, sand the floors, or make curtains for the fledgling Women's Center in Lakeview. In North Side lakefront neighborhoods, they built women-owned bars, coffeehouses, collective bookstores, restaurants, and drop-in

FIGURE 15. *Lavender Woman* cover, 1973. Courtesy of Chicago History Museum.

centers. Some wrote and published materials that helped connect women in crisis with help and resources, including the collectively run *Lavender Woman*, which was one of the most important and longest-running of the lesbian-feminist newspapers founded during the 1970s (see Figure 15). Some women simply showed up when pioneers of the new "women's music"— groups like Family of Woman and the Chicago Women's Liberation Union

Rock Band, which represented one of the key institutional sites for the formation of urban lesbian-feminist communities—performed at venues
around the city.

Many young lesbians not only could not afford to go out as often as
gay men but also were more likely to reject the bar scene. Even more than
gay-male liberationists who criticized the male bar subculture for being
commercial, hierarchical, or shallow, many young lesbians rejected the stylization of gender difference that had long characterized the lesbian bar subculture, especially among working-class and poor women. They sometimes
rejected the overt sexuality and physicality of the bar scene. A member of
Chicago Lesbian Liberation complained at a meeting, "Gay bars are as bad
as straight ones. You go to talk to your friends, and right away you're
approached by a lesbian on the make. 'May I buy you a drink?' 'Is she
bothering you? When you're with me, I'll take care of you.'" The neighborhood newspaper reporter who covered this Chicago Lesbian Liberation
meeting said that most of the participants "dressed in feminine fashion"
and that "the idea that the participants are female and feel feminine was
probably the most recurrent one."[9] Rejecting the institutions of an older
generation of lesbians who mostly did not strongly identify as feminists,
these younger women also rejected the "roles" with which they associated
them.

However, bars remained important, even to lesbian feminists. Many
women continued to patronize women's bars and they maintained ties to
the bar-based lesbian subculture. "On Monday nights," noted one woman
in describing a weekly lesbian meeting that arose out of Gay Liberation in
Hyde Park in 1970 and continued for several years, "all the girls from Chicago Lesbian Lib go to the Bradberry."[10] In Chicago, as Claudia Scott put
it, "I've met more women who've called Irene through the switchboard and
are now part of the regular crowd at a bar or Susan B.'s or are working the
switchboard itself."[11] Social worlds and new community spaces were thus
both social and political, just as they were for gay men.

Lesbianism and Socialist Feminism

Even though self-identified lesbian communities remained more distant
from electoral politics, an unsigned article in *Lavender Woman* noted that
Alderman Clifford P. Kelley's antidiscrimination ordinance was "of special

importance to lesbians," by virtue of their vulnerability as women in the job market.[12] Indeed, the struggle for equal pay for women itself had helped pry open the growing antidiscrimination apparatus of the state that would, in time, expand its reach to include some job protections based on sexual orientation. In the aftermath of the passage of the Civil Rights Act of 1964, working women had increasingly come to view their exclusion from certain jobs in a new way. Title VII of that act prohibited employment discrimination on the basis of sex as well as race; this made possible "a conceptual transformation that relocated disparate treatment because of sex from the venue of tradition to that of discrimination," as historian Alice Kessler-Harris aptly puts it.[13]

Chicago was the epicenter of the socialist feminist union movement that spread to more than a dozen cities in the 1970s, largely ignored by a national media that tended to seek out prominent individuals, usually living in New York City, as the voice of the women's movement. The Chicago Women's Liberation Union (CWLU), founded in the fall of 1969, was the largest grassroots feminist organization in the United States in the 1970s.[14] It drew a considerable lesbian membership, and its projects ran a very wide gamut. "In response to the success of the CWLU model and its theoretical initiatives," Sara Evans states, "over the next few years 18 women's unions formed, primarily on the East and West Coasts and in the industrial Midwest."[15] The CWLU's activist projects ranged from winning the right of women's softball teams to use the diamonds in local parks to the direct provision of low-cost, safe abortions through a secret collective known as Jane. It was perhaps the most distinctive organization on Chicago's lesbian feminist scene, as well as the longest-lived, and by far the most diverse ideologically and philosophically.

The structure of the CWLU allowed it to serve as an umbrella under which members could pursue a variety of projects, which included a formal "Gay Group" in 1972–1973 and a "Lesbian Group" in 1975. Lesbians were also active in Women Employed, a grassroots group founded in March 1972 "by working women to fight for working women" and affiliated with the CWLU. Like many other New Left groups, Women Employed actively sought attention from the news media, obtaining front-page newspaper coverage, for example, when the group met with a representative of Loop employers.[16] Women Employed targeted large corporate employers in metropolitan Chicago, like Kraft Foods and Sears, demanding specific actions. At Sears, the group alleged, "White men have all the high commission items and black women all the menial ones."[17] The group also held unofficial public hearings into job discrimination at an auditorium in the Loop.[18]

Lesbians benefited from the era's breakthrough advances for women in the areas of employment equity and reproductive freedom. These reforms reduced the authority of husbands over wives both during marriage and upon its dissolution; prohibited employment discrimination against women; and, crucially and controversially, won new freedoms for women to make their own reproductive choices.[19] Some lesbians reacted against the rigid marital expectations of postwar America or rejected the idea of the family altogether. Seeking to remove sex from the interlocking domains of capitalism and patriarchy, and encountering sexism in the gay movement, some pointed to gay men as embodying everything they wanted to reject. At its best, finding one's way into lesbian feminist communities in the 1970s could be intensely thrilling. One woman wrote exuberantly about attending a concert by Linda Shear, a pioneer of "women's music," with five members of a "rap group" she had recently joined. "When we left the concert," she wrote, "we walked back to our bus with our arms around each other."[20] The nascent institutions of the lesbian movement had enabled this woman to imagine ways of living that were different from those sanctioned by the dominant culture.

Members of the CWLU penned some of the most important articulations of lesbian feminist thought in the 1970s. The Gay Group's position paper "Lesbianism and Socialist Feminism" was circulated in radical feminist circles nationwide. The paper directly linked lesbianism to birth control and abortion, arguing that all three helped sever the long-standing association between sex and reproduction. The group also positioned lesbian experience as fundamentally reflective of the status of women more broadly on the grounds that "many lesbians have been able to choose whether to have children and so have control over the reproductive aspects of their lives" and that "most lesbians work for pay because of the exclusion from the family and the economic advantage of having a husband."[21] By treating lesbian experiences as emblematic rather than marginal to the wide range of women's lives, and without rejecting straight women, the Gay Group tied its values to those of the larger women's liberation movement.

At the heart of lesbian feminist politics was a critique of patriarchy. As one writer put it, "Our landlords, bosses, and fathers have stuck different knives into us."[22] Lesbian politics, including the strand that developed into lesbian separatism, must be understood as emerging out of a historical period—the United States in the postwar decades—in which procreative, heterosexual nuclear families acquired an unprecedented cultural importance. The analysis offered by lesbian feminism enabled many women to come to understand the gendered forces that had shaped and diminished their lives. Confronting a job market overwhelmingly segregated by sex and premised on post–New Deal family-wage ideology, lesbians faced widespread discrimination both as women and as lesbians.

Lesbian Feminism in Black and White

Both the power of lesbian feminism and the limits of its appeal were rooted in a critique of patriarchy that was sometimes premised on an implicit assumption of whiteness. A black lesbian complained, "[P]eople don't understand that I didn't give up men. I go out with men I like as friends, not because I have to but because I want to."[23] "There is no time for naïvely believing that because we are all gay we are for each other's well being," wrote Elandria V. Henderson, in a manifesto for black gay liberation that appeared in *Lavender Woman*.[24] Susan Jill Kahn recalled, in the early 1980s, "[T]here started being a standard for what a dyke was," a standard that included "not too much involvement with your family, which I think was really hurtful to people who have racial, cultural, family connections—Jews, Black women, you know, maybe all of us, but the sense was that you didn't need your family. They would just fuck you over. They had straight privilege. If you related to your family, you had straight privilege. Stuff like that."[25] Many black and white lesbians believe that the rise of separatism led black women to drop out of *Lavender Woman*, as well as other lesbian-feminist groups in Chicago.

Racial conflict looked different, of course, to black and white women. The Monday Night Meetings in Hyde Park, which were a rare instance of a queer community institution taking root on the South Side and then moving north, were an early source of racial conflict because of the different routes women had to travel around the city to get to and from the meeting places. After meetings in Hyde Park, the women initially went to the King's Ransom, "a primarily faggot bar very near downtown," as Michal Brody put it. The bar was eventually changed to Up North, on the far North Side, "in an all-white neighborhood. It was a long way home from there to anywhere else in the city except the predominantly white north side. Many south-siders, mainly dark women, objected to the choice, but the Up North prevailed," Brody recalled. "Based on atmosphere and hospitableness alone, that probably was the best of the limited choice of bars, but making the decision solely on those grounds further polarized the baby lesbian community along racial lines."[26]

The racial politics of separatism were complex. In criticizing a lesbian bar, Chez Ron, Loretta Mears wrote, "I am hurting because I stood in an oppressive, rip-off bar and watched as my sisters came in wearing men's suits and shoes and men's haircuts and with what they hope is a man's identity."[27] But other black women found that separatism's complete rejection of the family simply did not resonate with their life histories and present-day concerns. In her 1972 book *Lesbian Nation*—a landmark manifesto for "dyke nationalism" and "a separate (amazon) state"—Jill Johnston wrote that women "haven't had the ghetto experience like the blacks, a whole language etc., that binds you together." Johnston's language exemplified the racial blindness of some white feminists; by treating women and blacks as mutually separate categories, her reasoning seemed to deny the very existence and experience of black women.[28] A generation earlier, in analyzing women's status, Simone de Beauvoir, an early philosophical voice of the feminist "second wave," wrote that women are not "herded together in the way that creates community feeling among the American Negroes, the ghetto Jews, the workers of Saint-Denis, or the factory bands of Renault"; rather, "They live dispersed among the males, attached through residence, housework, economic condition, and social standing to certain men—fathers or husbands—more firmly than they are to other women."[29] The middle-class feminists who had written tracts widely viewed as the central works of modern feminist thought sometimes envisioned a sisterhood of women like themselves.

Black lesbians, like black gay men, were often more concerned with making themselves visible within black communities—of men *and* women—than with universal sisterhood. Like white lesbians, they sought acceptance and visibility in their communities of origin, but unlike white women they often remained connected to those communities by a shared experience of racial discrimination and segregation. Although the decline of the interracial drag balls meant that sexual and gender minorities were less visible in the black press in the 1970s than they had been in the 1950s, black women nonetheless sought out visibility. In the fall of 1970, for example, the *Chicago Defender* published a photo of Edna Knowles and Peaches Stevens, two women who held a wedding ceremony at a gay bar on Cottage Grove Avenue of the South Side. Under the headline "Unusual Union," the newspaper published the following account: "Happiness is reflected on the faces of the 'bride,' Edna Knowles and her 'groom,' Peaches Stevens, whose 'marriage' was solemnized at the Mark III Lounge, on S. Cottage Grove av. by the Rev. J. Yates. The couple—both females—embrace fondly following the ceremony. The Daily Defender was advised by the state's attorney's office that such marriages are not legal under the Illinois marriage statutes."[30] The national black magazine *Jet* picked up the story and published its own photo of the newlyweds. "The new Mrs. Stevens told *Jet* her mother-in-law was, at first, reluctant to sanction the marriage but now gives her blessings to the couple," noted the magazine, in language that seemed to assimilate the women's "unusual" qualities to the urban black community in which they lived. It was as though, in reporting the mother's gradual acceptance of the couple, the newspaper was confirming their membership in a larger community. The article concluded with this remarkable pair of sentences: "The Illinois attorney general's office explained to *Jet* that there is no state statute that either bans or sanctions such marriages. Although the duo has a type of 'marriage license' in their possession, the state's official marriage license bureau reported it has no record of their license."[31] Even as it bracketed the term in quotation marks, *Jet* reported not only that the state did not recognize the marriage but also that the couple had created for themselves something they regarded as "a *type* of 'marriage license.'"

For all that they embraced a concept of female sisterhood that alienated some black women, Chicago's lesbian and feminist subculture was more racially mixed than the highly segregated neighborhoods where many black and white women had been raised. In a series of interviews with women who participated in the *Lavender Woman* collective that were completed a decade later, many of the white women expressed regret for what sometimes became ugly racial conflicts within the organizations. "Most of us who were white," recalled Betty Peters Sutton in the 1980s, "had never really been around that many black people before in shoulder to shoulder contact." Noting that "many of us were very naïve," she said: "Some of us would live in white areas, not realizing when we moved there that they were so racist. And then black friends would come to visit me and my white neighbors would get upset."[32]

The racial politics of lesbian-feminist organizations in the 1970s was probably characterized by more collaboration between blacks and whites— and *also* by more racial conflict—than male-dominated gay organizations. Conflict between black and white lesbians in the 1970s emerged partly because more of these women were interacting than ever before. Moreover, the lesbian-feminist movement was at least partly open to racial dialogues that were of an intensity rarely seen in the broader society. For example, in an eloquent, angry missive published in *Lavender Woman,* Margaret, a black lesbian, directed her remarks to her white sisters:

experience of being lesbian is different for white and black women

What have you got to offer us? You wonder where we are and we say right in front of you. . . . You cry dry tears while we bleed. You like to watch us dance for you but you never ask us to dance with you. You imagine/think/fantasize we fuck better which either keeps you on our backs or miles away. You assume we are mostly all dykes and the fem in us you try to butch. You use our blackness as an excuse more than we do and you never try to see the pain behind all our laughter. When you are around us you talk black and we find ourselves talking white and you even come to our parties bringing a 1969 Aretha Franklin record and when we confront you, you say we're too powerful to deal with and you don't come to our neighborhood after dark except in groups when *your* men have raped us (you too) for over 300 years. I can't call you my sister until you stop participating in my oppression. You can't have a struggle without all oppressed people—and black women, particularly black lesbians, have struggled harder than anyone.[33]

Testifying to the frustrations black women faced within lesbian feminist circles, the letter also reflected a certain sense of comfort on the author's part in giving voice to her feelings. The notion of universal sisterhood had seemingly crashed against African American women's continuing frustrations with the casual racism they encountered from white women. Still, the lesbian-feminist movement at its inception was strikingly interracial. Margaret's letter conveyed that even if they did not ask women like her to dance, white lesbians were at least dancing in the same spaces.

The pages of *Lavender Woman* included far more discussion of black and white racial issues, and of often passionate conflicts, than did its contemporary, the *Chicago Gay Crusader*. The tiny, community-based publishing projects that lesbian feminists built in the 1970s attracted more black women than male-dominated gay political groups did. There was also a difference in ethos between the two communities. Many white women who sought the company of other lesbians were also committed to racial and economic justice. Renee Hanover, the radical lawyer, had a long record of civil rights activism going back to her days in the Communist Party underground, and she continued to advocate for people of color in the judicial system in the 1970s.

Black women objected to white women's racism within the movement and sometimes won attention for their concerns, as in the case of discriminatory carding at Augie and C.K.'s discussed earlier (though only after many years of commentary on the discrimination). In the late 1970s, African American women organized to protest the discriminatory requests for multiple forms of identification from black women at Augie and CK's, one of the most popular lesbian bars on the North Side. Pat Love, a spokeswoman for the Black Lesbian Discrimination Investigation Committee, said, "There are many white women on those picket lines, sisters who agree that racism hurts all of us."[34] Such a protest was sometimes successful at raising the consciousness of white lesbians. When Chicago Lesbian Liberation debated whether to sign a lease for a space at 1015 W. Armitage, one argument made against it was "the question of whether Black Women would use the Center because of the neighborhood and its problems." The group voted overwhelmingly not to sign the lease.[35] As it had before, and would again, Chicago's extraordinary degree of residential segregation made organizing across the color line difficult.

"Any Alder Tree [Would] Make a Better City Council Member than the Aldermen"

Lesbian feminists correctly diagnosed Chicago's political landscape as overwhelmingly male and imbued with masculinist values. They often viewed electoral politics as unalterably corrupt or as just another mechanism of male domination, and they rejected the very idea of staking a claim to such an institution. When some lesbians testified at city hall in favor of the proposed antidiscrimination ordinance in the 1970s, others criticized them for their collaboration with gay-male "politicos": "Setting a goal like legal-izing gayness by picketing city hall or ann landers," wrote one activist, "is the result of a straight myth that says that's the way to get anywhere. All it does is keep women's minds from exploring life in an original creative manner."[36] Even within their own groups, many lesbian feminists rejected the election of officers and other standard organizational practices as patri-archal and hierarchical. The lack of formal structure in many lesbian orga-nizations may have exacerbated tension over several issues, particularly whether to work with men.

Only months after the first two female Chicago aldermen were elected in 1971, an article in one lesbian feminist newsletter declared, "We were gonna run a candidate for alderperson, but since we're trying to deal with our human chauvinism, we reconsidered and decided to [run] some alder trees," noting that "any alder tree [would] make a better City Council member than the aldermen who presently monopolize the City Council."[37] Lesbian feminist political thought thus borrowed not only from the New Left but also from the counterculture and its stance of skepticism toward official institutions.

At the same time, lesbians also objected to the marginalization they experienced from straight feminists. They were, one woman declared, "the concubines of the women's movement."[38] Another writer complained that "the lesbian psychological ghetto is becoming as familiar as the flashing blue lights of Chicago's Brutality Department," while, by contrast, "the ERA [Equal Rights Amendment]," which she saw as the embodiment of straight feminist activism, "is somewhere outside, somewhere where *nice* women gather to speak of equal rights and sip tea." Indeed, she noted, the very idea of working with straight feminists "conjures up images of stuffing envelopes and bleary-eyed big-jowled Springfield legislators." As a tiny number of lesbian activists and writers achieved national celebrity, she complained, "So what are my options? . . . Work for the ERA and wait like women used to wait until after the revolution for lesbian equality?"[39]

Linda Shear, who became a nationally known icon of the women's music scene, described the lesbian feminist communities she was a part of in the 1970s as having adopted "a range of orthodoxies." Invoking the landscape of lesbian separatism in Chicago, Shear recalled, "Some women involved in separatism had many other community connections at the same time, and others shunned association with straight men, gay men, and straight women as much as possible."[40] Some women simply preferred the company of other women to that of men. Others enjoyed all-female spaces but retained male friends and associates. A few women rejected even associating with other lesbians who did not share their views on women's autonomy.

If the CWLU was Chicago's most broad-based feminist organization in terms of class and sexuality, the most racially diverse one might have been the collective that created *Lavender Woman*, the justly celebrated lesbian-feminist newspaper. The newspaper's pages presented fierce, sometimes brutally raw sentiments, political arguments, poems, and illustrations. In 1972, two young lesbians in Chicago made a short film called *Lavender*, which focused on their relationship and has been called the first nationally distributed lesbian-made lesbian film. Like participants in many New Left movements, lesbian feminists spoke often of "roles." Predominantly young, white, and middle class, they disdained the butch-femme system of gender stylization that they associated with older lesbians. One of the women in *Lavender* says to the other, "If you wanted a guy, you should've married one, right?" Her partner, a seminarian, responds, "Yeah: I'm a lesbian because I love women, not because I either want to pretend to be a guy or I want to love a pseudo-man. It just doesn't make sense that way."[41]

Some women who were older and veterans of the homophile movement viewed these women-only organizations with suspicion. Indeed, in 1970, Valerie Taylor casually noted in a column in the *Mattachine Midwest Newsletter* that she had a "wish that DOB would integrate," because as far as she knew "it's the only homophile organization that still practices sexual discrimination."[42] Younger women, for their part, reinterpreted the Chicago Daughters of Bilitis chapter's "Gab 'n' Java" weekend meetings, assimilating them into new political framings: "In the early 1960's the Daughters of Bilitis held womon only coffeehouses in various wimmin's houses," declared an article in a lesbian feminist newsletter in the late 1970s. Queer politics in Chicago was already becoming history.[43]

"We Hesitate to Call You Brothers"

In the early 1970s, there was both more conflict between lesbians and gay men and more cooperation, as both subcultures expanded dramatically. To be sure, the question of whether lesbians should identify primarily with the women's movement or the gay movement had been the subject of debate at least since the American homophile movement began in the postwar period. "Lesbians are not satisfied to be auxiliary members or second class homosexuals," Del Martin, the San Francisco lesbian activist, had declared at a 1959 Mattachine Society convention.[44] Yet relations between gay men and lesbians were never as fiercely debated as they were in the 1970s.

In the first flush of their twin emergence in 1970 and 1971, participants in the women's liberation and gay-liberation movements often saw their causes as deeply intertwined.[45] Binding the two together was a certain vision of acquiring an identity that was not necessarily culturally taught. Both movements mobilized a group whose sense of "groupness" was not assured in advance by familiar boundaries of family, inheritance, and caste. The philosophy of "consciousness-raising" and the associated practice of the "C-R group" or "rap group," which arose first among women's liberationists, quickly became central to gay liberation as well. Lesbians soon came to feel that the difficulty of carving out autonomous spaces in a hostile society made autonomy itself a prized and hard-won resource—in effect, a *scarce* one.

In some respects, politically active gay men were more receptive to feminism than were straight men, especially at the height of the gay-liberation era. One collective household of radical gay men wrote about their experience this way: "Living together is a struggle to find new ways; together we can support each other in exploring our feelings and strengthening ourselves. One of the best ways is through consciousness-raising, which we learned from Women's Liberation."[46] Some gay men learned to practice solidarity with lesbians: "I remember that the largely male gay liberation group did a lot of feminist reading, like they read *Sisterhood Is Powerful* and had a discussion about it," recalled Hannah Frisch of the gay-liberation chapter at the University of Chicago. "They were serious, and it's not that they were just PC, it was that feminism was the ideology that justified what they were doing and gave them [access] to the gay male world."[47]

For all that it drew on radical feminist ideas, however, the gay-liberation movement remained dominated by men and their concerns. Most gay men had access to jobs that paid a male wage, even if their careers suffered as a consequence of their outing themselves or being outed. Lesbians resented this state of affairs. "Lesbians are economically oppressed not only as homosexuals, but much more as women," a column in *Lavender Woman* argued in 1975. "What a gay man must realize is that the average lesbian is trying to survive on an income that is probably half of his own."[48]

Lesbian feminists argued with one another about whether to remain in the same organizations with gay men. "We hesitate to call you brothers as long as you participate in our oppression," declared the founders of Chicago Lesbian Liberation (CLL), in their 1971 manifesto titled, "Why We Left Chicago Gay Alliance." Inspired by the model of black nationalism, the manifesto continues, "We had hoped that you would appreciate this need, analogous to that of blacks during the first stages of their liberation."[49] Chicago Lesbian Liberation included in its official goals not only consciousness raising but also "initiating, supporting, and promoting legislative action for the freedom of women *and* homosexuals," male and female.[50] Its members were, however, willing to *work* with men in other organizations, unlike separatists who later broke off from the group.

Tensions between gay males and lesbians in Chicago's politics during the 1970s are perhaps best illustrated by the dramatically different relationships of those groups to Chicago-based *Playboy*. Women's liberationists viewed *Playboy* as a major culprit in society's acceptance of the sexual objectification of women. In 1970, women's liberationists protested in front of the *Playboy* building after a secretary there was fired for photocopying confidential memos.[51] By contrast, the Playboy Mansion on Chicago's Near North Side hosted in 1973 an evening fund raiser where "the ACLU raised enough money to start the Sexual Privacy Project, a national task force aimed at eliminating laws regulating private sexual activities between consenting adults and 'eliminating discriminatory practices which flow from such laws.'"[52] In 1976, following the formation of the umbrella Gay and Lesbian Coalition of Metropolitan Chicago, meeting minutes note that the Playboy Foundation (a separate organization from the magazine, though funded by the publisher's money) had offered the use of the ballroom in the Towers hotel for use "at no charge" for a Coalition-sponsored forum. "There was concern expressed regarding the community's association with Playboy, however, the Hotel is now a separate business and the name 'Playboy' is no longer affiliated with Towers Hotel."[53] Many gay-male activists nonetheless viewed the magazine's popularity—especially its celebration of nonprocreative sex—as a boon to the gay movement.[54]

The tensions between lesbians and gay men escalated in the first half of the decade. Some lesbian organizations even adopted a strict policy that men were excluded from participating in any of their events. In September 1974, a group called Dyke Patrol came to a concert of women's music at DePaul University and told men they were not welcome.[55] A member of the local lesbian rock band Mother Right told *Lavender Woman*, "We play for mixed groups reluctantly. Our music does not speak to men in any way."[56] Finally, in 1974, it was announced that "[t]he former Women's Center has now become the Lesbian Feminist Center. . . . Men are not welcome in the Center and will be asked to leave if they come in."[57]

In 1974, *Lavender Woman* noted, most lesbian organizations had withdrawn from participating in Gay Pride Week, with CLL the only exception. One woman in her mid-twenties told a writer for the newspaper that she did not plan to participate in Gay Pride Week, because "I'm basically tired of doing anything run by the patriarchy—whether faggot pigs or straight pigs—doing what they say and when they say." She added, "[F]aggots are the denial of women having any role at all. They simply don't need women for any reason. As far as I'm concerned Gay Pride means Faggot Pride. Faggotry is an illogical extension of men's incredible hatred for women." She noted that some of her "feelings have changed about Gay Pride," because, she said, she had "lifted some more of the fleece from my eyes."[58] In the following two years, Chicago lesbians held a separate Lesbian Pride observance, a month later than the gay-pride march, first held in June 1970 on the first anniversary of the Stonewall uprising. In 1976, Lesbian Pride Week was moved to a different date, in August, two months after the Stonewall anniversary.

Yet separatism likely caused as much conflict within the lesbian community as it did between lesbians and gay men. In 1973, for example, the editorial staff of *Lavender Woman* announced it was breaking off from CLL. The two groups signed a formal contract, specifying that CLL could submit one page for inclusion in each issue of *Lavender Woman*, over which it would have exclusive editorial control.[59] In the summer of 1974, CLL submitted a cartoon by Wanda Owen showing a distant character labeled Amazon refusing to assist Ms. Dyke and Fairy May, who are shown behind bars in "County Jail." To their call, "Help us, sister!" she responds, "Sorry, I'm a separatist." The newspaper's editors refused to print the cartoon, substituting a statement that it was "divisive and inflammatory." CLL announced with some fanfare that because of the breach of its contract, the title "Lavender Woman" reverted to its control, and the group proceeded to publish its own newsletter with the same title. "At least one bar has refused to carry either paper because of the confusion," observed Marie Kuda, in covering the conflict for the *Chicago Gay Crusader*. In addition, she added, "The Gay Law Students Association has offered to act as arbitrators in any negotiation, if asked."[60] The controversy surrounding the cartoon's deletion led to lasting personal bitterness and threats of litigation between members of the two organizations.

"Gay Life Is Split into Factions"

"Gay life is split into factions," observed *Chicago GayLife* in June 1975—with the biggest split of all being the "animosity" between men and women.[61] Even so, the gendered conflicts of the 1970s helped set the terms for a crucial shift: the wide adoption of the notion of a "gay and lesbian" community served by joint institutions. The new Gay and Lesbian Coalition of Metropolitan Chicago, founded at the end of 1975, included detailed regulations in its constitution to ensure parity between men and women.[62] In 1977, for the first time, the city's Pride celebration was known as Gay/ Lesbian Pride Week.[63] Gay and lesbian groups thus adopted a range of policies meant to lessen or counteract sexism internally, and to forge integrated organizations serving both men and women.

In fall 1975, an awkward and strikingly gendered conflict over strategy generated an attention-grabbing news story that led to structural changes in how gay Chicagoans managed their political aspirations. Two radical young women in their early twenties were so adamant in their quest to obtain a marriage license that they refused to leave the Cook County marriage bureau when their request was denied. The effort of these young women, Nancy Davis and Toby Schneiter, to demand the "civil right to marry" worried other activists, including Cliff Kelley, who feared that however noble their goals might be, they would jeopardize the chance for passage of the gay-rights bill in the city council. Members of several groups called a press conference where they labeled the young women's actions "irresponsible and nonrepresentative of the Chicago gay community."[64] After being arrested several times at the same office, Davis and Schneiter eventually were sentenced to a year in jail. Once in jail, they went on a hunger strike, and their friends organized several demonstrations in solidarity with them. The repeated arrests of Davis and Schneiter led to multiple press conferences, and in turn these catalyzed the formation of a mechanism for coordinating activities among Chicago's wide array of gay and lesbian organizations.[65]

The founding impetus of the Gay and Lesbian Coalition of Metropolitan Chicago, as a result, was to make sure that the same-sex marriage advocacy of Davis and Schneiter—marginal to the gay movement though it was and linked more to their involvement in revolutionary socialist activism—would not be the brush with which the whole gay movement would be tarred.[66] The coalition was founded at the end of 1975 as an umbrella group with both businesses and organizations under its aegis, and it sponsored regular caucus meetings of gay voters in the North Side's 43rd and 44th Wards. The coalition structure put in place during that crisis proved useful in the face of the antigay backlash that developed in 1977, and it coordinated the demonstration against Anita Bryant's visit to Chicago that spring.

The group's constitution included an elaborate, internal arbitration process in the event of disputes between its member groups. Activists began to use the term "gay and lesbian" or "lesbian and gay," making explicit their vision of lesbians and gay men building a movement together that would not simply replicate the gender inequalities of society at large. At one late 1976 meeting, Elaine Wessel of the Chicago Women's Liberation Union gave a presentation called "Sexism I," "speaking pointedly, but with great delicacy," as *GayLife* put it, about the status of women, emphasizing job discrimination and the lack of equal pay for equal work.[67] The group began to splinter just as it initiated a survey among community members about the extent of racial discrimination in North Side gay bars.[68] Some bar owners and activists disagreed about how much the group should devote energy to ensuring the equitable treatment of people of color. The group was unable to agree on whether to police racial discrimination on the part of member businesses.[69] And by the middle of 1977, it was clear the coalition would need to devote more attention to protecting its recent gains from conservative backlash.

*   *   *

As "coming out of the closet" became central to lesbian and gay-male politics, lesbians and gay men fought intense political battles over their own treatment of one another. Yet it was in part because gay men and lesbians developed new points of contact—not just because of the gay-movement groups but because many more of both were out at work and elsewhere—

that they clashed so much more frequently.[70] Working at a downtown Hyatt hotel around 1975, Linda Rodgers recalled, "I had to threaten to sue them and I had to take them to the union arbitration boards," in order to win the right to work behind the bar instead of as a cocktail waitress. In the course of taking her bosses to arbitration, Rodgers befriended a male coworker, "a flagrantly gay man" who "took an awful . . . verbal beating from people" at the Hyatt. It was he who introduced Linda to the lesbian bar world: "He took me to a bar called the Closet. I ended up working there six months later."[71] She took to the lesbian world immediately. By the end of the 1970s, Rodgers co-owned a music production company that produced citywide dances for lesbians; later she ran Paris Dance, the city's biggest lesbian bar.

Queer politics remained gendered, even as the period of separate gay-male and lesbian organizational growth came to an end and the news media began to report on the organizing gay men and lesbians did together. It is telling that the spring 1977 cover article in the alternative *Chicago Reader* about gay politics described "three very visible members of the north-side gay community," and posed the question, "Which of these *men* will be Chicago's first gay elected official?" The absence of any female candidate—or of gender politics at all—went unmentioned.[72] Some lesbians lobbied their elected officials for pay equity for women, for job protections for gays and lesbians, or for passage of the Equal Rights Amendment, but the few gay organizations in Chicago that sought to enter into ongoing relationships with elected officials in this period were *all* largely male in both leadership and foot soldiers. However, lesbian feminists paved the way for the social construction of a "gay and lesbian" community served by joint institutions. Some gay organizations changed their rules in the second half of the 1970s to increase women's access and participation and to institutionalize gender equality. After experimenting with mobilizing both separately and together, an influential subset of politicized gay men and lesbians decided by the late 1970s that they did share a common set of interests. In a smart commentary on gendered conflict, Susan Edwards wrote that it was important for both men and women to avoid thinking along the lines of "You're the bad guys, we're the good guys." She said, "Life is not an old Tom Mix western reenacted on Halsted Street."[73]

By the second half of the 1970s, gay male and lesbian activists had begun to unite, as they began to reach toward a more prominent role in the city and to seek enactment of their shared goals. The Planning Committee for

Gay Pride Week 1977 decided that the events should be cochaired by a man and a woman, and further decided to rename it Gay/Lesbian Pride Week. "It also appears," noted an article in the lesbian newspaper *Blazing Star*, "that there are more women active on the Planning Committee this year than in several recent years."[74] In a thoughtful series of articles on gay life in the city that appeared over the course of that week, the *Sun-Times* reported on the name change, under a headline, "Lesbians Charge Bias by Gay Men," that emphasized women's unwillingness to suffer discrimination within the gay movement in silence.[75] At the turn of the 1980s, then, gay men and lesbians had begun to realize they needed to work together, as well as to reach beyond the community for political allies.

6

Balance of Power

IN THE 1980s, at the same time that gay men and lesbians learned they needed each other, a black-gay political coalition achieved a greater degree of political integration than ever before. In this decade, in the nation's largest cities, gays and lesbians made their first well-organized, effective attempts to influence the outcome of citywide elections. Big-city black mayors like Chicago's Harold Washington cemented the inclusion of gays and lesbians in the politics of the Democratic Party. In less than a decade, gay Chicagoans went from having their bars raided by police to having their votes calibrated by politicians. Washington needed, and pursued, gay votes. Although only some politicized gays and lesbians backed his first mayoral candidacy in 1983, Washington's upset victory in the mayoral primary that year transformed Chicago's gay politics because, in office, he welcomed gays to city hall. Bloc voting was especially significant in political off-years and in local elections in which turnout was far lower than in presidential years.

Chicago's first black mayor thus broke something of a logjam: Not until his candidacy had gays and lesbians been acknowledged as potentially serious players in a citywide race. The Washington election was a watershed in that Washington recognized, and tried to benefit from, gay bloc voting. His candidacy reflected the emergence of authentic African American political power in a city that had grown increasingly black—and seen increasing racial tensions—over the past half century. His mayoralty symbolizes the high-water mark of a certain kind of urban progressive politics. It also set the stage for the first serious debate on the city-council floor about enacting a gay-rights ordinance. Black aldermen held the balance of power in large

gay rights
as big part
of hi law

part because white aldermen's votes were already spoken for, locked as they almost all were in the two council blocs that either supported or opposed the first-term mayor.

In Chicago as in other cities, as city councils held the first legislative debates and votes on sexual-orientation nondiscrimination—that is, on including gays and lesbians under the broad purview of civil rights laws, especially those prohibiting job discrimination—black politicians frequently held the balance of power. The effort to enact municipal employment nondiscrimination laws in the 1980s, like the fight to end police harassment in the 1970s, focused the gay movement on a policy issue that black activists had broached first. The enactment of gay rights thus depended not only on the example of black activism but also on the configurations of power that the struggles of the 1960s and 1970s had helped to bring about. By the 1980s, African Americans were still, by some metrics, underrepresented relative to their share of the city's population. Yet they had attained a degree of influence and respect citywide, they had secured the cooperation of the courts in protecting their rights to elect their own, and they had, in 1983, elected a mayor.[1]

As mayor of Chicago, Washington faced, for most of his time in office, a hostile, all-white bloc of city-council members, which led to gridlock that the press came to call the "Council Wars." Nonetheless, he took many steps in support of gay rights. Concretely, he became the city's first mayor to ask gay leaders to help set policy priorities during his transition to office, the first to endorse a gay-rights ordinance, the first to name a liaison to the gay community, and the first to appoint a Committee on Gay and Lesbian Issues and ask gay leaders to serve on it.

In Chicago's deeply Catholic, machine-driven political culture, it took a highly placed patron like Harold Washington to open the possibilities for gay organizing at city hall. Washington's support for gay rights was based not only on idealism but also on a pragmatic recognition of the potential for gays to affect electoral outcomes. Gay politics increasingly focused on the effort to pass a gay-rights ordinance, a struggle in which race, gender, and religion became critical factors. Several women council members, black and white, played key roles in supporting the gay-rights ordinance. By 1988, as the effort to pass the ordinance grew, involving multiple organizations, gay activists had adopted the strategy that had enabled Washington's own election five years earlier, by raising funds to sponsor a voter-registration drive, led by a paid political operative.

But Washington was not unique: In a remarkably large number of big cities, African American mayors pushed through gay-rights ordinances and advanced gay political incorporation in an effort to build their electoral coalitions. Although whites were fleeing for the suburbs at record rates, white gays and lesbians continued to migrate to cities, and black leaders, needing at least some white votes to win citywide, saw their votes as essential.[2] Black gay activists helped mediate these ties.

"A Little More Compassionate"

When Richard J. Daley died suddenly at the end of 1976, gays and lesbians had no formal voice in city hall, and there was little sign that they would acquire it anytime soon. Michael Bilandic, Daley's successor, was given positive credit merely for his lack of antigay hostility. In a testament to the marginality of gays and lesbians, the editor of *GayLife*—which took up in 1975 where the *Chicago Gay Crusader* left off as the city's regularly scheduled community-based gay newspaper—noted that although Bilandic did not return the paper's questionnaire, his mayoral campaign was "not hostile" to gays and lesbians. "Before," said the *Chicago Reader*, "he had been somewhat hostile."[3] Thus the bar was set low in the sense that a candidate's acknowledging gays and lesbians' existence was considered a major achievement.

The following decade saw gay politics in Chicago transform beyond recognition. Between the mid-1970s and mid-1980s, gay activists for the first time gained a seat at the table in city hall. In the mid-1980s, gays and lesbians even gained a mayoral liaison. Activists increasingly imagined gay bloc voting in local and state elections. The gay press played an important role in this effort at political mobilization. *GayLife*, which was now owned by Chuck Renslow, had become a full-fledged commercial venture. As the mainstream *Sun-Times* reported, "That it must serve a community not easily defined by street boundaries makes the job a little tricky."[4]

In Chicago, as elsewhere, gays and lesbians had marched in the streets in growing numbers over the course of the 1970s. Urban gay communities flourished, and the new annual tradition of the gay-pride parade transformed gay politics. Lesbians had fought a sometimes quite bitter battle to secure the inclusion of their agenda in that of feminist organizations, and by the late 1970s they had largely won that battle. At a landmark 1977

White House meeting, ten activists from the National Gay Task Force, including Bill Kelley from Chicago, met with Midge Costanza and other members of President Jimmy Carter's staff about their concerns. And in October 1979, gay men and lesbians had for the first time marched on Washington.[5]

A transitional figure, and an opening with respect to gay inclusion, came in the form of Mayor Jane Byrne, elected in 1979. Byrne's defeat of the incumbent Michael Bilandic seemed to signal a turning point—a defeat of the machine, a promise of a more inclusive city, and the first woman mayor of any of the nation's largest cities. Byrne received overwhelming support from black voters. Elected on an antimachine platform despite having been a protégé of Mayor Daley himself, Byrne quickly rehabilitated her ties to the Regular Democrats she had run against, and alienated African Americans by replacing two black school-board members with reactionary whites. In remarkably short order, she became once again associated with the machine politics she had ostensibly defeated.[6] Her upset victory had seemed to herald the collapse of the Chicago machine, but her electoral base—especially blacks—soured on her mayoralty after she reneged on many campaign promises and quickly reconciled with the machine bosses she had once called a "cabal of evil men."

Byrne changed the tone of city government's relationship to gay voters. Men such as Chuck Renslow, who felt connected to the Daley machine and who liked being able to be out of the closet, and were increasingly able to be out, were more enamored of Byrne than lesbians were. Her flamboyance, and her persona as an outspoken Irish Catholic woman with a diva personality, seemed to endear her to gay men.[7] Yet although Byrne was not hostile to gays and lesbians and seemed at times cognizant of her gay backers, she did little to advance gay equality in city government, and this was largely in keeping with her broader record on questions of inclusion. In 1982, she signed an executive order banning discrimination based on sexual orientation in city hiring. But it came without an enforcement mechanism.[8] Even though she did not deliver gay-friendly public policy, she did change the tone in city hall. She was willing—if sufficient pressure were applied—to say the word *gay* in public.

Bar raids continued under Byrne, but, unlike her predecessors, she could be induced to speak out against them. She did so after a dramatic Civic Center protest attended by an estimated 1,500 gay and pro-gay protestors in June 1979, following a series of raids on North Side bars, including the popular Carol's Speakeasy on North Wells Street. As a result of that protest, and again more vocally after a raid on the Rialto Tap in the South Loop, Byrne publicly chastised police, said they should stop targeting gay establishments, and announced her support for a gay-rights ordinance, though she took no steps toward passing it.[9] In February 1980, the *Tribune* reported that police harassment of gay bars seemed to be continuing.[10] Continued arrests of men in Lincoln Park for public sex, by contrast, aroused less controversy, despite vocal complaints from some gay activists. Police officials told the Illinois Gay and Lesbian Task Force in 1981, "What you do is your business—where you do it is our business."[11]

In one major area, the training of police officers, the Byrne administration oversaw significant progress. In 1981, for the first time, all cadets at the Chicago Police Academy were required to attend a one-hour presentation by gay and lesbian speakers from the Illinois Gay and Lesbian Task Force. The speakers planned on a series of points to emphasize: that most child molesters are straight, that not all gays and lesbians are gender non-conforming, and that gays do not attempt to recruit or convert straight people. Above all, the speakers worked to convey the impression that "gays fear police more than they fear the crime or the criminal." The cadets were impressed with the courage and forthrightness of the presenters. "It takes a certain amount of courage to stand up in front of a group of police officers and admit you're gay and talk about it," one cadet wrote.[12] The police brass had finally accepted the notion that officers should have some sort of training on the particular needs of gay Chicagoans.

Efforts were also made to train existing officers, although it is not clear these made much difference outside the areas of the city where gays were most visible. The police department issued a training bulletin the following year titled "The Gays and the Police," which was distributed during roll call at every police station in the city. Al Wardell, an official with the group, commented that "we aren't saying things are perfect here in Chicago but we have made real progress." He went on to say that "plans are being made to speak at all the roll calls in all the police districts in the city that have significant gay populations," but he added that presentations to current officers as well as recruits was a "longstanding goal," suggesting that it remained elusive.[13]

By 1985, the city police department had ceased to conduct or countenance gay-bar raids. Harold Washington faced questions from his gay supporters when bar raids occurred on his watch. Such raids were, as under

Byrne, often conducted by agents of nonmunicipal government, such as the
state police. It had been a federal prosecutor who had aggressively attacked
the regime of gay-bar raids in the 1970s by prosecuting police graft. Federal
prosecutions had reduced the opportunities for city police officers to extort
money from gay bar owners. The last raid to be conducted in the old style
occurred in 1985. That year, fifteen agents of a state-funded drug-
enforcement agency joined several Chicago police officers in raiding Carol's
Speakeasy, on Wells Street in Old Town, on allegations of drug dealing on
the premises. Patrons were made to lie down on the floor for up to two
hours, they were verbally harassed, and they were photographed. The
names of some patrons present were published in the *Sun-Times*, a particularly offensive step given the history of such treatment, and one gay man
reportedly lost his job as a result. The incident led to protracted litigation,
and four years after the raid, the city and state agreed in an out-of-court
settlement to pay as much as $227,000 in damages to those present during
the raid.[14] The outcome thus raised the potential cost to the police department of forms of harassment that had once been routine.

Gays had made enormous strides politically from the mid-1970s to the
mid-1980s. As urban gay communities flourished, the tradition of the gay-
pride parade expanded. The women's movement embraced many of the
concerns of gays and lesbians. The late 1970s had even brought a White
House meeting with a member of the president's staff, and a march on
Washington.[15] By the beginning of the 1980s, Chicago had seen the first gay
candidates for office and the first legislative votes on gay rights—and
although both were defeated by overwhelming margins, the public sphere
had been irreversibly opened to gay mobilization.

"You Ennoble Yourself"

When gay activists won an extremely circumscribed inclusion in the Democratic Party's platform in 1980, that step built on the party's earlier
explicit welcoming of African Americans, Latinos, and women, as well
as more-tentative gestures toward gays, in the 1970s.[16] At the 1972 party
convention in Miami Beach, in accordance with the new "McGovern
rules," Daley's Illinois delegates had been unceremoniously kicked out
in favor of reformers—notably, blacks and women—who challenged

traditional structures of power and won. It was African American municipal politicians, however, who most powerfully secured the position of gays
and lesbians in the party's new electoral coalition.[17] Feminism was a crucial mediator. "The people who stood with us in the '60s are asking us to
stand with them in the 1970s to ratify ERA," said Representative Larry S.
Bullock in 1980, turning down the request of a group of black pastors
from Chicago hoping to turn him against the Equal Rights Amendment.[18]
Black leadership in the 1980s helped forge a pragmatic coalition around a
progressive politics of sexuality and gender, which would move into even
greater national prominence in the 1990s.

When Congressman Harold Washington ran for mayor of Chicago in
1983, the particular circumstances of his primary campaign made white
lesbians and gay men a key constituency whose votes he sought during the
general election. The white vote had been split in the primary between Jane
Byrne, the incumbent, and Richard M. Daley, the State's Attorney and son
of the former mayor. Ahead of the February primary, Jane Byrne had spoken before a gay North Side audience and promised to march in the gay-
pride parade if she was reelected. Both Washington and Richard M. Daley,
the other major candidate, had sent representatives to that event.[19] Most of
Washington's votes in the primary had been cast by blacks and Latinos, but
the votes of a small number of liberal whites, concentrated in five wards
stretching north of the Loop along the lakefront, were crucial to his narrow
primary victory.[20] The weeks since the primary had proven a difficult education for Washington and his backers, however, bringing to a sudden end
three decades during which the nominee of the Democratic Party had easily
won the general election. No other mayoral nominee had faced a seriously
contested general election in almost thirty years. Washington had won the
black vote overwhelmingly, yet he could not now win citywide in the general election without some white support.

Facing this predicament—a very tight mayoral race, a divided city, and
the circumstance of being a black candidate facing an ugly, reactionary
white backlash—Washington came to speak before a gay audience for the
first time. "I remember back in 1973 when the ERA first came up down in
Springfield," he said, speaking before an audience of 300 that was packed
into a church on the North Side on the evening of April 5, 1983. "Henry
Hyde came up to me," he recalled, referring to an arch-conservative legislator from a suburban Chicago district, "and said, 'why would you be concerned with the rights of women when blacks haven't got their rights?' I

said, 'Henry, when a person defends his or her own rights, it's just courageous and smart. But when you defend the rights of other people, you
ennoble yourself.'" Washington acknowledged that Chicago gays and lesbians had "suffered at the hands of brutal policemen." Most important, citing
his decade-long record of support for state and federal bills to protect gay
men and lesbians from job discrimination, Washington asserted that as
mayor he would fight for "the gay rights ordinance that's been pending
before the Council for so long." He supported the rights of all people, he
said, "philosophically, legislatively, activistically, and otherwise."[21]

If Washington represented a seeming paradox—an antimachine politician who had come up through the machine—it was not an entirely surprising one for Chicagoans. He had worked with his father, a precinct
captain in the 3rd Ward, and attended the city's multiracial and largely
working-class Roosevelt University. He had been the only African American
in his Northwestern law school class, in which Dawn Clark Netsch, later a
beloved figure in statewide Democratic politics, was the only woman.
Beginning in 1964, Washington served in the Illinois general assembly. In
1980, he ran for the U.S. House seat previously held by Ralph Metcalfe,
who had split from Daley over police brutality in the early 1970s. Despite
being a freshman in the U.S. House of Representatives, Washington was
made the national spokesperson for reauthorizing the Voting Rights Act.[22]

Through massive new-voter registration and turnout among African
Americans, and with most white votes divided between two other candidates,
Washington had eked out an upset victory in an unusual three-way Democratic primary. The white vote had been split between Byrne and Richard M.
Daley. In the weeks after the February 1983 primary, however, most of the
city's white Democratic Party establishment abandoned the nominee of their
party and endorsed instead the Republican, Bernard Epton, whose campaign
adopted the controversial slogan "Before It's Too Late."

During the racially charged general-election campaign, the gay columnist Jon-Henri Damski decried "a number of white, Hispanic, and Asian
gays who have come down with a bad case of negrophobia," sharing in the
widespread white fear that "they might treat us like we have treated them."
Washington was unusual in that he had a record: He had voted for gay-
rights proposals in both Springfield and the nation's capital. But Damski
recalled gay men on election night expressing sentiments like, "If that
power-hungry, lazy Southern demagogue wins, I'm leaving for San Francisco."[23] More subtly, the newspaper *GayLife* reported, in endorsing the

nominee, some white gays voiced a "worry that Washington's pro-gay positions would be thwarted by his religious backers." Here the word "religious" operated in part as a code word, referencing assumptions about black opinion: Would a *black* mayor really support gay rights?[24]

There had been pro-gay candidates before Washington, of course. Indeed, not only that, six white and two black gay men ran for office as openly gay candidates between 1972 and 1987, although no openly gay candidate would win a primary or general election in Chicago until 1994, when Thomas R. Chiola won election as a circuit court judge. Gay organizing had forced officeholders in many of Chicago's North Side lakefront council wards and state legislative districts to pay attention to gay concerns, and thereby helped reshape North Side lakefront politics. Liberals Elroy Sundquist and Susan Catania had recognized a gay voting bloc in state legislative races, and community activist Charlotte Newfeld held campaign events in gay bars in her very narrowly defeated effort to unseat a machine alderman, Jerry Orbach, in the 46th Ward in 1983.[25]

Washington went on to win the April general election by fewer than 50,000 votes of nearly 1,300,000 cast. In office, his embrace of gays and lesbians took formal shape. In 1985, he created the Mayor's Committee on Gay and Lesbian Issues (COGLI) (Figure 16). The organization was meant to be analogous to similar committees representing the interests of Latinos, blacks, and Asians. Its sixteen members, balanced under its bylaws between men and women with "as a minimum four racial minority seats," were chosen by a selection committee and appointed by the mayor.[26] The members were recruited through a community-based process. Perhaps almost as important, Washington's police superintendent, Fred Rice, the first African American in that role, appointed its first liaison to the gay community.[27] "The rainbow coalition has become the rainbow administration," Washington declared at the end of his first year in office.[28]

The mayor's embrace of gay rights reflected a mix of principle and pragmatism. On the one hand, he certainly couched his backing for gay rights as a part of his broader commitment to civil rights for all citizens. He often depicted his support as a part of this broader commitment to equality. In October 1987, he backed the Chicago contingent at the second gay and lesbian March on Washington. His endorsement called the march "consistent with the historic thrust of struggles for civil rights in this country."[29] On the other hand, his backing for gay rights reflected more practical considerations: the long-standing antimachine politics of Chicago gay men

FIGURE 16. Mayor Harold Washington (at head of table) with members of his
Committee on Gay and Lesbian Issues, 1986. Courtesy of Gerber/Hart Library
and Archives.

and lesbians, the related politics and ideologies of the "lakefront liberals,"
and the groundwork within the existing machine that had been laid by the
growing "ethnic" gay voting bloc in earlier years.

As Washington faced implacable obstruction from an all-white bloc on
the city council, the North Side lakefront wards where gay voters were
concentrated were one of the areas of the city most visibly up for grabs.
White liberals on the North Side lakefront were considered a critical swing
constituency. In both 1983 and 1987, Washington's citywide primary and
general mayoral campaigns were very close. He needed the votes not only
of gays but also of straight lakefront liberals—many educated and socially
progressive, including the city's largest concentration of Jewish voters—
who were pro-gay and had gay friends. "With Chicago's north lakefront—
which contains the city's most visibly active gay community—designated
the official battleground in the 1987 mayoral race, the need for politicians
to hawk their wares at gay functions becomes more pronounced," as one

reporter put it.[30] In short, if gays and their gay-friendly neighbors in the North Side lakefront liberal wards were to vote as a bloc, they could even conceivably decide close citywide races.

At the midpoint of Washington's first term, Byrne announced she would attempt a political comeback in 1987; that year, she also marched in the gay-pride parade. Washington was thus somewhat at pains to shore up his reputation among gay voters. Referring to Byrne, he declared, "I am the first mayor in Chicago's history—regardless of the vague promises and loose talk of certain of my glib predecessors—to appoint a mayoral liaison to the gay and lesbian community." Contrasting Byrne's vision of gay inclusion with Washington's, journalist Albert "Bill" Williams pointed out that Byrne's speeches to gay audiences involved "no mentions of tenants' rights or Coors boycotts; even the gay rights bill is downplayed." Instead, Byrne regaled her mostly gay male audience with an elaborate tale about gay men who volunteered to redecorate her campaign office during her first campaign for mayor. For many white gay men, Washington's oratorical gifts were admirable, but, as one man complained, the incumbent mayor tended to use "20-dollar words that you can't understand."[31]

In Chicago, as elsewhere, enacting gay rights was difficult, and ordinances were rarely passed on the first attempt—and, until 1988, when gays proved that they could vote as a bloc by launching a well-organized voter-registration drive, doubts persisted about whether they were capable of doing so. In 1985, David Axelrod, who had left his post as the *Tribune*'s local political reporter and managed Paul Simon's victorious 1984 campaign for U.S. Senate, expressed doubt about "to what extent that's a bloc vote." He added, "[I]f you're asking me whether it's worth a full-scale assault [in an effort to win gay voters], my hunch is it isn't, if only because of the numbers involved. You're not going to be elected to an office in Illinois on a gay-rights platform."[32] But the fact that he was asked the question reflected the sense that a new level of mobilization was in the offing.

Washington's support for gay rights was particularly courageous because there had long been whispers and rumors suggesting that he himself was gay. He had been divorced after a brief marriage early in life. Asked by a reporter in 1983 about his marriage plans, he said, "Buried? I've lived in Chicago all my life and intend to be buried here." He added, "Oh, you said married," and reportedly "laughed it off." While running for mayor, Washington became engaged to a woman, Mary Ella Smith. "He had given in to the political requirement to have a fiancée," wrote one biographer, "but he would not be intruded upon."[33] On his death four and a half years later, she remained Washington's fiancée. In the supremely dirty 1983 general election campaign, anonymous leaflets alleged that he had been arrested for sodomizing a teenager. Once, seeking to speak on the city-council floor, Alderman Ed Vrdolyak addressed the mayor and said, "To someone of your gender I should say 'pretty please.'" Gary Rivlin, a journalist and biographer of Washington, called the mayor's sexuality a "strange preoccupation" of the Vrdolyak bloc.[34]

The rumors that Washington had gay associates were not without basis. One year into Washington's first term, the author of a *New York Times* profile reported that "members of his inner circle are supposed to be homosexual." In fact, Washington's chief of staff, William Ware, was gay and would die the following year from complications of AIDS. The reporter even complained, "He refuses to announce a wedding date despite much goading." Washington was gay-baited during his mayoralty most often by whites, but on at least one occasion by an African American city official.[35] Still, many colleagues recall his longtime secretary Delores Woods as having said, "If every woman Harold slept with stood at one end of City Hall, the building would sink five inches into LaSalle Street."[36]

In addition to wards with many gay voters being up for grabs, there was also the matter of citywide races, in which Washington or his supporters needed as many voters as they could find. At first it seemed that both sides in "Council Wars" included some supporters and some opponents of gay rights—and this created pressure for Washington to make his support more visible.[37] When Washington appeared at a gay-rights rally in early July 1984, it was partly in an effort to outflank two alderman from the city council's Vrdolyak bloc. The incumbent aldermen in the heavily gay 44th and 46th Wards, both supporters of Vrdolyak, had marched in the gay-pride parade the week before. In addition, it had been Orbach—not a Washington backer—who had proposed a $100,000 budget item to fund AIDS education.[38]

In 1986 and 1987, struggling to gain and then keep a supportive majority on the city council and to win reelection, Washington began aggressively to pursue gay voters, most of them white, who were concentrated in a few key North Side lakefront wards. Lakefront liberals constituted the white part of Washington's coalition, and gays and lesbians were perhaps the best-organized group within this constituency.[39] He sat down with Tracy Baim, editor of the city's leading gay newspaper, for a wide-ranging interview

FIGURE 17. Mayor Harold Washington meets with lesbian journalist Tracy Baim, 1986. Courtesy of Tracy Baim/*Outlines* and *Windy City Times* newspapers.

(Figure 17). Pro-Washington gay activists also secured the mayor's attendance at a dramatic Pride rally in Lincoln Park attended by some 6,000 people in June 1987 (Figure 18). To be sure, there were limits to Washington's embrace. For example, until his final year in office, he resisted entreaties from members of the Committee on Gay and Lesbian Issues to meet with them. The police department, under Superintendent Rice, refused to track hate crimes against gays and lesbians.[40] Many gays and lesbians remained invisible to their neighbors, to each other, and even to themselves.

With limited resources, Washington did not enact gay rights at the municipal level. When the gay-rights ordinance came to a vote in 1986, while he was mayor, it was defeated. Achy Obejas, a journalist and member of COGLI, recalled the trajectory of Washington's overall agenda in these terms: "Harold's legislative record is actually better than you might think, considering he only served one term and that he was stymied for the first two years of it." On any number of matters concerning the reform of city

FIGURE 18. Harold Washington at a gay-pride rally, 1987.
Courtesy of Chicago Public Library.

agencies and electoral politics, she noted, "black aldermen who would have normally opposed these measures had no choice" but to cast their lot with him. "But on the gay and lesbian thing, he wasn't holding their feet to the fire," making gay rights a rare vote on which they could "signal my independence" from the mayor and "hide behind the churches in my ward which are all opposed to this."[41] Faced with many difficult struggles in the council, and with passage of the ordinance unlikely, Washington viewed the gay-rights ordinance as an issue on which his verbal support would suffice.

Yet that verbal support made a world of difference to the gay movement locally. At a time when gays and lesbians faced a hostile administration in the nation's capital, Washington's voice—like those of other urban politicians, many of them African American—represented an increasingly important counterweight. In his second inaugural address, much of it devoted to an angry denunciation of Ronald Reagan's dramatic cuts in federal support to cities, Washington explicitly mentioned gays and lesbians, along with Muslims, the disabled, and others formerly without a political voice who he had worked to include at city hall.[42]

Following the 1986 defeat, in the tumultuous period between 1986 and 1988, several organizations were created in order to push the gay-rights ordinance, most notably Gay and Lesbian Town Meeting. The anger generated by the federal government's sluggish response to AIDS, along with the devastating Supreme Court decision in *Bowers v. Hardwick* upholding state sodomy laws, aided the cause. "We're deeply embarrassed for our city," declared Chicago activist Jonathan Katz, at the second gay and lesbian march on Washington, "the largest city in the nation without gay and lesbian civil rights."[43] Of the five most populous cities in the 1980 census, only Chicago had never passed a gay-rights ordinance—although Houston had passed such an ordinance in 1984 only to see it repealed in a ballot referendum the following year.[44] Washington, Detroit, Minneapolis, San Francisco, and Los Angeles had passed such ordinances in the 1970s, along with the downstate college towns of Champaign and Urbana, where the University of Illinois was located. Philadelphia joined the list in 1982 and Oakland in 1984. But it was, as Katz's comment implied, the passage of an ordinance in New York City in 1986, the same year gay Chicagoans faced defeat locally, that fueled Chicago activists' frustration.

"If the Cardinal's Against It, I Ain't for It"

Religion proved a pivotal issue as Chicagoans began to debate passing the ordinance. Gay and antigay mobilization occurred among both blacks and whites. Yet gay activists' most powerful and most effective religious antagonists were representatives of overwhelmingly white, not black, religious communities. Though its influence in city hall was markedly on the wane, the Roman Catholic Archdiocese of Chicago had held on to enough political power to delay passage of a gay-rights ordinance for more than two years, between 1986 and 1988, during the Washington era. (Though Washington himself, like many black Chicago politicians, was Catholic, he bucked the church's teaching on gay rights.)

Although black opposition to gay rights got more press, white religious opposition played the larger role in blocking enactment of gay-rights

HOW DO YOU FEEL ABOUT HOMOSEXUALS IN CHICAGO?

This Wednesday, September 12th, the Chicago
City Council will vote on a bill that permits:

1. Homosexuals to be Chicago Police Officers.
   How do you feel about that?
2. Homosexuals to be Chicago Public School Teachers.
   How do you feel about that?
3. Homosexuals to be Chicago Firemen.
   How do you feel about that?
Most likely this bill will be passed!
   How do you feel about that?
We feel this issue is too important to be
voted on without your opinion being heard.
   If you feel the same way, there's only one
course of action.
   You must call or send a telegram to the
Mayor *and* the President Pro Tem of the
Chicago City Council requesting 30 days of
public hearings and a city-wide referendum.
   Don't send letters.
   There are only two days left.

THE HONORABLE JANE BYRNE   THE HONORABLE EDWARD R. VRDOLYAK
MAYOR, CITY OF CHICAGO   PRESIDENT PRO TEM, CHICAGO CITY COUNCIL
CITY HALL   CITY HALL
121 N. LA SALLE STREET   121 N. LA SALLE STREET
CHICAGO, 60602   CHICAGO, 60602
PHONE: 744-4000   PHONE: 744-6822

Why are we paying for this advertisement?
   The Plymouth Foundation is a group of
Chicago citizens committed to Judeo-Christian
and democratic beliefs.
   We believe this moral issue must become
a public issue.

FIGURE 19. Full-page antigay print advertisement paid for by
the Plymouth Foundation, September 1979.

measures. In September 1979, a white-led Protestant group headquartered
in suburban Lake Forest called the Plymouth Foundation paid for identical
full-page antigay advertisements to run in the Sunday newspapers in
advance of the date when Cliff Kelley planned to bring the gay-rights ordinance up for a vote for the first time (see Figure 19). In bold type, the ad
asked, "How do you feel about homosexuals in Chicago?" These ads asked
readers to contemplate the thought of a bill allowing "homosexuals to be
Chicago Police Officers," "homosexuals to be Chicago Public School
Teachers," and "homosexuals to be Chicago Firemen," adding, "Most likely

this bill will be passed! How do you feel about that?" Pro-gay activists and aldermen said later that this single print advertisement, the appearance of which none had foreseen, from a foundation that few had heard of, nixed any chance of the measures' passing.[45]

Historians have often painted "the black church" with a broad brush, as a force pushing solely in one direction when it comes to sexual politics—a conservative direction. In fact, black religious authorities took a wide range of positions in Chicago's debate over gay rights. There were mainstream pastors who condemned homosexuality from the pulpit as a sin. Black opposition to gay rights took culturally specific forms, reflecting the broader politics of family and respectability in black churches and communities. Some perceived the visibility of queer people as a consequence of the breakdown of black families through the absence or departure of men.[46] As the legal scholar Harlon Dalton observed in 1989, the content of black religious rhetoric more often centered on managing male-female relationships, not controlling eroticism.[47] At Liberty Baptist Church at 49th Street and Martin Luther King Drive, for example, a young visiting minister "denounce[d] unisex fashions as a craze," noted a reporter covering a 1985 sermon. "We are trapped in a gender twilight zone, somewhere between male and female," said the minister. The reporter added, "Given the growing role of gays in choirs at many black churches, one wonders whether someone should warn this young preacher to exercise some restraint."[48] In the city council, Alderman Robert Shaw, who was African American, repeatedly asked whether the ordinance would create "another sex in the state" or would create "a third sex and a third class based upon sex."[49]

In addition, the white religious right stoked black religious opposition to gay rights. The most visible figure who organized petition drives and rallies against the gay-rights ordinance, the Reverend Hiram Crawford, saw opposing gay rights as a deeply felt religious duty. "I call it a holy war," he said. "It's a satanic deception to say they are born that way. If they become a political power, [Chicago] will become another San Francisco, another Sodom and Gomorrah."[50] Within the black Pentecostal and Holiness revival that flourished in the 1980s, Crawford was emblematic of one strand that was closely linked to the rise of black neoconservative politics. Strikingly, he served as president of the Illinois chapter of Jerry Falwell's largely white conservative religious coalition, the Moral Majority.[51]

Churches were key anchors politically on the South Side, and Crawford had proven that he could convince other pastors to lobby their legislators against gay equality. In 1985, he led a contingent of black fundamentalists to Springfield to lobby against the Illinois gay-rights bill, "concentrating their efforts on black legislators more sensitive to pressure from the many churches in their districts." Carol Moseley Braun, who was then a state representative from Chicago, recalled that Crawford and six other ministers came to her office in the state capitol, where they "condemned me to hell and damnation and prayed and preached up and down. . . . It was a very, very ugly scene." Braun noted that although almost all of her fellow black caucus members supported the gay-rights bill, "they're taking their political future in their hands on this because the black community has so many churches." She added, "Most of us do support them out of a sense of conviction that it's the right thing to do."[52] After the vote, though, the bill's chief sponsor, Representative Woods Bowman of Evanston, observed, "Half of Black legislators voted against it this time. All of Black legislators voted for it last time."[53] Herein lay the point that white gays and lesbians did not always grasp: that black legislators were often persuadable in either direction on gay rights and did not represent a monolithic bloc vote on either side of the issue. They were less likely than white aldermen to have preexisting alignments *either* with the Catholic Church or with the North Side lakefront liberal groups, and as a result they tended to hold the balance of power.

Pentecostal and Holiness congregations could also be found at the other end of the political spectrum, however. Reverend Willie T. Barrow, a black feminist Holiness pastor at the Vernon Park Church of God, two and a half miles southeast of Crawford's church, was a longtime civil rights activist who became a crucial supporter of the ordinance.[54] Moreover, black antigay lobbying was less effective in city hall than it had been in Springfield, precisely because Washington was in charge at city hall. The mayor's adhesion to the black electorate was mediated by personal charisma, not religious networks. Indeed, at the start of the 1983 mayoral primary, Washington, Byrne, and Daley each had the backing of a cadre of black ministers, and it had been congregants who had pushed their pastors in many cases to side with Washington.[55] In 1986 in the city council, Crawford went up against Washington, who asserted, "It is not a gay rights bill. It is a civil rights bill, and I have spent all of my life fighting for the rights of everyone. I won't back off on that." He added that Crawford was a "spear-carrier" for Falwell, who was then being widely criticized by African American activists and politicians for his opposition to U.S. sanctions against South Africa's apartheid government.[56] Every black alderman knew that close to 99 percent of his or her constituents had voted for Washington. Crawford may well have influenced his own 6th Ward alderman, Eugene Sawyer, to vote against the ordinance in 1986, but he lacked clout beyond the ward boundaries. Later, Ron Sable, a gay physician and activist, told his fellow COGLI members that Washington had assured him, "Hiram Crawford should not be a political problem for the community."[57]

Where a white Protestant group had scuttled Cliff Kelley's gay-rights ordinance in 1979 before it reached the floor, the Roman Catholic archdiocese, working powerfully behind the scenes, blocked enactment of a similar ordinance in 1986. That year, when the ordinance was brought to the floor for a vote for the first time, it was the intervention of the Catholic archbishop, Joseph Bernardin, that ensured its defeat. The *Sun-Times* described Bernardin's last-minute opposition—believed to have been prompted by the urging of the conservative alderman Ed Burke—as "the greatest single outside influence" on the defeat of the measure.[58]

Because of the intransigent opposition of the Roman Catholic archdiocese to gay equality, antigay politics had a more powerful and unified institutional base among white than among black Chicagoans in the 1970s and 1980s. In the words of the nationally syndicated columnist Clarence Page, speaking in an interview with the gay *Windy City Times*, once Bernardin made clear his opposition to the bill, "Suddenly almost all of the white aldermen were chiming in Me too. . . . Even Berny Stone, who is Jewish, was saying: If the Cardinal's against it, I ain't for it." Page observed, moreover, "Cardinal Bernardin has won in the sense of having this amount of demonstrated influence over legislation in Chicago, whereas Cardinal [John J.] O'Connor in New York lost when he tried to stop their gay rights bill." Jim Flint, a long-time gay bar owner with machine ties, who had recently run unsuccessfully for the Cook County Board, charged that Burke had called Bernardin, asked him to speak out against the ordinance at the last minute, and then distributed his opinion on the stationery of the City Hall Finance Committee. Page said he had "little reason to doubt" this, "considering the context of Chicago politics," and that he was unsurprised the Church could block the ordinance.[59] The power of the Catholic archdiocese was on the wane in 1986, but it was sufficient to block job protections for gay and lesbian Chicagoans.

FIGURE 20. ACT UP/Chicago protest of Joseph Bernardin. Courtesy of Rex Wockner/
Outlines and *Windy City Times* newspapers.

"A 'Queer' Almost Beat Bernie Hansen"

The movement for gay equality faced new tensions as it grew. As gay activists in Chicago regrouped in the wake of the defeat of the antidiscrimination bill, a division emerged among North Side gay activists that became bitter, over whether to focus on lobbying for legislative change or on electing one of their own. One group wanted to focus all its energy on lobbying for the ordinance. This group became Gay and Lesbian Town Meeting, and it held a series of mass gatherings in Lakeview to discuss possible strategies for converting some of the council's "no" votes to "yes" votes—regardless of where the aldermen with whom they might have to work stood on Council Wars. The group had named elected officers by 1987, and in 1988 four of them—who became known as the "Gang of Four"—emerged as the key public figures in the campaign.

The other group instead launched an effort to elect a progressive, openly gay alderman in the 44th Ward: Ron Sable, a member of COGLI and a left-leaning gay doctor at Cook County Hospital who had helped found the

FIGURE 21. Aldermanic candidate Ron Sable in gay-pride parade, 1986.
Courtesy of Marc PoKempner and Gerber/Hart Library and Archives.

AIDS clinic there with his colleague Renslow Sherer. This group included
many who were invested in 1980s progressive politics, including gay rights
but also other social causes. Many were also dedicated, officially or unofficially, to the effort to reelect Washington in 1987. Sable challenged the
44th Ward's incumbent alderman, Bernie Hansen, in the February 1987
Democratic aldermanic primary, which coincided with Washington's own
reelection campaign. The campaign had gotten underway in earnest when
Sable supporters marched in the 1986 Pride parade on his behalf.

The defeat of the gay-rights bill that same month had revealed where
each incumbent alderman had stood. The Vrdolyak bloc was antigay, yet
the durability of the stereotype of black homophobia made this much less
widely known among white gays than it might have been. As one activist
who had coordinated volunteers in some wards later wrote, "The media
has described the gay rights issue as 'bipartisan' with supporters on both
sides of the Council Wars. The City Council vote clearly shows that this is
not the case." In fact, only *two* members of the Vrdolyak bloc—Bernie
Hansen and Jerome Orbach, who represented lakefront liberal wards with

many gays and lesbians—had voted yes. By contrast, "Although Mayor Washington failed to line up all of his supporters for the bill, with one exception (Marlene Carter) every one of the black, Hispanic and white reformers closest to the mayor voted for the bill. Every one of the black votes against us was cast by the machine-oriented blacks." Her conclusion was that gay activists should work to reelect Washington—and that they should back Sable's challenge to Alderman Hansen.[60]

Gay progressives found the incumbent 44th Ward alderman objectionable both because his support for gay rights seemed equivocal and also because he was part of the Vrdolyak bloc. The race thus pit a gay progressive against a longtime machine alderman. As one observer put it, "If someone ordered Central Casting to send over a Chicago alderman, the result most likely would be a clone of Bernie Hansen."[61] Before 1987, Hansen's support for gay rights had seemed halfhearted. As late as 1984, asked to attend a major rally for the gay-rights ordinance, Hansen had said "he'd try to be there if his schedule permits."[62] He rankled some gays and lesbians by explaining his support for the gay-rights ordinance by declaring that gay people in his ward were clean and orderly; others felt, however, that it was intended as the highest possible compliment from a man who had risen through the ranks of the city's streets and sanitation department.[63] In the spring of 1987 primary campaign, Hansen's machine background made some gay business owners reluctant to back Sable against an incumbent who was, at least nominally, pro-gay. As one gay commentator asked, would Sable be able to get potholes filled in the ward?[64] Sable's electoral strategy, for his part, emphasized registering new voters, inspired in part by Washington's demonstration in 1983 that unregistered voters could become a hidden weapon to help unseat an incumbent.

During the 1987 Democratic primary in the 44th Ward, gay issues were widely recognized, for the first time, as central to deciding a particular race and the geographic distribution of gay votes was articulated as an element of campaign strategy. Sable's margins on the day of the primary were highly concentrated in the middle section of the ward—in densely populated apartment buildings located near gay bars. The middle portion of the ward voted for Sable, as indicated by a diagram produced by Sable's campaign staff after the election.[65] This area, in the words of the progressive, Boston-based magazine *Gay Community News*, was "heavily populated by yuppies, lesbians/gay men and people of color." Sable's largest margins came in a group of precincts, centered on the intersection of Halsted and Cornelia, where gay people and renters were concentrated. Hansen showed a slight lead in most of the wealthier, and less gay-dominated, lakefront precincts, and racked up significant margins in the western portion of the ward. There, according to one journalist, "Many probably turned out to vote specifically against mayoral incumbent Harold Washington, a Black liberal, but stayed to vote against Sable as well."[66] That this campaign coincided with Washington's reelection, in which lakefront liberals again proved critical, helped cement the notion that the 44th Ward as a whole, and its eastern precincts in particular, could serve as a proxy, however imperfect, for the gay vote citywide.

Though Sable was defeated, the margin was so close that the election compelled a dramatic political transformation in Hansen, the incumbent. As Joe Alongi, a member of Sable's campaign staff, explained, "At city hall they're amazed that a 'queer' almost beat Bernie Hansen. Very few incumbents lost in this round of elections, and Hansen was close to being one of them."[67] Thus, in the season of Washington's reelection, gay voters in the North Side's 44th Ward proved they could play a role in choosing whether to vote out a hostile incumbent or elect a friend of the community. Sable's gay and lesbian backers succeeded in pushing the incumbent alderman to drop his hostility toward Washington's agenda and indeed his membership in the anti-Washington bloc. The alderman quickly became a far more effective advocate both for municipal funds to address the AIDS crisis and, especially, for the gay-rights bill. He was, one observer said, "suddenly aware of whom he was representing and what they wanted."[68] Hansen even attended the October 1987 gay March on Washington, illustrating how far this straight alderman had traveled politically.

Even more significant, by nearly unseating an incumbent alderman in the North Side's 44th Ward, the Sable campaign drove Hansen to become the first member of the Vrdolyak bloc to switch sides in the racially charged battle for control of the City Council.[69] The Washington bloc had finally won control of the city council in March 1986, as a result of special elections held in several wards redrawn because of a lawsuit by black and Hispanic voters who argued they were underrepresented under the new ward boundaries drawn in 1981.[70] However, it was the Democratic aldermanic primary in the spring of 1987 that brought about the first fracture in the membership of the hardline, all-white Vrdolyak bloc that had bedeviled the mayor. "The solidarity of City Council opposition to Mayor Washington finally will be broken today when the first of his adversaries formally switches sides," declared the *Sun-Times*, calling it Harold Washington's "first triumph beyond his old political base" and "his opening shot at consolidating power." Sable ran against Hansen again in 1991, but because Hansen had become such a strong supporter of gay rights in the interim, many more gay activists backed Hansen than in the first campaign.

The Sable campaign failed to elect an openly gay aldermen, but it succeeded in changing the trajectory of ward and even citywide politics. As a political matter, then, the "gay vote" had become complexly interwoven with the citywide white liberal vote. For progressive activists, the Sable campaign signaled the possibilities for gays and lesbians not only to benefit from Washington's "rainbow coalition" but also to contribute to it. At the same time, the episode highlighted the role of black leadership in the incorporation of gays and lesbians into municipal government not only citywide but also, and more dramatically, in ward-level politics, even in white areas.

"You Are Criticizing God's Own Handiwork"

Meanwhile, Town Meeting adopted more brass-tacks strategies to enact the ordinance than any previous group. First, the ordinance was rewritten to prohibit discrimination based on thirteen separate categories, including disability, ancestry, marital status, and veteran status. Second, Town Meeting members decided to stop accepting invitations from radio and television programs to appear jointly with antigay religious leaders to debate the issue, on the theory that such appearances only drew attention to the religious leaders' message. Third, they decided to stop trying to negotiate with the archdiocese and instead to lobby Catholic aldermen directly—eventually bringing in nuns to speak with the aldermen individually.[71]

The increasing centrality of gay rights to citywide electoral politics was demonstrated in the political scramble following Washington's sudden death in November 1987. Alderman Eugene Sawyer, who became his successor, declared that although he had voted against gay rights the previous year, he would now push hard for its passage if selected by his colleagues. For a black alderman viewed by progressives as loyal to the machine, taking up gay rights was a way to burnish his image as someone who could cement Washington's legacy. It was also a way to sell his mayoralty to white lakefront voters—and with Richard M. Daley expected to run against him in a spring 1989 special mayoral primary, he desperately needed a pitch to this constituency. Indeed, his success in passing the gay-rights ordinance in December 1988 became a major factor in his campaign for a full term as mayor.

Those aldermen who were on the fence or seemed persuadable also tended to be African American. This had as much to do with the larger context of Chicago's polarized racial politics as it did with the public meanings of gayness in the 1980s. In part, as gay activists were forced to become more sophisticated and strategic about their efforts, they recognized that black aldermen were potentially a bloc vote. "The thing is that the people that we had to move were the black aldermen," recalls Achy Obejas, a journalist and member of COGLI. "The white aldermen who were going to vote for us were already on board. The white aldermen who were against us were the same bloc that was against Harold. And they moved in unison." Though many black aldermen were not known as progressive, there was "nowhere else to go," she added.[72]

The mayor's committee was also unofficially involved in the push to get the ordinance passed. That many black and Latino aldermen were on the fence, and thus held the balance of power, made it necessary to recruit blacks and Latinos to lobby them. But such work was delicate and often difficult. Black aldermen were less likely than white aldermen to represent openly gay constituents. In reaching out to individual aldermen, the committee as a whole "felt that the delegation should reflect the ethnic or racial constituency of the alderman whenever possible."[73] This would require recruiting black and Latino citizens living on the South and West Sides to speak to their aldermen. The people of color who belonged to COGLI formed a Third World Caucus and wrote a letter to Peggy Baker, then Mayor Washington's lesbian and gay liaison, that there were "constant references to the diversity within our community" and recognition of "the impact that minority aldermen will have on our future." Yet, they complained, "while there is much talk, little information and even less input is being sought from minority lesbians and gays."[74] The need for queers of color to join the ordinance push made some feel they were being asked only to accommodate preexisting political goals, not for their input in shaping new ones.

The two Latino aldermen were both viewed as swing votes as well. One was Luis Gutiérrez, who had been elected in a bitter primary fight between two Latino candidates to represent a new majority-Latino district, drawn in 1986 by court order, and who quite publicly became a swing vote on gay rights because there were many evangelical churches in his ward.[75] "We were all shocked when Louie said he wasn't sure he wasn't gonna vote for it," recalled Obejas, "because his ward was full of gay people and he was so comfortable with gay people that it seemed stunning that there was any question." Alderman Chuy Garcia, for his part, "had to be hauled in and sort of beaten by the union people who had historically supported him," and told he had no choice but to vote for the ordinance, Obejas recalls.[76] Gay Latinos who were acquainted with them made a point of coming out to these two aldermen, even if they did not live in their wards.[77] In the end, both voted for the ordinance.

Activists had difficulty identifying black gay people living in some of the African American wards, all of which were on the South and West Sides. Gayness was, as we have seen, increasingly associated specifically with affluent areas on the North Side, where there were openly gay lawyers, doctors, and small-business owners. The South Side had comparatively very few openly gay professionals. As Obejas noted, "Part of the problem that we had was that we didn't have a lot of people on our side who were black. Who could go talk to those aldermen? We realized that when we tried to appeal to them, that we very rarely knew somebody in their ward," Obejas recalled. When someone could be located, she said, "we couldn't always count on those people to come out cause their lives were in danger if they did depending on the ward. And not in danger like, 'Oh I'm gonna get killed on the streets,' but [it would] really wreck their lives if they came out." The very fact that there was no gay-rights ordinance itself meant openly gay people were not protected in the workplace.[78]

In the unsuccessful 1986 vote, three of the five female aldermen had voted yes, and two—Anna Langford, who was black, and Helen Shiller, who was white—played key roles in persuading their colleagues to vote in favor of gay rights. Shiller, who represented the 46th Ward in Uptown, north of Lakeview, was perhaps the council member who had the greatest degree of trust of both Washington and his inner circle and also of gay activists. She had a reputation as a left-liberal whose votes were cast based on principle rather than the horse trading, and she was a crucial broker and mediator because she was trusted by multiple constituencies. Her influence helped obtain the third female vote, that of Alderman Dorothy Tillman, an African American progressive from the South Side.[79]

By 1988, Cliff Kelley was out of the picture, having pled guilty to a federal bribery indictment the previous year, resigned, and gone to prison. Among the African American aldermen, Cliff Kelley's mantle as leading advocate for the gay-rights ordinance fell to Langford, who represented the South Side's 16th Ward. As a black woman alderman closely identified with the cause of civil rights, she was able to invoke the moral legacy and vocabulary of the civil rights movement to lend weight to her strong support for the gay-rights ordinance. She was thus positioned to influence the opinions of her black colleagues, as well as white liberals, on and off the council, and both the city's white-controlled press and the city's black press (whose influence had declined, as the city's major white-owned newsrooms began to employ talented black reporters).

In 1988, crucial testimony in support of the ordinance was delivered on the council floor by the Reverend Willie Barrow, a high-ranking official in Jesse Jackson's Rainbow/PUSH Coalition. Barrow's son Keith had died of AIDS-related causes in 1983. "Discrimination against any of God's children," she said, "means you are criticizing God's own handiwork." She reportedly supported the measure even though she expressed concern about "the veterans' protection provision" in the legislation, "which she feared would slight women and racial minorities." Barrow delivered "one of the strongest affirmations of the ordinance," the *Tribune* reported.[80] With her unquestioned spiritual authority and her earthly ties to South Side political power brokers, Barrow helped make gay equality a cause for which some council members could feel comfortable casting a vote.

When opponents of the ordinance, too, chose African Americans to represent their cause, Langford offered important pushback. During the council hearings in the summer of 1988, Concerned Women for America sent an African American woman, Denise Whitehurst, to testify against the ordinance on the city-council floor. "I think it's important for all of us here, particularly we who are black," Whitehurst said, "to understand that while a person has no choice in the matter of race, the homosexual has a choice in the matter of his or her sexual orientation."[81] Langford had no patience for Whitehurst's remarks. "I am a human being," she said, "and I am a woman and you [too] are a black woman. Are you trying to tell me that we didn't need legislation to get our rights in this country, Ma'am?"[82] Langford's response thus helped to certify gay rights as a legitimate extension of the black freedom struggle.

"The City's All-Time Voter Registration Champion"

Although principle might have brought a few aldermen into the pro-gay camp, gay activists worked to appeal to their self-interest as well, through a well-publicized voter-registration campaign. In the year after Washington's death, a project called Lesbian/Gay Voter Impact, with Carole Powell as a paid organizer, registered 17,225 new voters in Chicago. About 150 people were trained as volunteer deputy registrars. In 50 heavily gay precincts in the 44th, 46th, 48th, and 50th Wards, the project sponsored informational leafleting that contributed to unexpectedly high voter registrations in those precincts. Of course, no one could be sure whether voters, who registered outside supermarkets and El stops and on the sidewalk outside Loop office buildings, would later cast ballots in elections, and demographic information about those signed up was not released. Rather, the impact on the city council took the form of the prospect it raised in their minds of gay voters who would, on election day, cast ballots to reward their political friends and punish their enemies. Ward elections were low-turnout affairs, and wards were small, which meant, as every alderman knew, that a small number of highly motivated voters might well decide a politician's fate.

In choosing to hold a voter-registration drive, activists adopted the very tool that Harold Washington had used with tremendous effectiveness in the run-up to the 1983 mayoral primary and that Ron Sable had used to challenge Hansen. Lesbian/Gay Voter Impact was in part modeled on the Sable campaign's demonstration of the electoral power of gays and lesbians when they voted in a bloc. The project drew volunteers not only from those who had been involved in the Sable campaign and the earlier efforts to pass the ordinance but also from the organizers of the Chicago contingent at the March on Washington, as well as the Lesbian and Gay Progressive Democratic Organization and a new gay political action committee, IMPACT, which also raised funds to support the campaigns of pro-gay candidates. The effort was meant to put aldermen on notice that gays were watching how they voted on the measure and that they would seek to punish their opponents. The idea was to raise the potential cost in the minds of the aldermen of voting "no" on gay rights by drawing their attention to the existence of politicized voters who cared specifically about the gay-rights issue—while, at the same time, working to politicize and inform those voters about the proposed ordinance.

The gay press played a key role, as the foundation laid by Renslow's newspaper *GayLife* in the 1970s began to bear fruit. The *Windy City Times*, owned by Jeff McCourt, now prodded gay readers, week after week, to ask their aldermen to vote for the ordinance. Publicity from the mainstream press was equally important. Norm Sloan, a white working-class man who moved to Chicago from Detroit in 1984, briefly attracted a great deal of publicity in the fall of 1988. He had volunteered for the Sable campaign, registering voters, and continued working to register them after election day with a new group called the Lesbian/Gay Progressive Democratic Organization, whose members were mostly Sable campaign veterans. Six or seven days each week, Sloan signed up new voters, using a folding table he carried with him on the subway. "I was working second shift," he recalled, describing his nighttime job at a printing company, "so I could do things during the day downtown [during] the lunch hour."[83]

In September 1988, almost a year after Washington's death, the revised ordinance was brought to the council floor again. That morning, the city's most widely read gossip columnist, Michael Sneed, wrote about Lesbian/Gay Voter Impact, using Sloan as his hook. "It boggles the mind," wrote Sneed, but Sloan "has just become the city's all-time voter registration champion," having registered just shy of 3,500 voters since March. "He is currently logging 200 registrations per day," he quoted Carole Powell, the director of Lesbian/Gay Voter Impact, as saying, adding that she believed Sloan had registered closer to 6,500 new voters. Based on his calculations from election data, Sneed concluded that "one man, Sloan, has registered 10 percent of all new voters since March."[84] The gossip column got the attention of a number of the aldermen. "Aldermen who never fucking talked to us," Rick Garcia recalled, "didn't know we existed, came up to me that morning as I was going into City Council: 'I read that article today; were any of those people registered in my ward? How many in my ward were registered?' And I thought, 'Jesus.'"[85]

The floor debate that day was characterized by vicious antigay rhetoric by a few aldermen, both black and white. The ordinance's supporters came up short—though by a much closer vote, 26 to 21, than the vote two years earlier. Mainstream reporting focused on the opposition of the black aldermen. Alderman William Beavers, said, "In the words of the great Reverend Crawford, 'God made Adam and Eve, not Adam and Steve.'" Another black alderman, Marlene Carter, proclaimed, "We don't raise no sissies— we raise men." Hiram Crawford, the pastor and Moral Majority official, testified before the council that "sodomites eat human waste."[86] The *Sun-Times* ran on its front page a stand-alone photograph of Robert Shaw—a black alderman, who vividly and loudly expressed his opposition on the council floor—holding a Bible, while the *Christian Science Monitor* reported that "aldermen from wards where black Protestant churches campaign against the measure led fierce opposition at the last vote." To be sure, Shaw had offended gay Chicagoans, yet once again the media had given black antigay opposition a higher profile than it deserved. It had been George Hagopian, a white alderman from the Northwest Side, whose words spoken on the council floor circulated in the city's gay communities afterward, who had testified in great detail about his opinion that gays and lesbian were nothing more than "animals."[87] Invoking Carl Sandburg's famous description of Chicago as the "city of big shoulders," the *Windy City Times,* one of the city's two gay newspapers at the time, greeted the vote with a front-page editorial, "No Shoulders Big Enough for This Shame."[88]

The organizers of Lesbian/Gay Voter Impact, though frustrated by the failure, took pride that they had run the most successful voter-registration drive conducted anywhere in Chicago in 1988. Indeed, an internal report on the project noted, "The fact that every announced candidate for mayor in the upcoming election is actively soliciting gay and lesbian votes and has expressed support for the Human Rights Ordinance is compelling evidence that those seeking power concede the existence of a new force in city politics."[89] Gay activists thus redoubled their lobbying, examining what would be required to shift each of the votes they needed. Town Meeting's Gang of Four—Jon-Henri Damski, Art Johnston, Rick Garcia, and Laurie Dittman—redoubled their efforts. Garcia recalls researching which Catholic elementary school individual aldermen had attended, and arranged for them to meet with nuns from the same order.[90]

From late 1987 to early 1989, gay rights became a central issue in Chicago's mayoral campaign. In the wake of Washington's death, in November 1987, seeking to be chosen as his successor, Sawyer had promised to pass the gay-rights ordinance—*Washington's* gay-rights ordinance—which Sawyer had voted against in 1986. Now, as he contended with the son of Richard J. Daley in the spring of 1989 primary, passing the gay-rights ordinance became a test of his mettle. Between September and December 1988, when the ordinance finally passed on the third try, eight aldermen changed their votes from "no" to "yes," allowing the ordinance to pass even though the makeup of the council was unchanged. Four of the eight were African

FIGURE 22. Eugene Sawyer at Lesbian/Gay Progressive Democratic Organization.
Courtesy of Tracy Baim/*Outlines* and *Windy City Times* newspapers.

Americans, and Sawyer was widely credited with persuading these four to change their votes. Even Carter, whose language just a couple of months earlier had reflected a profound degree of homophobia, was swayed. Sawyer "bluntly told the cheering audience at the ordinance victory party that he deserved some credit" for its passage. He campaigned hard on the measure afterward.[91]

There were also four white converts that fall. Mayor Sawyer also took credit for the "yes" vote of another white alderman, Berny Stone—the same Jewish alderman who, two years earlier, had been reportedly influenced by Cardinal Bernardin's opposition to the measure. Sawyer claimed to have arranged a phone conversation between the alderman and a particular Orthodox rabbi in his ward, whose opinion Stone had told him would be decisive, and who assured him he would accept his decision to vote in favor.[92] The most startling conversion was that of Ed Burke, the devout Roman Catholic who had once invited Anita Bryant to testify before the city council. In changing his vote to "yes" in December 1988, Burke bowed to what he called the "reality" that gays were well-organized enough to exact a price should he remain intransigent in his opposition. Gay rights was fast becoming a nationally visible issue—and yet, in the famous maxim of the Boston Irish Democrat who rose to become Speaker of the House of Representatives, Tip O'Neill, all politics is local.

* * *

By catalyzing the gay vote, gay activists in the 1980s expanded the state antidiscrimination apparatus in an age when the federal government was scaling back enforcement of such protections. They did so partly by making the enactment of gay rights into a pragmatic necessity. At the same time, urban politics remained a male game, and it was largely by winning inclusion in that game, rather than by transforming it, that gay people won a seat at the table. Gay rights came of age in city halls around the country, where African Americans had achieved an unprecedented degree of control. Harold Washington was only one of a number of nationally prominent African Americans closely identified with civil rights who began to explicitly endorse gay rights in the 1980s as part of a broader "rainbow coalition."[93] Indeed, Washington's stamp on the trajectory of urban politics may have been less that he drove blacks into the mayor's office—a move pioneered by Cleveland's Carl Stokes more than fifteen years earlier and already undertaken in 232 other municipalities—than that he successfully formed a progressive multiracial collection that included white gays and lesbians.[94] Though he was cast in the role of "black mayor," a black candidate could not win a citywide election with black votes alone in Chicago or in most big cities.

It was Washington's 1983 mayoral triumph in Chicago that persuaded the Reverend Jesse L. Jackson, Sr., to mount a presidential campaign in 1984. Inspired in part by Washington's aggressive pursuit of Latino and white liberal voters, Jackson, too, became a vocal supporter of gay rights. In particular, Jackson railed against President Ronald Reagan's neglect of AIDS, noting that 25 percent of its victims were black, roughly twice the proportion of African Americans in the general population.[95] He spoke from the podium at the second gay and lesbian March on Washington in October 1987, by far the highest-profile politician and the sole presidential candidate to do so.

Yet for all the movement's progress in the 1980s, homosexuality remained politically radioactive for many people and in many places.

Shortly after Washington's death, the rumors about his sexuality burst into public view more spectacularly than they ever had during his life, when the Art Institute of Chicago exhibited, as part of a student art show, a painting of the late mayor in which he was depicted watering his garden while wearing women's lingerie. In an episode that Chicagoans would remember vividly long afterward, several black aldermen marched into the museum, removed the painting from the wall, and walked out of the building with it.[96]

After Ron Sable was defeated in 1987, he turned his campaign's energies into creating IMPACT, the political action committee that sought to elect gay and pro-gay candidates to office throughout Illinois. But here too the gay movement faced extraordinary obstacles to organizing as an interest group, as citizens and officeholders alike were reluctant to risk having their names publicly associated with homosexuality. In the spring of 1988, for example, when IMPACT sent a donation to a pro-gay downstate legislative candidate, she returned their $150 check, explaining, "I would like to request that your check be resubmitted in the amount of $149.00." The reason, she explained, was that contributions of under $150 did not have to be filed for public inspection at the State Board of Inspections, and thus could not be used by her opponent to tar her with the brush of being a gay-rights supporter.[97]

Big-city politicians, especially black and white liberals, increasingly saw political advantage in backing gay rights. For Eugene Sawyer, Washington's successor, the gay-rights ordinance epitomized the late mayor's unfinished business, and its successful passage was among the chief accomplishments he touted on the campaign trail in the 1989 special mayoral primary. Sawyer, however, did not reap the political benefit that he might have for passing the ordinance. Instead, he lost to Richard M. Daley in the heavily gay precincts of the 44th Ward. The reason was no mystery. Although the gay-rights ordinance remained profoundly important to many gay Chicagoans, they found less than satisfactory Sawyer's handling of another policy matter, one that, to many, felt even more urgent.

7

A New Disease Is Not Welcome Here

"JUST AS CITY HALL was beginning to recognize growing political power in the gay community," wrote Clarence Page, the *Chicago Tribune* columnist, "along came AIDS bigotry."[1] Between 1980 and 2010, almost forty thousand Chicagoans were diagnosed with HIV and AIDS, of whom about fifteen thousand died.[2] The urgency of the HIV/AIDS epidemic brought into stark relief the class and racial divisions in gay politics that had been slowly emerging, especially after the unifying enemy of the police was no longer present. First, the crisis forced gay activists to confront questions of economic inequality—resource distribution, welfare provision, and health care. Second, it revealed the fissure, at once economic and racial, that always threatened to divide black and white in the gay movement, but it had been temporarily patched by the need to cooperate in fights against the police and by the sense of unity engendered by the Washington coalition.

Gay politics, with a few exceptions, had focused throughout the 1970s on gaining civil liberties and rights-based protections grounded in sexual identity. Though these issues had clear economic ramifications, particularly in the case of job discrimination, the gay movement rarely raised explicit critiques of economic inequality, such as the wage disparity that women, including lesbians, faced in the workplace. Gay activists had not fully faced critical issues of class and racial differences within their own movement, but HIV/AIDS rendered this silence impossible. Even as it decimated the male membership of gay organizations, the disease put into stark relief the unequal access to social services and medical resources between white and black, affluent and poor. While intensifying antigay hostility, the AIDS crisis also hurt business in the bars whose owners often funded the movement.[3] And it generated a desperate need to raise money, in the process accelerating the gay movement's professionalization.

Although the city of Chicago made incremental steps in addressing AIDS, the crisis increasingly consumed the gay movement, and the second half of the 1980s saw the emergence of radical AIDS activism. A small group dating to the early 1980s, Dykes and Gay Men Against Repression/Reagan/ the Right Wing (DAGMAR), later joined others in founding Chicago for AIDS Rights (C-FAR), which disrupted the 1988 annual meeting of the Chicago-based maker of pentamidine, a drug widely used to treat the most common opportunistic infection in AIDS patients, *pneumocystis carinii* pneumonia, after the company quadrupled its price for the drug.[4] In October 1988, C-FAR changed its name to ACT UP/Chicago, adopting the name coined by New York activists the previous year—AIDS Coalition to Unleash Power—and joining what was becoming a nationwide movement that had gained momentum from the second gay March on Washington in the fall of 1987.[5] After Richard M. Daley was elected mayor in 1989, local gay politics was dominated by his bitter and confrontational relationship to Danny Sotomayor, a gay AIDS activist, person with AIDS, and charismatic leader of ACT UP/Chicago. In cartoons, speeches, rallies, and meetings, Sotomayor denounced the mayor's failure to fund AIDS services and prevention adequately. At the height of gay activists' conflict with Daley, Chicago police lifted the ailing Sotomayor by the neck during a sit-in at city hall.

During the 1980s, this new disease took a human and political toll just as city budgets bore the brunt of a conservative effort to shrink the public sector. In Chicago, the AIDS crisis unfolded not only in city hall but in the county's decaying public hospital, in fledgling volunteer-run organizations operating on a shoestring, and in municipal health departments and other public agencies already overwhelmed by cuts to social services. Though the crisis hit San Francisco and New York first, and hardest, by the second half of the 1980s it was clear that the epidemic was a multifaceted crisis for all large U.S. cities. The AIDS crisis so radicalized gay Chicagoans, and so reoriented gay politics around health-care provision, that not even his having finally enacted a gay-rights ordinance could redeem Mayor Eugene Sawyer in the eyes of activists deeply frustrated by the failures of his health commissioner.

FIGURE 23. Arrest of Danny Sotomayor during ACT UP protest at Chicago city hall, December 1989. Courtesy of Associated Press.

"Say That I Had AIDS"

For the first fifteen years of the epidemic, before protease inhibitors became available in 1996, AIDS meant large numbers of people getting sick and dying. The public's response to the emergence of a new disease was rooted in the sense that the disease was always fatal.[6] In the early years, the most common opportunistic infection, present in 64 percent of Chicago's AIDS patients through the end of 1985, was *pneumocystis carinii* pneumonia, which often required the use of a mechanical ventilator to relieve the symptoms.[7] A nurse with years of experience reported that she burned out on working in the medical intensive-care unit at Cook County Hospital, where inpatients with AIDS were concentrated. "It is the most horrible death. It's hideous," she said, describing the difficulty of caring for patients with end-stage disease who needed ventilators to breathe. "There were some nights when I would feel as if I was doing nothing more than torturing them. I wished that what I was doing to them would make them better—I was wishing that I didn't have to suction them and cause them pain, even though I had to, to take out the secretions so they could breathe."[8] Interviewed on 47th Street, on the city's South Side, one heroin addict who had been shooting up for decades said that, although he didn't fear dying itself, "I'm afraid of the way I'm gonna die, and I don't want to die from no AIDS."[9] Everyone diagnosed with AIDS was forced to confront the likelihood of a gradual decline in his or her immune system followed by death from an opportunistic illness.

The fact that there was not one but two common means of transmission —each with strong and highly stigmatizing behavioral connotations, and yet medically indistinguishable—profoundly shaped the racial, sexual, and class politics of the epidemic. In Chicago, as in the other large cities affected by the crisis, men who had sex with other men, many of whom understood themselves to be gay, made up a large majority of cases. A second group of cases was intravenous drug users, a majority of whom were poor and either African American or Hispanic. City surveillance data showed that white men living on the North Side, and concentrated in and around the lakefront Lakeview neighborhood, made up the largest cluster of HIV and AIDS diagnoses, while African Americans living on the South Side made up the second-largest cluster. The two hospitals where the most AIDS diagnoses occurred in the early years were Cook County Hospital, the public hospital serving the largely black and Hispanic poor and uninsured, followed closely by St. Joseph Hospital in Lincoln Park, because of its proximity to the Lakeview gay enclave.[10] By 1987, gay people of color made up fully 70 percent of AIDS patients at Cook County, according to the doctor who founded the first AIDS clinic there, Renslow Sherer.[11]

Because it was lethal, AIDS added a new layer of even higher-stakes decisions about self-disclosure. One of the most painful dimensions of the epidemic was the rejection many people with AIDS experienced from family members. Some parents and relatives refused to see or care for their children or loved ones who were dying; others were more accepting but concealed some or all information about their illness from others, or from themselves. When Harold Washington's 37-year-old chief of staff died in May 1985 after a brief hospitalization, for example, it was reported that he died "of complications resulting from pneumonia."[12] One Chicago man wrote in his last will and testament, "It is imperative that the word AIDS be printed in my obituary. If I die from some other unrelated cause, say that I had AIDS."[13] The early years of HIV/AIDS added another strand to the growing bundle of cultural markers that signified homosexuality as an element of the urban landscape while simultaneously reinforcing its whiteness.

Particular shades of stigma and political powerlessness were attached to these "risk groups." Intravenous drug use was more visible in black neighborhoods and more familiar to many African American Chicagoans than to middle-class whites. One black gay activist told a National Public Radio interviewer in 1989 about a joke he said had circulated in black communities: "The bad news is I have AIDS, the good news is I'm an IV drug user."[14] The political scientist Cathy Cohen opened her pathbreaking book about AIDS and black politics by telling the story of a young man who found it easier to tell his family that he was an injection drug user than the truth, which was that he was gay.[15] Disclosing one's HIV status or AIDS diagnosis was risky for everyone, but it was not always risky in the same way.

In cities like Chicago, with large numbers of both blacks and gays, the news media reinforced this subjective framing by almost constantly conflating race with risk groups: whites who had HIV/AIDS were gay, while blacks were drug users. In Chicago, more than 80 percent of AIDS cases in African Americans that were reported to the health department through mid-1987 were attributed to sexual transmission between men; while there are serious limitations to these data, they nonetheless point out that the conflation is flawed as well.[16] Some of these men identified as gay, while others did not. Nationwide, although the conflation was less of a distortion of the underlying epidemiological reality than it was in Chicago, sex between men was "the predominant AIDS risk category among black and Latino males, accounting for 45 and 47 percent of cases respectively," according to the Centers for Disease Control and Prevention (CDC) surveillance data through 1990, accounting for more transmissions in this population than shared needles.[17]

For different reasons, many actors—not only white heterosexual reporters but also black gays and lesbians, black heterosexuals, and white gays—engaged in this sleight of hand. Black neighborhood newspapers described blacks as "a high-risk group, especially in the category of IV drug users, women, and children." That statement was partially true; blacks, especially black women, were overrepresented among those contracting the virus through shared needles, and later through heterosexual sex. Chicago's health department conflated race with risk group in a request for proposals in 1988, making reference to "the growing number of AIDS cases and the ically that "in actuality" a large majority of both Hispanic and African

American people diagnosed with AIDS had contracted it through "homo-

The focus on white gay men in the coastal meccas in existing accounts of the early AIDS crisis reflects not simply scholarly inattention to African Americans but also the fact that blacks were less likely to identify politically as gay. The immense toll on the lives of queers of color has, as a result, been largely neglected. Many of the epidemic's victims of all races died amid their family members, embedded in local networks and traditions of caregiving, but this may have been more the case among urban blacks than among other groups. Although there were visible gays and lesbians in the South Side, the premise of the gay-liberation movement that preferring same-sex intimacy should lead to adopting a gay identity, and risking one's family ties by disclosing that identity to relatives, had not achieved the same popularity in America's hypersegregated urban black communities as among whites.

"A Federal War on the Cities"

An Early Frost, the first feature film on the subject of AIDS, which centered on a gay couple living in Chicago and was broadcast on NBC in November of 1985, depicts a heartbreaking scene involving fearful paramedics. To be sure, the Windy City was less hard hit by the AIDS crisis than the two or three cities with which AIDS is most associated. "No one knows how fast AIDS infections are spreading in Chicago," wrote a reporter in late 1985, two months after the death of movie star Rock Hudson drew the nation's attention to the crisis, "but the city appears to be about two to three years behind New York and San Francisco."[19] By the end of that year, fewer than three hundred cases of AIDS had been reported to the local health department.[20] The mainstream press increasingly and anxiously reported on the financial impact of AIDS on the public sector, in terms that reflected Reagan's attack on the welfare state.[21] Newspaper editorials argued that those with a deadly disease should not be protected from an insurance marketplace to which the general public remained subject.[22] In the 1980s, most people with AIDS died in hospitals—often in public hospitals in an era when these institutions faced a profound budgetary crisis. From the beginning, AIDS was an expensive disease that revealed the weaknesses of the U.S. health-care system. "Because of the complex, multiorgan involvement in AIDS, the cost of care was high—double that of other infectious diseases," according to one medical historian.[23]

In ways large and small, the politics of AIDS often came down to money and access to resources. No city illustrates better than Chicago the convergence between AIDS and the Reagan administration's huge cuts in aid to urban areas. "We are facing a federal war on the cities," declared Harold Washington in a 1986 speech to business leaders, "that is going to be harder on us here in Chicago than any war ever waged by a foreign power."[24] For many middle-class gay men, AIDS rapidly drained their savings, sooner or later cost them their jobs, and led their insurance companies to cancel their coverage.[25] It forced those who were sick to come out to family members, coworkers, and friends, thus risking the possibility of isolation. The AIDS crisis made middle-class people, once they got sick and could not work, suddenly poor, and it left the already poor and marginalized desperate for already limited public services. Strikingly, by mid-1987, 70 percent of patients with AIDS treated at the gay-run Howard Brown Memorial Clinic, the city's largest provider of outpatient AIDS services, lived only on Social Security and public assistance.[26] As the number of people with AIDS began to rise sharply in the second half of the 1980s, the crisis strained existing public resources, creating an especially severe need for housing.

In Chicago, the largest number of deaths attributed to AIDS occurred at the sole public hospital—Cook County Hospital, often called "County," a sprawling, deteriorating complex on the West Side. County had long taken uninsured patients, many of them African Americans, that other private hospitals would not accept. Renslow Sherer, a doctor at County who went on to become Chicago's best-known AIDS specialist, believes he saw his first AIDS patient there, in 1982: a young black gay man "who could no longer do his daily six-mile run."[27] In 1983, Sherer cofounded the city's first AIDS clinic, located at County, together with a colleague, Ron Sable, who was openly gay (and who would later die of AIDS). Sherer recalled being told by hospital administrators, "A new disease is not welcome here. There's not enough space for the ones we've already got, and there are too few resources." Sable and Sherer's clinic initially operated on Thursday mornings, but remained constrained by the financial pressures County faced.[28] By 1992, the hospital was treating fully one-third of all people with

AIDS or HIV in Illinois.[29] The director of County's trauma unit reported, at about this same time, that almost 5 percent of the hospital's overall patient population, and 10 percent of trauma patients requiring surgery, were HIV-positive.[30]

The urban experience of AIDS unfolded not only in the world of politics and public policy but in the fabric of daily life. Not long after taking a job as a housekeeper at Cook County Hospital, Jewell Jenkins, an African American woman and a lifelong resident of the South Side, realized she could switch to a coveted day shift if she volunteered to work on the AIDS ward. "At the time, nobody wanted to work up there," she said. She found the ward a rewarding place to work. Her tendency to befriend the patients repeatedly got her in trouble, however. She had become especially close to one young gay man with AIDS who had spent six months as an inpatient on the ward and whose parents had rejected him because he was gay. "Nobody came up to see him, nobody wanted to be bothered with him." Jenkins talked with him and brought him food, books, and cigarettes from home, but her supervisors drew the line when she took him on an illicit wheelchair trip around the hospital's outdoor campus. "All I did was put him in the wheelchair, took him downstairs, and rolled him around the complex," recalled Jenkins. "I don't know exactly who told." Jenkins was reprimanded and suspended for three days. Later, Jenkins recalled, she found out her nephew had AIDS and she was in a position to offer assistance that other family members could not. "It gave me a chance to be close to him," she said.[31] Jenkins's story offers a metaphor for a crisis that wove together strands of devastating stigma and unexpected intimacies, and created a micropolitics of coming out that rippled across the political landscape.

"Volunteering Is a Sign of Status"

The AIDS crisis had significant economic repercussions for the gay movement. In addition to exposing the cleavages of race and class within the movement, the needs of the sick and dying created an urgent need for fund raising. Gay bar and bathhouse owners, long crucial to funding gay organizations, faced intensifying antigay hostility from their neighbors, even as they struggled as patronage declined.[32] Gay organizations thus began to compete with AIDS organizations for private funding that grew scarcer as more men became sick, lost their jobs, and died.[33] The crisis also produced a far more intimate relationship between the state and gay and lesbian activists, often in the context of the many overlapping bureaucracies that regulated and governed American health-care provision.[34] For a significant number of lawyers, doctors, and other professionals who were positioned to advocate for the public-policy changes that the fight against AIDS required, it was a politicizing experience. But because of the scarcity of resources, the life-and-death stakes, and racial and spatial marginalization, AIDS brought about conflict within queer communities, and it brought much higher-profile conflict with public officials.

This dearth of resources led to the emergence of a whole array of new nonprofit organizations devoted to AIDS, which drew on volunteer labor of gay men—as well as lesbians, who heroically aligned themselves with their gay brothers despite their own very low rate of HIV infection. The earliest of these took the form of "buddy" programs, which gay volunteers formed to combat the social isolation and family rejection that people with AIDS often experienced. These programs sometimes succeeded in serving queer people of color. In October 1984, at age thirty-six, Robert Washington, a black psychologist in Chicago who believed he had the virus that causes AIDS, was assigned to a twenty-year-old African American man with little in the way of family support. Over nine months, as the younger man's condition deteriorated, Washington became his closest companion. "More than anything else, he was quite afraid he was going to be damned to hell," and Washington tried to comfort him despite not sharing his religious fear. Eventually Washington took him to County, where he died shortly after his twenty-first birthday.[35] Often, however, buddy programs met the needs of white and middle-class gay men more successfully than they did those of queer people of color.

Fund raising became a major priority for the gay movement, forcing activists to focus to a much greater extent than previously on public relations. "Volunteering to help agencies such as Horizons or the Howard Brown Memorial Clinic is a sign of status," reported the *Tribune* in 1987.[36] Broadway and Hollywood stars played a pivotal role in raising funds to support AIDS charities. In the fall of 1987, an unprecedented fund raiser in Chicago, emceed by Angela Lansbury and starring Chita Rivera, Peter Allen, and Oprah Winfrey, raised a million dollars for the AIDS Foundation of Chicago, which in turn funded a range of local AIDS service organizations.[37] In 1989, Open Hand Chicago was founded, delivering meals to people with AIDS, mirroring a similar program begun four years earlier in San Francisco.[38] Still, these agencies found themselves stretched thin even as they expanded. As costs soared out of proportion to the capacity of local government to meet them, in a time of federal budgetary austerity, fund raising became the only means of ensuring that the many needs of people with AIDS and their loved ones would be met.

The most important AIDS service organization in the city was the Howard Brown Memorial Clinic. The clinic had been established on the North Side by medical students in the 1970s for gay men seeking a more gay-affirming alternative to private doctors and public clinics for obtaining treatment for sexually transmitted diseases.[39] The clinic was located on the North Side near the lake, in the part of Chicago most strongly associated with the AIDS crisis and with the greatest concentration of cases. There, an existing gay community-based health infrastructure responded to the crisis as it emerged.

And yet Howard Brown's location also came to pose a serious and permanent problem. The clinic served almost two-thirds of the AIDS patients living on Chicago's North Side, but just over one-third of those living on the West and South Sides.[40] As new service organizations were established in Chicago to handle the epidemic, they too were located on the North Side lakefront. For example, Chicago House, an eight-bedroom house for people with AIDS who had lost their jobs or homes, accepted its first two patients in a North Side lakefront area in February 1986.[41] "When an IV drug user is diagnosed with AIDS, he is often referred to a gay clinic on the North Side for help," said Curtis Winkle, an urban-planning professor at the University of Illinois at Chicago, in a 1988 interview. "If he is straight and from the West Side or she is a mother with a sick baby, he or she might not feel comfortable going there or have the transportation to get there."[42] Often the unavailability of appropriate health care within a reasonable distance from one's neighborhood made health care difficult to access.

For many black and Latino Chicagoans, AIDS was embedded in the problems of industrial decline, unemployment, poverty, and addiction. A decade of hospital closures had disconnected South and West Side residents from health care and treatment for drug and alcohol dependency.[43] In the 1970s and 1980s, as manufacturing jobs left the city, Chicago's South and West Side black ghettoes had grown increasingly concentrated, segregated, and poor. In the 1980s, with sharp cuts underway to federally funded social services, hospitals, and public-health programs, IV drug users tended to be among those least connected to any sort of institutions or resources. In many black and Latino neighborhoods, churches were the strongest community institutions. Shelton Watson, a black gay activist on the South Side, recalled that the funerals of black gay friends with AIDS varied widely in how their families and communities handled their illness and its source. "I went to some funerals where you could never tell that the person was gay." In other cases, a preacher might say, "He led that sinful life and he got what he deserved" and "he paid the price."[44] As Cathy Cohen has argued, the AIDS crisis shifted the most visible and urgent arenas of progressive policy innovation away from issues that black churches were relatively well-equipped to address, such as poverty, and toward others—sexuality, morality, illegal drug use—where they more often fell short.[45]

Despite these obstacles, black gays and lesbians organized against AIDS on the South Side, where the first gay mobilization against AIDS emerged not out of a community health agency but rather out of a religious group. Max Smith, long active in the Metropolitan Community Church, the national network of predominantly gay congregations founded in Los Angeles in 1968, helped found United Faith Affinitas, a black gay religious group, in late 1979. In August 1983, while in the nation's capital to attend a twentieth-anniversary celebration of the March on Washington for Jobs and Freedom, Smith heard stories about AIDS from gay men living in New York. On his return to Chicago, he and other members of United Faith Affinitas held a series of twelve weekly workshops about how to educate the gay community, all held in black gay bars. "It was every Saturday in September of '83 that we were at Foster's bar," Smith recalled. "Then the next month, in October, we moved to Martin's Den," another South Side bar. "In November we moved to Nexus North," he said, a popular downtown disco with a clientele of predominantly black gay men. "We said, you know, we don't know a whole lot about this, but this is going on in New York."

Sponsored by a religious group and held in gay bars, these first workshops to prevent HIV on Chicago's South Side lasted for two hours each. "The bars didn't have people there at 2 o'clock on Saturday afternoon, so they were cool with getting people in." After the workshops, "people would stick around and buy drinks, so they benefited from having an early crowd, we benefited from having a free place to do these workshops, and encourage people to come to United Faith Affinitas."[46] Another group of African Americans later organized the Kupona Network, a tiny South Side volunteer-based service organization that worked primarily in black churches—but it was riven by a dispute in 1986 over whether to partner with Howard Brown in seeking federal funds.[47] In black political circles, the Reverend Willie Barrow, the longtime staff member at Jesse Jackson's Rainbow/PUSH Coalition whose city-council testimony had been so crucial to passing the gay-rights ordinance, was perhaps the first to break the silence about losing a family member to AIDS. Her son Keith, who had grown up singing in their church choir, had moved to New York and become a modestly successful disco recording artist before returning home to Chicago to die at the South Side's Michael Reese Hospital in 1983 at age twenty-nine. As she came to terms with her grief, Barrow became an AIDS activist, speaking at a health-department event in 1988 about the "crisis of avoidance" among black clergy. "I know what AIDS can do to a family," she said.[48] When a portion of the NAMES Project AIDS Memorial Quilt was first displayed in Chicago, at Navy Pier, Barrow joined Mayor Eugene Sawyer in reading from a list of names of people lost to the epidemic, beginning with that of her son.[49]

"No One Died Last Year from Catching Dutch Elm Disease"

The effects of the failure of the Reagan administration to take seriously the need for medical research on AIDS have been well documented, but the nation's rightward turn during the 1980s affected the crisis in other ways as well. Reagan's sharp budget cuts to urban hospitals and social services also hurt the capacity of the nation's big cities to react—particularly at a time when they were facing the ongoing depletion of their tax base because of white flight. Ron Sable saw the effects of the Reagan budget cuts on the ground at his workplace, Cook County Hospital. Not long before his own death from AIDS in 1993, Sable said that "one of the biggest tragedies of AIDS is that it arose just as Ronald Reagan was being elected for the first time, and it suffered from the neglect—the grotesque neglect—of that administration and the one that succeeded it."[50]

Harold Washington's liaison to the gay and lesbian community, Kit Duffy, laid out the problem starkly in a 1987 letter to a top mayoral aide. Although the need for direct services for people with AIDS was growing rapidly, money from the federal government was available to the city only for "educational programs of questionable effectiveness," she said—a reference to the Helms Amendment stipulating that AIDS-prevention materials could not "promote" homosexual acts—while the state of Illinois was "earmarking most of its funds for antibody testing." Not only did the government fail to sponsor medical research quickly or react quickly to prevent the spread of the virus, but the conservative ascendancy in Washington also shaped the epidemic's trajectory in this more indirect way.

Municipal government, like its state and federal counterparts, fell short in responding to the crisis, even within the limits imposed by the Reagan administration's starving the cities of funds. Duffy, for example, noted that Community Developments Block Grants "and other funding sources the city might use have been cut," a reference to one of the most flexible forms of federal aid to cities, which the Reagan administration had reduced sharply in the 1987 and 1988 budget years. But Duffy also warned that gay activists were likely to "look at the difference between the corporate budget for tree trimming and that for AIDS, and remember that no one died last year from catching Dutch Elm disease."[51] The public-health emergency could not wait for regime change in Washington or Springfield; for those affected, AIDS made all else seem relatively trivial.

When a Chicago alderman proposed using vacant Chicago Housing Authority units as a housing option of last resort for indigent people with AIDS, the agency's director of security, Francine Washington, complained that its resources were already stretched to the breaking point. "I don't have nothing against AIDS patients, but I'm already in trouble with the rats and roaches. I ain't got time for AIDS."[52] Remarkably, she continued, "Anyway, these people need a clean environment," and she had one in mind—"like Lake Shore Drive. Put 'em there." In proposing that AIDS patients be dumped in the part of the city with the highest real-estate prices, she was perhaps expressing her resentment of the continual displacement of poverty and attendant social problems onto public housing. (It is true, though, that because of their susceptibility to opportunistic infections, people with AIDS need a clean and sterile environment.) Homeless shelters, agency officials reported, were "unprepared to manage the panic of staff and residents" should it become known that someone present was infected with the AIDS virus. Paralleling the Chicago Housing Authority security director's remark, the agency staff noted, "Shelters are also inappropriate centers for people at risk of opportunistic infection."[53]

The near-exclusive focus on the federal government in existing scholarship has obscured the role of municipal and state governments in shaping the policy response to AIDS. Just as at the federal level, political leaders at the local and state levels overruled public-health authorities in accommodating a panicky public. Some such stumbles were minor: Chicago's police department briefly recommended that officers wear latex gloves when coming into contact with persons who might be infected with AIDS, a policy that was quickly rescinded.[54] Of far more serious concern, Cook County Hospital, which depended on the support of the politicians on its board, many of whom were Republicans or conservative Democrats from suburban areas of the county, removed a doctor with AIDS from seeing patients, only to reinstate him following criticism from civil liberties groups and experts. In response, the Cook County Board forced the hospital to adopt a policy, over strong objections from the American Medical Association and the state's public-health director, giving patients the right to refuse to be treated by people who had tested positive for HIV.[55]

The biggest failure at the local level was that of the Chicago Department of Health. Even as Harold Washington was pushing gay rights to a floor vote in mid-1986, frustrations were mounting over his health commissioner, Lonnie Edwards, the first African American in the position, who became a major liability for the mayor's relationship with gay Chicagoans. It was reported in the gay press as early as 1984 that "'red tape' has kept the city from hiring two AIDS researchers, even though federal funds for their salaries [were] available."[56] Edwards became the target of protests by AIDS activists in Chicago over the next three years. Early in 1986, the mayor's Committee on Gay and Lesbian Issues complained to the mayor about Edwards, when, during his first press conference on AIDS, Edwards emphasized the purported risk of contracting AIDS faced by men who patronized female prostitutes. This was a risk experts believed to be negligible in the United States. More egregiously, he also discussed the possibility of quarantining persons with AIDS if authorities judged them likely to infect others.[57]

Gay activists could not do anything about Reagan, but they could do something about Edwards. Attempting to recover, the health commissioner hosted a conference about AIDS that brought his counterparts from cities nationwide to Chicago later in the spring of 1986. "In addition to being the most critical public health problem of our time, AIDS is primarily an urban problem," said Edwards, welcoming conference participants. The cities, he

Lonnie Edwards = Problem

noted, represented some 70 percent of the nation's diagnosed HIV infections to date.[58] But gay organizations escalated their criticism. By the spring of 1987, the city had failed to make payments to agencies, including the Howard Brown clinic, with which it had signed contracts to provide AIDS services.[59] Several gay groups demanded that Edwards resign, beginning with the previously marginal gay Republican organization but soon also including a gay physicians' group and the Illinois Gay and Lesbian Task Force (IGLTF).[60] The spokesperson for the IGLTF flatly said his handling of AIDS "borders on criminal."[61] The board president of Kupona Network—then the city's only black gay AIDS agency—wrote a letter defending Edwards and claiming he "has been very responsive to Black people," though the private letter of support was not echoed by any public statement.[62] By May, the members of COGLI felt the health department's delays in disbursing both federal and state funds posed a major and needless difficulty for the city's AIDS service organizations.[63]

In August 1987, Washington finally acceded to gay activists' demands and announced that Edwards would resign—but, in what unexpectedly proved to be a consequential detail, with an effective date six months in the future.[64] When Washington's sudden death in November led to a furious struggle over the appointment of his successor, the promise to find a replacement for Edwards was sidelined—and Eugene Sawyer, who succeeded Washington, asked Edwards to remain in the job.[65] By mid-1988, the health commissioner still remained in office, and reports of incompetence and mismanagement continued. Key staff members for the city's AIDS office resigned.[66] Even though Sawyer had managed to push through the gay-rights ordinance in December 1988, his refusal to fire Edwards, to whom he apparently felt personally loyal, became his Achilles' heel with the gay community and provided white candidate Richard M. Daley an opening to court white gay voters. Daley, the Cook County State's Attorney, denounced Edwards for his "lack of professionalism" on the campaign trail and promised to appoint "a professional" to the post."[67]

Before 1989, gay and lesbian AIDS activists engaged in direct-action protests more often against the state of Illinois than against the city of Chicago. Illinois lawmakers often proved more eager to pass legislation mandating testing and criminalizing HIV transmission than to appropriate public funds for health and public services. In 1987, Illinois lawmakers passed a package of AIDS bills, some of which activists called the most extreme in the nation in their infringement on the civil rights and privacy

[handwritten note] Man Shepard → took into his story → brutally murdered in Wyoming

of people with AIDS.[68] The chief advocate for the measure, Penny Pullen, was a social conservative and passionately antigay legislator from Park Ridge, a northwest suburb of Chicago and an associate of the antifeminist Phyllis Schlafly. (President Reagan, in a move that infuriated gay activists, had appointed Pullen to his commission on HIV and AIDS.) The package included mandatory antibody testing of all applicants for marriage licenses, hospital patients between thirteen and fifty-five years old, prison inmates, and people convicted of sex crimes; a statewide registry with names and addresses of anyone diagnosed with AIDS or who tested positive for HIV; a requirement to trace the sexual partners of anyone diagnosed with AIDS for the past seven years; and a mechanism for officials to seek a court order to quarantine someone with AIDS deemed to be at a high risk of transmitting the virus to others. The package also included two more-progressive provisions: financial incentives for nursing homes to accept AIDS patients and a guarantee that test results would remain confidential.[69]

Activists began targeting Governor James Thompson while he mulled whether to sign these laws. With a rising death toll, an indifferent federal government, and no end in sight to the crisis, gay activists grew increasingly mobilized and militant, especially in the aftermath of the Supreme Court's 1986 antigay ruling in *Bowers v. Hardwick*. In August 1987, six members of DAGMAR chained themselves to the fence around Thompson's North Side mansion, demanding that he veto the repressive bills passed by the legislature.[70]

Thompson vetoed the worst of the bills, including those that would have required testing all prisoners and hospital patients, which would have cost the state millions of dollars annually, as well as the tracing bill with its quarantine provision, the proposal gay activists found the most outrageous. However, he did sign a law requiring marriage-license applicants to show proof they had, at their own expense, obtained an HIV antibody test. (It was repealed two years later, without controversy, when Illinois politicians noted that it had sharply increased the rate of Illinois couples traveling to towns just over the state line, to towns like Kenosha, Wisconsin, where they could marry without obtaining the blood test.[71]) The following year, though, Thompson signed one of the first of many state laws criminalizing the intentional transmission of HIV. Such laws have proven harder for gay activists to resist than measures that impose new costs on strained public institutions—and they have served largely to reinforce existing inequalities in the justice system.[72]

"Daley Did Nothing at All"

At the municipal level, keeping Lonnie Edwards as health commissioner had cost Sawyer gay votes in the 1989 special mayoral primary. Sawyer was also hurt by the presence of another black candidate on the ballot, Alderman Tim Evans, who had backing from progressives who had objected to the compromise selection of Sawyer—a black machine alderman with few progressive bona fides—as Washington's successor. The 1989 race was thus the mirror image of the 1983 race: The black vote was split between two candidates, and Daley outperformed Sawyer on the lakefront.[73] Activist Rick Garcia said that gay voters "told me they couldn't vote for Sawyer because of Edwards. When your friends and family are dying, who cares about anything else?"[74]

Yet conflicts over city funding of AIDS services went from tense to explosive after Daley took office. The Chicago Transit Authority had refused an AIDS-prevention advertisement that showed a naked man with his arm around a woman holding a condom package, calling it too sexually explicit.[75] Referring to Nancy Reagan's controversial antidrug campaign, the city's approach to prevention was "tagged by activists and the media as a useless 'Just-Say-No' approach to the problem." More important, Daley also reneged on a promise to increase the city's budget for AIDS. In addition, members of COGLI felt they had been frozen out in favor of a hand-picked Daley adviser on gay issues, Nancy Reiff, whom they felt was his crony and unable or unlikely to represent the larger community's views.[76] As tensions between gay and AIDS activists and the mayor reached a breaking point, the chairman of COGLI under Daley, Larry Rolla, complained, "I'm tired of sitting at the bar trying to get the Irish boy's attention. I'm tired of sending over little notes and free drinks."[77]

Enraged over multiple slights, gay community leaders demanded that the mayor attend a public forum at the Ann Sather restaurant in Boystown, owned by longtime gay political activist and community leader Tom Tunney. The meeting was to be presided over by Mike Savage, the president of Dignity, the gay Catholic organization. At the November 20, 1989, forum, Daley read his prepared remarks, defending his record on AIDS—and reminded listeners of their frustrations with the health commissioner kept in office by the previous two mayors. He was taken aback by the depth of the anger among the several hundred gay men and lesbians present. Daley was incensed when he was publicly charged with using COGLI as a political tool. Rolla said he had been "told" by the mayor's operatives "that COGLI had better get on board . . . there was one agenda and one agenda alone, one purpose for our existence, that purpose was the reelection of the mayor." His voice shaking with anger, Daley replied, "I really object to the sense that it's just a political system. It's not a political system, I ran on professionalism." Repeating his objection to the "political" charge, Daley made reference to the death of his infant son, who had been born with spina bifida and died at two years old in 1981. "You know, my son died, my son died of an illness," he said, and as a result, it should be clear that he would be sensitive "about people's illness in this city."

An extraordinary and bitter confrontation followed. Apparently sensing that the mayor was on the verge of leaving the podium, Savage, the moderator, warned him to stay: "It's heated. Stay here and take the heat with us." But Daley did not stay. Seven months into his first term, having struggled mightily to distance himself from his father's reputation for corruption and patronage politics, Daley was visibly enraged by the charge that he had attempted to commandeer the nonpolitical Committee on Gay and Lesbian Issues to work for his reelection. The crowd of hundreds, nearly unified, chanted "Shame!" as the 47-year-old mayor, first son of the city's late political boss, stormed out of the restaurant. At the urging of Danny Sotomayor, who had become the spokesperson of ACT UP on matters concerning Daley, protesters the next day at city hall chanted: "History will recall / Daley did nothing at all!" They were joined by Laurie Dittman, a member of COGLI and one of the Gang of Four whose insider negotiations with aldermen had helped push through the gay-rights ordinance less than a year earlier. Referring to Daley's assistant, Nancy Reiff, Dittman said, "We do not need any house queers speaking for us," a phrase that at once disparaged the mayor's gay supporters and implied that, under him, gay Chicagoans were living in bondage.[78]

Within a couple of weeks, Daley capitulated to the demands for increased funding and all the other demands made by the protesters. And though AIDS continued to cause intermittent conflict for most of Daley's first three years as mayor, he gradually incorporated some AIDS activists into his governing coalition, in part by launching new initiatives, like an annual Pride reception, to cultivate gay community leaders. Still, a decade into the AIDS crisis, perhaps no American big-city mayor had a worse relationship with his or her gay constituents than Daley of Chicago. If AIDS activists saw New York as worse than San Francisco in its response to the crisis, Chicago may have been worse still, in part because gays and lesbians had less power.

Daley managed to incorporate his opposition to an extraordinary degree. He honored Danny Sotomayor posthumously, not unlike the way his father, after battling Martin Luther King, Jr., in life, renamed a twelve-mile stretch of South Parkway after him four months after the civil rights leader's assassination. In 1991, the mayor created the Chicago Gay and Lesbian Hall of Fame to honor the contributions of gays and lesbians to the city. Each fall, those selected to join the Hall of Fame by a committee appointed by the mayor were to be inducted at a city-sponsored ceremony in a public building downtown. "Ironically," the *Chicago Tribune* noted in covering the first such ceremony in 1992, "one of the inductees this year, Daniel Sotomayor, was known for his angry confrontations with Daley over what many felt was the city's lax response to the AIDS crisis."[79]

*   *   *

By the late 1980s, the gay movement's encounter with Chicago police no longer centered on raids on gay bars but rather emerged from militant direct action and civil disobedience. Members of ACT UP targeted not only public officials but also insurance companies and the American Medical Association (AMA), headquartered in the city. Over one thousand protest-ers marched on the Loop and held a die-in in front of the headquarters of the AMA, with several chaining themselves to the building's entrance, to protest the organization's opposition to universal health care and anony-mous HIV antibody testing; 129 people were arrested.[80] Another demon-stration during the annual meeting of the AMA's governing body in 1991 led to twenty arrests and a brutality lawsuit that the city paid tens of thou-sands of dollars to settle.[81]

Conflict between gay and AIDS activists and city hall died down after 1989, partly because Daley capitulated in the face of increasing pressure from gay activists and partly because the federal government assumed a larger role in funding AIDS services. Title I of the Ryan White CARE Act in 1990, presented to congress as a form of disaster relief by Elizabeth Taylor, a crucial lobbyist on its behalf, provided direct aid to the cities hardest hit by the epidemic. In its initial five-year cycle, the law directed funds to sixteen urban areas; Chicago's CARE award under Title I during the first year was $3.2 million.[82] In its first two years, the law provided "$847 million to fund

AIDS services nationwide," transforming the fiscal environment in which direct-service providers for people with AIDS operated.[83] The law's very name—Ryan White was an Indiana teenager with hemophilia, who became an icon of HIV infection among pediatric patients, hemophiliacs, and others who contracted the virus "innocently" through blood transfusions— reflects the strategy of AIDS activists to "de-gay" a disease that still mostly affected gay and bisexual men.

Despite the funding that the law provided, AIDS continued to cause racial tension in gay communities around resources for prevention and services.[84] The transportation needs of South Side residents who required access to AIDS care on the North Side remained often unmet. Linda Benson, head of the Kupona Network, reported in 1992, "Education and a strong service delivery system are our strongest weapons, and they are weakest on the West and South Sides of the city."[85] In 1994, assessing how the landscape of service provision had changed under the new law, researchers noted that three-quarters of people with AIDS who fell under the IV drug user category required transportation for health services under the act, compared with less than half of gay men with AIDS. In addition, these researchers noted, "African Americans and especially Hispanics/ Latinos are significantly more likely to have needed housing in the last six months than are whites."[86] As federal funds became available, some leaders of white gay organizations felt that local government officials were reluctant to spend scarce city dollars on "gay" agencies. The chairman of the Howard Brown Health Center said in a mid-1990s interview that he resented what he described as the local government's view of Howard Brown: As a gay agency, they seemed to believe, "they have more money and more resources, and they should support themselves—they shouldn't rely on city dollars."[87]

In 1990, for the first time, more blacks than whites were diagnosed with AIDS in Chicago, as has been the case in each subsequent year. More research is needed on how the epidemic unfolded among IV drug users and those who may not have had a gay identity but who had sex with men.[88] At the same time, it is clear that after 1996, as the introduction of protease inhibitors dramatically improved HIV/AIDS survival rates in the city, "the drop in mortality occurred almost entirely among non-Hispanic Whites," as according to one report.[89] African Americans continued for many years to benefit significantly less than whites from the new drugs, which could cost tens of thousands of dollars annually. Indeed, in the 1990s, black–white health disparities widened in Chicago even as they narrowed nationwide.[90] Access to health insurance and particularly to prescription-drug coverage became yet another axis of unequal distribution.

The problems caused by the spatial concentration of AIDS services on Chicago's North Side endured even three decades after the passage of the Ryan White law. In Chicago, the rise of HIV and AIDS in the 1980s coincided with the reversal of prior small improvements in black-white health disparities. The uninsured and those treated in public hospitals—who tended to be African American or Latino—received poorer care.[91] The federal government's belated decision to assist municipalities in responding to the AIDS crisis could not undo the broad effects of the nation's uneven mechanisms for distributing health care—and so in Chicago, as elsewhere, the "new disease" continued to amplify those very forms of inequality. Nonetheless, gay men would reach the apex of their political power in the wake of, and partly as a result of, that crisis.

↳ How did this come to be?

8

Flexing Gay Economic Muscle

GAYS AND LESBIANS came out of the closet in far greater numbers in
the 1990s than in the 1970s. In many places, openly gay candidates were
elected to office for the first time: Thomas Chiola won election as a judge
of the Cook County circuit court in 1994, though it would be almost a
decade before the city of Chicago would have an openly gay alderman. In
the closing decade of the twentieth century, politicians treated gays and
lesbians as an interest group whose needs were no longer tied to a broader
transformative agenda. Money became more central, in part because of the
AIDS crisis and in part simply because gay organizations reflected the
broader political culture of the age—a time of increasing economic
inequality—in which they flourished. The professionalization of AIDS service organizations and the influx of money required to cope with the
impact of the virus on gay male communities helped pave the way for a
more corporatist organizational style in gay politics. Federal funds began to
flow, after passage of the Ryan White CARE Act in 1990, into AIDS service
organizations. Competing with such organizations for a limited pool of
individual donors, gay political groups, too, began to hold annual fund-
raising galas and to cultivate high-dollar donors.

The gay movement's political failures also pushed its leaders toward
hiring professional lobbyists and establishing political action committees to
channel donations to pro-gay legislators. A tidal wave of new antigay legislation was enacted at both the federal and state levels in the mid-1990s,
after the Hawaii Supreme Court suddenly thrust the issue of same-sex marriage onto the national political agenda, and this drove the movement's
professionalization and created a sense of urgency. The federal government

and many states passed so-called defense-of-marriage legislation. In Illinois, Public Act 89–459, passed in 1996, for the first time enshrined in state law that a same-sex marriage was contrary to the public policy of the state.[1] Many state legislatures and city councils alike remained opposed to enacting pro-gay legislation that would protect these men and women from repercussions in the workplace.

Openly gay people, most of them men, won election in Chicago for the first time in the 1990s. After Chiola was elected to the bench in 1994, Larry McKeon was elected to the state Senate in 1996; in 2006 he was succeeded by his longtime aide Greg Harris. In the first decade of the new century, more were elected, including the first Chicago alderman in 2003. Strikingly, not one of the city's first three openly gay aldermen—two men and one woman—was notably aligned with progressive politics beyond gay rights, abortion rights, and HIV/AIDS. On the issues of taxes and real-estate development, their gayness, and their involvement with the gay movement, became seemingly immaterial to their representation of the interests of property owners. As a political constituency preoccupied with electing its own and demanding recognition from politicians at its annual parade and community festival, gays and lesbians continued to resemble the fading white-ethnic politics of the old Chicago.

In the 1990s, as gays and lesbians gained entrée into municipal politics, the "gay vote" was increasingly capable of shaping candidates' positions and electoral outcomes not only in the areas most identified as so-called gayborhoods, but in other liberal enclaves as well. Chicago's gayborhoods included Boystown, as the section of Lakeview centered on Halsted Street was known by the 1990s, as well as Andersonville farther to the north, a former Swedish enclave that had a residential concentration of lesbians and later of gay men. Although gays remained weak as an organized political force at the state and federal levels, unable to prevent passage of a newly codified ban on gays in the military and the federal Defense of Marriage Act, at the municipal level in cities around the country the gay vote became an effective political force.

The entrenchment of the gay movement as an interest group made radical dreams of emancipation from gender and sexual norms harder to keep in view. To the extent that it became identified with lakefront liberalism, gay politics increasingly reflected the city's growing inequality and pattern of uneven economic development. This shift was embodied by Richard M. Daley, the first Daley mayor's eldest son. Elected in 1989 to the first of six mayoral terms, Daley combined progressive views on abortion and gay rights with support for low property taxes, corporate tax abatements, privatizing city services, and tough new anticrime policies. Daley's policies resembled not those of his socially conservative father but those of other neoliberal white mayors who used the crime issue to defeat black incumbent big-city mayors in the late 1980s and early 1990s, such as Republicans Rudolph W. Giuliani of New York and Richard J. Riordan of Los Angeles.

As their wards gentrified, beginning in the 1980s, Chicago's lakefront liberal politicians, as well as the old-line machine functionaries who soon learned to emulate them, often supported race and class diversity more in theory than in practice, at least when it came to real-estate development in their own districts. The 44th Ward's machine alderman Bernie Hansen, despite having been the first white alderman to eventually join the Washington coalition in 1987, reportedly helped ensure the closure of the North Side's only black gay disco. Club LaRay was, in the words of the local gay columnist Jon-Henri Damski, "the first full-size disco in New Town to cater to black gays." He said, "Many black gays made the trek nightly from their homes on the South Side to the bar because they found the chance to dance and party on the North Side in a club of their own liberating." The club's liquor license was revoked. Hansen was open about his desire to use his clout to have the club shut down. "I want them gone," he told Damski, "because they have caused nothing but trouble in the ward." Damski wrote, "Club LaRay's customers, in the main, did not live in the ward where they partied and they could not exercise the same kind of political pressure and clout white gays do, when they party and live in the same ward." The efforts of Damski and ACT UP were futile.[2]

Where Harold Washington had tried to shift resources away from downtown and toward the neighborhoods, partly by trying to shore up manufacturing jobs, in Daley's city hall real-estate capital was firmly in charge. Real-estate developers, who had opposed Washington's desire to tax them and to subsidize economic development in the neighborhoods at the expense of downtown, were the largest donors to Daley's campaigns.[3] Daley benefited from the boom of the Clinton presidential years, increasing revenues but keeping city spending parsimonious in order to maintain low property tax rates.[4]

Even as the public sector continued to shrink, Daley embraced the new law-and-order politics of the 1990s. Under his leadership, the payroll of all city agencies shrank except for the police force, which expanded with federal support from Congress and the Clinton administration, as many big-city police departments did in the 1990s.[5] And just as the lesbian, gay, bisexual, and transgender movement has won unprecedented changes to daily life, tensions have developed *within* urban queer communities over inequality and policing. White gay elected officials have frequently responded to antigay violence by advocating intensified policing, a response that in many of the nation's large cities has led to criticism from queers of color and others who question this growing rapprochement between the gay movement and the state.

Building and sustaining gay institutions took money, know-how, and boldness, yet by the 1990s the ambitions and capacities of government had atrophied to the point that seemingly only tax abatements and streetscape renovation funds could be provided. Over the preceding three decades the North Side had developed a variety of gay institutions; now, with the Halsted Street pylons, came official recognition from the city as well. The emergence of visible and officially recognized gay institutions on the North Side lakefront did nothing to alter existing patterns of segregation, which played on and also worsened inequities in the availability of resources with which to respond to AIDS.

Daley courted gay voters through appointments, further gay-rights legislation, and significant symbolic gestures. To make up for his decision after his first year in office not to attend events on Sundays anymore—which kept him from marching in any more Pride parades—Daley held a Pride reception downtown on a weekday, which became a popular annual event. While openly gay employees of downtown white-collar firms likely predominated among the attendees, the reception also drew a wide variety of lesbian, gay, bisexual, and transgender Chicagoans. In 1991, soon after winning election to his first full four-year term, Daley launched the Chicago Gay and Lesbian Hall of Fame and presided over its first annual induction ceremony.[6] The idea came from his Advisory Council on Gay and Lesbian Issues, under the leadership of one of its members, Thom Dombkowski, and Daley signed onto it. Alderman Bernie Hansen of the 44th Ward, transformed by his near-loss in 1987 to Ron Sable, became a key advocate in the city council for enacting measures like bereavement leave for gay city employees.

At first Daley's support for gay equality seemed to many, at least by comparison to the benchmark set by Harold Washington, merely pragmatic rather than principled. But over time he came to evince a strong personal devotion to the issue. The council passed a hate-crimes ordinance covering gays and lesbians in 1990.[7] In the spring of 1993, a group of four gay activists, who had been dubbed by the press the "Gang of Four," appeared in a photograph, standing together on a city sidewalk, on the cover of the *Chicago Tribune* magazine under the superimposed text, "Gays and Lesbians in Chicago: Into the Mainstream" (see Figure 24). In the cover article, journalist Grant Pick emphasized the police department's efforts to recruit gay officers and its improved efforts to track hate crimes. He described the police raids of the postwar decades, in the process quoting Richard M. Daley as saying, "My father was not homophobic," and suggesting that police action was justified because "the public bathhouses were questionable—there were a lot of problems." Pick also acknowledged that "although the nation is witnessing a rising tide of openly gay and lesbian elected officials, Chicago has yet to see one such candidate lifted into office."[8] The Windy City was once again contrasted to coastal cities deemed more advanced in their embrace of gay equality. Still, progress continued. In 1993 Daley signed the measure providing bereavement leave for city employees, and in 1997 he pushed through the council equal benefits for same-sex domestic partners of city employees.[9]

Daley cultivated gay voters through outreach to gay business owners and an alertness to the symbolic. For the political scientist Larry Bennett, it was through his "appearances" [sic] in the Pride parade that Daley "most strikingly distinguishes himself from his father."[10] In fact, however, Daley rode in the parade only in his first year in office, in 1989. The decline of the Catholic Church and the rise of gay politics were reflected in the younger Daley's embrace of gay equality, which enabled him to cast himself as more than simply his father's son. Rick Garcia, one of the Gang of Four, who had become political director of Equality Illinois, told a reporter for the *Advocate* in 1995, "Clearly, the mayor gets on our issues not ahead of everyone else but when we have the votes." [11]

Daley projected inclusion and welcoming, but by a method with many drawbacks. Crucial to the shift from Washington to Daley was Latinos' realignment from being part of a black-led insurgent political coalition with white liberals to being part of what amounted to a white-Latino machine coalition. As Latino migration to Chicago grew between the 1970s and the 1990s, Chicago's Latino residents became increasingly concentrated in areas "in between" black and white neighborhoods.[12] Daley helped to establish the Hispanic Democratic Organization, which was fiercely loyal both to

FIGURE 24. *Chicago Tribune Magazine* cover, February 7, 1993.

him and to Democratic Party machine regulars.[13] In each of Daley's five reelection campaigns, Latinos and whites both strongly backed Daley against an African American primary challenger who won only majority-black wards. With respect to their share of public-sector jobs—long the central issue in urban ethnic politics, but one of declining importance as the public sector shrank and the courts limited the use of patronage—Latinos made rapid gains, while black Chicagoans barely held onto the gains they had made under Washington.

As we have seen, down to the parades, the rainbow flags, and the tavern keepers as power brokers, the contours of gay politics by the 1990s bore more than a passing resemblance to white ethnic politics of the early and middle twentieth century.[14] Daley, who did not have funds for schools and who secured huge federal grants to transform, through demolition, the city's public housing, found a relatively modest sum of city money to spend on strengthening his ties to the gay community. Like his father, he backed downtown redevelopment; unlike his father, he supported the privatization of schools and, eventually, the destruction of all of the city's high-rise public housing (of which the elder Daley had overseen the construction) without a serious attempt to relocate the communities displaced. He made extensive use of tax increment financing (TIF) districts to provide public support to private developers based on anticipated increases in tax revenues resulting from their projects.

"Homophobia Is like Racism"

Though black-led progressive politics moved to the margins of municipal governance, it did not disappear in the 1990s; indeed, it was notably central to the successful 1992 U.S. Senate campaign of Carol Moseley Braun. As floor leader in the Illinois House in the 1980s, Braun had championed gay rights, and her Senate campaign harkened back to Washington's 1983 campaign, bringing black and gay activists together on a scale that no other candidate previously had done. Braun hired Carole Powell, who had served as the sole full-time staffer for Lesbian/Gay Voter Impact in 1998, in a campaign fund-raising role. While generating an unprecedented effort within black-church networks to raise the funds needed to support a costly statewide advertising effort, Braun also secured a contribution of $6,000 from IMPACT, the statewide gay political action committee. It is a testament to the fledgling character of gay politics in the 1990s that this was the largest amount the group (or any organization seeking to advance the status of Illinois gays and lesbians) had yet contributed to any candidate.

Braun, who became the first woman in American history to defeat an incumbent U.S. senator, as well as the first and so far only black woman senator, was also the chamber's first to appoint a liaison to the LGBT community, Troy Ford. Once in the Senate, Braun compiled an extraordinary record as a backer of gay rights. In her first summer in Washington, she clashed with conservative North Carolina Republican senator Jesse Helms not only when she attempted to stop the renewal of a congressionally awarded design patent by the United Daughters of the Confederacy but also when Helms held up Senate confirmation of Roberta Achtenberg, the first openly gay presidential appointment. In 1996, Braun cast one of twelve Senate votes against the antigay Defense of Marriage Act.[15] Perhaps unready for the spotlight that her meteoric rise to national prominence provided, Braun struggled to manage fallout from controversial actions taken on behalf of some of her associates. Still, though she lost her bid for a second term, her 1992 campaign reflected a maturing gay electoral activism in which progressives and centrists agreed on a candidate in whom many saw great promise.

The rightward turn in the nation's politics, beginning in the 1980s, was mirrored in black politics to a limited extent. In Chicago, as elsewhere, Pentecostal and Holiness congregations grew rapidly, while the mainline Baptist and Methodist denominations more strongly associated with the post–civil rights black political establishment, stagnated.[16] Over time, Daley drew into his orbit not only the "patronage-oriented" ministers associated with the Regular Democratic Organization but also a striking number of "reform-oriented" ministers as well.[17]

The social politics of the black church was shaped by national policy priorities such as those that provided funds for policing, the war on drugs, and faith-based programs.[18] But none of these was as important, with respect to sexual politics, as the emergence of gay marriage as a political issue in the 1990s. Many black religious leaders who had long been willing to back gay equality in employment and housing found same-sex marriage harder to support, in part because the connotations of marriage made it easier to see gay issues as a matter of morality rather than a question of rights.[19] When a gay organization applied to march in the Bud Billiken

FIGURE 25. Black gay activists in Bud Billiken Parade. Courtesy of Israel Wright.

Parade, the nation's largest African American parade, in 1993, its application was initially denied. After a complaint to the city's Human Relations
Commission and a series of meetings, Chicago Defender Charities agreed
to allow a small group called Proud Black Lesbians and Gays to march in
the parade in 1994 and for several years afterward (see Figure 25). Approximately thirty-five men and women marched that year. To be sure, this
effort succeeded far more quickly than gay activists' attempts to join the St.
Patrick's Day Parade in New York City, but the right to march as a gay
organization in the nation's largest African American parade was hard-
won.[20]

The linkage of gay rights with civil rights was further legitimized in
1998, when Coretta Scott King, speaking at Chicago's Palmer House hotel
under the auspices of the Lambda Legal Defense and Education Fund,
delivered her most forceful statement to that date advocating gay equality
(see Figure 26). Flanked by Maggie Daley, the wife of the mayor, King
declared that "homophobia is like racism and anti-Semitism and other
forms of bigotry," adding that gays and lesbians who joined her husband's

FIGURE 26. Coretta Scott King at a Lambda Legal Defense and Education Fund
event in Chicago, 1998. Courtesy of Israel Wright.

Montgomery and Selma campaigns "were fighting for my freedom at a
time when they could find few voices for their own."[21] Seated next to the
daughter-in-law of the man who had so dramatically stymied her husband's
quest for justice in the urban North, King's words represented an affirmation of what had become by then the forceful support for gay equality on

the part of the urban black establishment. In conferring legitimacy on the gay movement, the widow of the best-known martyr of America's black freedom struggle powerfully rebuked the nascent efforts of white social conservatives to cultivate allies among black religious leaders. The historical moment was encapsulated by another gesture as well: Mrs. King's security for the event was provided by a contingent of openly gay and lesbian police officers.[22] As recently as 1991, Chicago's department had had no such officers.[23]

"Don't Equate Sex with a Plate of Spanakopita"

Daley reshaped the city in ways that prioritized capital and pushed economic and social deviance to the margins. Where his father had famously remained in the same bungalow in the blue-collar 11th Ward that he had built in 1939, Daley moved to a townhouse in the rapidly gentrifying South Loop, built under a new tax-increment financing ordinance passed by the city in April 1990.[24] The development boom in the South Loop and West Loop generated new forms of inequality and marginalized queers of color and others living outside nuclear families. The homes of single people living in single-room-occupancy (SRO) hotels—in both the South Loop and Lakeview—were either demolished or renovated into higher-end residential buildings.[25]

In the Daley years, Chicago became more unequal. The lakefront "gay ghettos" on Chicago's North Side, like other predominantly white areas, enjoyed a renaissance, as crime declined and real-estate values rose, while the metropolitan landscape became, if anything, even more economically segregated. Areas adjacent to the Loop and stretching northward along the lake saw a construction boom linked to the flourishing of white-collar industries. Residents of Chicago's North Side lakefront areas commuted to office jobs either in the expanding downtown finance, insurance, and real-estate industries or in suburban office parks. Even as the mayor promoted Boystown, the Daley administration supported the removal of poor residents from gentrifying neighborhoods, including Lakeview.

Daley embodied the new Democratic Party of the Clinton era that embraced harsh policing and punishment. Like Clinton, he made crime a signature campaign issue. He instituted random sweeps of public-housing residents' apartments for drugs, a policy Clinton praised on the campaign trail in 1992 and that was imitated by other cities. He also launched electronic surveillance by private contractors of crime "hot spots" in high-crime locations, and prodded the city council to enact a sweeping antiloitering ordinance under which 45,000 mostly black and Latino young Chicagoans were arrested in two years before the U.S. Supreme Court struck it down as unconstitutionally broad.[26] Like many big-city mayors, Daley embraced the so-called community policing promulgated by the 1995 Clinton crime bill, which enabled him to expand the police department without additional municipal expense by drawing on federal funds.[27] Although harsher policing received strong criticism from civil libertarians, gay organizations by the 1990s generally did not see reining in the police as part of their agenda, and single-issue gay groups did not challenge the policies.

In this neoliberal era, lakefront areas on the North Side, including the gay enclaves of Boystown and Andersonville further north, instead saw luxury high-rise buildings and high-end grocery stores built.[28] Black neighborhoods on the West and South Sides were shaped most visibly by the large-scale demolition of the high-rise public-housing projects built only a few decades earlier, rendering these areas what Lawrence J. Vale has called "twice-cleared communities."[29] As the urban scholar Jason Hackworth has argued, "Gentrification is much more than a politically neutral expression of the real estate market; it involves the replacement of physical expressions of Keynesian egalitarianism like public housing with a privately led segmentation of inner city space."[30]

In the face of the financial burdens that AIDS imposed on gay organizations, however, Chicago's gay community proved unwilling to accommodate Daley's imposition of austerity. Conflict over AIDS funding continued to be a source of friction between Daley and gay activists into 1991 and 1992.[31] Like Washington and Sawyer, Daley was criticized by AIDS activists over his choice of health commissioner. In this case—notwithstanding whatever symbolic distancing from his father's faith his 1989 Pride-parade appearance may have accomplished—the appointee was a Catholic nun, Sister Sheila Lyne. Given the federal government's hostility to sexually explicit AIDS educational materials, AIDS activists were skeptical that Lyne was sufficiently supportive of sex-positive teaching in schools; pro-choice activists were equally troubled by her record and demanded assurances that she would not roll back existing programs. ACT UP members believed that Lyne was unwilling to use the word "condom" or to support the distribution of condoms in public schools. When she received an award from

Daley, they distributed leaflets demanding, "Make her say condom before you give her that award."[32] In 1992, Daley's relationship with AIDS activists again flared up. ACT UP protesters were forcibly removed from the city-council chamber when they disrupted it to protest the deferral of an AIDS spending measure. Daley eventually relented by agreeing to a $2.5 million increase in city spending on AIDS for the 1992 fiscal year and also to a rollover of any unspent funds appropriated for AIDS from one fiscal year to the next.[33]

As gay agencies grew in number and the city began to study their effectiveness, it found their North Side location a problem. In a study commissioned by the semigovernmental Human Relations Foundation of Chicago, city workers convened focus groups to study the issue of race and ethnicity among gay Chicagoans. The study's final report delivered a moral indictment of the ethnic model of gay politics: "The greatest concentration of agencies and organizations dedicated to the needs of gays and lesbians exists in the North Side community area of Lake View. This concentration implies that many of the city's lesbians and gays, disproportionately persons of color, must travel significant distances to Lake View to receive services." The report was equally definitive in its assessment of how the Daley administration itself served the queer people of color who call Chicago home, saying that city leaders "fail to understand that this population does not exclusively live in a North Side cluster."[34]

By a $3.2 million renovation of the North Halsted streetscape, Daley perhaps worsened this problem instead of ameliorating it, given the recommendation that more gay-related services be located on the South Side. Certainly the North Side lakefront wards were more important to his political coalition than the predominantly black wards that he could expect to lose to black insurgent candidates. At the beginning of his third term, Daley's incorporation of gays and lesbians into his electoral coalition was given a physical shape. The Halsted streetscape project, in the words of one architectural critic, was "both hailed and denounced as the first permanent government-sponsored marker of gay community."[35]

The mayor framed the project as an expression of his gratitude to Lakeview gay business owners for their political support. In May 1997, months before the project was disclosed to the public, Daley invited about a dozen North Halsted Street business owners to a luncheon, where he announced the project. Rudy Johnson, the owner of the North End, a gay sports bar in the neighborhood and the president of the Northalsted Area

Merchants Association, recalled, "The mayor and the city had money and he felt it was time to put something back into Halsted Street for commercial development. He told us he would give us the city's architects and planners and we could have whatever we wanted."[36] Business-driven but with a civil rights aspect as well, the project's political benefits for the mayor seemed clear.

Contractors widened the sidewalks along North Halsted Street; installed planters, trees, and public art; and erected eleven pairs of 23-foot-tall metal pylons, decorated with what the city described as "colored rings which pay tribute to the gay and lesbian community in Chicago and to the rainbow of diversity that has historically been the great strength of the Lakeview community."[37] Funds came from Neighborhoods Alive, Daley's $800 million bond-spending program for infrastructure, which also paid for ethnic-themed street improvements in Chinatown and Greektown.[38] The even bolder initial proposal for Halsted had drawn enormous controversy, reportedly generating some seven thousand pieces of mail delivered to the city council—more than any other single issue in Chicago's history.[39] Much of the controversy revolved around the legitimacy of the analogy between gayness and ethnicity. A *Tribune* columnist, for example, complained, "The city spends money defining many of its neighborhoods, they say, and an ethnic enclave is the cultural equivalent of one based on sexual identity. This claim rings wrong to those of us who don't equate sex with a plate of spanakopita."[40] Daley defended this project in the face of homophobic opposition. "I won't let the homophobes run this city!" he declared.[41]

The city agreed, in the face of the controversy, to "tone down" the proposal—a step that for gays and lesbians brought associations with the experience of having to calibrate the manifestation of one's queerness in response to the notion that visibility itself would constitute excess. The two massive rainbow-decorated archways that were to extend over the intersection at each end of the designated stretch of Halsted Street were replaced with smaller-scale trellises mounted on the sidewalks, with a neutral bronze color and no rainbow. The gates would bear the words "Lakeview" and "Northalsted," branding the neighborhood but without specifically referring to homosexuality. "Northalsted" was the name of the neighborhood merchants' association.[42]

Daley's North Halsted streetscape project, completed in 1998, masterfully secured the loyalty of gay politicos in an era of gentrification while solidifying the incorporation of gays and lesbians into Chicago's political fabric. The Halsted Street streetscape project affirmed gay identity, inclusion, and legitimacy, and it also spatialized it in a way that linked gayness and whiteness powerfully and permanently. The gay man has long been imagined as the consummate pioneer gentrifier, who portends an upgrade, first in taste and later in property values. We imagine gay space as a highly commercialized gayborhood, site of high-priced condominiums, gift and tourist boutiques, and entertainment venues. Chicago's Boystown, like San Francisco's Castro district and New York's West Village, appears as the template of emancipated gay life, rather than more affordable gayborhoods, in places such as Jersey City, Hell's Kitchen, Jackson Heights, or Nyack; or North Oakland; or, in Chicago, Rogers Park or Logan Square. (Indeed, the classic lament has been that gays fix up an affordable neighborhood and then must move because it becomes chic, and thus unaffordable, as nongay residents are attracted to move in and hike property prices.) But to view the most visible gay neighborhoods as the natural and inevitable locus of gay residential concentration and to look to them as expressions of gay "difference" and evidence concerning its nature is ahistorical. Boystown's prosperity was not brought about by some innate trait of gay people, popular sociological accounts notwithstanding. Because Chicago is so racially bifurcated, Boystown is more strongly linked with whiteness than are comparable neighborhoods in other large cities.[43] Even if Boystown's propertied white residents may be less committed to white supremacy than those of other neighborhoods, they have disappointed queer activists who see the liberation of people of color, women, and LGBT people as interrelated goals.

The Boystown streetscape renovation project illustrates that gay clout was intertwined with pro-growth development policies and with the neoliberal fashioning of urban space through capital improvements that distribute only basic facilities to poorer areas and more elaborate developments to more prosperous neighborhoods. The rise of gay political power is part of a history of queer incorporation into municipal politics, as well as a history of building projects that leave intact the extraordinary legacy of racial apartheid, or even embed it in the built environment. The shift in the focus of lesbian and gay activism away from the classic focus on civil liberties and freedom from police harassment, along with the decision of the Daley administration to take up a portion of the gay community's political agenda, increased the visibility and power of Chicago's gay minority, but at a cost. Businesses in Lakeview have benefited from the city's economic

boom of the past two decades, while those in African American neighborhoods have been left behind.

The rainbow pylons very quickly became instantly familiar reference
points not only to people living or working in the area but also to visitors
from across the city and across the Midwest. The unveiling of the streetscape in 1998 received major praise from around the world. Christopher
Reed, an art historian, has argued that the project "extends the queer legacy
of the nineteenth-century *flâneur* or dandy as both creator and connoisseur
of pedestrian spectacle," building on a gay "renovation aesthetic."[44] The
British news magazine *The Economist* noted that the project "reflects the
shrewd politics of Mayor Richard Daley, who has shown a prodigious ability to add partners to his political coalition."[45] The upgrade to the district's
built environment enhanced Chicago's visibility as a tourism magnet for
gays and lesbians from across the Midwest. The rainbow pylons enhanced
Daley's reputation with gay business owners in the 44th and 46th Wards.
Equally, they conveyed a vision—to some, an inspiring and welcoming
vision; to others, a troublingly narrow one—of what it meant to be gay.

Ultimately, building the pylons was a one-time expense. Establishing
social services geared to the needs of gays and lesbian, however, required
ongoing fund raising. The agencies and services that developed in Chicago
in the late twentieth century were located on the North Side. The blame for
this lies in part with the fact that they developed after the neoliberal turn in
urban political economy, when establishing new publicly funded programs
became difficult. As a result, the programs and institutions that met the
particular community needs of gay city-dwellers were made possible largely
by private fund raising, not by the city or county. Gay community leaders
used the skills of raising money they had cultivated as a result of the AIDS
crisis. And they tended to locate those agencies in the parts of the city where
the funders lived, worked, and played.

Gay Wards, Gay Aldermen

So rapid has been the acceptance of gays into the political mainstream in
Chicago, in fact, that some have observed that the North Side enclaves have
begun to be "de-gayed." Will the gays leave what gay liberationists once
imagined as "*our* ghetto," now officially recognized by the city? In 2001,
undercover police issued citations to two men in the back room of Cell

Block, a bar in the Boystown strip, for engaging in sexual activity. The manager said it had been the first time in six years this had occurred.[46] More prominent, in a conflict that seemed rife with broader possible implications, nongay residents in a newly built condominium building near the Halsted Street commercial strip entered into a protracted conflict with an established gay nightclub, called Circuit, that they deemed too noisy but that predated their move-in.[47] As Amin Ghaziani puts it, "[T]hough gays and lesbians also have kids, the stroller was, and still is, a politically charged symbol of heterosexual invasion into queer spaces."[48] In Andersonville, a controversy arose in 2005 about a coffee shop's rule that the parents of rowdy children must remove them from the premises.[49]

The early 2000s saw the 44th Ward pass the torch from a pro-gay former trash man to an openly gay machine alderman. In 2002, Daley appointed Tom Tunney, a gay restaurant owner in the ward, to succeed Bernie Hansen as alderman—a notable first for the great midwestern metropolis. At Tunney's restaurant—still called Ann Sather after its founder, who sold it to him in 1981—many gay political and charitable events had been held over the years. Tunney had served as president of the Illinois Restaurant Association. A gay independent candidate, Rick Ingram, had already announced his candidacy to replace Bernie Hansen at the next election. The incumbent, however, made use of a common means of perpetuating the machine: Hansen resigned before the end of his term, allowing the mayor to appoint his replacement, thus enabling his replacement to run as an incumbent. (Eventually, more than half of the aldermen had been initially appointed to their seats by Daley.) Ben Joravsky, a *Reader* columnist and longtime Daley critic, suggested that perhaps "Daley wasn't trying to empower gays so much as use them as weapons against independents." Tunney "is being looked upon as an Uncle Tom," said Rick Garcia, who had helped orchestrate passage of the gay-rights ordinance in 1988. Still, running as the newly appointed incumbent and aided by his gayness as well as being a well-known neighborhood figure, Tunney won easily (see Figure 27).[50]

Even as he broke a barrier by becoming the first openly gay person to hold the position, Tunney was in many ways a quintessential Chicago alderman, a small businessman who won the respect of his community and then joined a larger citywide governing coalition. In his early years on the council, in addition to advocating for AIDS prevention, Tunney introduced several measures on behalf of gay Chicagoans that symbolically affirmed the city's sexual liberalism. These included a resolution urging Congress to

FIGURE 27. 44th Ward Alderman Tom Tunney after his election, 2003.
Courtesy of Associated Press.

repeal the ban on gays serving openly in the military and the repeal of a
zoning restriction under which venues for performances by male and
female impersonators were technically classified as "adult entertainment
cabarets" (though he noted at the time that the restriction had long since
ceased to be enforced). When California began allowing out-of-state same-
sex couples to marry in 2008, he proposed an amendment to clarify that a
couple's obtaining a California marriage license would not jeopardize their
inclusion in the city's domestic partnership registry.[51]

Tunney lined up with Daley on economic and labor issues, however.
During a 2006 debate over a proposed living-wage ordinance covering "big
box" chain stores, which would have made it difficult for Wal-Mart to open
its first stores in Chicago, Tunney was among the measure's most vocal
opponents. Though the council passed it, Daley vetoed it, one of his few
vetoes cast in six terms as mayor. In summarizing Tunney's approach to
ward and city politics, the *Reader* said, "Who he's not: A progressive gay

politician a la Harvey Milk—Tunney acts like a Rotarian. And a machine boss."[52]

Chicago's second openly gay alderman, James Cappleman, was elected in 2011 in the 46th Ward, just to the north of Tunney's. Unlike Tunney, Cappleman not only joined the Daley coalition but was elected explicitly on a platform of cleaning up the neighborhood to fight crime and make it safer for condominium development. In his first campaign for the seat, Cappleman had demonized his opponent, Helen Shiller, who had been so crucial to brokering the city's gay-rights ordinance in the 1980s, using flyers that charged that her strong support for public services in the ward had brought gang violence, graffiti, crime, and poverty into the ward.[53] Though he lost by only a narrow margin in 2007, Cappleman's "clean up Uptown" campaign worked in 2011 when Shiller declined to run for a seventh term. In both the 44th and 46th Wards, Tunney and Cappleman faced protests from affordable-housing activists who claimed the aldermen wanted to close SRO hotels in the wards. Cappleman was especially vocal in complaining about the behavior of residents at SRO hotels, even occasioning a protest at his ward office by demonstrators who believed the purpose of his public complaints was to shut down the facilities.[54] Each man has welcomed the opening of a Wal-Mart location in his ward—among the first such locations in the city.[55] In 2013, Chicago's first out lesbian alderman, Deb Mell, was appointed by Mayor Rahm Emanuel to inherit the 33rd Ward seat on the city's white, working-class Northwest Side that had long been held by her father—a diehard member of the nearly all-white Vrdolyak bloc.[56]

Queers of color have an ambiguous place in today's Chicago—increasingly visible, especially if they belong to professional classes, yet still marginal. Many black, Latino, and Asian American gays and lesbians, particularly those who are middle class, have carved out space for themselves that is partly or fully anchored in the gay communities of the North Side. Once a year, during Pride, as Lakeview fills with tourists from across the Midwest, African American and Latino queers from across metropolitan Chicago join the throngs attending the Pride parade. But, alongside the growth of the mainstream North Side Pride festivities, activists have also created alternative forms of mobilization.

Though Pride became highly commercialized by the 2000s, new and separate "outsider" Pride events also developed—the Dyke March and Black Pride events—that have something of the grassroots feel that the first Pride celebrations had in the early 1970s. Beginning in the late 1970s, many black and Latino gays left Boystown after Pride and gathered instead along the lakefront on the North and South Sides. In a low-key and relaxed summer evening of barbecuing and socializing with family and friends, queer people of color have created a grassroots and low-cost alternative to the event's commercialization and the channeling of attendees into Boystown restaurants and bars. Beginning in 1999, community leaders also began to organize citywide Black Pride celebrations, held on a summer weekend not coinciding with the North Side Pride festivities, and for several years these were held in Sherman Park on the South Side. The organizers of Chicago's Dyke March, created in the mid-1990s as a deliberately noncommercial alternative to the Pride parade, has been held in various locales, including South Chicago and Pilsen, a Mexican American neighborhood on the South Side.[57]

Several community-funded gay organizations strove to provide services to whoever needed them, even if their funders and volunteers primarily lived on the North Side. In 2007, the nonprofit Center on Halsted, an LGBT community center, opened in Boystown, and since then it has been the site of a youth program that provides important after-school services primarily to adolescents of color living in neighborhoods across the city (see Figure 28). The city contributed the land for the center, but its operating expenses are paid by an independent revenue stream, including ongoing contributions by the building's "retail anchor," Whole Foods Market. These young people, however, can only attend the program by traversing the city on a crumbling public transit system.

However, the center's youth programs led to controversies in Lakeview over race, youth, and crime. Because they were under 21, participants could not legally enter the gay bars on Halsted Street and had nowhere to go nearby when the center closed its doors for the evening. Some of these teens hung out on the street in Boystown and some gay property owners—and most of the district's property owners were white—called on the Chicago police to clear them from the streets. In 2011, the tensions boiled over. Nearly eight hundred Chicagoans crowded into the auditorium of the Inter-American Elementary Magnet School, two blocks east of Wrigley Field, on July 6. Over the holiday weekend, a stabbing incident had been caught on video camera and then circulated among neighbors in the adjacent Boystown district.[58] The following hours saw, according to one news report, "a debate so heated that it often turned into a screaming match across auditorium aisles." Some residents of Boystown called for an increased police presence. As the meeting began, Tunney confirmed a

FIGURE 28. Center on Halsted and rainbow pylon, 2007. Courtesy of Associated Press.

request he had issued earlier in the day for a special nighttime "entertainment detail" to be assigned to the 19th and 23rd police districts, to supplement the activities of beat officers in his ward; other measures proposed at
the meeting included "police call boxes, neighborhood bike patrols, curfew
enforcement, and, most frequently, more police on the street."[59]

At the same time, critics, other neighborhood residents, and visitors argued that more policing would create more problems than it would solve. A youth-led group called Gender JUST, made up of queer youths of color and their adult allies, called attention to racist comments posted by a Facebook group called Take Back Boystown. Departing from the views of white gay leaders, members of Gender JUST argued that these calls for more aggressive policing of the neighborhood reflected a racist backlash against the center youth programs, not simply a rational response to increased crime. To many African American and Latino LGBT activists, calls for more policing by white gay male leaders were complicit with society's criminalization of youth of color since the 1990s, when Daley pursued his antiloitering ordinance, and with the broader history of police repression of young people on Chicago's city streets.

Though media coverage reduced the 2011 Boystown controversy to a debate over whether crime or racism was the larger problem in the neighborhood, it also illuminates the changing dynamic in the politics of crime and sexuality. When many whites were drawn to a new politics of "law and order," white gay activists in Chicago had borrowed from black activists' challenges to police brutality. The gay movement's successes, however, have reconciled its white constituents to state power as it is most intimately exercised.

*   *   *

Gays and lesbians continued to become still further incorporated as a constituency of the Democratic Party. In Chicago, Cliff Kelley was the first African American Democrat whose commitment to prying open the door to equality for other groups—the political move by which, according to Harold Washington, "you ennoble yourself," and which was taken up as well by Anna Langford and Carol Moseley Braun—extended to lesbian, gay, bisexual, and transgender citizens. When a statewide gay-rights bill was enacted in 2005, still more evidence of the key role of black politicians emerged, as state Senate leader Emil Jones, the dean of the South Side's delegation and a former city sewer-department employee, pushed through a statewide gay-rights bill nearly three decades after it was first proposed. Jones reportedly personally persuaded two of the final three Democrats whose votes were needed to pass it.[60] Media representations to the contrary notwithstanding, African American politicians have continued to be the

FIGURE 29. Barack Obama at an AIDS Foundation of Chicago gala, 2003.
Courtesy of Israel Wright.

most influential backers of gay rights whenever they have come up for a
vote, including votes on marriage equality.[61]

By 2004, when state Senator Barack Obama ran for the U.S. Senate,
cultivating gay donors was an important element of his campaign strategy.
A longtime supporter of gay equality, Obama had attended his first Equality
Illinois gala in January 2001, on the heels of the crushing defeat of his
attempt to unseat incumbent Congressman Bobby Rush. Obama attended
along with several dozen politicians, including U.S. Senator Dick Durbin,
three actors from the Showtime television show "Queer as Folk," and 1,200
paying guests.[62] In 2003, Obama attended the annual gala of the AIDS
Foundation of Chicago, where organizers acknowledged his role in supporting state AIDS programs as chairman of the state Senate's health and
human services committee (see Figure 29). That year, he also joined most
of the other Democratic primary candidates for U.S. Senate in marching in
Chicago's Pride parade. The role played by gays and lesbians in Obama's
2004 U.S. Senate race also reflected the increasing prominence of well-
heeled gays and lesbians as Democratic campaign contributors. In 1992, for
a gay political action committee to raise $6,000 for Carol Moseley Braun's

Senate race (a relatively small sum even by the standards of the day) had been an unprecedented achievement. In May 2004, a single LGBT fundraiser for Obama's Senate campaign at a downtown restaurant alone netted nearly $100,000.[63]

By the 1990s, although gays had begun as a disruptive insurgency in big-city politics, gay men especially became not only powerful and respectable but even symbolic of economic and social privilege. Gay politics was increasingly identified with entrepreneurs and small-business owners. In a January 2004 interview with the longtime gay journalist and publisher Tracy Baim, Obama, then running for U.S. Senate, observed, "[Y]our readership not only has a lot of small business owners in it, but it also has a lot of people who may be self-employed."[64] Two years later, at an event for his wife's South Side aldermanic campaign, Congressman Jesse Jackson, Jr., praised the role of LGBT people in developing neighborhoods: "Without the GLBT community, it's impossible to develop an area to its full potential."[65] In 2006 Laura Washington, a prominent black columnist for the *Chicago Sun-Times*, wrote, "Speaking of money, the gay pride movement is a model for African-American activism," calling it "an annual showcase of the ferocious flexing of gay economic muscle" and suggesting that if this once "apolitical constituency" could be mobilized, there would be lessons in that transformation. "We have a lot to learn from gays."[66] Having latched onto black insurgent politics in the 1970s and 1980s, when African American politicians won control over city governments increasingly facing budgetary disaster, the predominantly white gay movement adjusted far more rapidly and easily than did black civil-rights organizations to an era in which campaign contributions played a more central role than ever.

In the first decade of the twenty-first century, the reach of gay clout continued to expand from city halls to statehouses and the nation's capital. If Obama differed most obviously from the previous postwar presidents in that he is black, the urban roots of his political career were critical to his perception of gay rights as an extension of black civil rights. He began his political career in a time and place where gays and lesbians were organized. It was during his first campaign for the Illinois state Senate, in 1996, that Obama's campaign faxed a questionnaire to the office of *Outlines*, a gay newspaper, on which he had written, "I favor legalizing same-sex marriages."[67] In the middle of a messy standoff with the incumbent, who was a progressive legislator in a progressive South Side district, he needed all the help he could get.[68] Later that year, Obama wrote on another questionnaire that although he had no legislative track record, he had worked with gay groups on a voter-registration project in 1992.[69] And that fall, Obama went to Springfield alongside McKeon, another new Democrat from Chicago, who had won election to the House as the first out gay state legislator in Illinois.

As America's first urban president in more than a century, the man that Jones helped put on the path to the presidency by giving him a prominent role in the state Senate, Obama accomplished more for gays and lesbians than any other politician in history. After announcing his support for marriage equality in 1996, a position that was publicized in the gay press, Obama gradually distanced himself from this stance during his meteoric rise to national visibility.[70] The 2004 and 2008 elections were both huge victories for Obama and crushing blows for gay rights in state-level ballot propositions. What had been a gap between America's liberal big cities and the national political debate became a chasm, as big-city mayors in growing numbers, including Daley of Chicago, endorsed marriage equality.[71] By the time he won the 2008 presidential election, Obama no longer publicly favored legalizing same-sex marriage. He became president-elect on the same day that voters in the most populous state reversed the five-month-old decision of their state's highest court to legalize same-sex marriage—an episode that significantly clouded perceptions of the relationship between black and gay politics in the United States.[72]

Obama, however, ultimately delivered for his gay backers. The increasing role of gays and lesbians in the Democratic Party coalition was reflected in Obama's high-profile announcement in mid-2012, as his reelection campaign was getting under way, of his support for marriage equality for same-sex couples.[73] That Obama reversed his position again in a televised interview moved gays and lesbians, particularly those who had watched Presidents Bill Clinton and George W. Bush swerve sharply to the right on gay rights—in fact, on gay marriage in particular—during their own reelection campaigns. Obama's willingness to do the reverse, to embrace same-sex marriage, symbolized queer clout. A key 2012 donor was the Chicago media executive Fred Eychaner, who served as a campaign bundler and was the largest individual donor to the pro-Obama "super-PAC" Priorities USA Action. In his second term, Obama nominated four openly gay major campaign donors, all white men, to ambassadorships.[74] For no other part of the

FIGURE 30. Vernita Gray (left) and Patricia Ewert with marriage license, 2013.
Courtesy of Associated Press.

Democratic Party base did Obama secure as many policy achievements during his first six years in office as he did for the LGBT community, despite
worries in 2009 and 2010 that he would not follow through on his campaign promises.

The nation's first president from Chicago has done more than any previous American leader to enact equality for gay and lesbian Americans,
ushering in a wave of progress at every level of government. When the
Illinois legislature enacted same-sex marriage legislatively in November
2013, after a long struggle, the bill's passage reflected the contradictions in
which gays and lesbians had vaulted remarkably quickly from pariah status
to an unprecedented degree of political incorporation. Marc Solomon, who
had led the legislative fight to preserve the *Goodridge v. Massachusetts* decision during the five-year period when Massachusetts was the only state in
the nation to afford equal marriage rights to gay couples, described Springfield as more transactional than other state capitals in which he had previously worked, saying that "lawmakers from both parties" had asked for

money in return for a vote. "It was never put as a quid pro quo for a vote, but Springfield wasn't known for subtlety either."[75]

Today queers of color, especially transgender women of color, remain underrepresented in the LGBT movement and in an era of increased gay visibility. Gay political empowerment has reshaped politics in the nation's heartland—and it remains to be seen how those gay and lesbian Americans who have acquired political clout will use that power. Perhaps no individual's life story more neatly encapsulated the shift from margins to center than that of the late Vernita Gray, who cofounded Chicago Gay Liberation in 1970 but missed the city's first Pride march in 1970 because she had to take care of friends who were "tripping their brains out." In late 2013, same-sex marriage in Illinois was passed with an effective date slated for the following summer, but Gray and her partner Patricia Ewert knew that because of Gray's terminal illness, that would not be soon enough. They filed a motion for an emergency injunction, asking to receive a marriage license immediately (see Figure 30). On November 25, 2013, Judge Thomas M. Durkin, an Obama nominee to the federal district court in Chicago, ruled in their favor, and the office of Cook County Clerk David Orr hand-delivered a marriage license to their home that evening.[76]

NOTES

Introduction

1. Oral arguments in *U.S. v. Windsor*, March 27, 2013, www.supremecourt.gov/oral_arguments/argument_transcripts/12-307_jnt1.pdf, 107–108; and Peter Baker, "Political Strides May Lead to Setbacks in Court," *NYT*, March 28, 2013.

2. Carl Wittman, "A Gay Manifesto, (1969–1970)," in *We Are Everywhere: A Historical Sourcebook of Gay and Lesbian Politics*, ed. Mark Blasius and Shane Phelan (New York: Routledge, 1997), 380–388, at 380.

3. Kath Weston, "Get Thee to a Big City: Sexual Imaginary and the Great Gay Migration," *GLQ: A Journal of Lesbian and Gay Studies* 2 (1995), 253–277.

4. "Sandi," interview with Sukie de la Croix, "Black Pearls," *BLACKlines*, November 1999, 26.

5. In the late 1980s and early 1990s, AIDS activists frequently faced arrest and police brutality during political protests, rather than during a night out at a bar or a walk through a cruising ground.

6. "Interview on Gold Coast Bar Raid, C.I., DSF #30, 9/29/67," box 10, folder 5, WS. The raid involved eight plainclothes detectives; seven patrons had been charged with indecency.

7. Kari Moe and Luz Martinez to Harold Washington, August 29, 1986, in box 4, folder 41, Community Services Series, MR.

8. Guy Charles, "A New National Gay Rights Platform," *Advocate*, March 15, 1972.

9. See Kate Sosin, "Hundreds Pack into Boystown Violence Forum," *WCT*, July 13, 2011; "Ald. Tunney Issues Statement on 44th Ward Crime," *WCT*, July 6, 2011; Sam Worley, "The Battle in Boys Town," *CR*, July 14, 2011; Joey L. Mogul, Andrea J. Ritchie, and Kay Whitlock, *Queer (In)justice: The Criminalization of LGBT People in the United States* (Boston: Beacon Press, 2011); and Christina B. Hanhardt, *Safe Space: Gay Neighborhood History and the Politics of Violence* (Durham, NC: Duke University Press, 2013).

10. David Sklansky, *Democracy and the Police* (Stanford, CA: Stanford University Press, 2007), 143.

11. A pair of op-eds appeared in the *New York Times* on February 10, 1978, arguing for and against "homosexuals as police officers." The case against gay cops was made by Samuel DeMilia, the head of the Patrolmen's Benevolent Association ("Homosexuals as Police Officers? No . . ."); the opposing position was argued "by a police officer"—a New York City cop whose name was withheld (". . . Yes"). See also Katy Butler, "The Gay Push for S.F. Police Jobs," *San Francisco Chronicle*, April 9, 1979; Randy Shilts, "Gay Police," *Police* (January 1980), 32–33; and Stephen Leinen, *Gay Cops* (New Brunswick, NJ: Rutgers University Press, 1993).

12. Tony Kushner, *Angels in America, Part I: Millennium Approaches* (New York: Theatre Communications Group, 1993), 51.

13. Community studies include John D'Emilio, *Sexual Politics, Sexual Communities: The Making of a Homosexual Minority in the United States, 1940–1970* (Chicago: University of Chicago Press, 1983); Marc Stein, *City of Sisterly and Brotherly Loves: Lesbian and Gay Philadelphia, 1945–1972* (Chicago: University of Chicago Press, 2000); Elizabeth Lapovsky Kennedy and Madeline Davis, *Boots of Leather, Slippers of Gold: The History of a Lesbian Community* (New York: Routledge, 1993); George Chauncey, *Gay New York: Gender, Urban Culture, and the Making of the Gay Male World, 1890–1940* (New York: Basic, 1994); Nan Alamilla Boyd, *Wide-Open Town: A History of Queer San Francisco to 1965* (Berkeley: University of California Press, 2003); and Martin Meeker, *Contacts Desired: Gay and Lesbian Communications and Community, 1940s–1970s* (Chicago: University of Chicago Press, 2006). State-centered studies include David K. Johnson, *The Lavender Scare: The Cold War Persecution of Gays and Lesbians in the Federal Government* (Chicago: University of Chicago Press, 2004); and Margot Canaday, *The Straight State: Sexuality and Citizenship in Twentieth-Century America* (Princeton, NJ: Princeton University Press, 2009).

14. Alice Echols, *Daring to Be Bad: Radical Feminism in America* (Minneapolis: University of Minnesota Press, 1989); Anne Enke, *Finding the Movement: Sexuality, Contested Space, and Feminist Activism* (Durham, NC: Duke University Press, 2007); Stephanie Gilmore, *Groundswell: Grassroots Feminist Activism in Postwar America* (New York: Routledge, 2012); and Beth Bailey, *Sex in the Heartland* (Cambridge, MA: Harvard University Press, 1999).

15. Two important exceptions are Jennifer Brier, *Infectious Ideas: U.S. Political Responses to the AIDS Crisis* (Chapel Hill: University of North Carolina Press, 2009); and Robert O. Self, *All in the Family: The Realignment of American Democracy Since the 1960s* (New York: Hill & Wang, 2012).

16. John T. McGreevy, *Parish Boundaries: The Catholic Encounter with Race in the Twentieth-Century Urban North* (Chicago: University of Chicago Press, 1996); Cheryl Lynn Greenberg, *Troubling the Waters: Black–Jewish Relations in the American Century* (Princeton, NJ: Princeton University Press, 2006); Winifred Breines, *The Trouble Between Us: An Uneasy History of White and Black Women in the Feminist Movement* (New York: Oxford University Press, 2007); Scott Kurashige, *The Shifting Grounds of Race: Black and Japanese Americans in the Making of Multiethnic Los Angeles* (Princeton, NJ: Princeton University Press, 2008); Jacquelyn Dowd Hall, "The Long Civil Rights Movement and the Political Uses of the Past," *Journal of American History* 91 (2005), 1233–1263; Nancy MacLean, *Freedom Is Not Enough: The Opening of the American Workplace* (Cambridge, MA: Russell Sage Foundation/Harvard University Press, 2006); and Kevin J. Mumford, "The Trouble with Gay Rights: Race and the Politics of Sexual Orientation in Philadelphia, 1969–1982," *Journal of American History* 98 (June 2011), 49–72.

17. For studies engaged with similar issues in specific cities, see Kwame A. Holmes, "Chocolate to Rainbow City: The Dialectics of Black and Gay Community Formation in Postwar Washington, D.C., 1946–1978" (Ph.D. dissertation, University of Illinois at Urbana-Champaign, 2011); and Julio Capó, Jr., "It's Not Queer to Be Gay: Miami and the Emergence of the Gay Rights Movement, 1945–1995" (Ph.D. dissertation, Florida International University, 2011). On urban civil rights struggles, see Arnold R. Hirsch, *Making the Second Ghetto: Race and Housing in Chicago, 1940–1960* (Chicago: University of Chicago Press, 1983); Martha Biondi, *To Stand and Fight: The Struggle for Civil Rights in Postwar New York City* (Cambridge, MA: Harvard University Press, 2003); Thomas J. Sugrue, *Sweet Land of Liberty: The*

Forgotten Struggle for Civil Rights in the North (New York: Random House, 2008); Heather Ann Thompson, *Whose Detroit?: Politics, Labor, and Race in a Modern American City* (Ithaca, NY: Cornell University Press, 2001); Robert O. Self, *American Babylon: Race and the Struggle for Postwar Oakland* (Princeton, NJ: Princeton University Press, 2003); Matthew J. Countryman, *Up South: Civil Rights and Black Power in Philadelphia* (Philadelphia: University of Pennsylvania Press, 2006); Andrew J. Diamond, *Mean Streets: Chicago Youths and the Everyday Struggle for Empowerment in the Multiracial City, 1908–1969* (Berkeley: University of California Press, 2009); and Beryl Satter, "Cops, Gangs, and Revolutionaries in 1960s Chicago: What Black Police Can Tell Us About Power," *Journal of Urban History* (forthcoming 2015).

18. Timothy Stewart-Winter, "Queer Law and Order: Sex, Criminality, and Policing in the Late Twentieth Century United States," *Journal of American History* 102:1 (June 2015), 61–72; Regina Kunzel, *Criminal Intimacy: Prison and the Uneven History of Modern American Sexuality* (Chicago: University of Chicago Press, 2008); Christina B. Hanhardt, *Safe Space: Gay Neighborhood History and the Politics of Violence* (Durham, NC: Duke University Press, 2013); Mogul et al., *Queer (In)justice*; Christopher Lowen Agee, *The Streets of San Francisco: Policing and the Creation of a Cosmopolitan Liberal Politics, 1950–1972* (Chicago: University of Chicago Press, 2014); Regina Kunzel, *Criminal Intimacy: Prison and the Uneven History of Modern American Sexuality* (Chicago: University of Chicago Press, 2008); and Whitney Strub, *Perversion for Profit: The Politics of Pornography and the Rise of the New Right* (New York: Columbia University Press, 2011).

19. Beth Bailey and David Farber, *The First Strange Place: Race and Sex in World War II Hawaii* (Baltimore: Johns Hopkins University Press, 1992); Martha Hodes, *White Women, Black Men: Illicit Sex in the Nineteenth-Century South* (New Haven, CT: Yale University Press, 1997); Martha Hodes, ed., *Sex, Love, Race: Crossing Boundaries in North American History* (New York: New York University Press, 1999); John Howard, *Men Like That: A Southern Queer History* (Chicago: University of Chicago Press, 1999), esp. 127–173; Rickie Solinger, *Wake Up Little Susie: Single Pregnancy and Race Before Roe v. Wade* (New York: Routledge, 2000); Siobhan B. Somerville, *Queering the Color Line: Race and the Invention of Homosexuality in American Culture* (Durham, NC: Duke University Press, 2000); Renee C. Romano, *Race Mixing: Black-White Marriage in Postwar America* (Cambridge, MA: Harvard University Press, 2003); Alexandra Minna Stern, *Eugenic Nation: Faults and Frontiers of Better Breeding in Modern America* (Berkeley: University of California Press, 2005); Michele Mitchell, *Righteous Propagation: African Americans and the Politics of Racial Destiny After Reconstruction* (Chapel Hill: University of North Carolina Press, 2004); Jane Dailey, "Sex, Segregation, and the Sacred After *Brown*," *Journal of American History* 91:1 (June 2004), 119–144; Susan K. Cahn, *Sexual Reckonings: Southern Girls in a Troubling Age* (Cambridge, MA: Harvard University Press, 2007); and Peggy Pascoe, *What Comes Naturally: Miscegenation Law and the Making of Race in America* (New York: Oxford University Press, 2009); Chad Heap, *Slumming: Sexual and Racial Encounters in American Nightlife, 1885–1940* (Chicago: University of Chicago Press, 2009).

20. Cathy J. Cohen, *The Boundaries of Blackness: AIDS and the Breakdown of Black Politics* (Chicago: University of Chicago Press, 1999); Russell K. Robinson, "Racing the Closet," *Stanford Law Review* 61 (April 2009), 1463–1533; Roderick A. Ferguson, *Aberrations in Black: Toward a Queer of Color Critique* (Minneapolis: University of Minnesota Press, 2004); Tavia Nyong'o, *The Amalgamation Waltz: Race, Performance, and the Ruses of Memory* (Minneapolis: University of Minnesota Press, 2009); Jeffrey Q. McCune, Jr., *Sexual Discretion: Black Masculinity and the Politics of Passing* (Chicago: University of Chicago Press, 2014); and C. Riley

Snorton, *Nobody Is Supposed to Know: Black Sexuality on the Down Low* (Minneapolis: University of Minnesota Press, 2014).

21. Perhaps related, authorities in both New York and San Francisco shuttered their gay bathhouses in the 1980s. Chicago's bathhouses suffered sharp declines in business but were never closed. See Eric Zorn, "AIDS Turns Gays from Bathhouses," *CT*, January 6, 1986.

22. Arthur S. Leonard, "The Gay Bar and the Right to Hang Out Together," in his *Sexuality and the Law: An Encyclopedia of Major Legal Cases* (New York: Garland, 1993), 190–196.

23. Washington, D.C., Detroit, Minneapolis, San Francisco, and Los Angeles passed such ordinances in the 1970s, as did the downstate Illinois college towns of Champaign and Urbana, where the University of Illinois was located. They were joined by Philadelphia in 1982; Oakland, California, in 1984; and New York in 1986. Houston had passed such an ordinance in 1984 only to see it repealed in a ballot referendum the following year. William N. Eskridge, Jr., *Gaylaw: Challenging the Apartheid of the Closet* (Cambridge, MA: Harvard University Press, 1999), 356–361. Chicago was the second-largest city in every decennial census from 1890 through 1980, before falling below Los Angeles in 1990.

24. Michael Miner, "Kelley Hits Council Hangups for Gay Rights Bill Failure," *CST*, November 16, 1975. Kelley did his time with former Illinois governor Dan Walker: Thomas M. Burton and Maurice Possley, "7 Indicted in City Hall Probe," *CT*, November 22, 1986. See also Dean Baquet, "Bribe Probe Focuses on Waste-Firm Boss," *CT*, February 9, 1987; Maurice Possley, "Kelley Pleads Guilty, Vows to Return," *CT*, April 25, 1987; William B. Crawford, Jr., "Kelley Gets Year, Will Help Probe," *CT*, June 12, 1987; Anne Marie Lipinski, "Jail Almost a Reunion for Former Ald. Kelley," *CT*, July 22, 1988; and George Papajohn, "Out of Prison, Ex-Alderman Is on the Air," *CT*, June 1, 1990.

Chapter 1

1. Alfredo S. Lanier, "Coming Out and Moving On," *Chicago*, November 1983, 238. One block east along Division Street, at Dearborn Street, was an intersection equally strongly associated with homosexuality, as the title of a documentary film attests: *Quearborn and Perversion: An Early History of Lesbian and Gay Chicago*, directed by Ron Pajak (Chicago: Quearborn & Perversion, 2010).

2. Quoted in Jonathan Gathorne-Hardy, *Kinsey: Sex the Measure of All Things* (Bloomington: Indiana University Press, 1998), 135.

3. William Simon and John H. Gagnon, "The Lesbians: A Preliminary Overview," in *Sexual Deviance*, ed. Gagnon and Simon with the assistance of Donald E. Cairns (New York: Harper and Row, 1967), 247–282, at 263.

4. *Tiny & Ruby Hell Divin' Women*, directed by Greta Shiller and Andrea Weiss (Jezebel Productions, 1988). Davis had won fame after touring with the all-women International Sweethearts of Rhythm in the 1940s. Union records in the possession of a former guitarist indicate the club was open by 1954. A fall 1955 gossip column mentions that Davis had "sold her Chicago nitery," though it is not clear whether it closed then or later. "Louis Armstrong and Tiny Davis, King and Queen of Horn Here," *CD*, December 25, 1948; Paul Garon and Beth Garon, *Woman with Guitar: Memphis Minnie's Blues* (New York: Da Capo Press, 1992), 102; and "Swinging the News," *CD*, October 29, 1955. See also Sherrie Tucker, *Swing Shift: 'All-Girl' Bands of the 1940s* (Durham, NC: Duke University Press, 2000), 37.

5. Hearing transcript, n.d., describing early 1952 investigation, in box 17, folder 3, REM. The officer's captain testified that on receiving this report at 2:30 A.M., "I ordered that the officers arrest the whole place, pull everybody in and charge them with being inmates—I think the technical charge is inmates of a disorderly house, including the management and everybody else." "Inmate of a disorderly house" was indeed the charge used by the police in enforcing what was then section 193–2 of the Municipal Code of Chicago, though the term "inmate" did not actually appear in the code section, which was eventually declared unconstitutional in *McTavish v. Spiotto*, 500 F. Supp. 703 (N.D. Ill. 1980).

6. Jack G. interview with the author, February 7, 2007. In her study of mid-1960s gay clubs in Chicago, Esther Newton described the "attempted assumption of upper[-class] patterns of speech, taste, dress, and furnishings" as characteristic of "lower-middle-class young men who were referred to me by my informants as 'ribbon clerks,' those who were 'paying for their Brooks Brothers suit on time.'" *Mother Camp: Female Impersonators in America* (Chicago: University of Chicago Press, 1972), 29.

7. Samuel Steward, interview by Gregory Sprague, May 20, 1982, audio recording in GAS.

8. Esther Newton, interview by Naomi Sobel, November 21, 2003, collection of the Lesbian and Gay Studies Project, Center for Gender Studies, University of Chicago (transcript in author's possession).

9. Renee Hanover, in Hanover and Marie Kuda, joint interview by Gregory Sprague, May 19, 1980, audio recording in GAS.

10. Valerie Taylor, *Unlike Others* (New York: Midwood-Tower, 1963), 86–87. See also Yvonne Keller, "'Was It Right to Love Her Brother's Wife So Passionately?': Lesbian Pulp Novels and U.S. Lesbian Identity, 1950–1965," *American Quarterly* 57:2 (June 2005), 385–410; and Meredith Miller, "Secret Agents and Public Victims: The Implied Lesbian Reader," *Journal of Popular Culture* 35:1 (Summer 2001), 37–58.

11. Samuel Steward, interview by Gregory Sprague.

12. St. Clair Drake and Horace R. Cayton, *Black Metropolis: A Study of Negro Life in a Northern City*, rev. ed. (Chicago: University of Chicago Press, 1993 [1945]); Davarian L. Baldwin, *Chicago's New Negroes: Modernity, the Great Migration, and Black Urban Life* (Chapel Hill: University of North Carolina Press, 2007); Adam Green, *Selling the Race: Culture, Community, and Black Chicago* (Chicago: University of Chicago Press, 2006); and James R. Grossman, *Land of Hope: Chicago, Black Southerners, and the Great Migration* (Chicago: University of Chicago Press, 1991).

13. Chad Heap, *Slumming: Sexual and Racial Encounters in American Nightlife, 1885–1940* (Chicago: University of Chicago Press, 2009).

14. Jack Lait and Lee Mortimer, *Chicago Confidential* (New York: Crown, 1950), 54.

15. "Female Impersonators," *Ebony*, March 1953, 64. See also Allen Drexel, "Before Paris Burned: Race, Class, and Male Homosexuality on the Chicago South Side, 1935–1960," in *Creating a Place for Ourselves: Lesbian, Gay, and Bisexual Community Histories*, ed. Brett Beemyn (New York: Routledge, 1997), 119–144; and Gregory Conerly, "Swishing and Swaggering: Homosexuality in Black Magazines During the 1950s," in *The Greatest Taboo: Homosexuality in Black Communities*, ed. Delroy Constantine-Simms (Los Angeles: Alyson, 2000), 384–394.

16. *Monroe v. Pape*, 365 U.S. 167 (1961). Justice William Douglas, writing for the majority, said, "Although the legislation was enacted because of the conditions that existed in the

South at that time, it is cast in general language, and is as applicable to Illinois as it is to the States whose names were mentioned over and again in the debates." See also "Rule Brutality Victim Can Sue in U.S. Court," *CD*, February 21, 1961; "$13,000 Won in Cop Beatings," *CD*, December 5, 1962; and Marshall S. Shapo, "Constitutional Tort: *Monroe v. Pape*, and the Frontiers Beyond," *Northwestern University Law Review* 60 (July–August 1965), 277–329.

17. J. D. Mercer, *They Walk in Shadow: A Study of Sexual Variations* (New York: Comet Press Books, 1959), 390–391.

18. "Female Homosexual Interview; Chicago; Tucker; R-lower class (D.D.)," box 11, folder 3, WS. At the time of this interview in 1967, she was a high school graduate and employed in the enormous Western Electric plant, where "maybe a half a dozen" coworkers knew she was gay. Because she mentions receiving *Ebony* magazine at home to the interviewer, she was likely African American.

19. Jim Darby, interview by the author, June 26, 2007.

20. "Kefauver Hits Chicago as U.S. Crime Center," *CT*, November 13, 1950.

21. Andrew Wender Cohen has suggested that these hearings reflected the adaptation of the 1934 antiracketeering statute to a more conservative era. "Accusers aimed less at protecting American institutions," Cohen argues, "than discrediting the New Deal or—in the case of Democrats like Kefauver and Kennedy—demonstrating to a middle class public their virtuous independence from their own core supporters." *The Racketeer's Progress: Chicago and the Struggle for the Modern American Economy, 1900–1940* (New York: Cambridge University Press, 2004), 299–300.

22. Lawrence M. Friedman, *Crime and Punishment in American History* (New York: Basic Books, 1993), 273.

23. "Bare Million a Year Racket in Horse Meat," *CT*, January 9, 1952; "Political War on Horse Meat Issue Starts," *CT*, February 4, 1952; "Governor Knew of Horse Meat Sale, G.O.P. Told," *CT*, February 10, 1952; and "Illinois Horse Meat Scandal News in Capital," *CT*, June 24, 1952.

24. My account of Chicago corruption scandals in this and the next two paragraphs draws on James L. Merriner, *Grafters and Goo Goos: Corruption and Reform in Chicago, 1833–2003* (Carbondale: Southern Illinois University Press, 2004); Len O'Connor, *Clout: Mayor Daley and His City* (Chicago: Henry Regnery, 1975); and Richard C. Lindberg, *To Serve and Collect: Chicago Politics and Police Corruption from the Lager Beer Riot to the Summerdale Scandal* (Westport, CT: Praeger, 1991).

25. Merriner, *Grafters and Goo Goos*, 161.

26. Paul R. Leach to A. T. Burch, March 27, 1953, in box 17, folder 2, REM; Jim Kepner, *Rough News, Daring Views: 1950s Pioneer Gay Press Journalism* (New York: Harrington Park Press, 1998), 50; William N. Eskridge, Jr., *Gaylaw: Challenging the Apartheid of the Closet* (Cambridge, MA: Harvard University Press, 1999), 72.

27. "Thirty-Sixth Police District" report citing December 17, 1952, letter to Commander of Police, box 58, folder 10, VWP.

28. Ibid., January 19, 1953.

29. "Turn Spotlight on Shady Areas in Bauler Wards," *CT*, January 30, 1953.

30. "2 Captains Face Quiz Today," *CT*, January 30, 1953.

31. John Vandermeer, interview by the author, August 14, 2006. Vandermeer was about twelve when Kinovsky's bar came under a cloud of investigation.

32. "2 Captains Face Quiz Today," *CT*, January 30, 1953.

33. "Thirty-Sixth Police District" report, citing information in June 2, 1953, letter to Commander of Police, box 58, folder 10, VWP.

34. John Vandermeer, author interview, August 14, 2006.

35. "35th Police District" report, n.d., folder 10, box 58, VWP.

36. Transcript of Virgil W. Peterson oral history interview (conducted in 1968), 20–23, in box 2, folder 3, VWP.

37. "Memorandum Re: 35th Police District," October 7, 1953, box 59, folder 10, VWP. The correct names were the Shoreline 7 and the Haig. The Shoreline 7 was particularly reputed to be connected to the Mafia. A former bartender believed the owner was closely tied to the Italian syndicate, and the bartender claimed once to have seen Republican U.S. Senator Everett Dirksen arriving to meet with the owner (Sukie de la Croix, "Chicago Whispers," *Outlines*, October 21, 1998). Hal Call, a California homophile activist, claimed the place was "owned by a man who was in the legislature of the state of Illinois and who regularly paid off the police department." James T. Sears, *Behind the Mask of the Mattachine: The Hal Call Chronicles and the Early Movement for Homosexual Emancipation* (New York: Harrington Park Press, 2006), 139.

38. "Kennelly Asks Study of Liquor License Upsets," *CT*, June 20, 1952.

39. Chuck Renslow, interview by the author, October 12, 2007.

40. Ibid.

41. Richard Wright, "The Shame of Chicago," *Ebony* (December 1951), 28.

42. See Arnold R. Hirsch, *Making the Second Ghetto: Race and Housing in Chicago, 1940–1960* (Chicago: University of Chicago Press, 1983); Thomas J. Sugrue, *Sweet Land of Liberty: The Forgotten Struggle for Civil Rights in the North* (New York: Random House, 2008); and Beryl Satter, *Family Properties: Race, Real Estate, and the Exploitation of Black Urban America* (New York: Metropolitan Books, 2009).

43. Chicago is more typical of postwar urban politics than its distinctive reputation might suggest. As one political scientist put it, "[C]ohesive organizations like Chicago's may be fairly uncommon, while pervasive favoritism and patronage—machine politics—are much less so." Raymond E. Wolfinger, "Why Political Machines Have Not Withered Away and Other Revisionist Thoughts," *Journal of Politics* 34:2 (May 1972), 365–398, at 377.

44. Patronage jobs, of course, were the entitlement of male breadwinners—and contingent on adherence to norms of respectability, from which visibly gay or lesbian people would have been generally excluded.

45. Adam Cohen and Elizabeth Taylor, *American Pharaoh: Mayor Richard J. Daley—His Battle for Chicago and the Nation* (Boston: Little, Brown, 2000), 145.

46. "Prisoner 29681 Tells of Life Here and How He Went Wrong!: Good Times Slip, He Begins to Drink and Steal" (by "29681, Stateville"), *Lakeview Booster*, January 12, 1955.

47. Minutes of the Workers' Meeting of the Hard-to-Reach Youth Project of the Northwest Side Community Committee, June 6, 1958, quoted in Andrew J. Diamond, *Mean Streets: Chicago Youths and the Everyday Struggle for Empowerment in the Multiracial City, 1908–1969* (Berkeley: University of California Press, 2009), 190.

48. Robert O. Self, *All in the Family: The Realignment of American Democracy Since the 1960s* (New York: Hill and Wang, 2012).

49. Print advertisement, *Booster*, February 16, 1955, p. 4, and handbill, both in box 53, folder 7, REM.

50. Advertisement, *Booster*, February 16, 1955, in box 53, folder 7, REM.

51. Richard J. Daley obituary, *CT*, December 21, 1976.

52. Quoted in Milton L. Rakove, *Don't Make No Waves, Don't Back No Losers: An Insider's Analysis of the Daley Machine* (Bloomington: Indiana University Press, 1975), 121. Rakove notes, "When Daley's daughter married a young man whose father was a physician, the good doctor was appointed to two part-time positions with the city and the county" (52).

53. Clean-government reformers had disliked Kelly's tolerance of corruption, and many whites objected to his at least theoretical support for open housing. Roger Biles, "Edward J. Kelly," in *The Mayors: The Chicago Political Tradition*, ed. Paul M. Green and Melvin G. Holli (Carbondale: Southern Illinois University Press, 2005), 111–125.

54. On policy gambling, see Mark H. Haller, "Policy Gambling, Entertainment, and the Emergence of Black Politics: Chicago from 1900 to 1940," *Journal of Social History* 24 (Summer 1991), 719–739.

55. "Mayor Kennelly and Rep. Dawson," *CT*, February 2, 1955; and Christopher Manning, *William L. Dawson and the Limits of Black Electoral Leadership* (DeKalb: Northern Illinois University Press, 2009), 126–129.

56. St. Sukie de la Croix, *Chicago Whispers: A History of LGBT Chicago Before Stonewall* (Madison: University of Wisconsin Press, 2012), 159, 164; "Bachelor Mayor Ponders Leap Year Letter Offer," *CT*, January 14, 1948; Thomas Morrow, "Kennelly Life Story Tribute to His Mother," *CT*, April 5, 1951 ("one of the most eligible of Chicago's bachelors"), both front-page articles; and "What's Your Question?" *CT*, June 20, 1952 ("the most famous bachelor mayor of America").

57. Cohen and Taylor, *American Pharaoh*, 125.

58. "Daley's Rise in Politics Impressive," *CT*, February 20, 1955; and Shirley Lowry, "Wives of Rivals in Mayor Race Face Job Ahead: Motherhood Role Biggest Task for Both," *CT*, February 24, 1955.

59. "Mayoral Foes Agree Crime Is Organized," *CT*, March 6, 1955; Robert Howard, "Foes Planning Wide Open City, Says Merriam," *CT*, March 7, 1955; and Robert Howard, "Daley Making Phony Pledges, Merriam Says," *CT*, March 21, 1955.

60. "No Area Is Safe in a Wide Open City: Merriam," *CT*, March 31, 1955.

61. "Daley Pledges All-Out War on Crime in City," *Booster*, March 23, 1955.

62. George Chauncey, "The Postwar Sex Crime Panic," in *True Stories from the American Past*, ed. William Graebner (New York: McGraw-Hill, 1993), 160–178; Estelle Freedman, "'Uncontrolled Desires': The Response to the Sexual Psychopath, 1920–1960," *Journal of American History* 74 (June 1987), 83–106. See, among other *Tribune* articles, "Hunt Sex Killer of Girl, 5," July 31, 1960 (front page); "Missing Boy Found Slain Near Home," October 29, 1960; "Link Girl Killing to Attacks," November 15, 1960; "Chiefs Split in Grimes Quiz," February 15, 1957; "Tells How He Beat, Choked Boy," August 8, 1958; and "Hold Suspect in Sex Killing," July 8, 1955. Estelle Freedman has identified two waves of sex-crime panics, the first from 1937 to 1940 and the second from 1949 to 1955. However, the postwar panic drew as well on continuing fascination with the 1924 Chicago kidnapping and murder of fourteen-year-old Bobby Franks, to which Richard Loeb and Nathan Leopold later confessed. Chicago saw calls for tougher policing of sex crimes as early as 1946 with the kidnapping and murder of six-year-old Suzanne Degnan. "Find Head, Parts of Torso of Kidnapped Chicago Girl," *NYT*, January 8, 1946; "Council O.K.'s Plea for 1,000 Extra Police," *CT*, January 17, 1946; "Degnan Murder Spurs Move for a Big Crime Lab," *CT*, February 1, 1946; "State Official Urges Drive on Sex Criminals," *CT*, February 3, 1946.

63. "Sex Degenerate of Sadist Type Slew Three Boys, Alienist for Court Believes," *CT*, October 19, 1955.

64. John Gavin, "9 Years Ago, 3 Dead Boys Shocked City," *CT*, October 18, 1964; John Gavin, "Cop Retires, His Hunt for Killer Ends," *CT*, December 5, 1966; Frank Zahour, "Murder of 3 Boys in 1955 Unsolved; Leads Dwindle," *CT*, October 17, 1971; Dan Egler, "No Leads to Killer of 3 Boys After 17 Years of Searching," *CT*, October 15, 1972; and "Mystery Killings Haunt Woods," *CT*, May 19, 1975. Nearly forty years after the killing, after an investigation of an unrelated case from the 1970s, Kenneth Hansen was arrested and charged with the murders. Hansen was convicted, had his conviction overturned on evidentiary grounds, and was convicted again in 2002. "Death Closes the Case of Boys' Murders" (AP), *NYT*, September 16, 2007.

65. "Sex Degenerate of Sadist Type Slew Three Boys"; "Seek Teen Sex Gang; 250 Hunt for Clews," *CT*, October 23, 1955 (subhead: "Hangout for Perverts"); "Why Did Twisted Mind Choose Youths as Prey?" *CST*, October 19, 1955; and "How Three Boys Battled Slayers for Their Lives," *CST*, October 21, 1955.

66. "New Hunt for Clues in Slayings," *CT*, October 28, 1955 ("police sex bureau . . . turned over the names of 90 paroled sex offenders"); "Triple Killing Probe Opens with 3 Aims," *CT*, April 10, 1956; and "Quiz Sailor in 3 Slayings," *CT*, October 24, 1955.

67. "Search for Slayer Widened," *Milwaukee Sentinel*, March 16, 1956.

68. Herb Graffis, "The Law Upside Down," *CST*, October 23, 1955.

69. Mrs. LeRoy L. Kohn, letter, *CST*, October 25, 1955.

70. "Ask Ike to Act in Dixie Death of Chicago Boy," *CT*, September 2, 1955.

71. "Peterson Boy Beaten with a Garden Tool," *CT*, November 15, 1955; "$26,000 in Rewards Spur Slayer Search," *CST*, October 24, 1955; Rushing T. Greer, letter to the editor, *CD*, November 19, 1955; and "Mrs. Bradley Wires Moms of 3 Slain Chicago Boys," *CD*, October 29, 1955.

72. Richard C. Lindberg and Gloria Jean Sykes, *Shattered Sense of Innocence: The 1955 Murders of Three Chicago Children* (Carbondale: Southern Illinois University Press, 2006), 87, 83. Two other recent books on the Schuessler-Peterson case are Gene O'Shea, *Unbridled Rage: A True Story of Organized Crime, Corruption, and Murder in Chicago* (New York: Berkley, 2005), which focuses on alleged ties to horse racing near the forest preserves, and James A. Jack, *Three Boys Missing: The Tragedy That Exposed the Pedophilia Underworld* (Chicago: HPH Publishing, 2006), a sensational and unreliable account, written by the detective who first spoke with one of the fathers of the murdered boys and blurbed by former U.S. attorney and Illinois governor James R. Thompson.

73. Justin Spring, *Secret Historian: The Life and Times of Samuel Steward, Professor, Tattoo Artist, and Sexual Renegade* (New York: Farrar, Straus and Giroux, 2010), 233–234.

74. Thomas Painter diary, March 7, 1957, Series II C.1., V. 14, KI.

75. "Tips Pour In on Limper," *CT*, July 12, 1957; and "Hunt 'Frankenstein' in Boys' Killing," *CST*, July 30, 1957.

76. John Gavin, "Years Go By, but Search Continues for Slayer of Three Boys," *CT*, December 20, 1959.

77. Clay Gowran, "Hunt for Boys' Killer Turns to Minds of Friends," *CT*, October 15, 1960.

78. L. P., "Editorial," *ONE* (February 1957), 5; and Carl J. Pelleck and Charles Gruenberg, "Seized on Plane from Europe in '55 Deaths of 3 Chicago Boys," *Mattachine Review* (March 1957), 12–13.

79. George Montgomery letter, "Third Sex," *CD*, April 13, 1957.

80. Joe Smith, *Sin Corner and Joe Smith: A Story of Vice and Corruption in Chicago* (New York: Exposition Press, 1964), 20, 22.

81. Quoted in de la Croix, *Chicago Whispers*, 86. See also Henry Gerber, "The Society for Human Rights—1925," *ONE* (September 1962), 5–11.

82. "Major," interview by Susan Stryker, January 29, 1998, transcript in the collection of the Gay Lesbian Bisexual Transgender Historical Society, San Francisco.

83. Interview with Shirley Willer, in Eric Marcus, *Making History: The Struggle for Gay and Lesbian Equal Rights* (New York: HarperCollins, 1992), 129–130. Willer said the incident occurred in the late 1940s or early 1950s. Willer later moved to New York; in 1964, she was elected national president of the country's first lesbian organization, the Daughters of Bilitis.

84. J.S., "Member Reports on San Francisco Trip," *CMSN*, October 25, 1954.

85. Karen C. Sendziak, "Pearl M. Hart (1890–1975)," in *Before Stonewall: Activists for Gay and Lesbian Rights in Historical Context*, ed. Vern L. Bullough (Binghamton, NY: Harrington Park Press, 2002), 56–62; *U.S. v. Witkovich*, 353 U.S. 194 (1957). See also "Miss Pearl Hart," in *Prominent Women of Illinois, 1885–1932* (Chicago: Illinois Woman's Press Association, 1932). At thirteen, Hart had attended a meeting of the Young Women's Suffrage Alliance in Chicago's Garfield Park. "Women Arrange Fall Campaign," *CT*, July 20, 1913. Her work on behalf of the homophile movement was a late development in a long and varied career of criminal legal work on behalf of the dispossessed. See "Pearl M. Hart Scores Again," *CD*, October 19, 1918 ("[S]he succeeded in having three Race boys, who had been indicted for robbery, released on probation on her recommendation"); "Woman Lawyer Fights 3 Years to Save Client," *CT*, June 17, 1921; "Women Demand Chancery Post for Hart," *CT*, July 20, 1927; "Woman Lawyer to Defend Girls in Morals Court," *CT*, July 19, 1931; "Attorney Sees Improvement in Chicago Woman's Courts," *Washington Post*, March 20, 1934; "Race Champion Honored at 60," *CD*, April 8, 1950; "400 at Meeting Here on Behalf of Rosenbergs," *CT*, January 9, 1953; and "Soviet Spy Suspect Freed by U.S. to Better Relations," *NYT*, March 25, 1961.

86. I. F. Stone, "Bleak Landscape of the Resistance," *I. F. Stone's Weekly*, December 21, 1953, quoted in Sendziak, "Pearl M. Hart," 56.

87. Renee Hanover, in Hanover and Marie Kuda, joint interview by Gregory Sprague.

88. "Chicago Area on Way to Firm Legal Footing in Illinois," *CMSN*, July 20, 1954.

89. "Mid-West Responds to Newsletter," *CMSN*, August 25, 1954.

90. J. B., "Fair Employment Practices and the Homosexual," *CMSN*, May 1955. The term "fair employment practices" was associated with the African American struggle for justice in Northern industry. The Illinois House had just overwhelmingly passed a fair employment practices bill. However, the full Illinois legislature did not enact a quite limited fair employment practices bill until 1961. "House Passes Illinois 'FEPC' Bill, 80 to 35," *CT*, June 1, 1955; and Joseph Minsky, "FEPC in Illinois: Four Stormy Years," *Notre Dame Law Review* 41 (December 1965), 152–181. Bill Kelley believes the writing style and subject matter suggest this may have been Jim Bradford, pseudonym of James Osgood, who had moved from New York to Chicago by this time. Kelley, e-mail communication to author, April 28, 2015.

91. Erving Goffman, *Stigma: Notes on the Management of Spoiled Identity* (Englewood Cliffs, NJ: Prentice-Hall, 1963), 25.

92. "The Heard Lecture," *CMSN*, July 1954.

93. "Art Sale Attracts Wide Audience," *CMSN*, September 28, 1954.

94. Homophile publications enthusiastically reported on Hooker's research even before it was published. The Chicago group's newsletter emphasized her core finding that "homosexual persons vary widely in personality structure and *do not constitute a distinct type.*" The editor enjoined readers to consider their own experiences. "Stop for a moment and think about the homosexuals you know," suggested one article. "What are they like? Are they cut from the same pattern? Of course not." "Finds Homosexual *Not* a Type," *CMSN*, August 25, 1954.

95. "Society's Chicago Research Program Shifts into Gear," *CMSN*, November 1954.

96. Evelyn Hooker, "A Preliminary Analysis of Group Behavior of Homosexuals," *Journal of Psychology* 42 (1956), 217–225. Hooker refers to being acquainted with gay men "in New York, Los Angeles, San Francisco, and Chicago" (222). Thanks to Stephen Vider for drawing this to my attention.

97. Sears, *Behind the Mask*, 419.

98. "Your Legal Rights" [n.d. but 1957], pamphlet in vertical file Sexual Freedom—Gay Liberation—Mattachine Society, Inc., LC.

99. "N.S. Politicos Lash Officials for Unsolved Murders," *Booster*, September 2, 1957.

100. Robert Wiedrich, "A Sex Killer is on the Loose on North Side!," *CT*, February 7, 1960.

101. Dal McIntire, "Tangents," *ONE* (July 1959), 14.

102. John Farris to Frank Kameny, February 3, 1963, box 3, folder 10, FK. In fact, the Front Page was raided at least once in the period between Farris's visit and the date of his letter; see "Police Seize 40 in Raid at Rush St. Inn," *CT*, March 27, 1962.

Chapter 2

1. Early in 1960, the Cook County Democratic organization slated Otto Kerner, who was tied to the machine but a Protestant, for governor. As Edmund F. Kallina, among others, has pointed out, this move lowered the risk that having a Catholic presidential nominee at the top of the statewide ticket would hurt the machine slate among Protestant voters, and thus likely indicated Daley had already made up his mind to back Kennedy. Edmund F. Kallina, Jr., *Courthouse over White House: Chicago and the Presidential Election of 1960* (Gainesville: University Press of Florida, 1988), 46.

2. Norman Mailer, *Miami and the Siege of Chicago* (New York: Signet/New American Library, 1968), 104. Much has been made of Daley's role in the Illinois recount following the controversial 1960 presidential election. Thirteen days after the election, the British journalist Alastair Cooke famously quoted an anonymous Cook County Democratic politician who invoked "one law of American politics: when a vote is stolen in Cook County, it stays stolen." Alistair Cooke, "Uncooking the Cook County Books," *The Guardian*, November 21, 1960. Kallina argues that Republican vote-fraud allegations in the aftermath centered on Illinois, rather than Texas, because in Illinois the Democratic and Republican parties were about evenly matched at the state level, and the Republicans controlled the state Board of Elections. By examining more than 300 reports written on election day by volunteers for a nonpartisan poll-watching organization, Kallina suggests that "although it may have been flawed by procedural irregularities of varying degrees of severity, the election was still essentially fair" (91–92).

3. "Predicts Catholic and Negro Vote for Jack," *CD*, October 20, 1960.

4. "U.S. Issues Rules on Halting Funds," *NYT*, December 28, 1965; Adam Cohen and Elizabeth Taylor, *American Pharaoh: Mayor Richard J. Daley—His Battle for Chicago and the*

Nation (Boston: Little, Brown, 2000), 349–353. The *New York Times* went so far as to call Daley's demands "a northern city's cry of 'states rights'—more precisely, 'city's rights.'" Austin Wehrwein, "Chicago Story—City Hall and Civil Rights," *NYT*, October 17, 1965.

5. On redevelopment, see Joel Rast, *Remaking Chicago: The Political Origins of Urban Industrial Change* (DeKalb: Northern Illinois University Press, 1999); Larry Bennett, "Postwar Redevelopment in Chicago: The Declining Politics of Party and the Rise of Neighborhood Politics," in *Unequal Partnerships: The Political Economy of Urban Redevelopment in Postwar America*, ed. Gregory D. Squires (New Brunswick, NJ: Rutgers University Press, 1989), 161–177; Cohen and Taylor, *American Pharaoh*.

6. A city prosecutor called this issue "[t]he lowest, filthiest, most hardcore pornography I have ever seen." "He Decides Where to Draw the Line," *CT*, n.d. (but September 1964), as reprinted in M. W. Newman and Robert R. Kirsch, *The Smut Hunters* (Los Angeles: All America Distributors, 1965).

7. Calvin Tomkins, "Mr. Playboy of the Western World," *Saturday Evening Post*, April 23, 1966; and Bill Osgerby, *Playboys in Paradise: Masculinity, Youth, and Leisure-Style in Modern America* (Oxford: Berg, 2001).

8. Del Martin, "New Illinois Penal Code—What Does It Mean?" *The Ladder* 6:6 (March 1962), 14; Morris J. Wexler, "Sex Offenses Under the New Criminal Code," *Illinois Bar Journal* 51 (October 1962), 152–159; and Charles H. Bowman, "The Illinois Criminal Code of 1961 and Code of Criminal Procedure of 1963," *University of Michigan Journal of Law Reform* 4 (Spring 1971), 461–475. See also William N. Eskridge, Jr., *Dishonorable Passions: Sodomy Laws in America, 1861–2003* (New York: Viking, 2008).

9. After Illinois in 1961, no other state repealed its sodomy law until Connecticut did so in 1969. In the 1970s, however, as the gay movement gained steam in the years after the Stonewall uprising, seeking legislative repeal or judicial invalidation of these laws became a major focus of gay activism; half the states repealed their sodomy laws in that decade. John D'Emilio, *Sexual Politics, Sexual Communities: The Making of a Homosexual Minority in the United States, 1940–1970* (Chicago: University of Chicago Press, 1983), 238. See also Ron Dorfman, "The 'Infamous Crime' Against Privacy," in *Out and Proud in Chicago: An Overview of the City's Gay Community*, ed. Tracy Baim (Chicago: Surrey Books, 2008), 70. The Supreme Court's affirmation of the constitutionality of such laws in *Bowers v. Hardwick* (1986) was a setback for gay rights, later reversed in *Lawrence v. Texas* (2003).

10. "ISR H Study Code Book," 146, Box 186, JG.

11. *Tentative Final Draft of the Proposed Illinois Revised Criminal Code of 1961* (Chicago: Illinois State Bar Association and Chicago Bar Association, 1960), 239, 255–256.

12. "The Article [on sex crimes] is not intended to proscribe any sexual conduct between consenting adults unless such conduct adversely affects one of the *key interests* sought to be protected." These "interests" included the regulation of public space and the protection of innocent women and children. *Tentative Final Draft*, 239, emphasis mine. As Bowman describes it, "The new Code revamped entirely the sex offenses so that sexual activity between consenting adults (18 and over) in private would not be a crime, and legalized sexual activity between humans and animals" ("Illinois Criminal Code," 466).

13. Only the last of the three succeeded in amending the proposed code, to limit the relaxation of the state's abortion prohibition. After the Council of Catholic Churches threatened to "denounce the provisions from the pulpit," the code's authors felt they were "not ready to jeopardize the entire Code just because of the abortion provisions," one of its members later wrote. Proposed legal defenses against the crime of abortion in cases of rape or

incest, or if the mother's health were in danger, or in case of known fetal defects, were all deleted, retaining only the existing defense in cases where abortion was necessary to preserve the mother's life. Bowman, "Illinois Criminal Code," 469–471, at 470; Eskridge, *Dishonorable Passions*, 126.

14. Eskridge, *Dishonorable Passions*, 126.

15. "New Criminal Code in Effect Jan. 1," *CST*, December 21, 1961. Carl Nash points out that in the ALI's own mid-decade proceedings, the sodomy-law repeal was by far the most controversial of its recommendations. Judge Robert Parker and Judge Learned Hand debated publicly whether such repeal alone would, as Parker feared, lead the entire code to be "misunderstood" and "discredited" by the legal profession and the public. Judge Hand replied that although he, too, "voted that [the prohibition of sodomy] should be retained, and I did it at that time because I feared the effect in general of its omission from the Code," nonetheless "I have always been in great doubt about that, and I have finally come to the conclusion that the chance of its prejudicing the Code is not sufficient to warrant opposition to making the law as we . . . think it should be." Hand prevailed, and his change of heart about sodomy law repeal was reported in *Time* and the *Mattachine Review*. Carl S. Nash, "The Decriminalization of Sodomy in the American Law Institute's Model Penal Code: A Legal History of Ideological Transformation" (unpublished paper in author's possession, 2002).

16. "Kerner Signs New Criminal Code Bills," *CT*, July 29, 1961.

17. Wexler, "Sex Offenses Under the New Criminal Code," 153.

18. Del Shearer to Jaye Bell, February 16, 1962, in box 15, folder 12, LM.

19. Martin, "New Illinois Penal Code," 14. *ONE* magazine called it "ironic" that this liberalization "should have been adopted only in an area long and traditionally considered to be the very heart of United States conservatism, our state of Illinois." Marcel Martin, editorial, *ONE* (May 1963), 4.

20. Chicago Gay Liberation, "Working Paper for the Revolutionary People's Constitutional Convention," *Out of the Closets: Voices of Gay Liberation*, ed. Karla Jay and Allen Young, 20th anniv. ed. (New York: New York University Press, 1992), 346–351, at 348.

21. "Daley Saloon License Bill Turned Down," *CT*, June 24, 1961.

22. "Senate Passes Chicago Tax Rate Ceiling; House OK's Daley's Saloon Bill," *CT*, June 28, 1961.

23. "Session Ends; No Remap!" *CT*, July 2, 1961.

24. "Senate Votes Daley Saloon Closing Bill," *CT*, July 1, 1961.

25. James L. Merriner, *Grafters and Goo Goos: Corruption and Reform in Chicago, 1833–2003* (Carbondale: Southern Illinois University Press, 2004), 170–171; Cohen and Taylor, *American Pharaoh*, 190.

26. Wilson, according to his biographer, had clashed with the university's president, Clark Kerr, who wanted to dismantle some of the school's programs. William J. Bopp, *"O. W.": O. W. Wilson and the Search for a Police Profession* (Port Washington, NY: Kennikat Press, 1977), 80–82.

27. Bopp, *"O. W.,"* 83–100.

28. David K. Johnson notes that although "the absolute number of homosexual dismissals had declined since the 1950s, they accounted for an increasing percentage of the total number of security dismissals" in the early 1960s. David K. Johnson, *The Lavender Scare: The Cold War Persecution of Gays and Lesbians in the Federal Government* (Chicago: University of Chicago Press, 2004), 197.

29. "Wilson Tells Cops to War on Hoodlums," *CT*, April 30, 1960; "Wilson Tells Police to War upon '26 Girls,'" *CT*, May 12, 1960; and "Wilson Orders War on Teen-Age Gangs," *CT*, July 16, 1960.

30. Bopp, "*O. W.*," 99. "Raid on Bingo Game a Test," *CT*, April 1, 1960; "Alderman, Irked by Bingo Raid, to Defend Women," *CT*, April 6, 1960; George Bliss, "Halt Bingo, Priests Told by Cardinal," *CT*, April 13, 1960; "Legion Urges Local Option 'Legal Bingo,'" *CT*, August 21, 1960; "Bingo Banned at Picnics in Forest Areas," *CT*, May 11, 1960; and "3 Seized as 450 Play Bingo," *CT*, April 30, 1960;

31. "Eight Seized in Bingo Game Raid on Hall," *CT*, February 6, 1961.

32. "Two Arrested as Police Raid V.F.W. Clubs," *CT*, July 10, 1961.

33. O. W. Wilson, *Police Administration*, 2d ed. (New York: McGraw-Hill, 1963), 303.

34. Wilson, *Police Administration*, 207.

35. O'Connor, *Clout*, 170–172; Diamond, *Mean Streets*, 254; and "Wilson Orders Police to Use Military Time," *CT*, April 20, 1960. In his discussion of Chicago's black and Latino youth gangs, Diamond perceptively notes, "The aggressive style of policing ushered in by Wilson made challenging beat cops a primary means of demonstrating manhood, as well as a way to claim the role of defending the community" (*Mean Streets*, 255).

36. Wilson, *Police Administration*, 313.

37. "Blast at Police 'Spying' Assailed by Captain Morris," *CT*, July 1, 1960.

38. Bopp, "*O. W.*," 94–95, at 95.

39. "3 Arrested in Vice Trap in Loop Hotel," *CT*, February 25, 1961.

40. "Ragged Cops Trap Ten Robbers," *CT*, October 9, 1961; Patricia Leeds, "Disguises and Dog Credited in Convictions," *CT*, March 24, 1964; and "Undercover Cops Nab 4," *CT*, December 13, 1964.

41. Larry Wolters, "Police at Finest in 'TUF Guys' Show," *CT*, February 3, 1963.

42. Wilson ordered the police to use a similar approach to suppressing "smut" by empowering individual officers to control pornography and obscene printed matter. "Every beat policeman in town is accredited as a smut-hunter," reported the *Chicago Daily News*, in addition to an on-staff vice officer in every police district. By threatening store owners with the loss of their livelihood, this campaign led to the closure of many shops selling such material along and beyond the southern edge of the Loop. Officers were encouraged to report even publications with only the "slightest indication" of obscenity. M. W. Newman, "Every Cop a Soldier in War on 'Filth,'" *CT*, September 1, 1964; and William Kling, "Chicago Gains in Its War on Smutty Books," *CT*, July 27, 1965.

43. Studs Terkel, *Coming of Age: The Story of Our Century by Those Who've Lived It* (New York: New Press, 1995), 310–311. In his discussion of various ways in which police officers in this period perceived the task of harassing gay bars and their patrons, Christopher Agee argues that they often "set their strategy according to the amount of physical contact they wished to have with the patrons." Agee, *The Streets of San Francisco: Policing and the Creation of a Cosmopolitan Liberal Politics, 1950–1972* (Chicago: University of Chicago Press, 2014), 80.

44. Virgil Peterson to O. W. Wilson, February 3, 1961, box 59, folder 3, VWP ("possibly through your legal advisers you may deem it advisable to have an ordinance introduced and passed by the City Council which would make it easier to enforce certain phases of the liquor license laws"); and "It's Aldermen vs. Wilson in Barmaid Bout," *CT*, May 10, 1961.

45. "Wilson Wars on B-Girls; 3 Bars Shut," *CT*, March 3, 1964 (quotation); and "Police Arrest 17 Persons in 4 Vice Raids," *CT*, January 8, 1965. See Amanda H. Littauer, "The B-Girl

Evil: Bureaucracy, Sexuality, and the Menace of Barroom Vice in Postwar California," *Journal of the History of Sexuality* 12:2 (2003), 171–204.

46. "Newsletter 3" (May 1960), in reel 16, MSNY. The group was reactivated with eleven charter members in the fall of 1959. "More Convention Agenda, 9/7/59," in Administrative—Meeting Minutes & Reports, 1958–1960 folder, Mattachine Society of Detroit records, box 1, Labadie Collection, University of Michigan Library. I have not been able to locate any surviving newsletters from the period between September 1959 and March 1960.

47. "Civic Virtue Triumphs Again," *CMSN* (March 1961); the raid is referred to, and the club in question named, in N. L. Shearer to John Stanton, May 27, 1964, copy in box 58, folder 2, GL.

48. D. S., letter to *The Ladder* (April 1961), 21–22.

49. Religion interview #12, November 19, 1967, in box 10, folder 5, WS.

50. Ron Vernon, "Black & Gay: Growing Up in Chicago," *CGC*, November 1973.

51. "Sissy in Prison: An Interview with Ron Vernon," in *Out of the Closets*, 99–112, at 100 and 103. In this period, "Social welfare personnel vociferously complained about the court's overzealous use of institutionalization for first-time, minor, and status offenders, particularly if they were African American." L. Mara Dodge, "'Our Juvenile Court Has Become More Like a Criminal Court': A Century of Reform at the Cook County (Chicago) Juvenile Court," *Michigan Historical Review* 26:2 (2000), 51–89, at 68.

52. "Ogilvie Says He'd Padlock Fun Lounge," *CT*, October 8, 1962; and Sandy Smith, "Rivals for Sheriff Both War on Hoodlums," *CT*, October 21, 1962.

53. "Wilson Wars on B-Girls"; "Daley Pledges Steady Fight Against Vice," *CT*, March 4, 1964; "Plan to Curb B-Girls Wins Council Test," *CT*, March 20, 1964; "Bickley Calls for Renewal of Sex Bureau," *CT*, March 23, 1964; and "Four Taverns Lose Licenses to Sell Liquor," *CT*, March 27, 1964; "Sheriff Pulls Vice Patrol Out of Cicero," *CT*, April 10, 1964.

54. "Daley Doesn't Want to Stop Crime: Bickley," *CT*, January 19, 1964.

55. "Bickley Calls for Renewal of Sex Bureau," *CT*, March 23, 1964. See also "Ward to Abolish His Stolen Auto and Sex Bureaus," *CT*, April 3, 1963.

56. "98 Arrested in Fun Lounge Raid Are Freed," *CT*, May 16, 1964.

57. Jack G., interview by the author, February 7, 2007.

58. "109 Arrested in Vice Den," *CT*, April 25, 1964. Of those with addresses in Cook County outside Chicago, seven lived in Des Plaines (including three of the six women arrested), six in Melrose Park (a predominantly Italian American suburb and long-reputed home of the Chicago Outfit), three each in Evanston and Oak Park, and two each in Franklin Park and Leyden Township (one of the latter being Gauger, who lived on the premises). Four were listed as residing in other states.

59. "8 Area Educators Off Jobs After Arrests in Raid," *CST*, April 28, 1964; and "Tangents: News & Views," *ONE* (July 1964), 12.

60. "109 Arrested in Vice Den."

61. Ellen Schrecker similarly describes the relationship between the state and the private sector in the anticommunist purges of the 1950s as follows: "The economic sanctions that made [McCarthyism] so effective followed a two-stage procedure. First, the politically tainted individuals were identified, usually by an arm of the state. . . . Then they were punished, usually by their employers." Schrecker, *Many Are the Crimes: McCarthyism in America* (Princeton, NJ: Princeton University Press, 1998), xvi. See also Johnson, *Lavender Scare*.

62. "2 More Teachers in Raid Quit; Others Off Duty," *CT*, April 28, 1964.

63. Russell Doll, "Double Standard for Teachers?" *CT*, May 7, 1964.

64. Larry Wolters, "'Bad Boy' of Radio, Sorkin, Airs Views," *CT*, April 29, 1964.

65. In particular, they were charged with perjury regarding testimony about a phony December 1963 raid apparently staged by the sheriff to protect a mob-connected gang of burglars. "4 Indicted Ogilvie Aides Given Leave," *CT*, September 27, 1964; Frank Hughes, "3 Deputies Found Guilty," *CT*, December 9, 1964; and "Cain Admits Perjury Plot, Gets 6 Mos.," *CT*, July 9, 1969. Cain ultimately avoided prison, but after losing his day job in law enforcement he remained a close aide to mob boss Sam Giancana, and was later killed by Chicago mob hit men in 1973. The treachery of Chaconas and Cain would seem to turn on its head the Cold War notion of homosexuals as "security risks" prone to disloyalty. "Double-Dealer's Death," *Time*, January 7, 1974. Cain's brother recalled, "Richard was pretty bigoted against gays, which was true of most cops at the time. When he was with the Chicago PD he considered them fair game for shakedowns and was pretty brutal with them at times. He killed a guy in 1959 who was a gay hustler and received a commendation for it. The raids that Richard led during his time with Ogilvie were generally not designed to clear vice from Chicago. He saw most all of them as shakedown opportunities." Michael J. Cain, e-mail communication to author, February 18, 2013. See also Michael J. Cain, *The Tangled Web: The Life and Death of Richard Cain—Chicago Cop and Mafia Hitman* (New York: Skyhorse Publishing, 2009), which includes a very useful discussion of vice policing. Ogilvie not only escaped the taint of his close association with Cain but also leveraged his aggressive tactics as sheriff, along with his well-publicized but unsuccessful prosecution of Accardo, to vault him to higher office. A Republican, he was elected Cook County board president in 1966 and governor of Illinois in a narrow victory over Democratic incumbent Sam Shapiro in 1968. In the gubernatorial campaign and in 1972, when Ogilvie lost to Dan Walker in a reelection bid, gay activists kept alive the memory of the Fun Lounge raid in urging gay and lesbian voters to reject Ogilvie. His biographer reports entirely uncritically on "the roughly 1,800 vice raids" as sheriff: "Dens of illegal activity, safe in the pre-Ogilvie years from bother by the sheriff's men, were hit again and again—just like Ogilvie's great-grandfather Reuben Spivey made life miserable for vice lords in the Kansas cattle town country in the previous century." Taylor Pensoneau, *Governor Richard Ogilvie: In the Interest of the State* (Carbondale: Southern Illinois University Press, 1997), 46–47; "Opposes Ogilvie Because of Fun Lounge," *MMN*, November 1968; and "Ogilvie Is Through in '72!" flier in WBK.

66. "The Tortured Course of Justice," *CT*, December 10, 1964.

67. Don Sullivan, "21 More Places Probed as Sex Deviate Hangouts," *Chicago's American*, April 28, 1964.

68. "3 Women, 6 Men Seized in Vice Raids," *CST*, April 29, 1964.

69. "33 Men Seized Thru Vice Raid on Bathhouse," *CT*, June 14, 1964.

70. Letter from H. B., *ONE* (July 1964), 31.

71. W. E. G. M., "Tangents: News & Views," *ONE* (July 1964), 14.

72. Letter from A. L., *ONE* (July 1964), 31.

73. Jeffrey Sweet, *Something Wonderful Right Away: An Oral History of the Second City and the Compass Players* (New York: Avon Books, 1978), 151–152 and 235–236; and Stephen E. Kercher, *Revel with a Cause: Liberal Satire in Postwar America* (Chicago: University of Chicago Press, 2006), 166.

74. William B. Kelley, interview by the author, March 18, 2007.

75. Edward C. Banfield, *Political Influence* (New York: Free Press, 1961), 148.

76. Cohen and Taylor, *American Pharaoh*, 293.

77. William B. Kelley, interview by the author, March 18, 2007.

78. "You can always stroll along Wells street in Old Town and observe the shaggy hippies . . . ," wrote one columnist, "altho some of the suburban kids imitating their wild way of dress, may fool you!" Mary Merryfield, "Should I Go with the Hippies?" *CT*, July 5, 1967.

79. Patricia Krizmis, "Find Togetherness on North Side," *CT*, August 28, 1966.

80. See, e.g., Robert Wiedrich, "9 Arrested in Vice Raids," *CT*, April 18, 1967. In one instance, on a night when eleven prostitutes were rounded up and arrested in and around Old Town, police superintendent James B. Conlisk said that the number was "slightly higher than average." "Push Near North War on Vice," *CT*, September 6, 1967.

81. Alan B. Anderson and George W. Pickering, *Confronting the Color Line: The Broken Promise of the Civil Rights Movement in Chicago* (Athens: University of Georgia Press, 1986); David J. Garrow, *Bearing the Cross: Martin Luther King, Jr., and the Southern Christian Leadership Conference* (New York: William Morrow, 1986); and Cohen and Taylor, *American Pharaoh*.

82. The issue gained traction in August 1963 over charges made following a Congress of Racial Equality demonstration against Superintendent of Schools Benjamin C. Willis and the use of aluminum portable classrooms and double-shift schedules at schools in black neighborhoods. See "No Police Brutality: Wilson," *CD*, August 15, 1963; and "Plan Protest for Jobs, Against Police Brutality," *CD*, August 20, 1963. See also, generally, Anderson and Pickering, *Confronting the Color Line*. For earlier *Defender* coverage of police brutality, see "Police Brutality in Pictures," *CD*, January 21, 1958; "Quiz Brutality Victim in Bed," *CD*, March 31, 1959; "ACLU Seeks to End Cop Brutality," *CD*, May 23, 1959; "Probe Police Brutality in Mystery Death," *CD*, December 26, 1962; "Dad of 2 Accuses Cop of Brutality," *CD*, December 31, 1962; and "2 Motorists Ask Probe of Police Brutality Here," *CD*, June 13, 1963.

83. "2 Debate Use of Baldwin Book," *CT*, January 19, 1965. See Whitney Strub, *Obscenity Rules: Roth v. United States and the Long Struggle Over Sexual Expression* (Lawrence: University Press of Kansas, 2013), 161–182.

84. Though the 1911 vice commission report focused on female prostitution, it also concluded that "the practice of sexual perversion" was "very prevalent and growing in Chicago." *The Social Evil in Chicago* (Chicago: Vice Commission of the City of Chicago, 1911), 39.

85. Morris Ryskind, "It's Been Acclaimed, But Is It Art?" *LAT*, February 10, 1965 (also reprinted in *CT*, February 14, 1965).

86. Jay McMullen, "Council Unit Rips Book by Baldwin," *CT*, January 9, 1965.

87. Jay McMullen, "Teachers Defended in Choice of Books," *CT*, January 8, 1965. At the beginning of the novel's third, and final, section, Vivaldo, a white male character who is romantically involved with Ida, a black woman, is the passive partner during anal intercourse with his gay friend Eric; the narrator describes this as Vivaldo's "first sexual encounter with a male in many years, and his very first sexual encounter with a friend." James Baldwin, *Another Country* (New York: Vintage Books, 1993 [1962]), 384. I thank Jordan Alexander Stein for very helpful discussions of the novel.

88. Testimony by Mrs. Kenneth Kantor, January 8, 1965, box 61, folder 4, LD.

89. "Baldwin Novel Is Criticized by an Expert," *CT*, January 8, 1965.

90. "Baldwin Case Letters Are Made Public," *CT*, January 21, 1965.

91. Jay McMullen, "Council Unit Rips Book by Baldwin."

92. "Book Controversy," *CD*, December 28, 1964. In a column touching on the "hysteria" over the novel, Lillian S. Calhoun noted that on a recent network show discussing the Baldwin controversy, the white radio personality Bob Considine had "soulfully lamented last week the death of family fare in the movies and theaters. However, he lumped two Broadway plays about miscegenation with a group he called 'sordid and revolting,' and that's a revealing notion." Calhoun, "Confetti," *CD*, December 28, 1964.

93. Mrs. Marion Turner of Evanston to Ald. Despres, January 16, 1965, in box 61, folder 5, LD.

94. "Council Attacks Freedom: Despres," *Woodlawn Booster*, January 13, 1965.

95. "Moral Responsibilities of Schools," *CDN*, December 30, 1964.

96. McMullen, "Council Unit Rips Book by Baldwin." On the role of Walt Whitman's homosexuality in a 1950s dispute over the naming of Philadelphia's Walt Whitman Bridge, see Marc Stein, *City of Sisterly and Brotherly Loves: Lesbian and Gay Philadelphia, 1945–1972* (Chicago: University of Chicago Press, 2000), 138–154.

97. "Unwelcome Presences," editorial, *CT*, December 12, 1964. The debate was even fodder for the conservative *Los Angeles Times* columnist Morris Ryskind, who wrote, "Boy Gets Girl, to Be Sure, but Boy also Gets Boy." Ryskind, "It's Been Acclaimed, But Is It Art?"

98. Specifically, a week after the pastor leaves, the hallway of this imaginary apartment building is flooded by "a swarming mass of tight-suited, girlish young men, some white, some colored, but all looking rather studious and serious, waiting to get in the apartment." The author continues: "They swish, they make dainty gestures with their delicate hands and the actual odor of their clinging feminity [sic] is so overpowering you hastily close your door and lean against it to regain your equilibrium. . . . Next to disappear from your floor is the doctor and his family." Dan Burley, "Why Not Legalize Redlight Districts, Part I" (originally published 1962 or earlier), reprinted in *New Crusader*, March 7, 1964.

99. "A Wise Decision," *CD*, February 1, 1965. See, for example, "Baldwin Gets Big *LIFE* Mag Spread," May 23, 1963; and "James Baldwin Here Thurs. Nite," August 28, 1963.

100. "Doesn't Like Baldwin's Book," *CD*, February 13, 1965. Marybeth Hamilton observes, "It's at exactly the time of the civil-rights movement that drag balls disappear from the black press," which is accurate for the glossy national magazines such as *Ebony* and *Jet*, though the *Defender* did continue to cover Finnie's Ball, in a limited way, into the 1970s, "Sexual Politics and African-American Music: or, Placing Little Richard in History," *History Workshop Journal* 46 (1998), 161–176, at 174.

101. "Moral Abdication," *CT*, January 30, 1965. ("Negro members of the school board refused to condemn the book, and a member of the city council who is a Negro was one of the two aldermen who blocked its prompt condemnation by the council.")

102. Alderman Despres and Charles Chew, an African American alderman "independent" of the machine—the only two council members who opposed Daley with any frequency—first blocked the body as a whole from taking up the measure condemning *Another Country*. In 1963, Despres and Chew had jointly introduced a fair-housing measure in the council. Shortly after the controversy over *Another Country*, in March 1965 during the voting-rights crisis in Alabama, they chartered two airplanes to fly 184 people from Chicago to join the civil rights march from Selma to Montgomery. James R. Ralph, Jr., *Northern Protest: Martin Luther King, Jr., Chicago, and the Civil Rights Movement* (Cambridge, MA: Harvard University Press, 1993), 279n.68; and Neil Steinberg, "Former Chicago Ald. Leon Despres Dead at 101," *CST*, May 6, 2009.

103. Jay McMullen, "Mayor Seeks to Save Our Image," *CT*, January 20, 1965. See also Jay McMullen, "Check Signals—Book Censure Voted," *CT*, January 13, 1965.

104. *Times Film Corp. v. City of Chicago*, 365 U.S. 43 (1961).

105. James Sullivan, "Baldwin Book Little Used in Top Colleges," *CT*, January 12, 1965. Richard Ellmann, a Northwestern University professor, testified to the council, "Whether we like his book or not, it is an important social barometer." Jay McMullen, "Teachers Defended in Choice of Books," *CT*, January 8, 1965.

106. *DOBCCN*, September 20, 1965.

107. *DOBCCN*, February 1966.

108. Indeed, more than a year later, a member of the president's Cabinet offered his resignation over his daughter's marriage to a black Stanford University classmate, and only later in the summer of 1967 did the Supreme Court strike down the remaining state laws prohibiting marriage across the color line. See Renee C. Romano, *Race Mixing: Black-White Marriage in Postwar America* (Cambridge, MA: Harvard University Press, 2003).

109. Del Shearer to "Marion," February 27, 1963, box 15, folder 12, LM.

110. Daughters of Bilitis Chicago Chapter minutes, box 15, folder 16, LM.

111. Del Shearer to Meredith Grey, December 2, 1963, box 15, folder 11, LM. Shearer was responding to a letter from Grey to the effect that she had heard from Randy Wicker that no one in Chicago was willing to appear on the program. Meredith Grey to Chicago DOB Chapter, November 24, 1963, box 15, folder 11, LM. Early in 1964, when David McElroy corresponded with Shearer to nail down the details of the taping, she provided a more precise reason for her change of heart. "You may recall my talking to you prior to your last program of this type, at which time I did not feel it wise to publicly represent myself," she wrote. "At present I am in a safer position, since I am no longer a suburban servant economically dependent upon city officials, chambers of commerce, and a newspaper that has eagerly backed politicians in their use of 'homosexuality' as a red herring." Delle Shearer to David McElroy, January 21, 1964, in box 15, folder 11, LM.

112. Special Report, "Off the Cuff," *The Ladder* 9:1 (October 1964), 9–12, at 11.

113. Special Report, "Off the Cuff," 9. Randy Wicker of New York had said, "Much more needs to be learned through legitimate research. Nevertheless, the same as the Negro or any other minority group member, I want my rights!"

114. Norman Ross to Delle Shearer, March 2, 1964, box 15, folder 11, LM.

115. Shearer also noted, "We had several inquiries here as a result of the article, though most apparently from people viewing us as a social club only." "Local Lesbians Also Fight for Integration; Open Office Here," *New Crusader*, July 4, 1964; Del Shearer to DOB Governing Board, August 15, 1964, box 15, folder 11, LM. See also Marcia M. Gallo, *Different Daughters: A History of the Daughters of Bilitis and the Rise of the Lesbian Rights Movement* (New York: Carroll & Graf, 2006), 71. As of May 1965, the *New Crusader*'s circulation was 27,000 (see clipping service stamp on "Senator Neuberger Speaks at Cancer Prevention Center's Victory Dinner," http://legacy.library.ucsf.edu/tid/fwv77b00/pdf).

116. Robert Wiedrich, "Raid Reveals Big Vice Bar Profit," *CT*, March 17, 1966; on the raids, "News Briefs," *MMN*, April 1966. Crime reporters such as Wiedrich enjoyed a cozy relationship with the police. Author's telephone conversation with Lois Wille, February 20, 2013.

117. Lois Wille, "The Homosexuals—A Growing Problem," *CT*, June 20, 1966.

118. Author's telephone interview with Lois Wille, February 20, 2013. John D'Emilio, "In the News," in Baim, *Out and Proud in Chicago*, 85.

119. Wille, "The Homosexuals—A Growing Problem."

120. Wille, "Police Watch Homosexuals' Hangouts Here," *CT*, June 22, 1966.

121. John Dreiske, "Senate Votes Study of Sex Deviation," *CST*, June 9, 1967.

122. "Sen. G. William Horsley (R-Springfield), sponsor of the measure, asserted that the problem concerning sex deviates is becoming acute in the state. He said, "[S]chool-age children are becoming 'hooked' on the practice and have been subject to blackmailing." Dreiske, "Senate Votes Study of Sex Deviation."

123. On the roughly contemporaneous exclusion of "sexual deviates" in the 1965 Hart-Celler Act, see Margot Canaday, *The Straight State: Sexuality and Citizenship in Twentieth-Century America* (Princeton, NJ: Princeton University Press, 2009), 247.

124. "Johnson Asks 'Good Life' for Big-City Americans," *CST*, April 24, 1964; and Robert Wiedrich, "Chicago Gives a Warm Hello to President," *CT*, April 24, 1964.

125. Open-ended interview (unnumbered), November 2, 1967, box 11, folder 3, WS.

Chapter 3

1. Mike Royko, *Boss: Richard J. Daley of Chicago* (New York: Dutton, 1971), 140.

2. Fewer than half as many respondents said they "often" felt the other three possible worries listed—"being publicly exposed," "being blackmailed," and "being robbed or rolled"—compared with the worry about the police. "ISR H Study Code Book," 142, box 186, JG.

3. Nan Alamilla Boyd, *Wide-Open Town: A History of Queer San Francisco to 1965* (Berkeley: University of California Press, 2003); Martin Duberman, *Stonewall* (New York: Plume, 1993).

4. ONE of Chicago, informational leaflet and correspondence describing its activities, box 16, folder 17, GAA.

5. James T. Sears, "Bob Basker (1918–2001): Selling the Movement," in *Before Stonewall: Activists for Gay and Lesbian Rights in Historical Context*, ed. Vern L. Bullough (Binghamton, NY: Harrington Park Press, 2002), 193–202, at 196. Lois Wille gave the final word in her 1966 article on police harassment to a man she describes as "the manager of one of the Clark-Diversey gay bars and a Mattachine Midwest officer." Lois Wille, "Police Watch Homosexuals' Hangouts Here," *CDN*, June 22, 1966.

6. Valerie Taylor, "Notes from a Lesbian Grandmother," *MMN*, 15th anniversary ed. (April/May 1980).

7. Esther Newton, "The 'Drag Queens': A Study in Urban Anthropology" (Ph.D. dissertation, University of Chicago, 1968), 24–25.

8. Joan Rivard and Del Shearer to Chicago DOB members, November 12, 1964, DOB Chicago Chapter newsletter file, LHA.

9. Beryl Satter, *Family Properties: Race, Real Estate, and the Exploitation of Black Urban America* (New York: Metropolitan Books, 2009).

10. "'No Police Brutality' Supt. Wilson Claims," *CD*, August 15, 1963; and "Police Brutality Getting Worse; Explodes Twice," *CD*, November 20, 1963.

11. Adam Cohen and Elizabeth Taylor, *American Pharaoh: Mayor Richard J. Daley—His Battle for Chicago and the Nation* (Boston: Little, Brown, 2000), 283–286 and 307–309.

12. An Illinois "mob action" law passed in 1965 gave the mayor latitude in handling suspicious gatherings, "allowing policemen to arrest anyone they believed capable of mayhem." The law was invoked in a spate of some 200 arrests of African Americans in Chicago

in the summer of 1967. Claude A. Clegg, "Nation Under Siege: Elijah Muhammad, the FBI, and Police-State Culture in Chicago," in *Police Brutality: An Anthology*, ed. Jill Nelson (New York: W. W. Norton, 2000), 102–131, at 121; and "County, City Accused of Negro Squeeze," *CT*, October 27, 1967. According to Clegg, the statute was rescinded in March 1968.

13. Frank Donner, *Protectors of Privilege: Red Squads and Police Repression in Urban America* (Berkeley: University of California Press, 1990), 131; and Lois Wille, "The Secret Police in Chicago," *Chicago Journalism Review* 2:2 (February 1969), 1–11.

14. Thomas J. Sugrue, *Sweet Land of Liberty: The Forgotten Struggle for Civil Rights in the North* (New York: Random House, 2008), 330.

15. Ibid., 327.

16. *Report of the National Advisory Commission on Civil Disorders* (Washington, DC: Government Printing Office, March 1, 1968), 93.

17. D. S. "Readers Respond," *The Ladder* (April 1961), 21–22.

18. William B. Kelley, e-mail communication to the author, July 26, 2014. The only pseudonym on this list, aside from the pen name Valerie Taylor (Velma Tate), was Don Blythe (1929–1982), whose real name was Donald Kornblith; Kelley, e-mail communication to the author, April 25, 2015.

19. Robert S. Basker to Clark P. Polak, April 5, 1965, in box 7, folder 21, MSNY.

20. "Chicago Chapter Meets Mattachine Midwest," *DOBCCN*, August 11, 1965; "The Mattachine Monthly Meeting," *DOBCCN*, October 11, 1965.

21. "Midwest Mattachine Society—Social Service Committee" meeting minutes, June 2, 1965, box 7, folder 21, MSNY.

22. Taylor, "Notes from a Lesbian Grandmother."

23. Andrew Patner, conversation with the author, July 20, 2009.

24. Jim Bradford, interview by Jack Rinella, December 9, 1995, transcript in Leather Archives & Museum.

25. Robert B. Ridinger, ed., *Speaking for Our Lives: Historic Speeches and Rhetoric for Gay and Lesbian Rights, 1892–2000* (Binghamton, NY: Harrington Park Press, 2004), 120.

26. Ibid., 117.

27. Kelley interview with the author, March 18, 2007.

28. Jim Bradford, letter to members, December 1, 1965, in folder: "Mattachine newsletters, direct mail letters," JR; and Taylor, "Notes from a Lesbian Grandmother." See also Martin Meeker, "Behind the Mask of Respectability: Reconsidering the Mattachine Society and Male Homophile Practice 1950s–1960s," *Journal of the History of Sexuality* 10:1 (January 2001), 78–116.

29. "The Missing Ingredient—Courage," *MMN*, June 1966. Unlike the ONE chapter's sponsor, the straight lawyer Paul Goldman, who was known for his willingness to pay off cops, the editors of the *Mattachine Midwest Newsletter* leaned toward the position that gays and lesbians themselves had a moral duty to appeal unfavorable rulings and attempt to overturn unjust legal precedents.

30. *MMN*, April 1966.

31. Karen C. Sendziak, "Pearl M. Hart (1890–1975)," in *Before Stonewall: Activists for Gay and Lesbian Rights in Historical Context*, ed. Vern L. Bullough (Binghamton, NY: Harrington Park Press, 2002), 56–62, at 59.

32. Jim Bradford, "President's Corner," *MMN*, December, 1966. See also John D'Emilio, "Gay Power!" in *Out and Proud in Chicago: An Overview of the City's Gay Community*, ed. Tracy Baim (Chicago: Surrey Books, 2008), 70–71, at 71.

33. "Police Begin 'Suspect' File," *CT*, January 17, 1966.

34. "The Police," *MMN*, June 1966.

35. "Entrapment, Harassment, Enticement Faces the Homosexual," *MMN*, August 1966.

36. "Klassen Field Notes, Mattachine Midwest (Chicago area homophile society), Pot Luck, May 28 (Sunday, 4 PM–7PM)" [n.d. but 1967], box 10, folder 4, WS.

37. Marc Stein, "'Birthplace of the Nation': Imagining Lesbian and Gay Communities in Philadelphia, 1969–70," in *Creating a Place for Ourselves: Lesbian, Gay, and Bisexual Community Histories*, ed. Brett Beemyn (New York: Routledge, 1997), 253–88.

38. "ISR H Study Code Book," 143, box 186, JG.

39. Code Book, 144.

40. Ibid.

41. Open ended interview #29, box 10, folder 6, WS.

42. "Yes, Virginia, There Is an MM Gremlin," *MMN*, June 1968. The commentary concludes, "But for those who fear the landlady may be more hip than she looks, hereafter your newsletter will arrive in a plain wrapper, as the pornies say, with only a chaste box number to identify it." William B. Kelley, who often worked on the newsletter with Taylor, says this language is identifiably Taylor's. E-mail communication to author, August 6, 2014.

43. Jim Bradford to Frank Kameny, July 23, 1968, in box 8, folder 3, FK.

44. Robert Wiedrich, "Nab 14 in Raid on Near North Side," *CT*, January 29, 1968. The floor manager had been "found hiding in a dumbwaiter between the first and second floors of the four-story building." According to William B. Kelley, "This was actually a public, licensed bar-restaurant, but on Sunday nights it closed itself to the public and admitted only persons who had joined the 'private club" it created for Sunday-night dancing purposes. At that time, Chicago police forbade same-sex dancing in public licensed premises. Police gained entrance to the Trip that Sunday by confiscating someone's club membership card on the street outside." Kelley, e-mail communication to author, April 25, 2015.

45. Kelley interview, March 18, 2007.

46. Wiedrich, "Nab 14 in Raid on Near North Side."

47. "'Lucky Jim' Bradford," *MMN*, July–August, 1968.

48. "The Dish Rag," *MMN*, July–August, 1968.

49. Dal McIntire, "Tangents," in *Tangents* (October 1968), 22, copy in WBK; and "Schedule for Remainder of NAHC, 8/14/68," box 5, folder 4, MSNY. On Kameny's emulating the slogan "Black Is Beautiful" when he formulated "Gay Is Good" earlier in the summer of 1968, see Toby Marotta, *The Politics of Homosexuality* (Boston: Houghton Mifflin, 1981), 62–63. On the conference's official adoption of "Gay Is Good," see Martin Duberman, *Stonewall* (New York: Plume, 1993), 222. Minutes of NACHO Fourth Conference, August 12–17, 1968, Chicago, IL, WBK. "Homosexuals Ask Candidates' Ideas," *NYT*, August 19, 1968.

50. *Rights in Conflict: The Walker Report to the National Commission on the Causes and Prevention of Violence* (New York: Bantam, 1968), 56–57.

51. D. J. R. Bruckner, "Tense Chicago 'Policed Up' for Convention," *LAT*, August 25, 1968. The article notes that "plainclothes detectives of the Chicago police force . . . are conducting surveillances on known radicals, Black Power leaders, [and] political leaders."

52. Jim Flint, interview by Jack Rinella, July 11, 1995, transcript in JR, GH.

53. "Annex Saves Its License," *CGC*, June 1974; and *Easy Life Club, Inc. v. License Appeal Commission of the City of Chicago*, 18 Ill.App.3d 879, 310 N.E.2d 705 (1974), 707.

54. "Cops Ride Again," *MMN*, September 1968.

55. Jim Bradford, at least, wrote that the group "owes an enormous debt of gratitude" to the visitors, especially those from San Francisco's Society for Individual Rights, for "helping us see some of our shortcomings as an organization." Jim Bradford, "The President's Corner," *MMN*, October 1968.

56. Letter to Superintendent Conlisk, August 21, 1968, reprinted in *MMN*, September 1968, emphasis in original.

57. "News Releases," *MMN*, September 1968.

58. "Petition Campaign Mounted to Protest Police Harassment of Homosexuals" (press release), box 67, folder 10, GL.

59. "Cops Ride Again."

60. "The adult homosexual is 1. a citizen, 2. a taxpayer, 3. a voter," and thus "entitled to all the guarantees of the Constitution," the petition stated. "Forgotten Citizens Unite," in WBK.

61. Genet's emotionally intense and angry article included deliberately shocking and sarcastic praise for the "superb thighs" and "imposing members" of the Chicago cops. Jean Genet, "The Members of the Assembly," *Esquire*, November 1968, 83–89, at 87. See also Edmund White, *Genet: A Biography* (New York: Knopf, 1993), 506–514, esp. 511–512; and Norman Mailer, *Miami and the Siege of Chicago* (New York: Signet/New American Library, 1968), 152–153.

62. Kelley interview, March 18, 2007. Ginsberg went on to be part of the small group of activists charged in the Chicago Eight (later Chicago Seven, after Bobby Seale was removed from the group) conspiracy trial.

63. *Rights in Conflict: The Walker Report to the National Commission on the Causes and Prevention of Violence* (New York: Bantam, 1968).

64. See, e.g., Terry Southern, "Grooving in Chi," in *Esquire*, November 1968, 83–86, at 84.

65. Steve Clark, quoted in Sukie de la Croix, "Chicago Whispers," *Outlines*, May 21, 2000.

66. De la Croix, "Chicago Whispers," November 19, 1997.

67. Earl Caldwell, "Violence Stirs Chicago Negroes," *NYT*, August 30, 1968. David Farber has argued that black Chicagoans' complaints about the Chicago police were deeply implicated—for the mayor, city officials, and ordinary police officers—in the dynamics of the convention-week conflicts. More generally, Farber argues that Daley viewed "the state of his streets and his parks and his neighborhoods as a matter of pride and personal accountability." Farber, *Chicago '68* (Chicago: University of Chicago Press, 1988), 123, 256.

68. Ian Lekus, "Losing Our Kids: Queer Perspectives on the Chicago Seven Conspiracy Trial," in *The New Left Revisited*, ed. John McMillian and Paul Buhle (Philadelphia, PA: Temple University Press, 2003), 199–213.

69. Vidal's biographer observes, "The ten million people watching had heard a first, something almost unbelievable in those censored and sensitive days." Fred Kaplan, *Gore Vidal: A Biography* (New York: Doubleday, 1999), 601. As Marcie Frank puts it, "The public invisibility of Vidal's sexual orientation ended . . . when he was outed on national TV . . . in an episode that was said to have rocked television." Frank, *How to Be an Intellectual in the Age of TV: The Lessons of Gore Vidal* (Durham, NC: Duke University Press, 2005), 99.

70. "Meetings Yes . . . ," *MMN*, October 1968.

71. "Meetings Yes . . ."; and Karen C. Sendziak, "Pearl M. Hart (1890–1975)," 59.

72. "Meetings Yes . . . ."

73. Bradford, "The President's Corner," *MMN*, October 1968.

74. "Meetings Yes . . . ," December 1968.

75. Jim Bradford to Barbara Gittings, September 24, 1968, box 67, folder 10, GL.

76. Bill Kelley, "Riot, Tree-Cutting Mark NYC Gay Scene," *MMN*, July 1969.

77. William B. Kelley, "Report on Attendance at Conference on Police Discretion, Held at University of Chicago Law School, April 12, 1969," WBK.

78. Andrew J. Diamond, *Mean Streets: Chicago Youths and the Everyday Struggle for Empowerment in the Multiracial City, 1908–1969* (Berkeley: University of California Press, 2009), 290–291.

79. Stienecker, "A Gay Deceiver, or Is He?," *MMN*, September 1969.

80. It was a memorial march in Johnson's honor that led to "the first angry rally in the park the week before the convention." Marie J. Kuda, "Chicago's Stonewall: The Trip Raid in 1968," in *Out and Proud in Chicago*, 79–83, at 81.

81. Ron Dorfman, "Mattachine Editor Arrested; Gays Picket Sergeant Manley," *Chicago Journalism Review* 3:4 (April 1970), 4; David Stienecker, interview by Jack Rinella, July 19, 1995, transcript in JR; "Mattachine Editor Arrested," *Gay*, no. 8, n.d., box 1, folder 10, Mattachine Midwest organizational records, GH; Peter Fisher, *The Gay Mystique: The Myth and Reality of Male Homosexuality* (New York: Stein and Day, 1972), 185.

82. David Stienecker, interview by Jack Rinella, July 19, 1995, transcript in JR, 14–15.

83. Jim Bradford and Bill Kelley, "Cops Hit More Bars," *MMN*, October 1969.

84. Lekus, "Losing Our Kids"; Dennis Altman, *Homosexual: Oppression and Liberation* (New York: Avon, 1973 [1971]), 180. See also Frank Kusch, *Battleground Chicago: The Police and the 1968 Democratic National Convention* (Chicago: University of Chicago Press, 2008).

85. Henry De Zutter, "Homosexuals Blast Foran," *CT*, February 28–March 1, 1970; "Less Talk—More Action," *CGAN*, February 1972, 6. See also Bill Kelley's letter to the editor, published with his initials, though he had signed the letter for publication: "Foran's Epithet," *Chicago Today*, March 9, 1970.

86. Loren Baritz, "Daley and Hoffman: Two Masks for One Phenomenon," *CT*, November 18–19, 1970.

87. Irv Kupcinet, "Kup's Column," *CST*, December 23, 1969.

88. See Faith C. Christmas, " 'It Was Murder,' Rush," *CD*, December 6, 1969; Ted Lacey, "Whites Up in Arms, Join Blacks in Protest Here," *CD*, December 9, 1969; "Negroes in Chicago Impose a Curfew on Whites," *NYT*, December 16, 1969; "Chicago Negroes Back Off on Curfew," *NYT*, December 17, 1969; "The 'War' Between Panthers and Police," *NYT*, December 21, 1969; "Emotions Flare at Hearing," *CD*, December 22, 1969; and "Hampton Neighbors to Face Bleak Yule," *CD*, December 24, 1969. The Chicago chapter of the Black Panther Party was distinct from chapters in other cities in that, before his murder, Hampton had prodded the group toward interracial coalitions, forging a particularly successful alliance among black, Latino, and poor white Appalachian migrant young people on Chicago's North Side. It was Hampton who coined the phrase "rainbow coalition" to describe it. The phrase was undeniably catchy—"an amalgam that combines the ambiance of 'West Side Story' with the theory and discipline of the National Liberation Front," as the *New York Times* put it. Jon Rice, "The World of the Illinois Panthers," in *Freedom North: Black Freedom Struggles Outside the South, 1940–1980*, ed. Jeanne Theoharis and Komozi Woodward (New York: Palgrave

Macmillan, 2003), 41–64, at 55–56. See also Michael T. Kaufman, "Black Panthers Join Coalition with Puerto Rican and Appalachian Groups," *NYT*, November 9, 1969.

89. "Ortez Is Free!" *Chicago Seed* 7:7 (1971), 10.

90. "'Female Impersonator' Killed by Cop in W. Side Street Brawl," *Chicago Defender*, November 28, 1970; "Why Should We Live in Fear?" *Chicago Seed* 7:10 (1971), 7; "Protest Police Harassment of Gays," *Chicago Seed*, 7:13 (1971), 6; Ferd Eggan, interview by the author, April 30, 2007; and John D'Emilio, *In a New Century: Essays on Queer History, Politics, and Community Life* (Madison: University of Wisconsin Press, 2014), 164–165.

91. Elandria V. Henderson, a member of Black Gay Liberation, "Black Gay Liberation," *Lavender Woman*, May 1972.

92. The Black Caucus of Chicago Gay Liberation became the group Third World Gay Revolution.

93. Liz Highleyman, "Peace Activism and GLBT Rights," *Gay & Lesbian Review Worldwide*, September/October 2004.

94. "Ortez Is Free!" As Regina Kunzel has shown, gay liberationists were quite concerned with the fate of gays and lesbians in prison as well. Kunzel, *Criminal Intimacy: Prison and the Uneven History of Modern American Sexuality* (Chicago: University of Chicago Press, 2008),

95. "Gays Get Zapped," *Chicago Seed* 7:12 (1971), 11.

96. "Community," *Chicago Seed* 7:11 (1971), 14.

97. Brian C. Mullgardt, "'Don't Come to Chicago': The Events Surrounding the 1968 Democratic National Convention as Experienced by Chicago Residents" (Ph.D. dissertation, University of Connecticut, 2008), 9.

98. Bob Olmstead, "100 Walk Out on Rochford at Police–Community Parley," *Chicago Sun-Times*, June 2, 1972; "Youths Harass Conlisk," *CT*, June 2, 1972; and Patricia Stewart, "New Latin Group Fights Alleged Cop 'Harassment,'" *Booster*, November 4, 1970.

99. Eventually participants marched out, shouting, "Power to the people." "Community Control of the Police . . . *Not* Police Control of the Community," *Chicago Seed*, 8:8 (1972), 16.

100. "How Far Have We Gotten?" leaflet, n.d., in Chicago Gay Liberation Memorabilia collection, box 1, GH.

101. Bud Schultz and Ruth Schultz, *The Price of Dissent: Testimonies to Political Repression in America* (Berkeley: University of California Press, 2001); part 4 of the book, titled "A Notable Reversal," focuses on Chicago's Alliance to End Repression.

102. Schultz and Schultz, *The Price of Dissent*, 406.

103. George Sikes, memo to "small group to begin plans for formation of Alliance Task Force on Gay Rights," June 12, 1974, in box 2, AER-GRTF folder, ACS.

104. "6 Arrested at Belmont Rocks," *Chicago Gay Life*, August 15, 1975.

105. "This," Bradford wrote, "is the part that provides for concentration camps for political dissenters." Jim Bradford, "Alliance Calls for Action," *MMN*, December 1970/January 1971, 4.

106. "Opposes Ogilvie Because of Fun Lounge," *MMN*, November 1968.

107. "City Revokes 8 Licenses; 6 Are Taverns," *CT*, June 7, 1968.

108. Kelley, e-mail communication to the author, April 25, 2015; "Chicago Only Close Law K-O'D.," *Beverage Dealer & Tavern News* 38:12, Illinois Diamond ed. (April 1969); and *Johnkol, Inc. v. License Appeal Commission of City of Chicago*, 42 Ill.2d 377, 247 N.E.2d 901 (1969). The state Supreme Court decided, "The same rules must apply in Chicago as Downstate." Burnell Heinecke, "Chicago-Only Tavern-Closing Law Killed," *CST*, March 28, 1969.

109. William B. Kelley, "Through the Swinging Doors," *MMN*, April 1969.

110. "Annex Saves Its License," *CGC*, June 1974; and *Easy Life Club, Inc. v. License Appeal Commission of the City of Chicago*, 707.

111. Nancy MacLean, *Freedom Is Not Enough: The Opening of the American Workplace* (Cambridge, MA: Russell Sage/Harvard University Press, 2006); Jacquelyn Dowd Hall, "The Long Civil Rights Movement and the Political Uses of the Past," *Journal of American History* 91 (2005), 1233–1263; and Kevin J. Mumford, "The Trouble with Gay Rights: Race and the Politics of Sexual Orientation in Philadelphia, 1969–1982," *Journal of American History* 98 (June 2011), 49–72.

Chapter 4

1. Bob Stanley, "Gay Pride Week, 1970: That Was the Week That Was," *MMN*, July 1970, 1; "Gay Liberation Stages March to Civic Center," *CT*, June 28, 1970; and Richard Larsen, "Gay Pride Week," *Chicago Seed* (1970), clipping in box 26, folder 5, CWLU. The other marches were in New York, Los Angeles, and San Francisco.

2. My discussion here both builds on and seeks to supply historical context for Cathy J. Cohen's important critique of the ethnic model of gay politics, which she argues has contributed to the "secondary marginalization" of lesbian, gay, bisexual, and transgender people of color. That model, Cohen argues, "with its assumption of whiteness as an essential characteristic of normativity, privileges from its inception white members of lesbian, gay, bisexual, and transgendered communities, while disadvantaging the people of color in these groups." Cohen, "Straight Gay Politics: The Limits of an Ethnic Model of Inclusion," in *Ethnicity and Group Rights*, ed. Will Kymlicka and Ian Shapiro (New York: New York University Press, 1997), 572–616, at 578.

3. "1,500 Gays 'Come Out of the Closet,'" *CST*, June 25, 1973.

4. Joan Zyda, "Gays Called 'Pioneers': 'Back-to-the-City' Trend Is Charted," *CT*, November 12, 1978.

5. Paul Varnell, "Being Neighbors Together," typescript, Media 1987 folder, box 2, ILGTF.

6. Lawrence Muhammad, "Aldermen Claim Black Clergy Oppose 'Gay' Issue," *CD*, September 15, 1979.

7. Nathaniel Clay, "Blacks and Gays: An Odious Comparison," *CD*, June 14, 1977.

8. They even had reason to fear that one's homosexuality could legally be recorded by a credit agency if a prior employer were to mention its having been the grounds for dismissal. A letter on this topic is answered in Paul R. Goldman's advice column, "Law and the Homosexual," *CGC*, November/December 1974, 2. Goldman's answer suggests that the job applicant's rights in this circumstance were limited to the right to obtain a copy of the contents of the credit report—but, he writes, ambiguously, "The only exclusion is medical reasons, and hopefully they will not contend that homosexuality is a disease."

9. John D'Emilio, "Let's Dance," in *Out and Proud in Chicago: An Overview of the City's Gay Community*, ed. Tracy Baim (Chicago: Surrey Books, 2008), 98. One planner of the dance recalled that he very much had the Democratic National Convention events of August 1968 and the risk of police brutality on his mind. Comments of Murray Edelman at "Gays in the Revolution: Lesbian and Gay Liberation in Chicago," a panel discussion in the Chicago History Museum's Out at CHM event series, April 19, 2007.

10. Renee Hanover, in Hanover and Marie Kuda, joint interview by Gregory Sprague, May 19, 1980, GAS.

11. Steve Rosenberg, interview by Jack Rinella, transcript in JR, 8; and "Gay Liberation Sponsors First City-Wide Dance," *Second City*, 2:7, n.d., in ephemera file, GH.

12. Bill Kelley notes that several years earlier, on a trip to Springfield, he discovered that a bar near the state capitol, Smokey's Den, "was already allowing same-sex dancing, albeit in a room closed off from the front bar by a curtain. Springfield was ahead of Chicago" (e-mail communication to author, August 6, 2014).

13. *MMN*, June 1970. Some scholars on the left seem almost to have the gay movement specifically in mind when they write, for example, "We've got an entire academic pedagogy devoted to the notion that symbolic dissent—imagining, say, that the secret police don't want us to go to the disco, but that we're doing it anyway—is as real and as meaningful, or, better yet, *more* real and *more* meaningful than the humdrum business of organizing and movement-building" (Thomas Frank, "When Class Disappears," *The Baffler* 9 [1997], 3–12, at 7). There was nothing imaginary about the Chicago police not wanting gays to go to the disco.

14. Gerald Nicosia and Richard Raff, *Bughouse Blues: An Intimate Portrait of Gay Hustling in Chicago* (New York: Vantage Press, 1977), 59.

15. "Schism in Gay Lib!" *Chicago Gay Liberation Newsletter*, 1:9 (October 1970), 1.

16. "Kup Denies Bigotry, Eyes Gays for TV" *CGC*, September/October, 1974; and William B. Kelley's letter to the editor, "Don't Knock Gay Liberation" ("gay liberation is talking about real people here and now, not Royko's mythical monkeys"), in *CT*, March 28, 1974.

17. Background report on Chicago Gay Liberation Front, October 8, 1970, Chicago Police Red Squad files, box 150, file 964-L/Organizations, 1970, CHM.

18. In 1973, the Chicago-based American Bar Association called for the repeal of the nation's remaining sodomy laws. *CGC*, August 1973.

19. David Stienecker, interview with Jack Rinella, in JR, 14–15. See also "100 Protest Harassing of Homosexuals," *CT*, April 17, 1970. *MMN* printed a bitter complaint in February 1970 after a board member of ONE of Chicago, the most conservative of the city's gay organizations, appeared on a local television talk show and downplayed the jobs issue. "We were . . . surprised to learn that Chicago homosexuals face no particular problems with employment. Despite his statements, we are still not convinced of the advisability of declaring your homosexuality on your next employment application." Steve Robertson, "Job, Police Problems Denied," *MMN*, February 1970.

20. Nancy Banks, "'Sexual Orientation' at City Hall," *CR*, November 2, 1973. A state bill to ban job discrimination by private employers on the basis of sexual orientation was first introduced in Springfield in 1975. A version of it eventually passed in 2005, by which time its language had been revised to incorporate gender identity as well as sexual orientation.

21. Patrick Butler, "Gays Becoming More Accepted, Local Activist Says," *Booster*, March 19, 1975.

22. Richard Chinn, "Brother Defends Gay Lib Tactics," *MMN*, October 1970.

23. Victor Varbo, "Statement of Purpose: Black Caucus/Gay Liberation," n.d. [but likely August 1970], in Chicago Gay Liberation Memorabilia, GH.

24. Elandria V. Henderson, a member of Black Gay Liberation, "Black Gay Liberation," *LW*, May 1972, 5.

25. Jan Faller, "Black Gay Movement," *CD*, October 29, 1977.

26. "Homosexuals Rap with Elk Grove High School," *Elk Grove Herald*, February 17, 1972.

27. Martin P. Levine, "Gay Ghetto," in *Gay Men: The Sociology of Male Homosexuality*, ed. Martin P. Levine (New York: Harper & Row, 1979), 182–204, at 188.

28. The most conservative of Chicago's daily papers, the *Tribune*, for example, devoted a long, sympathetic article to a gay-male weight-loss group in mid-1976. "If I were at a Weight Watchers meeting tonight," explained one twenty-five-year-old male member of the Lavender Elephants, "I couldn't get up before the group and say I went home and ate and ate because I was rejected at a [gay] bar. They'd be in shock." Joan Zyda, "They're Elephants and Proud of It," *CT*, June 14, 1976. See also "How Therapy Center Helps Gays Accept Themselves," *Booster*, March 24, 1976, and "Gay Ghetto Tenants Unite," *MMN*, September 8, 1972.

29. Denise DeClue, "Gays 'n' Pols," *CR*, May 6, 1977.

30. Ibid.; and Steve Rosenberg, interview by Jack Rinella, transcript in JR, GH.

31. I am grateful to Bill Kelley for helping me to describe this timeline accurately. William B. Kelley, e-mail communication to author, August 6, 2014.

32. Nancy MacLean, "Postwar Women's History: The 'Second Wave' or the End of the Family Wage?" in *A Companion to Post-1945 America*, ed. Jean-Christophe Agnew and Roy Rosenzweig (Malden, MA: Blackwell, 2002), 235–259.

33. D. Bradford Hunt, *Blueprint for Disaster: The Unraveling of Chicago Public Housing* (Chicago: University of Chicago Press, 2009), 149. Hunt argues that "structural forces later deepened problems in the 1970s, but social disorder was present in high-rises with large numbers of children right from the start" (146).

34. This was the section of Lakeview bounded by Diversey Parkway, Irving Park Road, Broadway, and Sheridan Road. Joseph Schwieterman and Dana M. Caspall, *The Politics of Place: A History of Zoning in Chicago* (Chicago: Lake Claremont Press, 2006), 62–63. "Citizens came out in droves to protest the construction of these boxy buildings, which exploded on the scene in the mid-to-late 1960s. Shoehorned into many residential blocks, four-plus-ones were built from lot line to lot line and consisted of four floors of efficiency or one-bedroom apartments elevated on pylons or columns to allow parking at or below grade. With the parking level (which was exempt from FAR [floor area ratio] calculations), these buildings stood five stories tall (hence their name, 'four-plus-ones')" (61–62).

35. Telegram from Lake View Citizens' Council, Carl Wirtz, President, to Richard J. Daley, October 9, 1969, in box 68, Lake View Citizens' Council Correspondence/Newsletters folder, LPCA.

36. Letter circulated in the fall of 1969, in box 68, Lake View Citizens' Council Correspondence/Newsletters folder, LPCA.

37. The stand-alone photo appeared with the headline, "To Avert Another 4 Plus 1," *CT*, July 15, 1968; and Kit Barrett, "Refuse to Indorse 445 Barry Avenue '4 Plus 1' Revision," *CT*, January 18, 1970.

38. The man added, "It's the old stereotype, 'Bring in a fag and let him fix up the place. After all, they're all good interior decorators, aren't they?'" Barbara Ettorre, "Gay Men Discuss Their Lives, Parents, Images," *Chicago Today*, June 27, 1972.

39. "Gays Can Find Housing—Fear Fact of Life on the Job," *CST*, June 29, 1977.

40. This is documented by Gilbert Herdt and Andrew Boxer in their book-length discussion of Horizons, the social-service agency for gay youth in Chicago. The residential population of the eastern half of Lakeview, more than 99 percent white in the 1950 census, increased its black population to 10.2 percent by 1980. In 1980, 84 percent of Lakeview's African American population lived in this eastern section where gays had their highest level of concentration. The area also saw a large influx of Latinos, but because the census changed the way it

counted Latinos between 1970 and 1980, from a question about "Spanish language" to one about "Spanish surname," it is unreliable for tracking this shift. Herdt and Boxer, *Children of Horizons: How Gay and Lesbian Teens Are Leading a New Way Out of the Closet* (Boston: Beacon Press, 1993), 40–41. A 1979 article described Lakeview as "a sandwich of ethnicities and economic strata," distinguishing between "the affluent sector on Lake Shore Drive"; a middle area populated by gays and Latinos where there were many "older homes being rehabilitated"; and, on the west side, "a crust of working-class ethnics." "44th Ward Vote Perils Independents' Toehold," *CST*, January 29, 1979.

41. Walter L. Lowe, "Sex in America: Chicago," *Playboy* (April 1979).

42. Max Smith, interview by the author, January 16, 2007.

43. Ibid., July 31, 2008.

44. This was true of a significant number of urban Universal Fellowship of Metropolitan Community Churches congregations founded in the 1970s.

45. Milton L. Rakove, *Don't Make No Waves, Don't Back No Losers: An Insider's Analysis of the Daley Machine* (Bloomington: Indiana University Press, 1975), 31, 33.

46. Stephen O. Murray, "The Institutional Elaboration of a Quasi-Ethnic Community," *International Review of Modern Sociology* 9 (1979), 165–177, at 170–171, quoting Raymond Breton, "Institutional Completeness in Ethnic Communities," *American Journal of Sociology* 70 (1964): 195–205, at 194 (emphasis is Murray's); Leonard Norman Primiano, "The Gay God of the City: The Emergence of the Gay and Lesbian Ethnic Parish," in *Gay Religion*, ed. Scott Thumma and Edward R. Gray (Walnut Creek, CA: Altamira, 2005), 7–29. Writing around the same time as Murray, Martin P. Levine indexed the spatial concentration of gay-male gathering places in several cities; as discussed above, he found that in Chicago's case 64 percent of them were situated in a few areas that together occupied less than 1 percent of the city's land mass. ("Gay Ghetto," 182–204, at 188).

47. "Black Lesbians Win Fight Against Chicago Bar Bias," comp. Emmy Goldknopf, *Gay Community News*, July 28, 1980.

48. Delegates-at-large were chosen only by those few dozen delegates already elected in Democratic primary balloting, making this a limited campaign (Kelley, e-mail communication to the author, August 8, 2014).

49. This paragraph is based on the audio recording by Morty Manford of much of the conference and of interviews conducted there, in Series 5, Morty Manford Papers, NYPL (quotation from Abney on Tape 1); Guy Charles, "A New National Gay Rights Platform," *Advocate*, March 15, 1972; Laud Humphreys, *Out of the Closets: The Sociology of Homosexual Liberation* (Englewood Cliffs, NJ: Prentice-Hall, 1972), 162–168; and Bill Kelley, interviews with the author. See also "N.Y. Gay Activists Disrupt Lindsay's Campaign Fund Raiser at Music Hall," *Variety*, January 26, 1972.

50. William J. Grimshaw, *Bitter Fruit: Black Politics and the Chicago Machine, 1931–1991* (Chicago: University of Chicago Press, 1992), 116–117.

51. Roger Biles, *Richard J. Daley: Politics, Race, and the Governing of Chicago* (DeKalb: Northern Illinois University Press, 1995), 169; Adam Cohen and Elizabeth Taylor, *American Pharaoh: Mayor Richard J. Daley—His Battle for Chicago and the Nation* (Boston: Little, Brown, 2000), 493. The campaign that elected Singer as an "independent" alderman from the 44th Ward—independent, that is, of the machine—also, according to Daley's biographers, "reflected a new fault line that was emerging in Chicago Democratic politics" (*American Pharaoh*, 494). Singer went on to join Jesse Jackson in spearheading an ultimately successful

challenge to the Daley machine's handpicked delegation before the Democratic National Convention's Credentials Committee in 1972, a challenge that went all the way to the convention itself and epitomized the challenge that young whites and blacks posed to the Chicago Democratic Party's long-standing exclusionary policies. Rick Perlstein notes that with the televised images of Jesse Jackson wearing a dashiki and demanding a seat in the Illinois section on the convention floor, Jackson "became a visual symbol of the reformers' theft of 'regular' Democrats' birthright, and a great political party's civil war." Perlstein, *Nixonland: The Rise of a President and the Fracturing of America* (New York: Scribner, 2008), 693. The Singer and Hubbard elections were the first of several over the next decade in which outsider candidates unexpectedly defeated machine incumbents, including the winning black-led campaign in 1972 to defeat State's Attorney Edward Hanrahan, who oversaw the 1969 killing of the Black Panther leaders Fred Hampton and Mark Clark.

52. Bill Kelley, "Through the Swinging Doors," *MMN*, April 1969.

53. Tracy Baim and Owen Keehnen, *Leatherman: The Legend of Chuck Renslow* (Chicago: Prairie Avenue Productions, 2011), 31–32.

54. Bruce Vilanch, "Man's Country, Hottest Spa in Town," *CT*, February 14, 1975.

55. Baim and Keehnen, *Leatherman*, 274.

56. DeClue, "Gays 'n' Pols." She concluded that, "as a working member of the regular organization, he's proving that he can get out the votes." Renslow is also described as a 43rd Ward Democratic precinct captain in "125 Gays Hold Rally in Daley Plaza," *CT*, June 25, 1977.

57. Barbara Ettorre, "Laws Are on the Books, But Gays Struggle On," *Chicago Today*, June 26, 1972.

58. Cohen and Taylor, *American Pharaoh*, 493–494, at 494; and L. F. [Lu] Palmer, Jr., "Daley's Black Votes Show Significant Dip," *CT*, n.d., in WBK.

59. "Old Law Puts Heat on Cops in Chicago," *Pittsburgh Press*, April 22, 1973.

60. Dennis D. Fisher, "New Hobbs Act Ruling Seen Broadening Corruption Probes," *CST*, October 28, 1973. See also Robert E. Hartley, *Big Jim Thompson of Illinois* (Chicago: Rand McNally, 1979), 64.

61. Bob Wiedrich, "Tower Ticker," *CT*, June 11, 1972.

62. Ibid., August 11, 1972.

63. Ibid., January 18, 1973.

64. *United States v. Clarence E. Braasch*, 505 F.2d 139 (7th Cir. 1974).

65. William B. Kelley, "Eye on the News," *CGC*, November/December 1974.

66. Quoted in Marie J. Kuda, "Cops, Bars, and Bagmen," in *Out and Proud in Chicago*, 82.

67. "Gay Bars Named in Cop Payoff Trial," *CGC*, September 1973.

68. "Gay Bars Here Multiply as Atmosphere Relaxes," *CST*, September 7, 1975.

69. "ISR H Study Code Book," 23, box 186, JG.

70. Barbara Ettorre, "Lesbians Live in a 'Twilight Zone,'" *Chicago Today*, June 28, 1972. Shear went on to become one of the most successful performers in the women's music movement of the 1970s. Richard Pfeiffer, a gay activist, told a reporter, "Today landlords and employers find other excuses for rejecting prospective workers or tenants than just coming out and saying it's because the person is gay." Yet the reporter noted that "as far as Pfeiffer is concerned, the mere fact that some businesses find it necessary to report [sic] to this kind of hypocrisy is evidence of some progress." Patrick Butler, "Gays Becoming More Accepted, Local Activist Says," *Booster*, March 19, 1975.

71. William Simon and John H. Gagnon, "The Lesbians: A Preliminary Overview," in *Sexual Deviance*, ed. Gagnon and Simon with the assistance of Donald E. Cairns (New York: Harper and Row, 1967), 247–282, at 266. In an e-mail to the author, December 12, 2013, Gagnon confirmed that the interviewees quoted in this article were all members of Chicago's Daughters of Bilitis chapter.

72. "Ask Ann Landers: A Christmas Both Merry and Gay," *CST*, November 25, 1970.

73. Denise DeClue, "Gays'n'Pols," *CR*, May 6, 1977.

74. "For the four per cent of American males who are exclusively homosexual, public knowledge of their sexual preference bars all but a few employment possibilities." "Government-Created Employment Disabilities of the Homosexual," *Harvard Law Review* 82:8 (June 1969), 1738–1951, at 1738.

75. "Homosexual Employment Questionnaire," ca. February 1972, WBK.

76. "Homosexual Employment Questionnaire" completed by Richard G. Rinder [?], Director of Personnel Relations, Helene Curtis Ind., WBK.

77. "A person's sexual orientation or practice shall not affect his eligibility for employment with federal, state, or local governments, or private employers," read the item. The other four "basic rights" were the right of adults to engage in private consensual sex; the right to be charged with solicitation only "upon the filing of a complaint by the aggrieved party, not a police officer or agent"; the right to equal access to security clearances, visas, and citizenship status; and the right to serve in the armed forces and obtain veterans' benefits. "Homosexual Bill of Rights," adopted by NACHO, August 17, 1968, in *Los Angeles Advocate*, October 1968, 6.

78. Samuel K. Gove and James D. Nowlan, *Illinois Politics and Government: The Expanding Metropolitan Frontier* (Lincoln: University of Nebraska Press, 1996), 75.

79. "Daley Acts to End Sex Bias in City," *CT*, October 28, 1971.

80. Comments of Chuck Lamont, tape 1 (control #02835), Series 5, Morty Manford Papers, NYPL.

81. "Rights Bills to Get Hearing!" *CGC*, October 1973.

82. "Gays Heard by Council," *CD*, October 11, 1973.

83. Robert McClory, "Clifford Kelley: The Outraged Alderman," *CR*, July 18, 1980.

84. Edward Schreiber, "4 Challenge Holman in 4th Ward," *CT*, January 31, 1971.

85. David K. Fremon, *Chicago Politics, Ward by Ward* (Bloomington: Indiana University Press, 1988), 136.

86. Derrik Thomas, "Ald. Kelley Calls for Caucus," *Chicago Metro*, June 22, 1974. See also McClory, "Clifford Kelley: The Outraged Alderman; "9 Black Backers of Daley Assail Police Brutality," *CT*, May 16, 1972; and Vernon Jarrett, "Clifford Kelley's School Board Plan," *CT*, September 8, 1978.

87. Joseph Longmeyer, "Gays Push for Rights Here," *CD*, October 10, 1973.

88. "Gay 'Kiss-In,'" *CD*, June 29, 1974.

89. Six of eleven cosponsors were black. William B. Kelley, "Gay Rights Bills Filed in City Council," *CGC*, July, 1973; and Nancy Banks, "'Sexual Orientation' at City Hall," *CR*, November 2, 1973.

90. Banks, "'Sexual Orientation' at City Hall," 1.

91. Ron Grossman, "Signed for the War's Duration," *Advocate*, April 23, 1975.

92. Grossman, "Signed for the War's Duration."

93. Cliff Kelley, interview with author, November 7, 2007.

94. Ibid.

95. Michael Miner, "Kelley Hits Council Hangups for Gay Rights Bill Failure," *CST*, November 16, 1975.

96. Grossman, "Signed for the War's Duration."

97. Muhammad, "Aldermen Claim Black Clergy Oppose 'Gay' Issue."

98. "Analysis of Voting," *GayLife*, May 27, 1977.

99. Gay Rights Task Force minutes for September 12, 1974, December 12, 1974, and January 30, 1975, all in box 2, AER-GRTF folder, ACS.

100. "Ald. Burke Attacks Gays," *CGC*, August 1974; "Chicago Gays Still Hope but Setbacks Dim Chances," *Advocate*, September 11, 1974 (Burke announced "he had just fired off what he called a 'blistering' letter to Chicago's John Cardinal Cody condemning the two gay rights bills"). Similarly, when gay Catholics in Chicago created the nation's first Mass specifically for gays, they were delighted when the archbishop, John Cardinal Cody, formally allowed the Mass to continue on April 8, 1971, little anticipating that this decision would later be reversed—permanently—in a crackdown by the church hierarchy. "Cardinal Allows Gay Mass to Continue," *CGAN*, April 1971, 2–3.

101. Gay Rights Task Force minutes, November 22, 1974, in box 2, AER-GRTF folder, ACS.

102. Les Trotter, "Illinois Rights Bills Go to Assembly," *GayLife*, February 18, 1977. One scholar contends, however, that elite antigay perceptions were at least as important as New Right mobilization. John Skrentny, *The Minority Rights Revolution* (Cambridge, MA: Belknap/Harvard University Press, 2002), 323. In support of this view, see Bob Secter, "Catcalls, Defeat Greet Homosexual Job Rights Bill," *CT*, May 23, 1977, describing the first vote on gay rights in the Illinois legislature.

103. Gay Rights Task Force minutes, November 22, 1974, in box 2, AER-GRTF folder, ACS.

104. William B. Kelley, letter to the editor, *CGC*, February–March 1975. When Mayor Daley died in December 1976, an editorial in Chuck Renslow's *GayLife* newspaper stated, "Many people have felt that Hizzoner [Daley] was the main obstacle to gay civil rights legislation in this city." *Gay Life*, December 24, 1976. See also "City Council to Get New Gay Rights Bills," *CGC*, April/May 1975, 3 ("Observers felt that the failure of the committee to meet [regarding the bills], even though its chairman was on the list of bill sponsors, was the result of failure on the part of the city administration to make a recommendation concerning the bills").

105. DeClue, "Gays 'n' Pols."

106. Sudbury, who worked on former Alderman Bill Singer's ill-fated 1975 mayoral campaign against Richard J. Daley, died from AIDS in 1984. IVI-IPO Independent Gay/Lesbian Caucus Dinner and First Annual Glynn Sudbury Awards program, May 18, 1985, in box 1, Allan C. Wardell Papers, GH.

107. Patricia Moore, "Susan Catania: Keeping Track of Home and House," *CT*, December 30, 1977. On the Hyde Amendment, see Rickie Solinger, *Pregnancy and Power: A Short History of Reproductive Politics in America* (New York: New York University Press, 2005), 200–210.

108. "But why," asked one columnist, "if homosexuality is just another handicap, the insistence on keeping it in the closet? The reason, I think, is fear. No one supposes that the

nonhandicapped, children or adults, will be influenced into short-leggedness or nearsightedness or heart disease." Bill Raspberry, "Understanding the Gay Rights Issue," *CST*, June 18, 1977.

109. "Caucus Head Charges Gays Rejected as Voter Registrars," *CST*, February 1, 1978.

110. "Analysis of Voting," *GayLife*, May 27, 1977.

111. DeClue, "Gays 'n' Pols."

112. Jane Fritsch, "8 Arrested as 3,000 Gays Protest Anita Bryant's Shriner Show Here," *CT*, June 15, 1977.

113. Photograph in *Blazing Star*, August 1977, 2.

114. Sukie de la Croix, "Chicago Whispers," *Outlines*, April 28, 1999.

115. "Gays: Homebodies to Hustlers," *CST*, June 26, 1977; and Ron Anderson, "1977 Was a Year of Challenges and Progress," *Gay Life*, January 6, 1978.

116. "Statement of Candidacy," January 8, 1978, in Gary Nepon Papers, GH.

117. George Estep, "Nepon Confident He Can Win in 13th Dist.," *CT*, March 15, 1978.

118. Robert Reidenbach to Gary Nepon, March 11, 1978, in Gary Nepon Papers, GH.

119. "LV's Gary Nepon Thinks It's Time for Gay Legislator," *Booster*, November 2, 1977.

120. Tom Peters, "Gay Candidate Announces Plans to Run for Office," *GayLife*, October 28, 1977.

121. Sally Ann Palmer, "Parties: Rip Gay Hopeful for Ingratitude to O'Brien," *Near North News*, October 29, 1977.

122. "Problems of the City" talk-radio program, WAIT-AM radio, audio recording in Gary Nepon Papers, GH.

123. "New Campaign Issues Attract New Candidates," *CST*, March 9, 1978.

124. Harvey Milk speech, March 4, 1978, audiotape in Gary Nepon Papers and transcribed by Karen C. Sendziak, copy in the possession of the author.

125. Rodney C. Wilson, "Why Gays Must Vote Gay," *GayLife*, March 10, 1978.

126. "A Machine Candidate over a Gay Candidate?" *GayLife*, March 17, 1978.

127. David Axelrod, "Four Chicago Independents Swept Out of Seats in House," *CT*, March 23, 1978.

128. "2d Gay Running for Office," *CT*, November 12, 1977.

129. "Renslow Runs for Democratic Delegate," *GayLife*, December 7, 1979.

130. "44th Ward Vote Perils Independents' Toehold," *CST*, January 29, 1979.

131. William Griffin, "Two Independent Candidates Withdraw," *CT*, February 2, 1979.

132. Sukie de la Croix, "Black Pearls," *BLACKlines*, May 1999.

133. Thomas R. Chiola, the first successful openly gay candidate for public office in Chicago, was elected as a Cook County circuit court judge in 1994.

134. Marcia Froelke Coburn, "Toward a Gay *Politik*," *Chicago*, October 1979, 224.

135. Alfredo S. Lanier, "Coming Out and Moving On," *Chicago*, November 1983, 239.

136. Sheehan went on to commend specifically those who had planned the Flag Day demonstration. "They were most co-operative," he said. "They wanted a lawful and orderly demonstration." "Chicago 'Better Than Most Places,'" *CST*, June 28, 1977.

137. GLCMC minutes, August 10, 1976, Gay and Lesbian Coalition of Metropolitan Chicago Records, GH.

138. "Presidential Hopefuls' Views on Gay Rights," *CGC*, January 1976; and "'No Anti-Gay Bias in State Jobs': Walker Aide," *CGC*, January 1976.

139. DeClue, "Gays 'n' Pols."

140. Coburn, "Toward a Gay *Politik*," 224.

Chapter 5

1. M. J. Kuda, "Media Montage," *MMN*, March 1970, 11.

2. Betty Peters, "Notes on Coming Out, i.e., They Mean to Kill Us All," *LW*, May 1972, 3.

3. As a contemporary popular book about lesbian liberation pointed out, "Lesbians, on all levels, identify their interests with their jobs in a more concrete way than other women, since for them Prince Charming is not going to come galloping up and, if and when he does, he will be rejected." Sidney Abbott and Barbara Love, *Sappho Was a Right-On Woman: A Liberated View of Lesbianism* (New York: Stein and Day, 1972), 47. Lesbian feminism developed in the context of a crucial "paradox" to which Nancy MacLean has drawn attention: "[D]espite having produced the world's strongest women's movement and the vastest public policy apparatus to fight sex discrimination, the United States still has one of the largest wage gaps between the sexes." "Postwar Women's History: The 'Second Wave' or the End of the Family Wage?" in *A Companion to Post-1945 America*, ed. Jean-Christophe Agnew and Roy Rosenzweig (Malden, MA: Blackwell, 2002), 235–259, at 237. Margot Canaday notes, "The regime of coverture and the regime of heterosexuality thus move along opposite arcs: as the first was coming undone, the second was rising in its stead. This was a ragged and uneven transition—one whose periodization is difficult to capture with exact precision—in part because the old regime left a sediment on the new." "Heterosexuality as a Legal Regime," in *The Cambridge History of Law in America*, vol. 3, ed. Michael Grossberg and Christopher Tomlins (New York: Cambridge University Press, 2008), 442–471, at 445.

4. "I Was a Flesh Peddler," *LW*, October 1974, 1.

5. "Lesbian Survival School," *LW*, October 1973, 6.

6. Bill Osgerby, *Playboys in Paradise: Masculinity, Youth, and Leisure-Style in Modern America* (Oxford: Berg, 2001), 4.

7. Katherine Sender, *Business, Not Politics: The Making of the Gay Market* (New York: Columbia University Press, 2004), 33.

8. Sue, "Dear Mother," *LW*, December 1971, 3.

9. Merle Kaminsky, "Lesbians Search for Sisterhood," *Booster*, October 10, 1972.

10. Sandy Skord, "Uniting Lesbians," *MMN*, July 1973, 7.

11. Claudia Scott, "929-HELP Helps Lesbians," *LW*, July 1974, 17. This was the Gay Switchboard created by Michael Bergeron, discussed in Chapter 4.

12. "Putting It to City Hall," *LW*, November 1973, 7.

13. Alice Kessler-Harris, *In Pursuit of Equity: Women, Men, and the Quest for Economic Citizenship in 20th-Century America* (New York: Oxford University Press, 2001), 246.

14. Anne Enke, *Finding the Movement: Sexuality, Contested Space, and Feminist Activism* (Durham, NC: Duke University Press, 2007), 12.

15. The CWLU operated "at one time or another projects focused on day care, women in prison, workplace organizing, political education, a liberation school, outreach, a journal (*Secret Storm*), a legal clinic, a lesbian rap group, a rock group, a poster and art collective, and several health care projects, including an abortion task force, pregnancy testing, and HERS (health evaluation and referral service)." Sara M. Evans, *Tidal Wave: How Women Changed America at Century's End* (New York: Free Press, 2003), 160–161. Evans argues that socialist feminism has been underemphasized in historical scholarship, which has tended, since Alice Echols's pioneering book *Daring to Be Bad*, to view "cultural feminism," characterized by an

essentialist view of femininity, as having replaced radical feminism as the prevailing strain of left feminist thought in the 1970s (*Tidal Wave*, 158).

16. Sheila Wolfe, "Job Equality Plea Made," *CT*, April 24, 1973; and "Labor Force Up, but Gals' Pay a Bad Second," *CT*, January 21, 1973.

17. Susan Edwards, "Women Employed," *LW*, November 1973, 6.

18. Margaret Wilson, "Lesbian Lore," *CGC*, September 1973, 3.

19. See, e.g., Winifred D. Wandersee, *On the Move: American Women in the 1970s* (Boston: Twayne, 1988), 127–130.

20. Fran Kozlik, letter to the editor, *LW*, November 1972, 5.

21. "Lesbianism and Socialist Feminism" (Chicago Women's Liberation Union position paper, "Written by the Gay Women's Group of the CWLU and adopted by the CWLU at its annual membership conference, November, 1972"), in Chicago geographic file, LHA, 6. See also Evans, *Tidal Wave*.

22. Judy Henderson, "And What If We Get into Listening," *LW*, November 1972, 15.

23. Barbara Ettorre, "Lesbians Live in a 'Twilight Zone,'" *Chicago Today*, June 28, 1972.

24. Elandria V. Henderson, "Black Gay Liberation," *LW*, May 1972, 5.

25. Michal Brody, ed., *Are We There Yet?: A Continuing History of Lavender Woman, a Chicago Lesbian Newspaper, 1971–1976* (Iowa City, IA: Aunt Lute Press, 1985), 55.

26. Michal Brody, "Some Historical Background," in Brody, *Are We There Yet?*, 6.

27. Loretta Mears, "I'm Hurt . . . I'm Angry," *LW*, July 1972, 4. From an interview with Loretta Mears: "So I get really angry when women—dark women or light-skinned women—talk about how early separatism and separatism now doesn't have anything to say to dark women, or that we didn't have anything to do with the theory and ideas that got developed. That's just not true. I know the kind of impact we had. Dark women have a herstory in lesbian separatism, and it should not be minimized or ignored." Brody, *Are We There Yet?*, 130.

28. Jill Johnston, "Dyke Nationalism and Heterosexuality" [first published October 12, 1972], in *Admission Accomplished: The Lesbian Nation Years (1970–75)* (London: Serpent's Tail, 1998), 172, 173.

29. Simone de Beauvoir, "Introduction" to *The Second Sex* (1953), in *The Second Wave: A Reader in Feminist Theory*, ed. Linda Nicholson (New York: Routledge, 1997), 15.

30. "Unusual Union," *CD*, September 30, 1970.

31. "Two Females 'Married' in Chicago—to Each Other," *Jet*, October 15, 1970.

32. Betty Peters Sutton, interview with Michael Brody, in Brody, *Are We There Yet?*, 30.

33. Margaret, "Blacklesbian," *LW*, November 1971, reprinted in Brody, *Are We There Yet?*, 13.

34. "A Study/Action Project: Chicago Gay Bars," *CLL Newsletter*, n.d. [but ca. November 1973], 3; and "Hazards, Bias in Bars to Be Investigated," *CGC*, November 1973.

35. Chicago Lesbian Liberation meeting minutes, June 11, 1973; and Lynn McKeever to Susan Edwards, June 12, 1973, both in CLL folder, Chicago geographic file, LHA.

36. Barbara Lightfoot, "*LW*," *Cries from Cassandra* 1:1 (June 1973), 5; I have retained the idiosyncratic capitalization of the original.

37. "Workin' Thru the System," *Killer Dyke* 1:1 (September 1971), 2.

38. "New and Improved Closet," *LW*, April 1975, 7.

39. Susan Edwards, "ERA and the Lesbian Ghetto," *LW*, November 1973, 6.

40. Jorjet Harper, "The Agony and the Ecstasy: Lesbian Separatism," in *Out and Proud in Chicago: An Overview of the City's Gay Community*, ed. Tracy Baim (Chicago: Surrey Books, 2008), 124–125.

41. Elaine Jacobs and Colleen Monahan, dir., *Lavender* (13 min., color; Perennial Education, 1972).

42. Valerie Taylor, "People Power," *MMN*, April 1970, 4.

43. "The Great Chicago History Quiz," *Lunatic Fringe: A Newsletter for Separatist, Anarchist, and Radical Feminist Lesbians in Chicago*, n.d. [but late 1970s or 1980], Chicago geographic file, LHA.

44. Quoted in Del Martin and Phyllis Lyon, "Lesbian Liberation Begins," *Harvard Gay & Lesbian Review*, Winter 1995, 16.

45. See, e.g., the flyer for a Women's Liberation/Gay Liberation Teach-Out in 1970 at Northwestern University, in vertical file, LC.

46. "New Gay Way," *CGAN*, December 1971, 11.

47. Hannah Frisch, interview by Ana Minian, November 21, 2003, collection of the Lesbian and Gay Studies Project, Center for Gender Studies, University of Chicago (transcript in author's possession). The book referred to is *Sisterhood Is Powerful: An Anthology of Writings from the Women's Liberation Movement*, ed. Robin Morgan (New York: Random House, 1970).

48. "Reflections on the Lack of Unity in the Chicago Gay Community," *LW*, December 1975, 5.

49. "Why We Left Chicago Gay Alliance," *LW*, December 1971, 2.

50. "Goals of Chicago Lesbian Liberation," n.d., CLL organizational file, LHA, emphasis mine.

51. "Women's Liberation Adherents Go to War with *Playboy* Again," *CT*, April 24, 1970. The secretary apparently said she could not promise not to do it again.

52. William N. Eskridge Jr., *Dishonorable Passions: Sodomy Laws in America, 1861–2003* (New York: Viking, 2008), 176. See also Rob Cole, "ACLU Launched on Major Gay Rights Project," *Advocate*, November 21, 1973, 18.

53. GLCMC minutes, April 13, 1976, GLCMC.

54. William B. Kelley, interview by the author, December 2, 2006.

55. "The Great Chicago History Quiz," 1.

56. "Mother Right Interview," *LW*, February 1975, 6.

57. "Chicago's Lesbian Feminist Center," *LW*, June 1974, 3.

58. "*LW* Interviews the Community: Lesbian Thoughts on Gay Pride," *LW*, June 1974, 1.

59. CLL meeting minutes, June 11, 1973, and Lynn McKeever to Susan Edwards, June 12, 1973, both in CLL folder, Chicago geographic file, LHA.

60. Marie Jayne Kuda, "Second *LW* Appears," *CGC* (September–October 1974), 8.

61. *Chicago GayLife*, June 20, 1975.

62. "Coalition News," *Blazing Star*, January 1977, 8; "Coalition to Organize, Vote on Proposed Procedures," *GayLife*, January 7, 1976; "Nat'l Gay Lobby Plans Made Here," *CGC*, April 1976; and Max Smith, interview by the author, January 16, 2007.

63. "Gay/Lesbian Pride Week," *Blazing Star*, January 1977, 7.

64. "Reject Lesbians' Bid to Wed, Sit-In Starts," *CDN*, October 20, 1975; Jeff Lyon, "Lesbians Protest at Marriage Office," *CT*, October 21, 1975; Lynn Sweet, "Prison Can't Crush Lesbians' Marriage Crusade," *CST*, 10 February 1977; and "Lesbian Pair Seized Again in

Marriage Bid," *CST*, October 22, 1975. According to one gay activist, it was "the first time that the combined sit-in and hunger-strike strategy has been used anywhere in an attempt to force the issuance of a marriage license to individuals of the same sex." Charles Nicodemus, "2 Lesbians to Seek License to Wed," *CDN*, October 18, 1975.

65. "Reject Lesbians' Bid to Wed"; "Lesbians Jailed in Marriage Protest at County Building," *GayLife*, October 29, 1975; and advice column, *CD*, November 27, 1975.

66. "Coalition to Organize; Vote on Proposed Procedures," *GayLife*, January 7, 1976; and "Nat'l Gay Lobby Plans Made Here," *CGC*, April 1976 (*Advocate* conference).

67. One gay man objected, asking why he must be "excluded from a gay women's coffee house in this city simply because I am male." Tom Peters, "Coalition Hears Clinic Report; Discusses Sexism," *GayLife*, November 26, 1976.

68. "Discrimination Within Our Community: Has It Happened to You?" and "Discriminación dentro de nuestra comunidad: ¿Le ha acontecido a usted?" both 1980, in Chicago geographical file, LHA.

69. Max Smith, interview by the author, January 16, 2007; and "Coalition News," *Blazing Star*, January 1977, 8.

70. Robert W. Bailey, a political scientist, in a study of the geographic concentration of gay men and lesbians, argued in the late 1990s that the two groups were "more separated socially than outsiders might expect but more closely linked politically than some insiders might perceive." Bailey, *Gay Politics, Urban Politics: Identity and Economics in the Urban Setting* (New York: Columbia University Press, 1999), 77.

71. Linda Rodgers, interview by Jack Rinella, July 17, 1995, in JR.

72. Denise DeClue, "Gays 'n' Pols," *CR*, May 6, 1977, emphasis mine.

73. "Something Old, Something New, Something Borrowed . . . ," *LW*, December 1975, 4.

74. "Gay/Lesbian Pride Week," *Blazing Star*, January 1977, 7.

75. "Lesbians Charge Bias by Gay Men," *CST*, June 27, 1977.

Chapter 6

1. Gary Rivlin, *Fire on the Prairie: Chicago's Harold Washington and the Politics of Race* (New York: Henry Holt, 1992), 347–361.

2. Robert O. Self, *All in the Family: The Realignment of American Democracy Since the 1960s* (New York: Hill and Wang, 2012), 236–237. Embracing gay rights helped a startling number of black mayors win election, including, early on, Tom Bradley of Los Angeles. It was Marion Barry in Washington, DC, however, who perhaps most effectively exploited this strategy before Harold Washington. Milton Coleman, "Barry Endorsed by City's Major Gay Rights Group," *WP*, March 21, 1978, and Kwame A. Holmes, "Chocolate to Rainbow City: The Dialectics of Black and Gay Community Formation in Postwar Washington, D.C., 1946–1978" (Ph.D. dissertation, University of Illinois at Urbana-Champaign, 2011).

3. Denise DeClue, "Gays 'n' Pols," *CR*, May 6, 1977.

4. Rick Kogan, "A Labor of Love," *CST*, June 25, 1981.

5. The meeting was held on March 26, 1977; see Dudley Clendinen and Adam Nagourney, *Out for Good: The Struggle to Build a Gay Rights Movement in America* (New York: Simon and Schuster, 1999), 285–291.

6. "If I'm not mistaken," Richard J. Daley is alleged to have told Byrne upon appointing her, in a tone of self-congratulation, "you'll be the first woman commissioner in any major city in the United States." Rivlin, *Fire on the Prairie*, 65.

7. Richard Foley, a professor at the University of Illinois at Chicago, told a reporter, "I think it's a sense of her style that is attractive to gays. A sense of class, a certain flamboyancy. I mean, you'd pick up a newspaper and one day she'd be on an elephant at the circus and four hours later she'd be at a fire-fighting situation." R. Bruce Dold, "Civil Rights Battle Looms as Gays Gain Political Power," *CT*, September 4, 1984.

8. "Chicago Mayor Signs Antibias Order," *Advocate*, August 5, 1982.

9. "Gays Protest Raids," *CT*, June 6, 1979; Bob Wiedrich, "Gays Turn Heat Back on Police," *CT*, June 19, 1979; John Gorman, "Mayor Endorses Gay Rights Plan," *CT*, August 31, 1979; and Robert Davis, "Byrne Hits Cops for Raid on South Loop Gay Bar," *CT*, January 1, 1980.

10. Bonita Brodt, "Gays Fear Resumption of 'the Raiding Game,'" *CT*, February 28, 1980.

11. Police Community Relations Committee report, June 8, 1981, box 2, Police Community Relations folder, ACS.

12. Evaluations in box 4, Cadet Reactions 1981 [Aug.] folder, ILGTF.

13. IGLTF press release, April 16, 1982, in "General Interest to Women" binder, box 2, Lesbian Community Center Records, GH.

14. William B. Crawford, Jr., "Suit Assails 1985 Raid on Gay Bar," *CT*, December 16, 1986; "50 Men in Raid at Gay Bar May Each Get $5,000," *CST*, August 18, 1989; William Grady, "Accord Reached in Gay-Bar Raid Suit," *CT*, August 18, 1989. "It might have been cheaper for state taxpayers if the agents had walked into Carol's Speakeasy that night, handed $1,000 to each of the customers and sent them all home," wrote one columnist. Bill Grady, Merrill Goozner, and John O'Brien, "Meter Still Going on State's Bar Raid," *CT*, May 30, 1989.

15. See Clendinen and Nagourney, *Out for Good*, 274–277.

16. Ibid., 416–420; Neal Peirce, "The Gay-Rights Cause Moves Forward," *Boston Globe*, August 4, 1980; and Eugene Robinson, "Gay Caucus Proud But Lacks Power," *WP*, August 13, 1980.

17. Self, *All in the Family*, 248–275.

18. William Currie, "Two Legislators Unswayed by Ministers Against ERA," *CT*, June 22, 1980.

19. Thom Shanker, "Byrne Gains Support as She Promises to March in Gay Parade," *CT*, February 11, 1983.

20. Brian J. Kelly and Basil Talbott, Jr., "Washington Win 'Iced' by Whites," *CST*, February 24, 1983; and see, four years later, Greg Hinz, "Lakefront Cinches Washington Bid," *Lincoln Park-Lake View Booster*, February 25, 1987.

21. Paul Cotton, "Washington Appears at Community Forum," *GayLife*, April 7, 1983. On Washington's gay-rights record, see Les Trotter, "Candidate Backs Gay Rights," *GayLife*, April 15, 1977. On Hyde's long-standing opposition to the Equal Rights Amendment, see Henry J. Hyde, "Equal Rights Amendment: The Losses Can Outweigh the Gains," *CT*, June 9, 1972, and David Axelrod and Daniel Egler, "ERA Issue Won't Go Away, Hyde Says," *CT*, June 12, 1982. For Washington's campaigning on women's issues, including his charge that female city workers remained underpaid under Byrne, see Mitchell Locin and Thom Shanker, "Mayor Candidates Target Women's Issues," *CT*, February 13, 1983. See also Rivlin, *Fire on the Prairie*; Paul Kleppner, *Chicago Divided: The Making of a Black Mayor* (DeKalb: Northern Illinois University Press, 1985); and Arnold R. Hirsch, "Harold and Dutch: A Comparative

Look at the First Black Mayors of Chicago and New Orleans," in *The Making of Urban America*, ed. Raymond A. Mohl (Wilmington, DE: Scholarly Resources, 1997), 265–282.

22. Jacky Grimshaw, interview with the author, November 4, 2007.

23. Jon-Henri Damski, "Looking Beyond Black Tuesday," *GayLife*, March 17, 1983.

24. Editorial, "Harold Washington: The Clear Choice for Chicago," *GayLife*, March 31, 1983.

25. Alfredo S. Lanier, "Coming Out and Moving On," *Chicago*, November 1983, 238–239.

26. COGLI bylaws, n.d., box 4, folder 38, MR.

27. "Chicago Police Chief Names Liaison to Gay Community," *Advocate*, March 6, 1984.

28. Thom Shanker, "Mayor Celebrates First Year in Office," *CT*, March 9, 1984.

29. Harold Washington to Julie Valloni and Victor Salvo, September 17, 1987, in box 4, folder 38, Community Services Series, MR; and Michael Briggs, "City Law for Gays Gets Push," *CST*, October 12, 1987.

30. Albert Williams, "Hustling the Gay Vote," *CR*, May 31, 1985.

31. Ibid.

32. Greg Hinz, "Political Clout Coming Out of Closet," *Lerner*, December 7, 1985 [?], in clippings file on Homosexuality—Chicago—Political Activities, MRL.

33. Florence Hamlish Levinsohn, *Harold Washington: A Political Biography* (Chicago: Chicago Review Press, 1983), 282. In the words of one account, Washington's fiancée Mary Ella Smith "suddenly materialized in the 1983 campaign." Melvin G. Holli and Paul M. Green, *Bashing Chicago Traditions: Harold Washington's Last Campaign, 1987* (Grand Rapids, MI: Eerdmans, 1989), 183.

34. Rivlin, *Fire on the Prairie*, 262.

35. "Love Gay-Baits Mayor," *WCT*; "Mayor Discusses Gay Rumors in N.Y. 'Times,'" *GayLife*, May 3, 1984; and E. R. Shipp, "Chicago Mayor Regrets Time Spent on His Rival," *NYT*, April 22, 1984.

36. Rivlin, *Fire on the Prairie*, 53.

37. "Chicago City Council Support for Gay Rights Ordinance Bridges 'Factions,'" *GayLife*, November 17, 1983.

38. Williams, "Hustling the Gay Vote"; and "Orbach Seeks AIDS Funding in '84 Budget," *GayLife*, December 15, 1983.

39. Williams, "Hustling the Gay Vote."

40. Raymond Risley to William Schneider, June 10, 1987, in Police-Community folder, box 4, ILGTF.

41. Achy Obejas, interview by the author, January 9, 2012.

42. "Cities are treated like failed industries, cut off from the central economy, left to sink or swim if they can, the survivors urged to 'vote with their feet' and migrate to defense industries in the Sun Belt, the halt and the lame callously discarded like so much worn-out furniture," Washington said. *Journal of the Proceedings of the City Council of the City of Chicago, Illinois,* May 4, 1987, http://docs.chicityclerk.com/journal/1987/050487INAUGURAL.pdf.

43. Michael Briggs, "City Law for Gays Gets Push," *CST*, October 12, 1987.

44. William N. Eskridge, Jr., *Gaylaw: Challenging the Apartheid of the Closet* (Cambridge, MA: Harvard University Press, 1999), 356–361. Chicago was the second-largest city in every decennial census from 1890 through 1980, so technically there remained only one larger city, New York, at the time.

45. William Juneau, "'Gay Rights' Bill Opponents Call for Citywide Referendum," *CT*, September 12, 1979; and Lawrence Muhammad, "Aldermen Claim Black Clergy Oppose 'Gay' Issue," *CD*, September 15, 1979. The Plymouth Foundation advertisement, which appeared in the *Sun-Times* and *Tribune* on September 9, 1979, listed a Chicago mailing address. However, the group's 1975 articles of incorporation apparently listed a Lake Forest address, and its executive director, Tony Ahlstrom, is described in news articles throughout the 1970s and 1980s, which touch on Ahlstrom's religious activism and long-distance runs for various causes, as a Lake Forest resident, and, by the early 1980s, as the pastor of Christ Church there. "Explain Antigay Ads, Group Told," *CT*, September 18, 1979. See also, e.g., James Robison, "Christian Booksellers Reporting Spirited Gains," *CT*, June 12, 1976; Thomas Schilling, "Faith a Steady Light for 2 Crash Burn Victims," *CT*, April 1, 1983; "5 More Injured in Crash at Edens-Clavey Corner," *CT*, April 29, 1983; and "Lake Forest Thrills to Gills by a Shower of Dead Smelt," *CT*, October 7, 1987. Earlier in 1979, the Associated Press reported that Ahlstrom had disturbed Illinois state senators by calling, during the normally uncontroversial opening prayer at a floor session, for "fewer laws—and especially ones with loopholes." "Power of Prayer Disturbs Senators," *Spokane Daily Chronicle*, May 5, 1979.

46. Winifred Breines, *The Trouble Between Us: An Uneasy History of White and Black Women in the Feminist Movement* (New York: Oxford University Press, 2007), 89–92.

47. Harlon L. Dalton, "AIDS in Blackface," *Daedalus* (Summer 1989), 205–227, at 215–216.

48. Leon Forrest, "Souls in Motion," *Chicago*, July 1985, 128–135, 148, at 133.

49. City of Chicago Committee on Human Rights and Consumer Protection, report of proceedings for December 1, 1988, copy in GH, 80, 137.

50. R. Bruce Dold, "Civil Rights Battle Looms as Gays Gain Political Power," *CT*, September 4, 1984. In 1987, WMAQ television, the local NBC affiliate, invited Crawford to debate gay rights with Max Smith, a black gay activist and the then treasurer of the Illinois Gay Rights Task Force. "Reverend Hiram Crawford was a black minister, and they probably wanted a black gay activist to debate him," Smith recalled. The two developed an awkward rapport. "He always recognized me when he saw me," Smith said, "and we always shook hands, and we learned a lot from each other from talking one on one." Max Smith, interview by the author, July 31, 2008.

51. The church historian David D. Daniels III has labeled Crawford as "an independent Holiness pastor in Chicago who has embraced elements of the black neoconservative platform," and a figure who "directly challenged those supporting the political agenda of Jesse Jackson." See Daniels, "'Doing All the Good We Can': The Political Witness of African American Churches in the Post–Civil Rights Era," in *New Day Begun: African American Churches and Civic Culture in Post-Civil Rights America*, ed. R. Drew Smith (Durham, NC: Duke University Press, 2003), 164–182, at 173.

52. "Moral Majority Hits Springfield," *GayLife*, May 2, 1985. The bill's sponsor, Representative Woods Bowman of Evanston, said, "A couple of supporters are weakening" because of the lobbying, adding, "A lot of these people have storefront churches on practically every block in their district."

53. IGLTF State Coordinating Committee meeting minutes, December 7, 1985, in Illinois Gay Network folder, box 3, ILGTF.

54. "'Doing All the Good We Can,'" 173.

55. Fredrick C. Harris notes that "in many instances church members themselves pushed their ministers to participate in Washington's campaign, as many Southern activists had done

during the civil rights movement." "Black Churches and Machine Politics in Chicago," in *Black Churches and Local Politics: Clergy Influence, Organizational Partnerships, and Civil Empowerment*, ed. R. Drew Smith and Fredrick C. Harris (Lanham, MD: Rowman & Littlefield, 2005), 117–136, at 128.

56. Chinta Strausberg, "Gay Bill Ignites Discord," *CD*, July 17, 1986.

57. COGLI minutes, May 27, 1987, folder 40, box 4, Community Services Series, MR.

58. Harry Golden, Jr., "Gays Lose, 30–18," *CST*, July 30, 1986; and author's conversation with Kit Duffy, November 4, 2007. For Catholic criticism of Bernardin, see letters in *Chicago Catholic*, August 15, 1986.

59. J. H. Johnson, interview with Clarence Page, *WCT*, August 7, 1986.

60. Hannah Frisch, "Targeting 'Machine' in Quest for Rights," *WCT*, August 7, 1986.

61. David K. Fremon, *Chicago Politics, Ward by Ward* (Bloomington: Indiana University Press, 1988), 294.

62. Greg Hinz, "Gays Plan Rally for Bill," *Booster*, June 27, 1984.

63. Stuart Michaels, interview by the author, January 12, 2007; and Arthur L. Johnston, interview by the author, January 8, 2008.

64. Jean Latz Griffin, "Despite Loss, Results Hearten Gay Leaders," *CT*, February 26, 1987.

65. Diagram, loose in Sable Papers, GH.

66. Michael C. Botkin, "Sable Lost the Race, but Chicago Gays Won," *Gay Community News*, March 8–14, 1987.

67. Ibid.

68. Achy Obejas, "Gay Rights, Gay Votes," *Chicago* (February 1989), 13–18, at 14.

69. Hansen's precinct captains had backed Washington in the 1983 general election. Basil Talbott, Jr., "Ald. Hansen to Break Ranks, Back Mayor," *CST*, March 29, 1987.

70. See Fremon, *Chicago Politics, Ward by Ward*, 8–10.

71. Rick Garcia, interview with the author, February 11, 2008.

72. Achy Obejas, interview by the author, January 9, 2012.

73. COGLI Legislative Subcommittee Meeting Minutes, September 9, 1987, in box 4, folder 40, Community Services Series, MR.

74. Art Brewer, Rhonda Craven, Chris Cothran, and Achy Obejas to Peggy Baker, August 22, 1987, box 4, folder 40, Community Services Series, MR.

75. One political journalist wrote, "No other alderman felt more heat over the 1986 gay rights vote than Gutiérrez. His liberal base (plus gay supporters who threw large sums of money into his campaign) insisted he support the bill. Equally adamant were Pentecostal church congregations, who provided strong support in his 1986 win." Fremon, *Chicago Politics, Ward by Ward*, 174.

76. Achy Obejas, interview by Tracy Baim, July 11, 2007, on Chicago Gay History website, www.chicagogayhistory.org.

77. Achy Obejas, interview by the author, January 9, 2012.

78. Ibid.

79. Ibid.

80. Cheryl Devall, "Mayor Seeks Bernardin's Support on Rights," *CT*, June 16, 1988; Jean Latz Griffin, "Gays Seek Black Help for Bill," *CT*, June 22, 1988; "Gay Rights Like Black Rights, Says Operation PUSH's Rev. Barrow," *GayLife*, March 7, 1985; and Phyllis Goldberg, "PUSH Leader Speaks Out on Black Empowerment, Gay Rights," *National Alliance*, March 1, 1985.

81. City of Chicago Committee on Human Rights and Consumer Protection, report of proceedings for June 23, 1988, copy in the collection of GH, 186.

82. Ibid.

83. Norm Sloan, interview by the author, January 5, 2012.

84. "Michael Sneed," CST, September 14, 1988.

85. Rick Garcia, interview by Jack Rinella, July 26, 1995, in JR.

86. "No Shoulders Big Enough for This Shame," WCT, September 22, 1988.

87. Front-page photo, CST, September 15, 1988; and Alf Siewers, "Efforts to Sign Up Voters May Help 'Gay Rights' Measure in Chicago," Christian Science Monitor, October 12, 1988.

88. Ray Hanania and Lynn Sweet, "Human Rights Bill Loses," CST, September 15, 1988; and "No Shoulders Big Enough for This Shame," WCT, September 22, 1988.

89. June–October 1988: "A Summary Report: Lesbian/Gay Voter Impact '88," box 1, folder 1, Carole Powell Papers, GH.

90. Rick Garcia, interview by the author.

91. Peter Freiberg, "Chicago Approves Gay Rights Bill," Advocate, January 31, 1989.

92. Ibid.

93. Dudley Clendinen, "Throughout the Country, Homosexuals Increasingly Flex Political Muscle," NYT, November 8, 1983.

94. The number of black mayors elected in the United States before Washington is from the preface by Chuck Stone, Senior Editor of the Philadelphia Daily News, to Florence Hamlish Levinsohn, Harold Washington: A Political Biography (Chicago: Chicago Review Press, 1983), 2.

95. Chinta Strausberg, "Jackson Says Reagan Ignoring AIDS," CD, June 16, 1987. Jackson's candidacy, in turn, forced Walter Mondale, the party's eventual nominee, to adopt more-progressive stances on matters of interest to black Democrats.

96. William E. Schmidt, "Chicago Aldermen and Police Seize Portrait That Blacks Deem Offensive," NYT, May 13, 1988.

97. Rebecca Drake to IMPACT, March 11, 1988, in box 1, Sable 1988 correspondence folder, IMPACT Records, GH.

Chapter 7

1. Clarence Page, "Acute Info Deficiency Syndrome," CT, October 27, 1985.

2. Tracy Baim, "AIDS: The Plague Years," WCT, April 6, 2011, 14.

3. See, among other works, Dennis Altman, "Legitimation Through Disaster: AIDS and the Gay Movement," in AIDS: The Burdens of History, ed. Elizabeth Fee and Daniel M. Fox (Berkeley: University of California Press, 1988), 301–315; Robert A. Padgug and Gerald M. Oppenheimer, "Riding the Tiger: AIDS and the Gay Community," in AIDS: The Making of a Chronic Disease, ed. Elizabeth Fee and Daniel M. Fox (Berkeley: University of California Press, 1992), 245–278; and Deborah B. Gould, Moving Politics: Emotion and ACT UP's Fight Against AIDS (Chicago: University of Chicago Press, 2009), 67, 156, 258.

4. Rex Wockner, "C-FAR Disrupts LyphoMed Annual Meeting," New York Native, June 6, 1988.

5. Gould, Moving Politics, 129, 221–222.

6. As Guenter B. Risse aptly put it, "[T]he myth of our perceived conquest of infectious diseases was shockingly pierced." Risse, Mending Bodies, Saving Souls: A History of Hospitals (New York: Oxford University Press, 1999), 660.

7. "Statistics 'AIDS' Cases Chicago," in box 24, folder 8, Central Office Records, MR.

8. Sydney Lewis, *Hospital: An Oral History of Cook County Hospital* (New York: New Press, 1994), 44.

9. William E. Schmidt, "In AIDS Battle, Hope for Addict Arises on Street," *NYT*, July 5, 1988.

10. Tom Brune, "15 Hospitals Diagnose Most Area AIDS Cases," *CST*, November 8, 1987.

11. Wes Smith, "Underclass Falling Victim to AIDS Siege," *CT*, February 17, 1987.

12. Philip Lentz and Manuel Galvan, "William Ware, Top Mayoral Lieutenant," *CT*, May 26, 1985.

13. Last will and testament of Roland Pena, May 13, 1992, box 1, Roland Pena Papers, GH.

14. Philip Brian Harper, "Eloquence and Epitaph: Black Nationalism and the Homophobic Impulse in Responses to the Death of Max Robinson," *Social Text* 28 (1991), 68–86, at 82. After the December 1988 death of Max Robinson, who as the nation's first black network news anchor had reported from the Chicago desk of ABC's *World News Tonight* from 1978 to 1983, Jesse Jackson said in his eulogy at the funeral that before his death, Robinson told him he had contracted HIV not from "homosexuality" but from "promiscuity," a statement he later repeated in a radio interview ("Eloquence and Epitaph," 79). See also Harper's important discussion of Magic "Earvin" Johnson's 1991 disclosure of his HIV-positive status and disavowal of homosexuality in Philip Brian Harper, *Are We Not Men?: Masculine Anxiety and the Problem of African American Identity* (New York: Oxford University Press, 1996), 25.

15. Cathy J. Cohen, *The Boundaries of Blackness: AIDS and the Breakdown of Black Politics* (Chicago: University of Chicago Press, 1999), 1–2.

16. Lisa Ely, "AIDS, the Black Community," *Chatham Citizen*, March 12, 1987; and "AIDS Cases Reported to Chicago Department of Health by Risk Behavior Within Racial/ Ethnic Group," n.d. but 1987 in box 28, folder 4, Community Services Series, MR. African American journalists, too, at times corrected the record; see, for example, Nathaniel Clay's response to New York congressman Charlie Rangel's incorrect assertion that the "primary source" of AIDS in African Americans is IV drug use in "Is AIDS a White Gay Disease?" *Chicago Metro*, October 10, 1987.

17. Committee on AIDS Research and the Behavioral, Social, and Statistical Sciences, National Research Council, *AIDS: The Second Decade* (Washington, DC: National Academy Press, 1990), 43.

18. Jenny Robles, "Health Department Reneges on AIDS Funding," *CT*, December 8, 1988.

19. Ronald Kotulak, "State Mapping Plan for AIDS Epidemic," *CT*, December 8, 1985.

20. By the end of 1985, 262 cases of AIDS had been reported to the Chicago health department for which risk-group data were available. Of these cases, 62 percent were white, 30 percent "black/not Haitian," and 8 Hispanic. The cases included one male hemophiliac; four women thought to have been infected by transfusions, and two by heterosexual contact; two children classified as "parent at risk"; and eleven male and two female IV drug users with "no history of homosexuality." Ten men and eleven women were listed as "none apparent/ unknown." All the other cases were men classified as "homosexual/bisexual." The most common opportunistic infection with which these patients had presented, *pneumocystis carinii* pneumonia, was common to 64 percent of cases. "Statistics 'AIDS' Cases Chicago," in box 24, folder 8, Central Office Records, MR.

21. Rogers Worthington, "Public May Bear Extra Costs of AIDS Burials," *CT*, August 22, 1987; and Joan Beck, "None Wants to Pay the Cost of AIDS, But All of Us Will Have To," *CT*, September 14, 1987.

22. "AIDS and Insurance Companies," *CT*, June 16, 1987.

23. Risse, *Mending Bodies, Saving Souls*, 661.

24. Harold Washington, speech to Chicago Association of Commerce and Industry, February 21, 1986, in *Climbing a Great Mountain: Selected Speeches of Mayor Harold Washington* (Chicago: Bonus Books, 1988), 111.

25. Jesse Green and Peter S. Arno, "The 'Medicaidization' of AIDS: Trends in the Financing of HIV-Related Medical Care," *Journal of the American Medical Association* 264:10 (September 12, 1990), 1261–1266; and Jonathan Engel, *The Epidemic: A Global History of AIDS* (New York: Smithsonian Books, 2006), 177.

26. Howard Brown Memorial Clinic, "PWA Client Population Data," July 31, 1987, in box 28, folder 22, Community Services Series, MR. On poverty and early AIDS cases, see Michelle Cochrane, *When AIDS Began: San Francisco and the Making of an Epidemic* (Routledge, 2004).

27. Tracy Baim, "Cook County Hospital's Sable/Sherer Clinic Offers Treatment, Support for AIDS Patients," *GayLife*, August 30, 1984; and John J. Accrocco, "Sable and Sherer: Two Doctors That Changed AIDS in Chicago," *CT*, February 15, 2012.

28. Ronald Bayer and Gerald M. Oppenheimer, *AIDS Doctors: Voices from the Epidemic* (New York: Oxford University Press, 2000), 97.

29. This percentage included 80 percent of the women and 40 percent of the children with AIDS or HIV in Illinois. Jean Latz Griffin, "AIDS Activists Beg for Funding," *CT*, March 10, 1992.

30. Lewis, *Hospital*, 25.

31. Ibid., 28–29.

32. Derek Regnier, "Emergency Shelter for PWAs Announced," *GayLife*, December 12, 1985; Jessica Seigel, "Brown Clinic, PUSH to Hold AIDS Benefit," *CT*, October 30, 1989; and Curtis R. Winkle and Andréa Carr, with the assistance of Shyamala Parameswaran, "Evaluation of Ryan White CARE Act Title I as Implemented in Chicago, Illinois," August 12, 1994, 46, in box 4, folder 4, ACT UP.

33. Jane Lowers, "The Funding Crunch: AIDS, Gay and Lesbian Organizations Compete for Limited Resources," *Outlines*, June 1995, 16.

34. For one of the earliest analyses of this, see Altman, "Legitimation Through Disaster."

35. John-Manuel Andriote, *Victory Deferred: How AIDS Changed Gay Life in America* (Chicago: University of Chicago Press, 1999), 119–120. Those who died in relative social and cultural isolation, like this young man, have been left out of scholarly narratives that have reinforced the popular notion of AIDS as a disease of white gays and intravenous drug users of color.

36. Tom Brune, "In Gay Bars, Reminders Abound," *CST*, April 28, 1987.

37. Sid Smith, "Stars Hit Chicago for AIDS Benefit," *Boston Globe*, September 23, 1987; and Tracy Baim, "$1 Million Raised at AIDS Benefit," *Outlines*, October 1, 1987.

38. Kate Sosin, "Open Hand Chicago Starts Rolling Out Meals," *CT*, November 23, 2011.

39. A double-blind trial conducted among gay men at Howard Brown and similar clinics in four other cities had proven the effectiveness and safety of the hepatitis B vaccine. David G. Ostrow and Dale M. Shaskey, "The Experience of the Howard Brown Memorial Clinic of

Chicago with Sexually Transmitted Diseases," *Sexually Transmitted Diseases* 4:2 (April–June 1977), 53–55; Alfred Baker, "Chronic Type B Hepatitis in Gay Men: Experience with Patients Referred from the Howard Brown Memorial Clinic to the University of Chicago," *Journal of Homosexuality* 5:3 (March 1980), 311–315; and Donald P. Francis et al., "The Prevention of Hepatitis B with Vaccine," *Annals of Internal Medicine* 97:3 (September 1982), 362–366. See also Chad Heap, *Homosexuality in the City: A Century of Research at the University of Chicago* (Chicago: University of Chicago Library, 2000), 38.

40. Howard Brown Memorial Clinic, "PWA Client Population Data," July 31, 1987, in box 28, folder 22, Community Services Series, MR.

41. Eric Zorn, "Home Open for Victims of AIDS," *CT*, March 12, 1986.

42. "City Has Failed Black and Hispanic AIDS Victims, Researcher Says," *CT*, November 17, 1988.

43. Gunnar Almgren and Miguel Ferguson, "The Urban Ecology of Hospital Failure: Hospital Closures in the City of Chicago, 1970–1991," *Journal of Sociology and Social Welfare* 26:4 (December 1999), 5–25.

44. Shelton Watson, interview by the author, January 15, 2007.

45. Cathy J. Cohen, "Service Provider or Policymaker?: Black Churches and the Health of African Americans," in *Long March Ahead: African American Churches and Public Policy in Post–Civil Rights America*, ed. R. Drew Smith (Durham, NC: Duke University Press, 2004), 103–126.

46. Max Smith, interview with the author, January 16, 2007.

47. Jo A. Moore, "Kupona Rift Revealed at COGLI Session," *CT*, February 2, 1986.

48. Maudlyne Ihejirika, "She Knows AIDS Up Close," *CST*, March 26, 1988.

49. "Performing . . . ," *CD*, August 17, 1974; Carol Kleiman, "Being a Woman Is Harder to 'Overcome' than Being Black," *CT*, April 28, 1975; "Songwriter, Singer Keith Barrow, 29," *CT*, October 27, 1983; and Andrew Davis, "Willie Barrow: 8 Decades of Activism, a Son Lost to AIDS," *CT*, December 29, 2004.

50. Lewis, *Hospital*, 187. The classic journalistic account of the Reagan administration's neglectful response to AIDS is Randy Shilts, *And the Band Played On: Politics, People, and the AIDS Epidemic* (New York: St. Martin's, 1987). In the sole published monograph by an academic historian on the AIDS epidemic in the United States, Jennifer Brier has complicated this picture, arguing that the Reagan administration was in fact deeply divided about how to respond to the epidemic. She also usefully and persuasively challenges the conventional distinction between AIDS service organizations and protest groups, instead referring to both as "AIDS workers." Jennifer Brier, *Infectious Ideas: U.S. Political Responses to the AIDS Crisis* (Chapel Hill: University of North Carolina Press, 2009).

51. Kit Duffy to Jacky Grimshaw, March 19, 1987, in box 28, folder 19, Community Services Series, MR. On the Reagan cuts to Community Development Block Grants, see Roger Biles, *The Fate of Cities: Urban America and the Federal Government, 1945–2000* (Lawrence: University Press of Kansas, 2011), 250–86, at 265–67.

52. Chinta Strausberg, "Batter Plan for Victims of AIDS," *CD*, July 17, 1987.

53. Travelers and Immigrants Aid of Chicago, untitled document on AIDS in Chicago, n.d., in folder 20, box 28, Community Services Series, MR.

54. "Chicago Police Chief Names Liaison to Gay Community," *Advocate*, March 6, 1984; Raymond Risley to William Schneider, June 10, 1987, in Police-Community folder, and CPD Department Special Order on Acquired Immune Deficiency Syndrome, January 11, 1984; and

David G. Ostrow, M.D., to Fred Rice, January 17, 1984, in Police/Rice folder; both in box 4, ILGTF.

55. "Doctor with AIDS Back at Hospital," *NYT*, February 5, 1987; "Chicago Patients Gain Curb on AIDS Carriers," *NYT*, September 22, 1988; Peter Freiberg, "Chicago Doctor with AIDS Allowed to Treat Patients," *Advocate*, September 1, 1987; Peter Freiberg, "Gay Doctor with AIDS Fights to Continue Seeing Patients," *Advocate*, March 31, 1987; and William Burks, "Politicos Oust PWA Doctor," *New York Native*, March 16, 1987.

56. "Sneed and Lavin, Inc.," *CT*, April 24, 1984.

57. COGLI to Harold Washington, January 14, 1986 [erroneously labeled 1985], in box 29, folder 9, Community Services Series, MR; Jennifer Kapuscik, "Commissioner on Prostitutes and AIDS," *GayLife*, January 9, 1986; and John A. Fall, "Midwest Health Official Denies Quarantine Plans," *New York Native*, February 10, 1986. See also Ronald Bayer, *Private Acts, Social Consequences: AIDS and the Politics of Public Health* (New York: Free Press, 1989), 173–186.

58. Lonnie C. Edwards, opening statement to AIDS roundtable, April 11, 1986, box 29, folder 8, Community Services series, MR.

59. Tom Brune, "AIDS Groups Hit City on Long-Overdue Funds," *CST*, March 27, 1987.

60. "2 more Gay Groups Ask City Health Chief Firing," *CST*, March 26, 1987; and Brune, "AIDS Groups Hit City on Long-Overdue Funds."

61. Tracy Baim, "City Announces AIDS Response, Pays Groups," *CT*, April 2, 1987.

62. Richard Gray to Lonnie Edwards, June 16, 1987, box 28, "Gay and Lesbian Book 4 of 4" folder, Community Services Series, MR.

63. COGLI minutes, May 27, 1987; Paul Varnell op-ed "Health Dept. Needs to Fix Flaws in Its AIDS Program," both in box 4, folder 40, Community Services Series, MR; and "Lonnie Edwards Should Resign or Be Fired," *CT*, August 6, 1987.

64. Ray Hanania, "Edwards Quits Top Health Dept. Post," *CST*, August 29, 1987.

65. James Strong, "City Health Commissioner to Quit March 1," *CT*, August 29, 1987; John Kass, "City Health Chief Asked to Stay," *CT*, January 7, 1988; Cheryl Devall, "City Health Department Firing Blamed on Politics," *CT*, June 16, 1988; and Albert Williams, Paul Handler, and Paul Tarini, "Abetting the AIDS Crisis," *CR*, December 22, 1988.

66. Deborah Nelson, "Fund Cuts, Staff Loss Cripple City AIDS Work," *CST*, September 11, 1988.

67. Peter Freiberg, "Chicago Approves Gay Rights Bill," *Advocate*, January 31, 1989; and Joel Kaplan and John Camper, "Daley Seeks to Prop Up Sagging Support," *CT*, February 19, 1989.

68. Frank E. James, "AIDS Bills in Illinois Reflect a Backlash Against Moderate Public-Health Policies," *Wall Street Journal*, July 3, 1987; and Dirk Johnson, "Broad AIDS Laws Signed in Illinois," *NYT*, September 22, 1987. Ron Sable charged that "the Illinois Legislature has enacted the worst AIDS related legislation anywhere in the U.S.": Sable et al. to March on Washington Executive Committee, n.d., box 1, Lesbian and Gay Voter Impact '88 folder, Ron Sable Papers, GH.

69. Johnson, "Broad AIDS Laws Signed in Illinois"; Peter Freiberg, "Illinois Governor Limits Coercive Action in Statewide AIDS Bills," *Advocate*, October 27, 1987; Susy Schultz, "Gay Protestors Ask Governor to Veto AIDS Bills," *CST*, August 17, 1987; Flyer asking Gov. James R. Thompson to veto four bills, in box 29, folder 10, and Illinois AIDS Interdisciplinary Advisory Council minutes, August 15, 1986, in box 28, folder 18, both in Central Office

Records, MR; Tom Brune and Howard Wolinsky, "New Jab at AIDS Testing," *CST*, June 22, 1987; Albert Williams, "'Veto!' Cries Ring as 70,000 Gather for Pride Parade," *CT*, July 2, 1987; Dirk Johnson, "Veto of AIDS Testing Bills Is Urged in Illinois," *NYT*, July 7, 1987; and Susy Schultz, "Prenuptial AIDS Tests Criticized by Scientists," *CST*, n.d. [fall 1987], clipping in MRL.

70. Gould, *Moving Politics*, 155, 162–63, 317.

71. Only a tiny number of positive antibody tests had occurred by this means, as far as officials could tell (couples were not required to present the results of the tests). "Illinois May End Premarital AIDS Testing," *NYT*, January 5, 1989. Cindy Patton offers a useful reading of the cultural meanings of such legislation: "Unlike contact tracing, which followed the vectoral line anywhere and everywhere, testing of marriage applicants was aimed at discovering whether the male partner had been to the territory occupied by homosexuals (or, more forgivably, that was occupied by prostitutes)." Patton, *Globalizing AIDS* (Minneapolis: University of Minnesota Press, 2002), 72.

72. "Other States Show Interest in Illinois 'AIDS' Law," *New York Native*, November 5, 1990; and Russell K. Robinson, "Racing the Closet," *Stanford Law Review* 61 (April 2009), 1463–1533.

73. Tom Brune, "City Gays Mobilize to Oust Health Chief," *CST*, December 23, 1988.

74. Jennifer Robles, "'Gay Precinct' Vote Results Show Lukewarm Support for Sawyer," *CT*, March 23, 1989.

75. Jack Houston, "Suit Challenges CTA for Barring AIDS Ad," *CT*, September 14, 1989.

76. Rex Wockner, "Mayor Daley Storms Out of Gay Meeting," *Outlines*, December 1989.

77. Mark Schoofs, "Politics: Gays and Daley," *CR*, November 17, 1989.

78. All quotations from both the Ann Sather's forum and the Daley Plaza protest were transcribed by the author from "The 10% Show," episode 10, video recording in 10% Show Collection, GH.

79. Neil Steinberg, "Gays Induct Activists into Hall of Fame," *CST*, November 17, 1992.

80. Chinta Strausberg, "AIDS Protest Sparks 129 Arrests," *CD*, April 24, 1990; Chris Bull, "Thrown for a Loop," *Advocate*, June 5, 1990; and Gould, *Moving Politics*, 267–271.

81. Marian Moore, "AIDS Demonstrators Clash with Cops," *CD*, June 25, 1991; and Gould, *Moving Politics*, 269.

82. G. Stephen Bowen, Katherine Marconi, Sally Kohn, Dorothy M. Bailey, Eric P. Goosby, Sonya Shorter, and Steve Niemcryk, "First Year of AIDS Services Delivery under Title I of the Ryan White CARE Act," *Public Health Reports* 107:5 (September–October 1992), 491–499, at 494.

83. Andriote, *Victory Deferred*, 232.

84. Terry Wilson, "Blacks Worry Funds Won't Reach Hard-Hit Group," *CT*, May 16, 1997.

85. Jean Latz Griffin, "AIDS Activists Beg for Funding," *CT*, March 10, 1992.

86. Winkle and Carr, "Evaluation of Ryan White CARE Act Title I as Implemented in Chicago, Illinois," 46.

87. Andriote, *Victory Deferred*, 312.

88. Tracy Baim, "Chicago HIV/AIDS Cases Pass 36,000," *CT*, April 20, 2011.

89. "AIDS Mortality Declines Sharply, Chicago Department of Public Health Finds," *Chicago Citizen*, September 18, 1997.

90. Helen Margellos, Abigail Silva, and Steven Whitman, "Comparison of Health Status Indicators in Chicago: Are Black-White Disparities Worsening?" *American Journal of Public*

Health 94:1 (January 2004), 116–121; and Girma Woldemichael, Demian Christiansen, Sandra Thomas, and Nanette Benbow, "Demographic Characteristics and Survival with AIDS: Health Disparities in Chicago, 1993–2001," *American Journal of Public Health* 99, Supplement 1 (March 2009), S118–S123. Jennifer Brier argues that one reason for the drugs' high cost is that pharmaceutical companies negotiated even more favorable trade and patent terms as part of the broader move toward deregulation in the George H. W. Bush and Bill Clinton years, while "treatment activists went from direct action to boardroom negotiations." Brier, *Infectious Ideas*, 185.

91. Charles L. Bennett et al., "Racial Differences in Care Among Hospitalized Patients with *Pneumocystis carinii* Pneumonia in Chicago, New York, Los Angeles, Miami, and Raleigh-Durham," *Archives of Internal Medicine* 155:15 (1995), 1586–1592.

Chapter 8

1. *Obama and the Gays: A Political Marriage*, ed. Tracy Baim (Chicago: Prairie Avenue Productions, 2010), 7–8; David Olson, "Fighting for the Right to Marry," *Windy City Times*, April 25, 1996; David W. Dunlap, "Fearing a Toehold for Gay Marriages, Conservatives Rush to Bar the Door," *NYT*, March 6, 1996; and Kurt Erickson, "Edgar Bans Gay Marriages in Illinois," *The Pantagraph* (Bloomington, IL), May 25, 1996.

2. Jon-Henri Damski, "Down for the Count," *CT*, August 10, 1989; and "ACT-UP Hits Racism in Chicago Bars," *BLK* (October 1989), 23.

3. Merrill Goozner and Stanley Ziemba, "Big Gifts to Daley Reflect City's Divisions," *CT*, July 20, 1989.

4. John J. Betancur and Douglas C. Gills, "Community Development in Chicago: From Harold Washington to Richard M. Daley," *Annals of the American Academy of Political and Social Science* 594:1 (2004), 92–108, at 100; see also Jason Hackworth, *The Neoliberal City: Governance, Ideology, and Development in American Urbanism* (Ithaca, NY: Cornell University Press, 2006).

5. Eric Klinenberg, *Heat Wave: A Social Autopsy of Disaster in Chicago* (Chicago: University of Chicago Press, 2003), 150.

6. Robert Davis, "City Plans Gay, Lesbian Hall of Fame," *CT*, May 4, 1991.

7. Jeffrey Fishman, "How to Win Enemies and Influence People," *CR*, August 30, 1996.

8. "Outward Mobility," *CT*, February 7, 1993.

9. Robert Davis and John Kass, "City Gives Funeral Leave to 'Domestic Partners,'" *CT*, December 16, 1993 (describing an executive action); Jacquelyn Heard and John Kass, "Gay Partners of City Workers in Line for Benefits," *CT*, February 27, 1997; and John Kass and Nancy Ryan, "Partners Plan Shows a New Daley," *CT*, March 20, 1997.

10. Larry Bennett, *The Third City: Chicago and American Urbanism* (Chicago: University of Chicago Press, 2010), 95.

11. John Gallagher, "Chicago Hope," *Advocate*, July 25, 1995.

12. Janet L. Abu-Lughod, *New York, Chicago, Los Angeles: America's Global Cities* (Minneapolis: University of Minnesota Press, 1999), 332, 417.

13. In the city council under Daley, race was the strongest predictor of an aldermanic candidate's ability to attract corporate campaign contributions, with black candidates receiving much less than either white or Latino candidates. Timothy B. Krebs, "Money and Machine Politics: An Analysis of Corporate and Labor Contributions in Chicago City Council Elections," *Urban Affairs Review* 41:1 (September 2005), 47–64.

14. The first book-length biography of the younger Daley devotes fully three pages to his appearance in the 1989 Pride parade, but it makes no mention of any other gay- or AIDS-related issue or policy that surfaced during any of his six terms in office. Keith Koeneman, *First Son: The Biography of Richard M. Daley* (Chicago: University of Chicago Press, 2013), 133–135.

15. David Olson and Louis Weisberg, "Braun Presents Strong Record on Human Rights," *CT*, March 12, 1992; "IMPACT Aids Braun Campaign," *CD*, June 17, 1992; Achy Obejas, "Capitol Hill or Bust," *Advocate*, November 3, 1992; April Lynch, "Senate Agrees to Vote Monday on Achtenberg," *San Francisco Chronicle*, May 21, 1993; and Fredrick C. Harris, *Something Within: Religion in African-American Political Activism* (New York: Oxford University Press, 1999), 12–26. In her floor speech opposing the Defense of Marriage Act, Braun compared it to miscegenation statutes and recalled a family member who had married across the color line. *Congressional Record* 142:123, September 10, 1996, www.gpo.gov/fdsys/pkg/CREC-1996-09-10/html/CREC-1996-09-10-pt1-PgS10100-2.htm.

16. For a useful side-by-side analysis of the religious rhetoric of the Reverend Jesse L. Jackson, Sr., and Alan Keyes, who represent different generations and political standpoints yet draw on the same prophetic tradition, see David Howard-Pitney, "'To Form a More Perfect Union': African Americans and American Civil Religion," in *New Day Begun*, ed. R. Drew Smith (Durham, NC: Duke University Press, 2003), 89–112.

17. For an indispensable analysis of this shift, see Fredrick C. Harris, "Black Churches and Machine Politics in Chicago," in *Black Churches and Local Politics: Clergy Influence, Organizational Partnerships, and Civil Empowerment*, ed. R. Drew Smith and Fredrick C. Harris (Lanham, MD: Rowman and Littlefield, 2005), 117–136.

18. Samuel K. Roberts, "On Seducing the Samaritan: The Problematic of Government Aid to Faith-Based Groups," in Smith, *New Day Begun,* 278–291.

19. Patrick Egan and Ken Sherrill, "Proposition 8: What Happened and Where Do We Go from Here?" (January 2009), report commissioned by the Evelyn & Walter Haas, Jr. Fund and released under the auspices of the National Gay and Lesbian Task Force Policy Institute, www.thetaskforce.org/downloads/issues/egan_sherrill_prop8_1_6_09.pdf. In the most comprehensive study of black-white differences in public opinion on gay-rights issues, combining data from thirty-one national surveys conducted between 1973 and 2000, Gregory B. Lewis concluded that "blacks appear to be more likely than whites *both* to see homosexuality as wrong *and* to favor gay rights laws." Lewis further notes that "religion actually appears to affect white more than black homophobia." Lewis, "Black-White Differences in Attitudes Toward Homosexuality and Gay Rights," *Public Opinion Quarterly* 67:1 (Spring 2003), 59–78, at 64, 75–76.

20. Karen Nolan, "Defender Denies Discrimination Charges," *CD*, July 22, 1993; Ethan Michaeli, "African Americans Show Lesbian and Gay Pride," *CD*, June 6, 1994; and Neil Steinberg, "No Room for Gay Group in Bud Billiken Parade," *CST*, July 21, 1993. Gay life had been significantly whitened since the 1950s, when the elected "mayor of Bronzeville" handed out prizes to black and white female impersonators in the presence of some 4,000 spectators each Halloween ("Heard and Seen," *CD*, November 3, 1958). On elections for "mayor of Bronzeville," see St. Clair Drake and Horace R. Cayton, *Black Metropolis: A Study of Negro Life in a Northern City,* rev. ed. (Chicago: University of Chicago Press, 1993 [1945]), 383.

21. Chinta Strausberg, "King Seeks to End Gay Bias," *Chicago Defender*, April 1, 1998; Terry Wilson, "King's Widow Stands Up for Gay Civil Rights," *CT*, April 1, 1998; and Mary

Houlihan-Skilton, "Wife Invokes Rev. King in Support of Gays," *Chicago Sun-Times*, April 1, 1998.

22. Strausberg, "King Seeks to End Gay Bias"; Wilson, "King's Widow Stands Up for Gay Civil Rights"; Houlihan-Skilton, "Wife Invokes Rev. King in Support of Gays"; Ron Dorfman, "Gays and the Police," in *Out and Proud in Chicago: An Overview of the City's Gay Community*, ed. Tracy Baim (Chicago: Surrey Books, 2008), 119.

23. David Sklansky, *Democracy and the Police* (Stanford, CA: Stanford University Press, 2007), 143.

24. David C. Ranney, Patricia A. Wright, and Tingwei Zhang, *Citizens, Local Government and the Development of Chicago's Near South Side* (Geneva: United Nations Research Institute for Social Development, 1997), 50.

25. On the South Loop and West Loop, see Chinta Strausberg, "Homeless, Mayor at Odds," *CD*, March 15, 1994; "Ethan Mitchell, "City's SRO Supply Shrinking; More Homeless Feared," *CD*, July 20, 1994; "Code Change Aimed at SROs," *North Loop News*, June 1, 1995; Brendan Shiller, "Number of SRO Units Declining, but Not as Much," *Streetwise*, October 1, 1997; Brendan Shiller, "City Considers Proposal to Make It Easier to Evict SRO Tenants," *Streetwise*, October 1, 1997; Bob Troy, "SRO Decline Slows, But Continues," *Streetwise*, April 14, 1998; La Risa R. Lynch, "Eminent Domain Invoked in Closing of SRO," *Streetwise*, January 5, 1999; Bob Zuley, "Two Local SRO Hotels Sold, Order Residents to Vacate," *Booster*, August 3–9, 2011; and Rex W. Hupple, "Single-Room Occupancy Hotels Disappearing Across Chicago," *CT*, August 31, 2011.

26. *City of Chicago v. Morales*, 527 U.S. 41 (1999); Nik Theodore, Nina Martin, and Ryan Hollon, "Securing the City: Emerging Markets in the Private Provision of Security Services in Chicago," *Social Justice* 33:3 (2006), 85–100, at 96; Bill Clinton AIDS and urban policies [faxed May 19, 1992], 7, in box 6, folder 16, ACT UP; and Jeff Chang, *Can't Stop Won't Stop: A History of the Hip-Hop Generation* (New York: Picador/St. Martin's, 2005), 390. Daley served as Cook County state's attorney from 1980 to 1989, and accusations have dogged him that he either failed to investigate adequately or may have helped to cover up reports of police torture of criminal suspects. Julilly Kohler-Hausmann, "Militarizing the Police: Officer Jon Burge, Torture, and War in the 'Urban Jungle,'" in *Challenging the Prison-Industrial Complex: Activism, Arts, and Educational Alternatives*, ed. Stephen John Hartnett (Urbana: University of Illinois Press, 2011), 43–71.

27. Eric Klinenberg, "Bowling Alone, Policing Together," *Social Justice* 28:3 (Fall 2001), 75–80; and Wesley Skogan and Susan Hartnet, *Community Policing, Chicago Style* (New York: Oxford University Press, 1997). For a critique of community policing, see Steve Herbert, *Citizens, Cops, and Power: Recognizing the Limits of Community* (Chicago: University of Chicago Press, 2006).

28. Richard Greene, "Strong Downtowns and High Amenity Zones as Defining Features of the 21st-Century Metropolis: The Case of Chicago," in *Chicago's Geographies*, ed. Richard P. Greene (Washington, DC: Academy of American Geographers, 2006), 50–74; see also David Wilson, "The Growing Socio-Spatial Polarization in Chicago," in Greene, *Chicago's Geographies*, 189–204; and Terry Nichols Clark, *The City as an Entertainment Machine* (Boston: JAI/ Elsevier, 2004).

29. Lawrence J. Vale, *Purging the Poorest: Public Housing and the Design Politics of Twice-Cleared Communities* (Chicago: University of Chicago Press, 2013).

30. Hackworth, *The Neoliberal City*, 99.

31. David Olson, "Chicago Rock Bottom in AIDS Spending," *CT*, December 26, 1991; "City Must Rectify Abysmal AIDS Record," *CT*, March 5, 1992; and Jean Latz Griffin, "AIDS Activists Beg for Funding," *CT*, March 10, 1992.

32. Jean Latz Griffin, "Nun Picked as City Health Chief," *CT*, February 8, 1991; Jean Latz Griffin, "Activists See Nun in New Light," *CT*, February 15, 1991; Terry Wilson, "Health Chief Leaves Abortion Foes Optimistic," *CT*, March 14, 1991; and PISD (People with Immune System Disorders), "Make her say condom before you give her that award," box 3, folder 7, ACT UP.

33. AIDS Foundation of Chicago to RMD, July 8, 1993, in box 3, folder 5, ACT UP.

34. John Blandford, "Voices of the Community: Issues of Race and Ethnicity Among Chicago's Gay Men and Lesbians," a report to the Human Relations Foundation of Chicago (May 1993), 6, 8, in pamphlet file, GH; and Center for Urban Research and Learning, Michael Leachman, and Philip Nyden, "Housing Discrimination and Economic Opportunity in the Chicago Region," Center for Urban Research and Learning, Paper no. 22 (2000), ecommons.luc.edu/curl_pubs/22.

35. Christopher Reed, "The Third Chicago School?: Marking Sexual and Ethnic Identity," in *Chicago Architecture: Histories, Revisions, Alternatives*, ed. Charles Waldheim and Katerina Rüedi Ray (Chicago: University of Chicago Press, 2005), 163–175, at 166.

36. Keith O'Brien, "Rainbow's End?" *NewCity*, October 23, 1997.

37. City of Chicago Department of Transportation, "North Halsted Streetscape: Project Description and Concept Design," 1997, quoted in Christopher Reed, "We're from Oz: Marking Ethnic and Sexual Identity in Chicago," *Environment and Planning D: Society and Space* 21 (2003), 425–440, at 427.

38. Patricia Callahan, Heather Gillers, and Jason Grotto, "Spending with Abandon," *CT*, November 6, 2013.

39. Christopher Reed, "The Third Chicago School?" 166.

40. Mary Schmich, "Gaytown Enters Gray Area of Community Naming," *CT*, August 20, 1997; and Mary Ellen Podmolik, "N. Halsted Streetscape Plan Drawing Attention," *CST*, August 26, 1997.

41. ex Wockner, "America's First Official Gay Neighborhood Debuts." *Stonewall Journal*, January 1999.

42. Stephanie Banchero, "Gay Theme Toned Down in Halsted St. Plan," *CT*, November 2, 1997; and Stephanie Banchero, "City Offers Toned-Down North Halsted Plan," *CT*, November 13, 1997.

43. In 1999, Chicago was unusual in that measures of gay residential concentration appeared to negatively correlate with black residents, whereas "most cities have a greater mix of African Americans and Anglos in 'gay domains,' or at least when viewed from the MSA's perspective if not in the core central city." Robert W. Bailey, *Gay Politics, Urban Politics: Identity and Economics in the Urban Setting* (New York: Columbia University Press, 1999), 144.

44. Reed, "The Third Chicago School?" 171.

45. "N. Halsted Streetscape Plan Drawing Attention," *CST*, August 26, 1997; Dirk Johnson, "Chicago Hails District as Symbol of Gay Life," *NYT*, August 27, 1997; and "Chicago Street Rockets Out of the Closet," *Advocate*, November 24, 1998.

46. Louis Barlow, "Police Cite 2 Men for Sex in Cell Block," *Chicago Free Press*, July 18, 2001.

47. Gary Barlow, "City Liquor Board to Hear Dispute Between Gay Club, Condo Owners," *Chicago Free Press*, June 26, 2002; and Gary Barlow, "Circuit, Condo Residents Seek 'Peace,'" *Chicago Free Press*, August 21, 2002.

48. Amin Ghaziani, *There Goes the Gayborhood?* (Princeton, NJ: Princeton University Press, 2014), 4.

49. Jodi Wilgoren, "At Center of a Clash, Rowdy Children in Coffee Shops," *NYT*, November 9, 2005.

50. Ben Joravsky, "How Could He?" *CR*, February 14, 2003.

51. Gary Barlow, "Chicago City Council Urges Repeal of 'Don't Ask, Don't Tell,'" *Chicago Free Press*, August 3, 2005; Fran Spielman, "No Limits for Female Impersonators?" *CST*, November 29, 2006; and Amy Wooten, "Tunney Introduces Domestic-Partnership Ordinance," *CT*, June 18, 2008.

52. Ben Joravsky and Mick Dumke, "Your City Council," *CR*, June 15, 2007; and *Journal of the Proceedings of the City Council of the City of Chicago*, July 27, 2006, 83061. See also Gary Washburn, "Daley Nominates Gay Restaurateur to City Council," *CT*, December 20, 2002; "Gay Alderman Blows into Windy City," *Advocate*, February 4, 2003; Fran Spielman, "Tunney Pushes for More AIDS Prevention Funds," *CST*, October 30, 2003; Mark J. Konkol, "Tunney Symbolizes Growing Empowerment," *CST*, July 16, 2006; Mark Brown, "Union Fine-Tuning List of Aldermen It Wants Out," *CST*, November 28, 2006; and Fran Spielman, "Gay Center Opens on Halsted," *CST*, June 6, 2007.

53. "Your Neighbor: Gangs," flyer in Jeff Edwards Papers, in author's possession.

54. Bob Zuley, "Cappleman Warns Chateau Hotel Residents over Behavior," *News-Star*, November 2–8, 2011; John Byrne, "In Uptown, Freshman Alderman Angers Advocates for the Needy," *CT*, March 9, 2013; and Kate Sosin, "Protestors Mourn Diversity in Action Against Cappleman," *CT*, March 22, 2013. On the 44th Ward, see Jessica Pupovac, "Diplomat Battles for Affordable Housing," *Booster*, August 14, 2008; Micah Maidenberg, "Developer Chosen for Viceroy," *Chicago Journal*, April 16, 2009; Kate Sosin, "SRO Residents' Hopes on Last Legs," *CT*, September 7, 2011; and Ethan Ross, "Lakeview Group Fights for Affordable Housing," *Streetwise*, February 27, 2013.

55. Dawn Rhodes, "Lakeview Residents Turn Out to Hear, and Jeer, Proposal for Wal-Mart Store," *CT*, April 11, 2011; and Elliott Ramos, "Wal-Mart Makes Inroads into Chicago's North Side with Lakeview Store Opening," WBEZ, November 30, 2011, www.wbez.org/blog/city-room-blog/2011-11-30/walmart-makes-inroads-chicagos-north-side-lakeview-store-opening-9444.

56. John Byrne, Ray Long, and Monique Garcia, "Deb Mell Faces Skepticism About Family Ties," *CT*, July 25, 2013. The council's sole Latino member from 1983 to 1986, Miguel Santiago in the 31st Ward, was also part of the Vrdolyak 29.

57. Teresa Wiltz, "Black Gays, Lesbians Begin to Fight Back," *CT*, August 15, 1993; Terry Wilson, "New Lesbian, Gay Magazine Targets Blacks," *CT*, January 23, 1996; Chinta Strausberg, "Black Homosexual Men Leading AIDS Cases," *CD*, January 25, 1996; Ytasha L. Womack, "Black Pride '99 Weekend Set for July 4th," *CD*, June 23, 1999; Audarshia Townsend, "Say It Loud—They're Black, Gay and Proud," *CT*, June 29, 2001; and Amy Wooten, "Chicago Dyke March Returns to Pilsen," *Chicago Free Press*, June 4, 2009.

58. Kate Sosin, "Hundreds Pack into Boystown Violence Forum," *CT*, July 13, 2011; and "Ald. Tunney Issues Statement on 44th Ward Crime," *CT*, July 6, 2011.

59. Sam Worley, "The Battle in Boys Town," *CR*, July 14, 2011.

60. Mark Brown, "How Emil Jones Became Unlikely Hero of Gay Rights," *CST*, January 19, 2005. Asked how he "squeezed" them to win their support, Jones said, "I don't squeeze people. It was just a little friendly persuasion." He claimed that it was the testimony of parents of gay children on the House floor in the 1970s that swayed him. "That convinced me," Jones said. "It was those hearings that were held in the House that made me a strong supporter for it."

61. When the Illinois House finally passed a marriage-equality bill in 2013, a slight majority of black legislators voted yes, while a slight majority of white legislators voted no. While there is far more scholarship in the humanities than the social sciences on black-gay political encounters, see, among other works, Devon W. Carbado, "Black Rights, Gay Rights, Civil Rights," *UCLA Law Review* 47 (2000), 1467–1519; Cathy J. Cohen, "Deviance as Resistance: A New Research Agenda for the Study of Black Politics," *Du Bois Review* 1 (March 2004), 27–45; and Russell K. Robinson, "Racing the Closet," *Stanford Law Review* 61 (April 2009), 1463–1533.

62. Karen Hawkins, "Stars & Pols Parade at Gay Gala," *Windy City Times*, January 24, 2001; and Baim, *Obama and the Gays*, 13.

63. Baim, *Obama and the Gays*, 27.

64. Ibid., 22.

65. Matt Simonette, "Sandi Jackson Talks with GLBTs at Jeffery Pub," *Chicago Free Press*, April 30, 2008.

66. Laura Washington, "Black Business Owners Have Much to Learn from Gay Entrepreneurs," *CST*, July 3, 2006.

67. Tracy Baim, "Obama's Marriage Views Changed"; and Timothy Stewart-Winter, "Putting Obama's Questionnaire in Context," *WCT*, January 14, 2009. See also Timothy Stewart-Winter, "Barack Obama, Gay Marriage, and Chicago Politics: A Brief History," in *Obama and the Gays*, 450–453.

68. After the highest court in Hawaii began seeking to force that state to grant marriage licenses to same-sex couples, legislators in statehouses nationwide stampeded to ban the practice preemptively. Two days previously, a Republican legislator had introduced a "defense of marriage" bill in the Illinois state Senate. It was signed into law in May 1996 by Governor Jim Edgar, a Republican.

69. Barack Obama, response to IMPACT questionnaire, September 3, 1996, in 1996 general election questionnaires binder, box 4, IMPACT Records, GH. The highly successful registration effort helped secure Illinois's electoral votes for Bill Clinton—the first time since 1964 that they had gone to the Democrat—and for Braun's election. In a profile in *Chicago* magazine afterward, Obama said the reason he had moved to Chicago in 1984 was "because of Harold Washington." Gretchen Reynolds, "Vote of Confidence," *Chicago* (January 1993), 53–54.

70. Baim, *Obama and the Gays*, 201.

71. "Daley Backs Marriage for Gays in Chicago," *NYT*, February 20, 2004, A12.

72. As black turnout surged because of enthusiasm for Obama, a National Election Pool (NEP) exit poll seemed to show disproportionate black support—as high as 70 percent—for Proposition 8, aimed at overturning the California Supreme Court's decision favoring marriage equality. To be sure, Obama opposed the measure, and political scientists later described the poll as an outlier relative to previous and subsequent polls, arguing that the true level of black support was in the ballpark of 58 percent. The Yes on 8 campaign was funded by the

overwhelmingly white Church of Jesus Christ of Latter-Day Saints. Still, some leading white gay commentators and columnists blamed black voters, and their high turnout in support of Obama, for the law's passage. Proposition 8 would still have passed even if every black voter in California had stayed home—but given the closeness of the outcome it is possible that, if black voters had opposed it more, it might have been defeated.

73. Jackie Calmes and Peter Baker, "Obama Endorses Same-Sex Marriage, Taking Stand on Charged Social Issue," *NYT*, May 10, 2012.

74. Dan Eggen, "Obama's Gay Marriage Announcement Followed by Flood of Campaign Donations," *Washington Post*, May 10, 2012; Jackie Calmes, "Obama Heads West for Dollars and Thanks from Gay Supporters," NYTimes.com, June 6, 2012; Associated Press, "Who Are Top 5 Donors to Obama, Romney Campaigns?" October 19, 2012, www.politico.com/news/stories/1012/82637.html; and Chris Geidner, "Senate Approves Several Out Gay Nominees, With No Opposition," *BuzzFeed*, August 1, 2013, www.buzzfeed.com/chrisgeidner/senate-approves-several-out-gay-nominees-with-no-opposition.

75. Marc Solomon, *Winning Marriage: The Inside Story of How Same-Sex Couples Took on the Politicians and Pundits—and Won* (Lebanon, NH: ForeEdge, 2014), xix.

76. Tracy Baim and Owen Keehnen, *Vernita Gray: From Woodstock to the White House* (Chicago: Prairie Avenue Productions, 2014), 47.

INDEX

Abney, John, 110
abortion, 16, 124, 137–38, 208–9, 246n13, 268n15
Achtenberg, Roberta, 214
ACT UP/Chicago (AIDS Coalition to Unleash Power), 172, 187–88, 203–4, 209, 218–19
Adamowski, Benjamin, 41
Adams, Polly, 75
Advocate, 120–21, 211
African Americans: and AIDS, 184, 186, 191, 195–96; aldermen, 6, 118–22, 153–55, 159–60, 173–79; antigay politics, 169–71, 283n19; Bud Billiken Parade, 214–15; gay candidates, 128–29; gay organizations, 90–91; gays, 19, 103–4, 107–9, 118, 139–43, 178, 193, 228; mayors, 2, 6, 153, 154, 184, 228–29, 276n94; and lesbian feminism, 142; migration to cities, 12, 14; press, 33, 62–63, 118, 140, 190; and police brutality, 19–20, 48; and respectability, 33, 62; in Richard J. Daley era, 113; women, 142, 179, 178. *See also* African American elected officials; AIDS; analogies; black church; black freedom struggle; Black Panther Party; coalitions; Latinos; Washington, Harold; whites
Afro-American Patrolmen's League, 87
AIDS (acquired immune deficiency syndrome), 3, 8–9, 164, 186–206, 219, 222; and African Americans, 184, 195–97; and city budget, 164, 191–92, 199, 209; and condoms, 202, 218–19; NAMES Project quilt, 197; *pneumocystis carinii* pneumonia, 187–88; policy response, 198, 200–201, 208; protease inhibitors, 188, 205; and queers of color, 179, 191; risk groups, 190–91, 205; and whiteness,

189–90, 205, 278n35; as urban problem, 199–90. *See also* ACT UP/Chicago; AIDS activism; AIDS Foundation of Chicago; AIDS service organizations; American Medical Association; Chicago for AIDS Rights; drugs; Edwards, Lonnie; federal government; Helms Amendment; HIV; Howard Brown Memorial Clinic; hospitals; racial segregation; Ryan White CARE Act; Sotomayor, Danny
AIDS Foundation of Chicago, 194, 229
AIDS service organizations, 193–97, 200, 205, 207, 222, 279n50; and racial segregation, 195
Alderson, Ortez, 90–91
Alliance to End Repression (AER), 92–93, 122–23
Alongi, Joe, 175
American Bar Association, 101
American Civil Liberties Union (ACLU), 77–78, 86, 147
American Law Institute (ALI). *See* Model Penal Code
American Medical Association, 101, 199; and ACT UP/Chicago, 204
analogies: between blacks and gays, 63–68, 96, 120, 147, 179, 215–17; between gayness and ethnicity, 10, 108, 111–12, 184, 213, 219; between gays and white ethnics, 162, 213, 220, 260n2; between gays, Catholics, and Jews, 83
Andersonville, 208, 218
Angels in America (Tony Kushner), 10
Annex, the (club), 83, 94
Another Country (James Baldwin), 59–63
antigay politics, 22, 207, 125, 150, 167–71, 176, 181–82, 201, 207–8, 214, 287n72. *See also* African Americans; federal government; whites

ACKNOWLEDGMENTS

IT IS A PLEASURE to be able to thank those who made this book possible. In particular, I wish to thank three individuals. The first is George Chauncey, whose command of the historian's craft is second to none. He offered unparalleled guidance and encouragement throughout the research and writing of this book. I admire his commitment to rigor and to making the past usable. Margot Canaday believed in this project and guided its path into print, offering smart and useful feedback at every stage. And Bob Lockhart has been a champion of my ideas, a careful and supportive editor, and has gone far above and beyond the call of duty.

Several other players were crucial in assisting me in reaching this point. Thomas J. Sugrue offered helpful comments as the work began to take shape. Most important, whatever merits this book might have are likely attributable to the generous and thoughtful critiques I received from the two external readers chosen by the University of Pennsylvania Press, Robert Self and Nancy MacLean (both of whom waived their right to anonymity). Also at the Press, Erica Ginsburg deftly shepherded the manuscript into production.

Over the years, I have benefited from the support of many people and institutions. I am grateful for funding received from the Jacob K. Javits Fellowship, the American Council of Learned Societies and Andrew W. Mellon Foundation, the James C. Hormel Fellowship, and the University of Chicago Center for Gender Studies, and for research grants from the Yale Fund for Lesbian and Gay Studies and the Rutgers University Research Council. A semester's leave from Rutgers University–Newark allowed me to complete the manuscript, and Jay Barksdale and the Frederick Lewis Allen Room at the New York Public Library provided a wonderful place to work. Domna Stanton was my New York City guardian angel.

The University of Chicago was my intellectual home for seven years. I thank Amy Dru Stanley, whose brilliance stretched my mind and whose curiosity was always encouraging; Jim Sparrow, whose grasp of modern U.S. politics is matchless; and William H. Sewell, Jr., who shaped the way I think about social change. I also appreciate conversations with Lauren Berlant, Mary Anne Case, Cathy Cohen, Tom Holt, Stuart Michaels, Mae Ngai, Gina Olson, Saskia Sassen, and Christine Stansell. There, too, I met Mike Czaplicki, Cassie Fennell, Joseph Fischel, Debbie Gould, Julian Hendrix, Moira Hinderer, Betty Luther Hillman, Alex Hivoltze-Jiménez, Allyson Hobbs, Molly Hudgens, Jonathan Levy, Toussaint Losier, Monica Mercado, Ana Raquel Minian, Carl Nash, Jessica Neptune, Kelly O'Brien, Sarah Potter, Gautham Rao, Ross Yelsey, Hillary Reser, Scott Richmond, David Spatz, Anthony Todd, Red Tremmel, Jennifer Vanore, and Kyle Volk. I could not have asked for more wonderful colleagues. A year spent as a visiting lecturer in LGBT studies at Yale University gave me a chance to try out many ideas. In the more distant past, Tim Burke, Bruce Dorsey, Pieter Judson, Lillian Li, and Marjorie Murphy introduced me to the historical profession.

I have been incredibly lucky to have a job teaching history at Rutgers University–Newark. My wonderful colleagues and interlocutors include Karen Caplan, Susan Carruthers, Kornel Chang, Ruth Feldstein, Eva Giloi, James Goodman, Mark Krasovic, Neil Maher, Lyra Monteiro, Stephen Pemberton, Mary Rizzo, Nukhet Varlik, and especially Jan Lewis, Beryl Satter, and Whit Strub. I am grateful as well for the privilege of having had the late Clem Price—though too briefly—as a colleague. Beyond the history department, Fran Bartkowski, Jyl Josephson, Tim Raphael, Robert Snyder, and Sherri-Ann Butterfield have helped me navigate life at Rutgers. Rabeya Rahman, Andy Lester, and Diana Schwartz ably provided research assistance. Christina Strasburger has served as a consistent voice of wisdom, a reliable friend, and has—often heroically—made many things possible.

More than thirty Chicagoans, past and present, allowed me to interview them formally in the course of my research, and I am grateful to all even though I could not include the voices of every one. Max Smith, Art Johnston, Kit Duffy, Cliff Kelley, Laurie Dittman, Rick Garcia, Mark Schoofs, and Achy Obejas were especially generous with their time and their willingness to explain nuances of Chicago politics. Ferd Eggan, Vernita Gray, and Renae Ogletree did not live to see this book's publication, but I hope it would make them proud.

I could not have written this book without help from many archivists and librarians. At Gerber/Hart Library and Archives, Karen Sendziak was indispensable during my research and Lucas McKeever helped with last-minute needs. At the Chicago History Museum, Lesley Martin and Jill Austin were steadfastly helpful, and I thank Peter Alter for letting me know about the newly processed William Simon Papers. I thank as well Morag Walsh at the Chicago Public Library's Harold Washington Archives and Collections, Désirée Yael Vester at the Lesbian Herstory Archives, and archivists at Stony Brook University, the New York Public Library, the GLBT Historical Society in San Francisco, the Leather Archives and Museum, DePaul University Special Collections, the University of Chicago's Special Collections Research Center, and the University of Michigan's Labadie Collection. I also thank Nancy Hanover-Reyes for permission to examine the papers of her late mother, Renee Hanover, even though constraints of time and space prevented my making full use of them, and Jeff Edwards for access to his own collection. And I am grateful to Tracy Baim, who kept her eye out for materials relevant to my project and assisted many times with tracking down people and information.

I have striven to make this book well illustrated. I thank Tracy Baim, Israel Wright, Mark PoKempner, and especially Margaret Olin for permission to reproduce their photographs, and Steve Fabus and Bill Kelley for allowing me to use materials they created at an earlier stage of life. I thank Ian Darnell for directing me to the 1955 campaign flyer for Richard J. Daley that appears in these pages. Michael Cain, John Gagnon, Jeff Graubart, Jacky Grimshaw, Anne Krook, David Ostrow, and David Sonenschein all assisted me with various aspects of the research.

For their collegiality, suggestions, and feedback at various points, I thank Farid Azfar, Wallace Best, Mia Bay, Jennifer Brier, Julio Capó, Jr., Mary Anne Case, Nathan Connolly, Andrew Diamond, Stephen Engel, René Esparza, Ann Fabian, Amin Ghaziani, Jessica Halem, David Halperin, Christina Hanhardt, Clay Howard, Nadine Hubbs, David K. Johnson, Seth Koven, Kevin Kruse, Aaron Lecklider, Martin Meeker, Joanne Meyerowitz, Darnell Moore, Khalil Muhammad, Kevin J. Mumford, Donna Murch, Tim Naftali, Yasmin Nair, Claire Potter, Graeme Reid, Brian Rojanasumaphong, Gabe Rosenberg, Dan Royles, Ken Sherrill, Marc Stein, Susan Stryker, Stephen Vider, Deborah Gray White, Michael Yarbrough, Julian Zelizer, and the members of the 2011–2012 Institute for Research on Women seminar at Rutgers University–New Brunswick. Sewell Chan, Gayle Rubin, John D'Emilio, and Heather Ann Thompson had many conversations with me about the ideas in these pages, for which I am a far better scholar.

I am grateful for the friendship of Brad Anderson, Tom Bachtell, Jeff Beeler, Matthew Berthold, Chris Blacker, Phil Blumenshine, Melissa Borja, John Alexander Burton, Tristan Cabello, Jennifer Callaghan, Seth Carlson, Saalim Carter, Payton Chung, Ryan Cook, Joanna Curtis, Robert Cole, Ryan Copi, Scott Dankert, Adrian Dimanlig, Scott Feldman, Jason Fleetwood-Boldt, Gill Frank, Greta Gao, Chris Geidner, Charles Gershman, Alvia Golden, Theo Greene, Philip Hales, John Havard, Peter Hill, Emily Hobson, Martha Hodes, Mark Horn, Ryan Hoshi, Chris Johnson, Dan Johnson, Padraig Johnston, Jonathan Kay, Gwen Kelly, Jeff Kosbie, John Kuhn, Patrick Kwan, Kevin Lees, Ian Lekus, Brian Lobel, Will Mackintosh, Michael Malecki, Ben Francisco Maulbeck, Samira Mehta, Chris Mitchell, Michael Moore, Mark Nattier, Tavia Nyong'o, Matt O'Connor, Richard Kim, Steve Kriz, Aaron Mertz, Mekado Murphy, Catherine Osborne, David Palmer, Frank Pasquale, Jerry Passannante, Atiba Pertilla, Justin Phillips, Joey Plaster, David Polk, Tim Retzloff, Robin Blair Riley, Patrick Roberts, Don Romesburg, Harish Shivde, Perry Simmons, Carroll Smith-Rosenberg, Dustin Stephens, Brad Stocking, Aaron Tabak, Nathan Tabak, Andrew Tangel, Morgan Tingley, Benjamin Toff, Mark Tyndall, Ed Wei, Claire Robbins, Jesse Sanford, Traci Schlesinger, Ian Shin, Nick Syrett, Elizabeth Tulis, Dennis Tyler, Ryan Viloria, Greg Walton, Josh J. Weiner, Carsey Yee, BG Wright, many friends made through the Chicago Gay Men's Chorus, and others too numerous to name. Dan Korobkin and Ben Wurgaft, thank you for your friendship and for your help in locating sources. Thanks also to the Floreen-Stewart clan, Bob and Penney Winter, Ulrica and David Perkins, Joan G. Stewart, the late Milton D. Stewart, and particularly my brother, Nicholas Winter, and my sister-in-law, Tucker Andrews Winter.

As this book was going to press, William B. Kelley died suddenly. It is difficult—perhaps impossible—to convey the depth of my gratitude to him. On Martin Luther King, Jr., Day in 2008, when I persuaded him to take me along to the storage unit where many of his boxes of files were stored, I knew I'd hit a gold mine. Bill joined a tiny social movement at a time when gay activism was risky and "queer clout" almost unimaginable, and I am grateful for his foresight, even then, in holding onto so many seemingly obscure scraps of paper. Bill let me interview him formally twice, tolerated a steady stream of queries over many years, and carefully reviewed and edited multiple drafts of the manuscript, always phrasing his reservations politely. He saved me from numerous embarrassing errors; I am responsible for those that remain. I also thank Bill's partner, Chen K. Ooi, for his good company and for putting up with the weeks I spent going through Bill's papers on the living room floor.

For countless conversations about my ideas and for being there through thick and thin, I thank Benjamin Eleanor Adam, Thomas Jessen Adams, Kathleen Belew, Gerry Cadava, Thom Cantey, Robert Chang, Brian Distelberg, Kathleen Frederickson, Gerard Cohen-Vrignaud, Moon Duchin, Elizabeth Emens, Justin Glasson, Kwame Holmes, Patrick W. Kelly, Alison Lefkovitz, Jeremy Posadas, Elliott Powell, Jordan Stein, Ben Steverman, and Brian Klinksiek and Byron Harrison, who generously offered me a home away from home in Chicago on numerous occasions.

Two others shaped this book profoundly but did not live to see it. My late grandmother, Dorothy Overlock Stewart, was the first native-born Chicagoan in my life, although she claimed to have never liked the city. I carry her memory in my heart every day. As this book was going to press, my friend Andrew Patner died suddenly. I met him in the course of my research on this project, and he shared his deep knowledge of Chicago, the city he loved, and racial politics in the United States. He also provided me what I'm certain was the best tour of Chicago's city hall that anyone's ever had. He helped me believe in this project.

Greg Edwards has been my partner and comrade as I've come down the home stretch. I am grateful for his daily backup; for his tolerating the time and space this book took up; and for his kindness, love, and way with words.

This book is dedicated to my parents, Abigail J. Stewart and David G. Winter. They inspire me every day with their curiosity and dedication to their own work; they have provided me with every kind of support; and they have believed in me even when the path seemed difficult. It is a thrill finally to have the opportunity to thank them in print.

CPSIA information can be obtained
at www.ICGtesting.com
Printed in the USA
JSHW031559190321
12631JS00002B/2